The Political Economy of
Tax Reform

NBER–East Asia Seminar on Economics
Volume 1

National Bureau of Economic Research
Korea Development Institute

The Political Economy of Tax Reform

Edited by Takatoshi Ito
and Anne O. Krueger

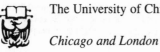

The University of Chicago Press

Chicago and London

TAKATOSHI ITO is professor of economics at Hitotsubashi University.
ANNE O. KRUEGER is Arts and Sciences Professor of Economics at Duke
University. Both are research associates of the National Bureau of
Economic Research.

The University of Chicago Press, Chicago 60637
The University of Chicago Press, Ltd., London
© 1992 by the National Bureau of Economic Research
All rights reserved. Published 1992
Printed in the United States of America

01 00 99 98 97 96 95 94 93 92   1 2 3 4 5 6

ISBN (cloth): 0–226–38667–8

Library of Congress Cataloging-in-Publication Data

The political economy of tax reform / edited by Takatoshi Ito and Anne
O. Krueger.
        p. cm.—(NBER–East Asia seminar on economics : v. 1)
    Includes bibliographical references and index.
    1. Taxation—East Asia—Congresses. 2. East Asia—Economic
policy—Congresses. I. Ito, Takatoshi. II. Krueger, Anne O. III.
Series.
    HJ2970.5.P65   1992
    336.2′0095—dc20   92-9001
                                                          CIP

Contents

Preface

The first National Bureau of Economic Research–East Asia Seminar on Economics was held in Seoul, Korea, in June 1990. This volume presents the papers and comments of discussants from that conference, revised for publication.

The seminar was jointly sponsored by the National Bureau of Economic Research and the Korea Development Institute with the support of the Chung-Hwa Institute. The Korea Development Institute was the host institution and provided amazingly efficient arrangements, hospitality, and secretarial support for the conference. A planning committee, consisting of ourselves, Dr. Koo Bon Ho of the Korea Development Institute, and the late Dr. C. M. Hou of Colgate University and Chung-Hua Institute, was responsible for organizing the program. We are grateful to Drs. Hou and Koo and to all three institutions for their support of this endeavor and believe that the outcome of the conference, as represented in these papers, provides evidence of the benefits of cooperation and of the fruitfulness of the approach.

Takatoshi Ito and Anne O. Krueger

Introduction

Takatoshi Ito and Anne O. Krueger

The rapid emergence of the East Asian region as an important geopolitical-economic entity has been one of the most visible and striking changes in the international economy. In that new role East Asia raises a number of issues of economic interdependence that call for considerable economic analysis and increased trans-Pacific understanding.

For the world economy as a whole, there were two major themes of the 1980s. A first identifiable trend was growing interdependence among countries, as communications and transportation continued to become quicker and cheaper. The growth in the volume of world trade continues to outpace the growth in world output, as exports and imports account for an increasing share of most countries' GNPs. At the same time domestic firms are increasingly sensitive to events in the world as a whole: changes of 1 or 2 percentage points in costs, which before would have been buffered by transport costs of 20 or 30 percent of factory price, instead have been reflected quickly and entirely through shifts in competitive position.

The second trend, evident in most industrialized countries, was heightened sensitivity to the implications for economic efficiency, living standards, and growth of incentives confronting individual producers. This was reflected in concerns with, inter alia, deregulation, removal of trade barriers, and changes in tax structure, as there was increasing recognition of the importance of the effects of these on productivity and "international competitiveness."

All of these concerns were reflected in the economic policy debates in East Asia and in the United States. Increased interdependence means that each individual's and each firm's competitive position is affected by all of the circumstances. When competitors are perceived to be producers in other countries,

Takatoshi Ito is professor of economics at Hitotsubashi University. Anne O. Krueger is Arts and Sciences Professor of Economics at Duke University. Both are research associates of the National Bureau of Economic Research.

concern focuses not only on what domestic economic policies are, but on how they position the individual relative to those foreign competitors.

Because East Asia has been so successful in economic terms, attention has turned to that region of the world perhaps more than to any other. It seemed natural, therefore, to focus the first NBER–East Asia Seminar on Economics on one such problem of interdependence and to investigate how the different countries addressed it: tax reform.

Because of heightened concerns with incentive effects on the functioning of markets and for other reasons, all of the major countries of East Asia and the United States considered and undertook major tax reform programs during the 1980s. Analysis of these programs is interesting in its own right. In addition, it sheds light on the ways in which interdependence interacts with domestic economic and political concerns in affecting issues as politically vital as tax reform. One of the interesting findings to emerge from the conference was that, in all countries, international considerations had become secondary when domestic political interests were focused on issues of tax structure and reform.

Part I contains two background papers. The first, by Assaf Razin and Efraim Sadka, provides a theoretical basis for considering some of the important issues of interdependence in tax policy. Razin and Sadka consider linkages between systems of taxation and domestic capital formation in open economies. They note that a great deal of attention has been paid to the ways in which exchange rate management and monetary policy are affected by integration of capital markets across countries, but that much less attention has been given to the effects of alternative tax structures in the presence of capital mobility. Investors may decide to invest abroad because of differences in tax structure (or in the enforcement of taxation of foreign source income) when the economic rate of return is higher on domestic investment if the tax structure is inappropriate. Razin and Sadka show how these considerations are likely to affect not only tax structures but also governmental fiscal policies, as countries' capital markets become increasingly integrated.

In the second background paper, Vito Tanzi and Parthasarathi Shome provide a survey of taxation structures in eight East Asian economies, Hong Kong, Indonesia, Korea, Malaysia, the Philippines, Singapore, Taiwan, and Thailand, paying attention to similarities and differences among countries as well as to tax reforms. On the basis of their analysis, they conclude that distortions in tax structure become important impediments to growth once macroeconomic stability has been achieved; it is probably preferable to have a distortionary tax that closes the fiscal deficit than to let the deficit persist. Interestingly, countries with macroeconomic instability included those with high and low levels of taxation: fiscal deficits were not necessarily associated with low levels of taxation. Once macroeconomic stability is achieved, Tanzi and Shome conclude that undertaking tax reforms that substitute other revenue sources (such as the value-added tax) for highly distortionary taxes (such as customs duties and high rates of income taxation) is worthwhile and can contribute significantly to growth.

Part II contains four papers, on Japan, the United States, Korea, and Taiwan. Each paper is designed to provide an analysis of the political-economic interactions that underlay the tax reforms undertaken in that country. Authors were requested to focus on both the economic considerations pertinent to the reforms in their countries, and the political factors that affected the outcome. An interesting observation made at the conference is that domestic political considerations were such an important element that international issues hardly surfaced in any of the four countries when decisions were being made. Of equal interest to conference participants was the extent to which the "political" considerations and behavior that apparently determined outcomes were similar in all four countries.

The Japanese tax reform, analyzed by Masaaki Homma, represents a ten-year struggle to introduce a value-added tax. The first attempt was made by Prime Minister Masayoshi Ohira in 1979. The effort was abandoned when the LDP was defeated in the next general election because of the tax reform issue. Opposition to reform arose both from distributors who believed that they would be forced to absorb the value-added tax and from consumers who believed that distributors would pass it on to them (see also the discussion in Yukio Noguchi's paper on the bases for opposition to the reform). The next attempt at introducing a value-added tax, then called a sales tax, was made by the Nakasone government in 1986 and also failed, again with serious political consequences. The third attempt, this time called a consumption tax, was introduced by the Takeshita government and won approval in 1988. However, the LDP was defeated in the next election. In his paper, Homma traces the history of the tax reform effort and analyzes the differences between the three reform proposals.

The American tax reform, analyzed by Charles McLure, had a very different history. It was believed to be politically impossible to remove a large number of very inefficient exceptions, complications, and special treatments that had been introduced into the American tax code over a long time. In the early 1980s, however, a group of technocrats was encouraged to start developing a tax reform package that would not change overall tax revenue but would simplify the tax structure. The technocrats were enabled to formulate their proposals without public scrutiny; once the proposals were public, the political appeal of simplification turned tax reform from political suicide to political necessity. The ensuing simplification of the tax structure and reduction of the high marginal rate of income tax constituted in fact a very significant tax reform.

In contrast to the Japanese and American tax reforms, which were aimed at major changes in the structure of taxation that would greatly reduce distortions emanating from the tax structure, Taiwan's tax reform represented a much smaller effort. The government introduced a business tax in 1986, which was presented as improving economic efficiency and social equity of the tax system. In fact, however, Chuan Lin considers the 1986 reform an important building block for the future, as Taiwan continues to have high income tax rates applied to a small base and high commodity taxes on a few items. The Taiwan reforms to date would thus appear to be much more partial than those of Japan and the United States.

Among the four countries, Korean tax reform has progressed least. Although there have been a large number of changes in the tax code and in tax administration during the period of Korea's rapid growth, Taewon Kwack and Kye-Sik Lee show that the tax system remains highly distortionary. In part, the problem is one of tax administration and compliance, as the absence of a "real-name system" in Korea prevents the identification of holdings and thus the tracing of assets and income. However, many of the tax changes to date have focused on the government's efforts to contain real estate speculation through increasing taxes on holdings of land and real estate. Until the time of writing, these taxes had not had their intended effect. Kwack and Lee conclude that more fundamental reform of the tax system, to make it less distortionary, is a task that still remains for the Korean government.

The tax reforms in the four countries (as in the eight surveyed by Tanzi and Shome) thus ranged from far-reaching attempts at simplification and unification of rates to more partial efforts to remedy particular problems. Taiwan and Korea are at earlier stages of their development than are Japan and the United States. Perhaps for that reason, they have still further to go in reforming the tax system. Interestingly, in light of the conference focus on the implications of tax reform for interdependence, it is significant that in none of the four countries did issues of interdependence have any political weight in the consideration of tax reform possibilities. Even in the United States and Japan, domestic political concerns seem to have entirely dominated consideration of the issue.

The final part of the volume contains papers on individual aspects of the linkages between tax structure, economic efficiency, growth, and interdependence. Tatsuo Hatta and Hideki Nishioka evaluate the efficiency effects of changing the effective marginal capital income tax rate by simulating the Nakasone-Takeshita reform. They estimate that the efficiency effect of eliminating the maruyu (exemption of taxation for interest income) was between -0.2 percent and 0.9 percent of consumption wealth; in addition, the maruyu had constituted a major avenue for tax evasion. Tax reform therefore was economically efficient and closed an effective tax loophole. However, taxation of other sources of capital income was not reformed. If the marginal capital income tax rate had been reduced to the average, Hatta and Nishioka estimate that there could have been an efficiency gain of 0.77 and 1.69 percent of consumption wealth without any loss in tax revenue.

Irene Trela and John Whalley analyze the linkages among the Korean tax structure, Korea's outward orientation, and its rate of economic growth. They show how the tax structure was modified over time to support Korea's growth strategy, shifting away from taxation of exportables and toward other sources of taxation as the growth orientation changed. They also develop a general equilibrium model with which to estimate the contribution of the tax structure to Korea's growth rate. Recognizing that tax structure is only one of many contributors to growth, they nonetheless note that the model does capture the resource reallocation effects of shifting from import substitution to export promotion, and conclude that less than 10 percent of growth, or 1 percentage point of the growth rate, was contributed by the tax structure.

Yukio Noguchi considers the impact on the Japanese need for savings, the aging population structure, and the tax reform. He notes that, despite the political discussion, a major issue that went virtually unnoticed was the need to finance future social security expenditures as the Japanese population ages. Noguchi traces the implications of the aging population for social security expenditures in the coming decades. He shows that tax comparisons with other countries currently indicate that Japanese taxes are low, but that this finding is questionable when the younger age structure of the current Japanese population is taken into account. In the coming decades, the demographic structure of Japan relative to other industrialized countries will change markedly. It is this phenomenon that made a reform of the Japanese tax system essential: in years to come the number of working people relative to the number of pensioners will decline so much that raising adequate revenue through an income tax would require extremely high marginal rates. Noguchi notes that there are also macroeconomic implications of the changing demographic structure, especially on the likely level of national savings and the current account balance, but he does not focus on those in the present paper.

Thomas Barthold and Takatoshi Ito describe and contrast the gift and estate tax systems of the United States and Japan, and calculate the magnitudes of intergenerational transfers induced by the two systems. Among the several differences between the two systems, the chief are that (1) the American tax is based on the estate, while the Japanese tax is based on the size of the bequest to each individual; (2) land and real estate is valued at very low rates in Japanese bequests relative to its true value, whereas there is no such bias in American taxation; and (3) spouses are entitled to receive an estate tax-free in the United States, whereas only half of the relatively large estate in Japan may be given to a spouse tax-free. Barthold and Ito show that three-quarters of Japanese taxable bequests consist of real estate, whereas only one-quarter of the value of American taxable bequests consists of real estate.

The implications of tax policy for foreign investment are important in all countries, but are often neglected. In his paper, Kun-Young Yun reviews the taxation of foreign capital in Korea and examines whether the tax system distorted resource allocation. He calculated the effective tax rate for investment financed with foreign capital and concluded that the overall tax burden on foreign investors appeared to be reasonable. Despite this, he regards the tax treatments provided in the Foreign Capital Inducement Law as being "extremely generous."

For Taiwan, Ching-huei Chang and Peter W. H. Cheng consider the same issue. In Taiwan, tax rates for foreign investors have been about two-thirds of those confronting domestic owners, as the authorities have sought to encourage foreign investment. Chang and Cheng obtained data covering both Taiwanese and foreign-owned firms and attempted to estimate the impact of these special tax incentives on rates of return. They found that, for all manufacturing industries, tax incentives appeared to have no effect on firms' net worth, with the exception of the electronics industry. They conclude that further work needs to be done before their findings can be translated into policy terms, although they note that, as the Taiwanese economy grows, the case against distorting treatment of capital from different sources grows stronger.

Three conclusions emerge from these studies. First, there is a striking similarity in the tension between political considerations and good economics in the formation of tax policy in all the countries covered. The political economy of tax reform is not well understood, and there is much in common across countries. Second, consideration of tax policy in the individual countries has thus far proceeded with little attention to the implications of interdependence for its formulation and administration. There is clearly a lag between the fact of increased interdependence and recognition of it in ways that result in modified policy discussions. Third, although the studies contained in this volume shed considerable light on the structures of taxation and their economic effects in the countries concerned, a great deal of work remains to be done to understand the effects of alternative tax structures on income distribution, resource allocation, and economic growth. We hope that the results reported here will stimulate further work on these issues.

I.

1 International Interactions between Tax Systems and Capital Flows

Assaf Razin and Efraim Sadka

1.1 Introduction

International capital market integration has become the subject of major theoretical and practical interest in recent times. Policymakers are becoming more and more aware of the potential benefits accruing from such integration, which allows more efficient allocations of investment and saving between the domestic and the foreign market. In particular, with the prospective comprehensive integration of capital markets in Europe in 1992, some key policy issues arise.[1]

The financial, monetary, and exchange-rate-management policy implications of capital market integration have been widely discussed in the context of the European Monetary System (EMS); see, for instance, the survey by Micossi (1988). However, capital market integration also has profound effects on the fiscal branch of each country separately and on the scope of tax coordination among them. These issues have not been dealt with extensively so far.[2]

One issue is the tax-induced distortions in the allocation of world savings

Assaf Razin is professor of economics at Tel Aviv University and a research associate of the National Bureau of Economic Research. Efraim Sadka is professor of economics at Tel Aviv University.

1. In a recent paper Micossi (1988, 26) provides a succinct survey of the proposed institutional arrangements for the 1992 European integration. He writes: "The European integration entails the elimination of restrictions and discriminatory regulations and administrative practices concerning: (i) the right of establishment and acquisition of participations by foreign institutions in domestic financial markets; (ii) permitted operations of foreign-controlled financial institutions; (iii) cross-border transactions in financial services. The first two items basically involve the freedom to supply services in EC national markets, the third, the freedom to move capital throughout the Community."

2. For an earlier discussion of the interaction among taxes, government consumption, and international capital flow, see Razin and Svensson (1938).

and investment. In a world with international capital mobility, the equality between savings and investment need not hold for each country separately, but rather for world aggregate savings and investment. This separation brings out new issues of taxation in theory and practice. In a closed economy a tax on capital income drives just one wedge between the consumer-saver marginal intertemporal rate of substitution and the producer-investor marginal productivity of capital. In a world of open economies two more types of distortions can be caused by capital income taxation: (1) international differences in intertemporal marginal rates of substitution, implying an inefficient allocation of world savings across countries; (2) international differences in the marginal productivity of capital, implying that world investment is not efficiently allocated across countries.

The fundamental result of the theory of second best suggests that adding distortions to already existing ones may very well enhance efficiency and welfare. To put it differently, reducing the number of distortions in the economy may lower well-being. Thus, even though there are in general gains from international trade, some restrictions on free trade may be called for in a distortion-ridden economy.

The opening up of an economy to international capital movements affects the size and structure of the fiscal branch of its government. Capital flows influence both the optimal structure of taxes on domestic and foreign-source income, and the welfare cost of taxation. As a result, the optimal size of government (the optimal provision of public goods) and the magnitude of its redistribution (transfer) policies are affected as well.

Another issue is capital flight. There is now substantial evidence that governments encounter severe enforcement difficulties in attempting to tax foreign-source income. Dooley (1987) estimates that in 1980–82 as much as $250 billion may be classified as capital flight by U.S. residents. Tanzi (1987) reports that tax experts were concerned that lowering the U.S. individual and corporate tax rates in the U.S. Tax Reform Act of 1986 would induce capital drain from other countries by providing a tax advantage to investments in the U.S. These concerns are based on an implicit assumption that the governments of these countries cannot effectively tax their residents on their U.S. income so as to wipe out the U.S. tax advantage. The issue of capital flight is even more relevant for developing countries. Cumby and Levich (1987) estimate that a significant portion of the external debt in developing countries is channeled into investments abroad through overinvoicing of imports and underinvoicing of exports. Dooley (1988) estimates that capital flight from a large number of developing countries amounts to about one-third of their external debt in 1977–84.

Finally, integration of capital markets brings up the issues of international tax coordination, harmonization, and competition. There are two polar principles of international taxation: the *residence* (of the taxpayer) and the *source* (of income) principles. According to the first principle, residents are taxed on their worldwide income equally, regardless of whether the source of income is domestic or foreign.[3] A resident in any country must earn the same net return on her savings, no matter to which country she chooses to channel her savings (the rate-of-return arbitrage). If a country adopts the residence principle, taxing at the same rate capital income from all sources, then the gross return accruing to an individual in that country must be the same, regardless of which country is the source of that return. Thus, the marginal product of capital in that country will be equal to the world return to capital. If all countries adopt the residence principle, capital income taxation does not disturb the equality of the marginal product of capital across countries, which is generated by a free movement of capital. If the tax rate is not the same in all countries, however, the net returns accruing to savers in different countries vary, and the international allocation of world savings is distorted.

According to the second principle, residents of a country are not taxed on their income from foreign sources, and foreigners are taxed equally as residents on income from domestic sources. Now, suppose that all countries adopt this principle. Then a resident of country H earns in country F the same net return as the resident of country F earns in country F. Since a resident in country H must earn the same net return whether she channeled her savings to country H or to country F, it follows that residents of all countries earn the same net return. Thus, intertemporal marginal rates of substitution are equated across countries, implying that the international allocation of world savings is efficient. If the tax rate is not the same in all countries, however, the marginal product of capital is also not the same in all countries. In this case the international allocation of the world stock of capital is not efficient.

Although there are two extreme principles of international taxation, in reality countries adopt a mixture of the two. Accordingly, countries partially tax foreign-source income of residents and domestic-source income of nonresidents, in which case the international allocations of world savings and of world investments are distorted.

These issues are of particular relevance for the Europe of 1992. The creation of a single capital market in the European Community raises the possibility of tax competition among the member countries, in the absence of a full-fledged harmonization of the income tax systems. Also, the possibility of capital flight from the EC to low-tax countries elsewhere has strong implications for the national tax structures in the EC. These developments renewed interest among public finance and international finance economists in the issue of tax harmonization and coordination, tax competition, the international structure of taxation, etc.[4]

3. A credit is given against taxes paid abroad on foreign-source income in order to avoid double taxation.
4. See, for instance, Alworth (1988), Bovenberg (1988), Giovannini (1988, 1989a, 1989b), Gordon (1986), Razin and Sadka (1989, 1990, 1991), Razin and Slemrod (1990), Sinn (1987), and Slemrod (1988).

1.2 Restrictions on Capital Mobility

1.2.1 The Analytical Framework

Consider a stylized two-period model of a small open economy with one composite good, serving for (private and public) consumption and for investment. In the first period the economy possesses an initial endowment of the good, and individuals can decide how much of it to consume and how much of it to save. Savings are allocated either to investment at home or to investment abroad. In the second period, output (produced by capital and labor) and income from foreign investment are allocated between private and public consumption. To finance optimally its (public) consumption, the government employs taxes on labor, taxes on income for investment at home, and taxes on income from investment abroad. For the sake of simplicity, we assume that the government is active only in the second period.

In practice, governments encounter severe enforcement difficulties in attempting to impose taxes on foreign-source income. For instance, many foreign experts worried that lowering the individual and corporate tax rates in the U.S. Tax Reform Act of 1986 would induce a capital drain from other countries since it would increase the net return to capital in the United States. They implicitly assume that governments cannot effectively tax capital invested abroad and thus cannot reduce the net return on that capital to the level of the domestic rate of return (see Tanzi 1987). Dooley (1988) estimates that a significant fraction of external claims and of external liabilities in various developing countries is unaccounted for due to capital flight.[5] Therefore, after briefly analyzing the case where foreign-source income is fully taxable, we concentrate on the more realistic case where such income is effectively taxed only partially.

We consider a representative individual with a utility function of the form

(1) $$U(c_1, c_2, L, G) = u^p(c_1, c_2, L) + u^g(G),$$

where u^p and u^g are the private and the public components of the utility function, respectively; c_1, c_2, and L are first-period consumption, second-period consumption, and second-period labor supply, respectively; and G is second-period public consumption.[6]

Denote savings in the form of domestic capital by K and savings in the form of foreign capital by B. Since the focus of our analysis is on the case where income from capital invested abroad cannot be fully taxed, we assume that the pattern of capital flows is such that the country is a capital exporter (i.e., $B \geq$

---

5. See also Dooley (1987), Cumby and Levich (1987), and Giovannini (1989b).

6. To ensure diminishing marginal rates of substitution between private and public commodities, we assume, as usual, that u^p and u^g are strictly concave. Notice also that the separability between private and public commodities embodied in equation (1) ensures that government spending on public goods does not affect individual demand patterns for private goods or the supply of labor.

0). Hence, the amount of savings channeled through domestic investment constitutes also the domestic stock of capital in the second period.

The private-sector budget constraints in the first and second period are given, respectively, by

(2) $$c_1 + K + B = \bar{I}.$$

(3) $$c_2 = K[1 + (1 - t_D)r] + B[1 + (1 - t_F)r^*] + (1 - t_w)wL,$$

where t_D = tax on capital income from domestic sources; t_F = tax on capital income from foreign sources; t_w = tax on labor income; r = domestic rate of interest; r^* = world rate of interest (net of taxes levied abroad); w = wage rate; and $\bar{I}$ = initial endowment.

Obviously in the absence of quantity restrictions on capital flows, the private sector must earn the same rate of return on domestic investment and on investment abroad, i.e.,

(4) $$(1 - t_D)r = (1 - t_F)r^*.$$

When quantity restrictions are imposed on investment abroad, the arbitrage condition (4) becomes

(4a) $$(1 - t_D)r < (1 - t_F)r^*.$$

As is common, we consolidate the periodic budget constraints in equations (2) and (3) into a single (present value) budget constraint:

(5) $$c_1 + qc_2 = I + B((1 + (1 - t_F)r^*)q - 1),$$

where

(6) $$q = (1 + (1 - t_D)r)^{-1}$$

is the consumer (i.e., after-tax) price of second-period consumption in present values. In order to highlight the issues associated with capital-income taxation (i.e., saving and investment incentives and government tax revenues), we abstract from issues pertaining to variable-labor supply and assume that the labor supply is inelastic. Accordingly, after-tax labor income is added to the initial endowment, and their sum is denoted by I in equation (5).[7]

The second term on the right-hand side of equation (5), namely $B((1 + (1 - t_F)r^*)q - 1)$, plays a crucial role in the analysis. In case there are no restrictions on capital exports, the arbitrage condition (4) must hold, and this term vanishes. Otherwise (when capital exports are restricted) condition (4a) applies, and this term becomes positive, representing inframarginal gains to the savings of the private sector that are channeled to investment abroad.

7. It is straightforward to show that efficiency considerations usually require taxing the inelastic labor income first before moving on to taxing capital income. We assume that the size of government is large enough so that the tax on labor income does not suffice to finance government consumption and thus a distortionary tax on capital income is also required. Formally, we conclude that $I = \bar{I}$.

A maximization of the utility function U, subject to the budget constraint in equation (5), yields the consumption demand functions:

(7) $c_o = c_i(q, I + B((1 + (1 - t_F)r^*)q - 1)), \quad i = 1, 2.$

The utility obtained from these demand functions (the indirect utility function) is

(8) $V = v(q, I + B((1 + (1 - t_F)r^*)q - 1)) + u^g(G).$

Domestic output (Y) is produced in the second period by capital and labor, according to a production function that exhibits diminishing marginal products. Suppressing the fixed labor input, we write the production function as

(9) $$Y = F(K).$$

The firm's demand for capital is determined by the marginal productivity condition:

(10) $$F'(K) = R.$$

Equilibrium in the first period requires that the demand for domestic capital (i.e., K) is equal to the supply of domestic capital (i.e., $I - c_1 - B$):

(11) $$K = I - c_1 - B.$$

Similarly, equilibrium in the second period requires the equalization of (private and public) demand for and supply of consumption goods:[8]

(12) $$c_2 + G = F(K) + K + (1 + r^*)B.$$

Substituting equation (11) into equation (12) yields the single (consolidated) equilibrium condition:[9]

(13) $c_2 + G - F(I - c_1 - B) - (I - c_1 - B) - (1 + r^*)B = 0.$

As mentioned previously, we employ the analytical framework to examine two distinct regimes. The first regime, which we may term the *optimum*, entails no constraints on the taxation of foreign-source income. This regime is considered a benchmark case. In the second, more realistic regime, which we may term the *suboptimum*, foreign-source income cannot be taxed as effectively as domestic-source income. To highlight the distinction between the regimes, we simply assume that in the second regime no tax can be levied on foreign-source income (i.e., $t_F = 0$).

---

8. This condition must hold because obviously there will be no savings and investment in the second (and last) period.

9. The government budget constraint is $rt_D K + r^* t_F B + F(K) - rK = G$. Note that the term $F(K) - rK$ represents the revenue from taxes on labor income. Notice also that by Walras's law this constraint is satisfied in equilibrium.

1.2.2   The Optimal Regime

This section deals with the case where the government can tax foreign-source income as effectively as domestic-source income. The question naturally arises whether it would be indeed optimal to levy the same tax rate on the incomes from these two sources and abstain altogether from quantity controls on capital exports.

Since there are distortionary taxes as part of the optimal program, the resource allocation is obviously *not Pareto-efficient*. In general, the intertemporal allocation of consumption, the leisure-consumption choice, and the private-public consumption tradeoffs are all distorted. Nevertheless, we show in this section that the optimal program (namely, the regime in which no constraints on taxation of foreign-source income exist) requires an efficient allocation of capital between investment at home and abroad, so that $F_1 = r^*$. That is, the marginal product of domestic capital must be equated to the foreign rate of return on capital.

To derive the optimal program, the government maximizes the indirect utility function in equation (8) subject to the equilibrium condition in equation (13). The control (policy) variables at the government's disposal are the tax rate on domestic capital income (t_D) or, more generally, the consumer price of future consumption (q), the tax rate on capital income from abroad (t_F), the level of public consumption (G), and the quota on capital exports (B). Carrying out the optimization problem yields the efficiency condition

$$(14) \qquad\qquad F' = r^*$$

(see Razin and Sadka 1991).
Accordingly, savings of the private sector must be allocated efficiently between investment at home and investment abroad. Since $F' = r$, the arbitrage condition is satisfied if the two tax rates are equalized, i.e.,

$$(15) \qquad\qquad t_D = t_F.$$

In such a case there is no need to impose any quantity restrictions on capital exports.[10]

1.2.3   The Suboptimal Regime

We turn now to a more realistic case where the government cannot effectively tax income from investment abroad. To highlight this phenomenon we set $t_F = 0$ and write $t_D = t$. In this case, if the government allows unlimited exports of capital, then capital will flow out of the country until the net return on domestic investment equals the net return on investment abroad:

---

10. Evidently this is an open economy variant of the aggregate efficiency theorem in optimal tax theory (e.g., Diamond and Mirrlees 1971, Sadka 1977, and Dixit 1985).

(16) $(1 - t)r = r^*$.

This means that $F' = r > r^*$, so that the domestic stock of capital is smaller than in the optimal regime (where $F' = r^*$), given that the marginal productivity of capital is diminishing. The mirror image of such an underinvestment in capital at home is an overinvestment in capital abroad.

Therefore, an interesting issue that arises in this context is whether it is now efficient from the society standpoint to restrict the exports of capital, and if so, how severe should the restriction be. One may ask, for instance, whether the restriction on exports of capital should bring the domestic capital stock all the way back to a level that is even higher than in the optimal regime (i.e., an overinvestment in domestic capital). Furthermore, is it possible that capital exports should be altogether banned when foreign-source income cannot be effectively taxed? We address these issues below.

To derive the effects of a change in the capital-export quota on welfare, we totally differentiate the indirect utility function in equation (8) with respect to B. This yields

(17) $$\frac{dv}{dB} = -v_y \frac{K}{q} \frac{dq}{dB} + v_y ((1 + r^*)q - 1),$$

where $v_y > 0$ is the marginal utility of income.

Similarly, total differentiation of the market-clearing condition in equation (13) yields the general equilibrium effect of a change in the capital export quota on the after-tax price of future consumption:

(18) $$\frac{dq}{dB} = (-((1 + r)c_{1y} + c_{2y}) ((1 + r^*)q - 1) + r^* - r)A^{-1},$$

where

(19) $A = (1 + r)c_{1q} + c_{2q} + ((1 + r)c_{1y} + c_{2y})(1 + r^*)B < 0.$

The terms c_{1y} and c_{2y} are the income effects on present consumption and future consumption, respectively, and the terms c_{1q} and c_{2q} are the gross (future consumption) price effects on present consumption and future consumption, respectively. Note that the specification in equation (18) implies that the government adjusts its budget in response to the change in the capital export quota only by altering tax rates and not through adjustment in spending. However, the derivations below show that welfare improves even with the restricted measures; a fortiori the welfare level should rise with the unrestricted measures.

Consider now the point where no restrictions on capital exports are imposed. We refer to this case as the laissez-faire case. The arbitrage condition in equation (4) then implies that

$$(20) \qquad\qquad q = (1 + r^*)^{-1}.$$

Hence, employing (17) and (18), we conclude that

$$(21) \qquad\qquad dv/dB = -v_y K(r^* - r)A^{-1}.$$

Since $r^* < r$ and $A < 0$, it follows from equation (21) that $dv/dB < 0$ at the laissez-faire point. This means that reducing B is welfare-improving. Namely, the government should impose a binding quota on capital exports in order to reduce the amount invested abroad. It can be shown that such a quota usually raises the stock of domestic capital.

Having established that some restrictions on capital exports are desirable when the government is unable to tax the income from the exported capital, we turn now to the question of how severe the restrictions should be. As a benchmark consider K^*, the stock of domestic capital exported under the optimal regime defined by $F'(K^*) = r^*$. Starting from this benchmark we now investigate the policy question, whether the restrictions on capital exports should be severe enough so as to bring the stock of domestic capital to a level that exceeds even K^*, or whether the level of domestic capital still remains below K^*. (See fig. 1.1; K^{**} is the second-best optimal capital stock, and K_{LF} is the laissez-faire capital stock.)

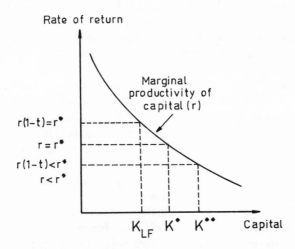

Fig. 1.1   Efficient stock of domestic capital with and without taxation of foreign-source income

Note: K_{LF} = laissez-faire stock of capital with no taxation of foreign-source income. K^* = efficient stock of capital with taxation of foreign-source income. K^{**} = efficient stock of capital with no taxation of foreign-source income.

To do this, we evaluate the derivative of the indirect utility function, dv/dB, at the point where $K = K^*$ (and consequently, $r = r^*$). This derivative is

(22) $$\left[\frac{dv}{dB}\right]_{K=K^*} = v_y((1 + r^*)q - 1)A^{-I}rt\, c^o_{1q},$$

where c^o_{1q} is the Hicks-Slutsky compensated effect of a change in the price of future consumption (q) on present consumption (c_1). Since two goods must always be net substitutes, it follows that $c^o_{1q} > 0$. Hence, $dv/dB < 0$ at the point $K = K^*$. This means that reducing B further, beyond the point where $K = K^*$ (and $r = r^*$), enhances individual welfare. This implies that the stock of domestic capital rises to a level that exceeds the corresponding level in the optimal regime, implying that $r < r^*$. Thus, when the government cannot effectively tax the income from the capital invested abroad, it is efficient to overinvest in capital at home up to a point where the marginal product (r) falls below the world rate of interest (r^*).

Finally, we turn to investigate an extreme possibility: should capital exports be altogether banned (i.e., $B = 0$) when the government cannot effectively tax the income from the capital exported? Obviously, if $dv/dB < 0$ at $B = 0$, then no capital exports should be allowed.

It turns out that the latter is a real possibility. To see this, notice that equations (17)–(19) imply after some tedious algebra that at $B = 0$ we have

(23) $$\left[\frac{dv}{dB}\right]_{B=0} = v_y A^{-I}(rtc^o_{1q}((1 + r^*)q - 1) - c_2(r^* - r)).$$

Now, when r is sufficiently close to r^*, then $dv/dB < 0$ because $A < 0$ and $c^o_{1q} > 0$. In this case, a total ban on capital exports is called for. The rationale for this result is straightforward. When r is close to r^*, there is very little gain for the society as a whole from investing abroad, because this gain is equal only to the difference between r and r^* (though the private sector can still gain considerably from investing abroad if $r(1 - t)$ is considerably below r^*). However, the government loses a significant amount of tax revenues from the outflow of capital. Therefore, in this case, it is not efficient to allow exports of capital.

Since there are distortionary taxes as part of an optimal fiscal program, obviously the resource allocation is not Pareto-efficient: the intertemporal allocation of consumption, the leisure-consumption choice, and the private-public consumption tradeoffs are all distorted. Nevertheless, when the government can tax its residents on their foreign-source capital income, it is optimal to allow capital to move freely in or out of the country. That is, optimal policy requires an efficient allocation of capital between investment at home and abroad so that the marginal product of domestic capital is set equal to the world rate of interest (net of foreign taxes). Evidently, this is an open economy variant of the aggregate efficiency theorem in optimal tax theory (see Diamond and Mirrlees 1971, Sadka 1977, and Dixit 1985).

Notice also that this production efficiency result implies also that it is optimal to have a nondifferential tax treatment of foreign and domestic sources of income. One might argue that the investment efficiency result (i.e., equating the return on capital at home to the return on capital abroad via free international capital flows) is not valid when the government is concerned about financing its debt. For opening an economy to international capital flows will raise the domestic interest rate to the world rate. In such a case, a government that is burdened by an ongoing deficit incurs a higher interest cost of financing this deficit. In fact, it loses some of its monopsony power in the domestic capital market. It can then be argued that the government may not wish to allow residents to invest abroad. However, in this case it can be shown that the investment efficiency result is still valid nevertheless, because the government can offset the cost of losing its monopsony power by an appropriate tax policy.

We have shown, however, that when the government cannot effectively tax foreign-source income, it should put severe restrictions on capital exports and bring the marginal product of domestic capital to a level that is even below the world rate of interest. The loss in the return to the private sector on their total investments (at home and abroad) due to the reallocation of capital from abroad to home is more than offset by the extra tax revenues accruing to the government on the income from the capital shifted to home.

An important issue concerning capital flight if capital mobility is effectively free is the vanishing of the capital income tax from the optimal tax menu. Optimal taxation of capital income is usually subject to two conflicting forces. On the one hand, the income from existing capital is a pure rent and taxing away rents is efficient. On the other hand, the taxation of the returns on current and future investments would retard growth, which may not be efficient. We have argued that the optimal policy, in the face of free capital mobility, calls for applying the residence principle of a uniform treatment of foreign- and domestic-source income. Consequently, if tax on foreign-source income from capital is not enforceable, the optimal tax on domestic-source income would vanish.

In summary, no capital income tax whatsoever can be imposed efficiently by a small open economy if capital flight to the rest of the world cannot effectively be stopped. Consequently, all the burden of taxes falls on the internationally immobile factors, such as labor, property, land, and so on. The global tax system becomes very much like a local and state tax system (within a federal system as in the United States), in which the largest share of revenue arises from taxes on property and excises. The capital-flight equilibrium is obviously welfare inferior to the residence-based system of capital taxation that ensues whenever the tax enforcement problem is solved.

1.3   The Cost of Public Funds and the Size of Government

The optimal size of government, or more precisely the optimal provision of public goods, must be determined by an appropriate cost-benefit analysis. Such analysis implies that the marginal cost of public funds must be equated to the marginal utility from public goods. To find the effect of liberalization in the international capital markets on the optimal quantity of public goods, we discuss here the effect of such a liberalization on the cost of public funds in a small open economy.

In calculating the cost of public funds, one must take into account the optimal response of the structure of taxation (on incomes from all sources) to the international capital market liberalization, because the cost of public funds is derived from a process of tax optimization. Therefore, we must also discuss the effect of liberalization on the structure of taxation. Of course, entangled with the structure of taxation is also the issue of the optimal size of income redistribution.

Suppose that the government can effectively tax income from capital invested abroad. In this case, a liberalization of the capital market is welfare-improving. Therefore such a liberalization entails an income effect. Such an effect usually tends to increase the marginal utility of public goods. In addition it may lower the marginal cost of public funds because the government benefits directly from the liberalization as it taxes the increased amount of income from the capital invested abroad and can therefore lower the tax burden on domestic sources. Therefore, the income effect tends to increase the provision of public goods and the size of income redistribution. On the other hand, the liberalization may change the internal terms of trade (e.g., the real wage, etc.) and affect directly the cost of producing public goods. The effect of this change in the terms of trade on the cost of public funds and the size of government cannot a priori be determined and should be examined empirically.

1.4   Feasible International Tax Structure

Capital market integration between two countries brings out the issue of the feasibility of their tax structures. When residents of one country invest in the other country, one must reckon with the possibility of tax arbitrage that may undermine the feasibility of integration.

To highlight this issue, consider a two-country world with perfect capital mobility. Denote the interest rates in the home country and the foreign country by r^H and r^F, respectively. In principle, the home country may have three different tax rates applying to interest income:

(i) t_{RD}^H = the tax rate levied on domestic residents on their domestic-source income;

(ii) t_{RF}^H = the tax rate levied on domestic residents on their foreign-source income;

(iii) t_{NRD}^H = the tax rate levied on nonresidents on their interest income in the home country.

The foreign country may correspondingly have three tax rates, which we denote by t_{RD}^F, t_{RF}^F, and t_{NRD}^F. Furthermore, assume that these rates apply symmetrically for both interest earned and interest paid (i.e., full deductibility of interest expenses, including tax rebates).

A complete integration of the capital markets between the two countries (including the possibility of borrowing in one country in order to invest in the other country) requires, due to arbitrage possibilities, the fulfillment of the following conditions:

(24) $$r^H(1 - t_{RD}^H) = r^F(1 - t_{NRD}^F)(1 - t_{RF}^H)$$

and

(25) $$r^H(1 - t_{NRD}^H)(1 - t_{RF}^F) = r^F(1 - t_{RD}^F).$$

The first condition applies to the residents of the home country and requires that they be indifferent between investing at home and abroad. Otherwise, they can borrow an infinite amount in the low (net of tax) interest–rate country in order to invest an infinite amount in the high (net of tax) interest-rate country. The second condition similarly applies to the residents of the foreign country.

Notice that unless

(26) $(1 - t_{RD}^H)(1 - t_{RD}^F) = (1 - t_{NRD}^H)(1 - t_{RF}^F)(1 - t_{NRD}^F)(1 - t_{RF}^H),$

the only solution to the linear system of equations (24)–(25) is a zero rate of interest in each country:

$$r^H = r^F = 0.$$

Thus, some feasibility conditions on the structures of taxes must be met in order to satisfy (26) and yield a sensible world equilibrium.

Somewhat surprisingly, the two polar schemes of source-based or residency-based taxation are examples of feasible tax structures even when the two countries do not adopt the same scheme. Consider first the case in which *both* countries adopt the source-based tax scheme. In this case, income is taxed according to its source, regardless of the residency of the taxpayer. This implies that

(27) $$t_{RD}^H = t_{NRD}^H, \ t_{RD}^F = t_{NRD}^F, \ t_{RF}^H = t_{RF}^F = 0,$$

so that (26) is satisfied and we can have a world equilibrium with positive rates of interest.

Similarly, consider the case where both countries adopt the residence principle: income is taxed according to the residency of the taxpayer, regardless of its source. This implies that

(28) $t_{RD}^H = t_{RF}^H, \; t_{RD}^F = t_{RF}^F, \; t_{NRD}^H = t_{NRD}^F = 0,$

so that, again, (26) is satisfied.

Next, consider the case in which one country adopts one tax scheme while the other adopts another one. Suppose, for instance, that the home country adopts the residence principle, while the foreign country adopts the source principle. In this case we have

(29) $t_{RD}^H = t_{RF}^H, \; t_{NRD}^H = 0, t_{RD}^F = t_{NRD}^F, \; t_{RF}^F = 0,$

and, again, (26) is satisfied.

However, if the two countries do not stick to one of the two polar schemes, then (26) need not hold and no sensible world equilibrium exists. Suppose, for instance, that each country levies the same tax rate on its residents (irrespective of the source of their income) and also all nonresidents investing in that country. In this case, we have

(30) $t_{RD}^H = t_{RF}^H = t_{NRD}^H, \; t_{RD}^F = t_{RF}^F = t_{NRD}^F.$

Hence, unless $(1 - t_{NRD}^H)(1 - t_{NRD}^F) = 1$, which is just a sheer coincidence, condition (26) is violated.

Thus, some feasibility conditions on the tax structure are essential for a full capital market integration. Any mutually beneficial tax coordination or harmonization must satisfy the tax arbitrage condition (26). There are two considerations. One concerns the indirect manipulation of the international terms of trade by various fiscal measures (other than explicit trade barriers such as tariffs and quotas), which is akin to the familiar "trade wars." Tax coordination is Pareto-improving when the terms of trade are subject to manipulation by national governments. The second consideration, which received less attention, concerns the international and domestic misallocation of resources that is generated by tax competition for given terms of trade.

This section focuses on the second of these two elements, since the first one has been exhaustively studied and has become by now a textbook case. Consider therefore a stylized model in which tax competition within the group of countries that we analyze cannot affect their terms of trade. This can be accomplished by assuming that this group of countries is small relative to the rest of the world, which effectively sets the international terms of trade.

Suppose first that fiscal policies are not harmonized internationally, so that the two countries are engaged in tax competition. Some minimal degree of coordination among the two countries and the rest of the world prevail, however, so that they can effectively tax their residents on foreign-source income.

It can be shown that it is not optimal from the individual country's standpoint to tax foreigners on their income from capital invested in that country.

Each one of the competing countries would tax its residents uniformly on their capital income from all sources, domestic as well as foreign. Thus, tax competition leads each country to adopt the residence (or worldwide) principle for the taxation of income from capital. This behavior implies that there are no gains from tax harmonization.

In order to implement effectively a policy of taxing worldwide income, a considerable degree of coordination among countries is required, such as, for example, an exchange of information among the tax authorities, withholding arrangements, relaxing bank secrecy laws, etc. Suppose that the competing countries can reach such coordination, which enables each to effectively tax its residents on their income from capital invested in the other country, even though they continue to engage in tax competition. However, assume now that they cannot tax the income from capital invested in the *rest of the world*, as they have no coordination (exchange of information, etc.) agreements with the rest of the world. This seems a rather interesting and realistic case that captures the essence of a problem hindering European integration, that of capital moving to low-tax countries in the rest of the world.

It can be shown in this case that the rate-of-return arbitrage condition prevents each one of the competing countries from taxing its residences on their income from capital invested in the other country, even though their tax authorities can cooperate on such things as tax withholding, etc. This may explain why the EC dropped the idea of imposing a withholding tax on capital income. Tax competition leads to an extreme situation where *no tax whatsoever* is imposed by any one of the competing countries on capital income from any source. All of the tax burden falls on the internationally immobile factors (unskilled labor, land, etc.). Here again it can be shown that tax harmonization among our initially competing countries will yield no gains for them.

In conclusion, there are no gains from tax harmonization among competing countries that constitute just a fraction of the world economy, regardless of whether or not they are coordinated with the rest of the world. However, the first case in which there is some coordination with the rest of the world yields a higher level of welfare compared to the second case where no such coordination exists. These propositions underscore the important role of tax coordination.

Bilateral double-taxation agreements are often in the form of credit and exemption provisions implemented by the residence country. These methods are close sometimes to the residence principle, but at other times to the source principle. Under the credit system firms typically pay the residence country tax when this country tax is higher than the tax in the source country. However, companies often defer the taxation of foreign subsidiary income until repatriation and can thus effectively choose to pay according to the source principle if the source country tax is lighter. If the source country tax is higher than the residence country tax, the tax system under the credit system effectively worked according to the source principle.

Tax exemption by the country of residence, at the company level, is often consistent with the source principle. Things become even more complex for multinational corporations with highly integrated activities across countries, by the conduct of various transfer price techniques to allocate profits so as to minimize the tax burden. In such cases the tax system is effectively consistent with the residence or the source principles, depending on whether the residence or the source country is the one that imposes the lower tax rate.

Table 1.1, which summarizes the corporate tax systems in the European Community, shows a large disparity in tax rates and the frequency of credit-exemptions provisions. Our analysis suggests that substantial convergence of rates and credit-exemptions provisions consistent with the residence principle is expected with the creation of the single capital market in Europe and the further integration of the world capital market in the 1990s.

1.5   Conclusion

We analyze three policy issues that arise with the international integration of the capital markets. One issue is the effects of the opening up of an economy to international capital movements on the size of government and the structure of taxes. A second issue is the incentive to restrict the size of capital exports in the presence of capital flight. A third issue is the provisions of the

Table 1.1   **European Community: Corporate Tax Systems (1989)**

	Statutory, Corporate Tax Rate	Investment Incentives	Taxation of Foreign Source Income
Belgium	43	13% reduction	Exemption
Denmark	50	—	Exemption or Credit[a]
France	39	—	Exemption
Germany	56	—	Deduction or Exemption[b]
Greece	35	—	Credit
Ireland	43	—	Credit or Deduction[c]
Italy	36	—	Credit
Luxembourg	36	12 % Credit	Credit or Exemption[b]
Netherlands	35	—	Credit
Portugal	36	—	Credit
Spain	35	5% Credit	Deduction Credit or Exemption[d]
United Kingdom	35	—	Credit or Deduction[e]

Source: A. Lans Bovenberg and George Kopits, Harmonization of Taxes on Capital Income and Commodities in the European Community, International Monetary Fund, October 1989.

[a]Exemption is from France, Germany, Ireland, Portugal, and Spain.
[b]Exemption under treaty.
[c]Credit.
[d]Credit on exemption under treaty.
[e]Deduction under treaty.

taxation of foreign-source income from capital that emerge from international tax competition and the advantages of international tax harmonizations. Our analysis suggests that a significant tax restructuring could follow the progressing process of integration of the world capital markets, and we highlight the significance of coordination between national tax authorities to enable the functioning of a worldwide system of taxing capital income.

References

Alworth, J. S. 1988. *The Finance, Investment, and Taxation Decisions of Multinationals*. New York: Basil Blackwell.

Bovenberg, A. Lans. 1988. The International Effects of Capital Taxation: An Analytical Framework. International Monetary Fund, Washington, D.C. Manuscript.

Cumby, Robert, and Richard Levich. 1987. On the Definition and Magnitude of Recent Capital Flight. In *Capital Flight and the Third World Debt*, ed. Donald R. Lessard and John Williamson. Washington, D.C.: Institute for International Economics.

Diamond, Peter A., and James Mirrlees. 1971. Optimal Taxation and Public Production. *American Economic Review* (March and June): 8–27, 261–78.

Dixit, Avinash. 1985. Tax Policy in Open Economies. In *Handbook on Public Economics*, ed. Alan Auerbach and Martin Feldstein. Amsterdam: North-Holland.

Dooley, Michael P. 1987. Comment on the Definition and Magnitude of Recent Capital Flight, by Robert Cumby and Richard Levich. In *Capital Flight and the Third World Debt*, ed. Donald R. Lessard and John Williamson. Washington, D.C.: Institute for International Economics.

———. 1988. Capital Flight, a Response to Differences in Financial Risks. *International Monetary Fund Staff Papers* 35(3):422–36.

Giovannini, Alberto. 1988. International Capital Mobility and Tax Avoidance. Graduate School of Business, Columbia University. Manuscript.

———. 1989a. International Capital Mobility and Capital-Income Taxation: Theory and Policy. Graduate School of Business, Columbia University. Manuscript.

———. 1989b. National Tax Systems versus the European Capital Market. *Economic Policy* 4(2):345–86.

Gordon, Roger H. 1986. Taxation of Investment and Savings in a World Economy. *American Economic Review* 76:1087–1102.

Micossi, Stefano. 1988. The Single European Market: Finance. *Banca Nazionale del Lavoro Quarterly Review*, no. 165:217–35.

Razin, Assaf, and Efraim Sadka. 1989. International Tax Competition and Gains from Tax Harmonization. Working Paper no. 37–89. Foerder Institute for Economic Research, Tel Aviv University.

———. 1990. Integration of the International Capital Markets: The Size of Government and Tax Coordination. In *Taxation in the Global Economy*, ed. Assaf Razin and Joel Slemrod. Chicago: University of Chicago Press.

———. 1991. Efficient Investment Incentives in the Presence of Capital Flight. *Journal of International Economics* 31:171–81.

Razin, Assaf, and Joel Slemrod, eds. 1990. *Taxation in the Global Economy*. Chicago: University of Chicago Press.

Razin, Assaf, and Lars E. O. Svensson. 1983. The Current Account and the Optimal Government Debt. *Journal of International Money and Finance* 2 (2):215–24.

Sadka, Efraim. 1977. A Note on Producer Taxation and Public Production. *Review of Economic Studies* 44 (2):385–87.

Sinn, H. W. 1987. *Capital Income Taxation and Resource Allocation*. Amsterdam: North-Holland.

Slemrod, Joel. 1988. International Capital Mobility and the Theory of Capital Income Taxation. In *Uneasy Compromise: Problems of a Hybrid Income-Consumption Tax*, ed. H. Aaron and H. Galper, and J. Pechman. Washington, D.C.: Brookings Institution.

Tanzi, Vito. 1987. The Response of Other Industrial Countries to the U.S. Tax Reform Act. *National Tax Journal* 4 (3):339–55.

Comment   Toshihiro Ihori

Assaf Razin and Efraim Sadka present a very clean theoretical paper that explains its assumptions and conclusions and leaves little for the discussant to do except to provide an intuitive explanation of the results. The paper provides a very neat analysis of the profound effects of capital market integration on the fiscal policy of each country separately and on the scope of tax coordination among them. This paper discusses two issues: tax-induced distortions in the allocation of world savings and investment, and the issue of tax coordination. I would like to comment on the first issue.

The main conclusion of section 1.2 is that when the government cannot effectively tax foreign-source income, it should put severe restrictions on capital exports. First, let me explain intuitively the results using a diagram. Suppose $G = 0$, and hence the government need not impose any taxes. In such a case there is no need to impose any quantity restrictions on capital exports, B. As shown in figure 1C.1, the laissez-faire is optimal. E^* is the optimal production point and F^* is the optimal consumption point. Figure 1C.1 may be regarded as the standard diagram with respect to gains from trade. c_1 may be regarded as an export good, c_2 as an import good, and B as the amount of exports.

Suppose now $G > 0$, and G is returned in a lump-sum manner. Note that if lump-sum taxes are available, F^* is still optimal. If lump-sum taxes are not available and the government can tax foreign-source income as effectively as domestic-source income, F_1 is the optimal point. This case corresponds to the optimal regime of section 1.2.2. On the analogy of trade theory, t_D may be regarded as a consumption tax on the import good, c_2.

Suppose the government cannot effectively tax income from investment abroad, $t_F = 0$. In figure 1C.2 E_2 is the production point in the laissez-faire case ($r^* < r$), and F_2 is the associated consumption point. On the analogy of trade theory the exporting industry, which is producing c_1, now receives subsidies because $t_F = 0$ is less than t_D. In figure 1C.2 E^* is the production point

Toshihiro Ihori is associate professor of economics at Osaka University.

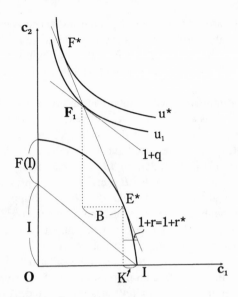

Fig. 1C.1   Gains from trade

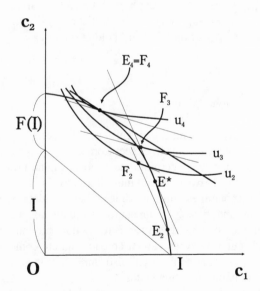

Fig. 1C.2   The case of $t_F = 0$

in the benchmark case ($r = r^*$), and F_3 is the associated consumption point. Utility at F_3 is less than utility at F_1 because q is larger in the benchmark case than in the optimal regime case. $E_4 = F_4$ is the equilibrium point under financial autarky ($B = 0$). Section 1.2.3 shows that utility at F_4 may well be higher than utility at F_2 or F_3.

Let me explain intuitively why a total ban on capital exports is called for. An increase in B means a decrease in K, and hence the revenue from taxes on labor income ($F(K) - rK$) will be reduced. In order to meet the government budget constraint, t_D has to be raised. This will raise q and hence reduce the welfare. Equation (17) implies that $dq/dB > 0$ is necessary for $dv/dB < 0$ if $(1 + r^*)q - 1 > 0$. The sign of dq/dB is crucial for the present analysis.

I have a question about the sign of dq/dB at $B = 0$. Suppose $t_F > 0$ and $t_w = 0$; that is, although the government cannot effectively tax income from investment abroad ($t_D > t_F$), the government can still impose a positive tax rate on B. And labor income taxes are not available. Then the government budget constraint is $t_D rK + t_F r^*B = G$. Suppose also for simplicity rK is independent of K. In such a case an increase in B and the associated decrease in K would mean an increase in tax revenues if t_D is fixed. A decrease in t_D is thus required to satisfy the government budget constraint, which means $dq/dB < 0$ at $B = 0$. If this case happens, from equation (17) $dv/dB > 0$ at $B = 0$. In the present paper, since labor supply is assumed to be fixed, t_w is raised to unity. However, if labor supply is highly elastic, t_w may be quite low. Would the main conclusion of section 1.2.3 still hold in such a case?

Comment   John Whalley

This is an extremely interesting and well-written piece by Assaf Razin and Efraim Sadka, as we have come to expect from this very distinguished pair of authors. It looks at issues concerning international capital flow and how they affect tax interactions between economies. It argues, in effect, that tax competition between economies will tend to lead them to adopt a residence principle for taxation, and in such circumstances there are no gains from tax harmonization. On the other hand, if various restrictions are introduced, such as the inability of countries to tax capital abroad, and are combined with arbitrage conditions, tax competition will also imply that there are no taxes on mobile factors, only on immobile factors.

As far as I know, this last proposition is certainly new, relative to previous literature on tax competition, and as this literature generally is quite limited, this work is especially important. My comments are threefold. First, it seems

John Whalley is an academic research economist at the University of Western Ontario, where he is director of the Centre for the Study of International Economic Relations. He is also a research associate of the National Bureau of Economic Research.

to me that in the paper there are some areas of institutional weaknesses that could be improved upon. Second, the discussion of tax instruments is worthy of comment. Finally, I will make some comments on the posture of the paper in the wider context of EC integration.

In terms of the institutional weaknesses, these may be relatively minor, but the discussion in section 1.4 of bilateral double-taxation agreements often being in the form of credits and exemption provisions implemented by the resident's country, seems to me to negate what double-taxation treaties are typically all about. While they may mutually specify some treatment within the country, double-taxation agreements usually focus on the withholding tax rates on dividends, interest, and royalties. The discussion of double-taxation treaties that follows is misfocused.

Second, there is discussion of the creation of a single capital market in Europe in 1992. In fact, the 1992 exercise, while it has discussed capital integration, has done so in a very limited way. The major focus has been on treatment of banking under the single banking license. Discussion of harmonization of corporate taxes has been separate from the 1992 exercise. This policy discussion, it seems to me, is also misplaced.

Furthermore, throughout the paper there are incorrect references to various features of arrangements. For instance, table 1.1 implies there is a single corporate tax rate in Germany, but because of the split credit imputation system, a 56–36 split in rates currently applies.

Beyond this, the discussion of instruments is worthy of further comment. Section 1.4 begins with a consideration of three tax rates t_{RD}, t_{RF}, and t_{NRD}. The first two of these, it seems to me, are typically treaty-bound and therefore usually the same, which places substantial limitations on the analysis that follows. In addition, it is misplaced to argue that these are the only instruments that countries use to control capital flows. Part of the Uruguay Round exercise, for instance, is about trade-related investment measures (TRIMs). These may include participation schemes commonly used in particular sectors, which guarantee participation of domestic equity owners. There are also tax holidays and many other such instruments. Thus, a full range of instrument substitution has to be acknowledged, even though it may be difficult to build into the analytical structure of the paper.

Finally, I have a few comments on European integration and how this fits into the wider discussion in the paper. Since the relative absence of tax competition in the European case is a particularly notable feature, it is interesting that thirty years after the Treaty of Rome there is still no agreement on a common corporate tax system. There have been repeated attempts to move toward a common imputation system, but at the moment no draft directive exists on what that common system will be. With the likely eventual move to an imputation system, however, there is also talk of the use of a refundable credit system with refundability limited to other EC countries, the echo of the restricted origin principle long discussed for the VAT.

In addition, besides the limited agreement on integration, the corporate tax rate reductions that have occurred in recent years across all the European countries seem to me, again, not to have been driven by tax competition effects but by a common intellectual climate under which it was widely believed that reductions in taxes to stimulate investment would be good. This began with the 1984 budget in the United Kingdom and continued with tax reductions in a number of other European countries. Thus, one might be tempted to conclude that, in the mid- to late 1980s, reductions in corporate tax rates were widespread among the European countries and were a reflection of tax competition. I would strongly disagree with that proposition. The European experience, it seems to me, even though it may have some relationship to the analysis in this paper, is more distant than the authors suggest.

2 The Role of Taxation in the Development of East Asian Economies

Vito Tanzi and Parthasarathi Shome

2.1 Introduction

This paper examines the role that taxation has played in the economic development of eight East Asian economies—Hong Kong, Indonesia, Korea, Malaysia, the Philippines, Singapore, Taiwan Province of China (henceforth, referred to as Taiwan), and Thailand. These include four so-called newly industrialized countries (Hong Kong, Korea, Singapore, and Taiwan), two oil exporters (Indonesia and Malaysia), and the Philippines and Thailand.[1] Much has been written on the tax systems of these countries, but a perusal of the literature indicates that it is difficult to identify the role that taxation has played in the development of these economies.[2] Indeed, the papers tend to focus more on the need to reform the existing tax systems than on the role that these systems may have played.

Vito Tanzi is director of the Fiscal Affairs Department of the International Monetary Fund and president of the International Institute of Public Finance. Parthasarathi Shome is division chief of the Tax Policy Division, Fiscal Affairs Department, International Monetary Fund.

This research paper is based on secondary sources. It does not necessarily reflect the official position of the International Monetary Fund and represents solely the views of the authors. The authors would like to thank Takatoshi Ito, Hitotsubashi University; Joseph Y. Lim, University of the Philippines; John Whalley, University of Western Ontario; Susan Schadler, International Monetary Fund; and an anonymous referee for comments and discussions that were very helpful in the finalization of the paper.

1. In this paper, the term *country* is used synonymously with *economy*. No legal significance should be attached to the use of this term.

2. For comparative studies, see Shome (1986). The most exhaustive set of recent papers was presented at a January 1990 symposium, "Tax Policy and Economic Development among Pacific Asian Countries," Institute for Social Sciences and Philosophy, Taipei. Of particular interest were the papers by Asher, Salih, and Salleh (Malaysia); Gillis (Indonesia); Kim and Lee (Korea); Lee (Korea); Richupan (Thailand); and Sicat (the Philippines). A February 1990 conference, "Fiscal System of Singapore: Trends, Issues, and Future Directions," offers another interesting set of papers, of particular relevance being Asher's paper on the fiscal system in an international perspective. See also Riew (1988) on Taiwan, and Asher (1989) on all the sample countries, including Hong Kong.

This paper has two distinct parts. Section 2.2 provides an informal summary of the main features of the tax systems of these countries that may have played a role in their economic development, with the objective of highlighting the major differences among the countries. In a way, this part looks at the past experiences of these countries to see whether any conclusions can be derived from them. Section 2.2 also includes a more forward-looking part that, after commenting on recent changes, assesses the direction that tax reform should take to increase the usefulness of the tax system as an instrument for development. Section 2.3 is a more speculative section that attempts to draw some lessons and some conclusions from the experiences of these countries.

2.2 Tax Structures, Tax Reform, and the Development of East Asian Economies

This section highlights some characteristics of the tax structures in the various sample countries, as well as major features of recent tax reform that might have helped or hindered their economic development. We will deal with three subgroups: (1) the newly industrialized countries (NICs);[3] (2) the two oil exporters; and (3) Thailand and the Philippines. Tables 2.1 and 2.2 will be used for reference.

2.2.1 Taiwan

General Characteristics

Taiwan's development strategy has been characterized by (1) a high saving rate, matched by appropriate interest rate policies; (2) an export orientation, supported by an appropriate exchange rate policy and by rapid industrialization financed by the high saving rate; and (3) an awareness of equity considerations as revealed by its land reform program, by the system of property taxation, and by the fact that this is the only country that seems to have generated official annual surveys of income distribution.

Having grown to about 20 percent in the early 1980s, the tax/GDP ratio fell back to about 15 percent by the late 1980s; such a level is now well below the world average especially for countries at Taiwan's level of economic development. Nevertheless, given the limited range of activities by the public sector and good public expenditure management, public revenue has been sufficient to meet the country's expenditure needs. Fiscal deficits were not allowed to develop, and revenue generation, per se, never became a major concern of the tax system. Thus, Taiwan did not experience the fiscally caused macroeconomic problems that have characterized many other countries.

Subnational taxes are important revenue sources, accounting for 45 percent

---

3. For a comprehensive analysis of the increasing economic maturity of the four NICs, see Banque Indosuez (1990).

Table 2.1 **Sample Asian Countries: Tax Revenue by Type of Tax (in percentage of total tax revenue)**

	Total Taxes	Income Taxes				Domestic Taxes on Good and Services				Foreign Trade				Social Security	Wealth and Property	Other
		Total	Individual	Corporate	Other	Total	General Sales, Turnover, VAT	Excises	Other	Total	Import Duties	Export Duties	Other			
Taiwan (1988)[a]	100	22.0	10.8	11.2	...	35.5	13.0	11.0	11.5	14.1	14.1	—	—	—	21.4	7.0
Hong Kong (1987)[a]	100	54.5	26.7	27.8	...	25.1	...	...	8.7	9.8	9.8	—	—	—	10.6	...
Korea (1986–88)	100	31.3	17.1	14.2	—	44.3	22.0	13.7	8.7	17.2	17.2	—	—	2.6	1.3	2.2
Singapore (1985–87)	100	42.9	15.1[b]	27.8[b]	...	27.5	—	9.0	18.5	6.1	6.1	—	—	—	17.1	6.5
Malaysia (1986–88)	100	48.7	12.8	35.8	0.1	24.4	7.9	9.5	7.0	23.2	14.4	8.8	—	1.0	0.6	2.2
Indonesia (1986–88)	100	61.0	4.6	55.0	1.3	28.2	19.5	6.5	2.3	8.0	6.0	0.6	—	—	1.6	0.9
Thailand (1986–88)	100	21.6	11.1	10.5	—	53.2	19.0	29.6	4.7	22.6	21.3	1.2	0.2	—	1.7	0.8
Philippines (1985–87)	100	28.0	9.0	14.3	4.7	44.0	10.0	24.8	9.3	25.2	23.1	0.9	1.2	—	0.7	2.1

Sources: International Monetary Fund; Asher (1900) for Taiwan and Hong Kong.

[a]The composition of the various taxes should be used as broad indicators.

[b]Assumed proportions from Asher (1990).

Table 2.2   **Sample Asian Economies: Selected Tax Characteristics**

	Taiwan	Hong Kong	Korea	Singapore	Indonesia	Malaysia	Thailand	Philippines
Maximum corporate income tax rate (%)	25	16.5	33[a]	33	35	40	35	35
Maximum personal income tax rate (%)	40[b]	15	50[a]	33	35	40	55	35
Treatment of capital gains[c]	S	E	S	E	S	E	S	S
Withholding taxes								
Dividend	20	—	10	—	20	—	20	35
Interest	20	—	10	33	20	20	25	20
Tax incentives	Important	Small	Important	Important	None	Important	Important	Important
Basic sales tax/VAT rate	5	None	10	None	0–35	5–10	0.5–10	10
Property taxes	High	Based on rent	Low	High	Low	None	Low	Low

Sources: MIER 1989, and updated information from national sources.

[a]If defense and inheritance surcharges are included, the effective corporate tax rate would be 42 percent and the top personal income tax rate would be 64 percent.

[b]Reduced from 50 percent in 1990.

[c]S = same as ordinary income; E = exempt.

of total tax revenue. They have strong implications for intragovernmental transfers; thus, studies on the Taiwanese tax system have tended to analyze both national and regional taxes (Riew 1988; Asher 1989). Of the tax composition presented in table 2.1, the national government collects customs duties, selected commodity taxes, personal income tax, and business income tax—there is no payroll tax—while the subnational governments levy monopoly charges on tobacco and wine (10 percent, of which the national government gets the lion's share at 6.5 percent), land-related taxes, and a flat 5 percent value-added tax, called the business tax.

Role of Selected Important Characteristics of Tax Policy

Incentives to Save and Invest. The fact that income taxes have not contributed significantly to tax revenue reflects the tax incentives given through the income tax system. Until 1981, there was an unlimited exclusion of both interest and dividend earnings from personal income taxation, at which time a ceiling was imposed (beyond which they would be taxed at a flat rate). Capital gains were exempt until 1989 (when a threshold was introduced that affects only large investors), thereby increasing the effective after-tax rate of return on capital. Expenditure allowances are relatively small, with no deductibility of interest on consumer loans and limited deductibility on mortgage loans.

It has been argued that such incentives to save and invest coupled with a lack of any tax-induced encouragement to spend have had a significant impact on the high savings performance of the economy; they also have helped to expand the corporate sector and to develop the capital market.

Investment incentives are also provided within the Statute for Promoting Investment (SPI), which applies to a wide range of "productive" enterprises[4] that are liable to the business income tax. Under the SPI, all research and development expenditures are immediately deductible. A five-year tax holiday or accelerated depreciation is provided for new and expanding enterprises, with additional preferences for "capital or technology-intensive" enterprises, together with a 20 percent effective tax rate ceiling (including surcharges) on "important" enterprises in basic metals, heavy machinery, and petrochemicals, and an additional tax credit worth 5–20 percent of investment in capital stock in "strategic" enterprises as determined by the government. Finally, mergers are encouraged by exempting the dissolved enterprise and providing a two-year, 15 percent tax credit to the merged enterprise. In sum, Taiwan has had a very finely tuned tax incentives scheme with the objective of rapid industrialization.

Land-based Taxes. Perhaps the most distinguishing feature of Taiwan's tax structure among the sample countries has been its ability to tap property val-

---

4. Most profit-seeking enterprises except those in trade, banking, and services.

ues—land as well as structures—as a significant source of revenue, a characteristic shared with Singapore. There are three main taxes: the land value tax (LVT), the land value increment tax (LVIT), and the house tax. Without going into the details of the individual tax structures, suffice it to say that the LVT is comparable to the property taxes of most other countries, that is, it is based on the assessed value of residential and industrial urban land. As might not be too surprising, its share in tax revenue has declined over time—from 4 percent in 1980 to 2 percent in 1987. Neither does the house tax, which is levied on the value of construction, generate much in terms of revenue.

The uniqueness lies in Taiwan's successful implementation of the LVIT on the *net increment to the transfer value* of land, levied at the rate of 40 percent on the first 100 percent increase, 50 percent on the next 100 percent, and a top rate of 60 percent. This is a kind of benefit-received tax, since the increase in the land value is assumed to reflect the growth of the economy and the provision of public services. Land is probably the main beneficiary of public spending on infrastructures. Apart from being a significant revenue generator, the tax is likely to have contained land speculation, raised regional autonomy, and improved the equity of the tax system.

In a country where income tax revenue is not high (in contrast to Hong Kong and Singapore), a relatively high contribution from property taxes has maintained the level of public revenue at an adequate level in spite of the granting of wide-ranging incentives from the income tax base. In a way, the land taxes have paid for the investment incentives. Also, in an environment of high savings and large trade surpluses there could be an incentive toward speculative investments, especially in the form of landholdings. LVIT discourages such investments and redirects financial resources toward more productive investments for which tax incentives are given.

The LVIT has been a much-needed instrument to counter the probable negative effect on the income distribution of the various savings incentives, the relatively small capital gains tax, and the special incentives for capital-intensive investment. The growth of LVIT revenues implies a rising share of subnational tax revenue in overall tax revenue and, consequently, a greater decentralization of the fiscal sector, bringing with it a more balanced regional development.

Customs Duties. In the early stages of development, customs duties usually account for a major share of tax revenue. This was the case in Taiwan. If growth and development proceed on the right path, the advantages of an open economy eventually become more apparent, thus leading to a decline in the share of customs duties. This has occurred in Taiwan; however, one is surprised that, in spite of its success as an international competitor, customs duties still remain important—their tax share declining rather slowly, from 24 percent in 1975 to 22 percent in 1980.

Tax Reform for Development

Strongly relying on a system of tax incentives to promote industry-led exports, Taiwan has felt the need neither to globalize income taxes nor to curtail significantly its incentives structures. This is not to say that it completely overlooked the need for tax reform or that it did not initiate some reforms. Reform measures were taken in 1986 when the value-added tax (VAT) was introduced and the top marginal personal income tax rate was reduced from 60 percent to 50 percent; in 1988 when the top business income tax rate was reduced from 35 percent to 25 percent; and in 1990 when the top personal income tax rate was reduced further to 40 percent. Thus direct taxes followed the international trend toward the lowering of marginal tax rates.

The most important reform action was perhaps the introduction of the consumption-based VAT with the dual objectives of reducing the distortions created by the existing commodity taxes and, as an added incentive to export, eliminating exports and capital goods from the tax base. Revenue generation was not an objective, and the VAT was introduced on a revenue-neutral basis at a single 5 percent rate. Therefore, while the schedular direct tax structure together with its multifaceted incentives schemes is still considered important to promote growth, the multirated commodity taxes were perceived as distortionary and were replaced by a VAT.

Taiwan has not had fiscal deficits; its direct tax and incentives system seems geared for its industry-led, export-oriented growth path that has certainly materialized; it has substituted the reduced role of direct taxes with increased land taxation; it has substituted a generalized VAT for distortionary domestic consumption taxes; and in answer to a large trade surplus, it has been reducing its customs tariffs (even though they still remain high). On the face of it, thus, taxation may have played a positive role in Taiwan's development. The tax structure that accompanied that growth reflected the philosophy of the 1960s and 1970s based on fine-tuning tax incentives and disincentives. Taiwan shows no particular inclination to move away from it and, given the success of its economy, it is easy to understand why.

There are some aspects of taxation that Taiwan probably cannot neglect in the future as its economy matures and enters the next stage of development. First, the complete absence of payroll/social security taxation will need to be replaced by some form of contribution system that addresses the issue of social insurance and social security. Second, pollution taxes will possibly have to be introduced to ameliorate environmental deterioration. Third, the levels of customs tariffs will have to be reduced, especially in view of Taiwan's large trade surplus. Finally, the large trade surplus may lead to strong reactions by other countries and force Taiwan to reassess its incentive policy toward exports.

2.2.2   Hong Kong

General Characteristics

Among the sample countries, Hong Kong's average tax level has been the smallest (together with the Philippines), though the tax/GDP ratio increased from around 9 percent in 1975 to 10 percent in 1980 and reached almost 12 percent by 1987 (Ho 1989). Revenues have been sufficient to meet public expenditure so that revenue generation has not been an objective requiring particular attention. The relative importance of direct taxes in total tax revenues has risen from the 52–54 percent range in 1974–76 to the 55–59 percent range in 1985–87.

Selected Distinguishing Features

Aspects relevant to development are the low tax level and the resilience of the tax structure itself. The main tax—the earnings and profits tax (EPT)—has remained basically unchanged since the mid-1950s, thereby imparting a stable tax environment for business operations. This has removed an important factor—tax uncertainty—that in other countries plays a role in reducing the incentive to invest.

Overall Tax Levels. The "standard" tax rate and the corporate tax rate of the EPT are low and result in low overall tax levels. Between 1975 and 1984, the standard tax rate was 15 percent; it rose to 17 percent in 1986 but was steadily brought back to 15 percent by 1989. Similar modifications apply to the corporate tax, the corresponding rates being 16.5 percent, 18.5 percent, and 16.5 percent. As a consequence of these low rates, the authorities have felt no need to grant tax incentives. However, depreciation allowances are quite liberal with high initial allowances, inventory valuation is on market-value basis, the nominal value of interest payments is deductible, and losses can be carried forward for an indefinite period of time. There are no taxes on dividends or capital gains, even at the personal level, and a tax on interest income was eliminated in 1989.

Indirect taxes are not high either. Import duties and excises which tend to be levied on a specific basis—resulting in low elasticities with respect to GDP growth—have fallen in terms of GDP from around 2 percent in 1970 to 1.5 percent in the mid-1970s and 1 percent in 1986. The dutiable commodities are few and include tobacco, alcoholic and nonalcoholic beverages, cosmetics, and hydrocarbon oils. Other indirect taxes are also selective and are levied on usually accepted sumptuary bases—bets and sweeps tax, entertainment tax, hotel accommodation tax, stamp duties, airport departure and harbor passage tax, and motor vehicles tax. In sum, the role of tax policy in the development strategy of Hong Kong has consisted in maintaining an environment of low interference with private sector activity matched by neutrality made possible by a policy of low government expenditure and taxation. It is not difficult to see why Hong Kong has been seen as the best example of a supply-side–oriented fiscal policy.

Resilience of the Tax Structure. Hong Kong's tax structure has remained relatively unchanged since the 1950s. The EPT, its direct tax umbrella, is a schedular system comprising salaries (after various forms of personal allowances), profits (both noncorporate and corporate), property (only rent is taxed), and interest (abolished in 1989). Different tax rates apply to each component. The fact that the bases remained more or less unchanged while the rates changed very little and remained very low by international standards over three decades is possibly the most important distinguishing feature of Hong Kong's tax system. If the tax system played a role in attracting and maintaining a high level of investment and in promoting growth, it must have been due to that feature.

Tax Reform

In its continuous endeavor to encourage efficiency and growth Hong Kong introduced a major change in its tax structure in 1989 by abolishing its tax on interest income, thus equating it, for tax purposes, to the untaxed dividends and capital gains. To a large extent, therefore, the tax base moved closer to consumption.

Hong Kong's main preoccupation for its future development is its tax structure after 1997. Several authors have suggested possible tax reforms in view of the forthcoming change. Asher (1989) has recommended increasing the base of indirect taxes rather than raising EPT rates at a time when the economy might be expected to undergo a recession. The 1988 Budget Speech also recommends a sales tax in the medium term. The Draft Basic Law for after 1997 emphasizes the continuation of a free port, low taxation, and balanced budgets. A related concern is the possible extension to Hong Kong of China's tax treaties with third countries.

To conclude, Hong Kong's future development comprises unique challenges. While its tax structure has remained viable for many years, the emerging circumstances are likely to oblige Hong Kong to introduce major modifications. Some of these modifications would inevitably raise the tax level. It must be recalled that the tax level of China is now about 20 percent of its GDP. It does not seem likely that Hong Kong would have the luxury of maintaining its present unusually low ratio.

2.2.3   Korea

Structural Characteristics

Korea's history of rapid GDP growth begs the question as to whether and to what extent that growth was supported by its tax policies. A glance at Korea's tax shares indicates that taxes on domestic goods and services yield almost half of total tax revenue, income taxes less than a third, and customs duties almost a fifth. Social security and property taxes contribute little. Tax shares have remained more or less stable since the mid-1970s in the face of various tax reforms.

Korea's tax structure has been changed many times since the 1960s in order to raise the elasticity of the tax system by increasing the share of broad-based, domestic indirect taxes and in order to promote specific objectives. This change accompanied the reduction in foreign trade taxes and the granting of wide-ranging tax incentives from corporate income taxes. The objective was the promotion of export-oriented industrialization—a strategy similar to that of Taiwan.[5] By contrast personal incomes continued to be taxed at high rates (the 70 percent top marginal rate, which was reduced only in 1989, was not only the highest in our sample, but was high by world standards—see table 2.2—and continues to be one of the highest in our sample). Furthermore, it yielded about a sixth of tax revenues (table 2.1)—the second highest proportion within the sample (after Hong Kong).

Selected Distinguishing Features

Among the distinguishing features of Korea's tax system are (1) the earliest introduction—among the sample countries—of a VAT in 1977; (2) the strong role given to tax incentives; (3) an early recognition of the important role of tax administration in revenue performance; and (4) a tax reform process that has been almost uninterrupted over the years as a part of what seems to be a policy of perennial fine tuning of the tax system to promote specific objectives. These aspects are discussed below.

The VAT has become the single largest contributor—at well over a fifth—to total tax revenue and has functioned remarkably well with little change since its introduction in 1977. It is levied at a single rate of 10 percent and generates over 4 percent of GDP, which is a very good yield for such a low rate. By providing the needed revenue, Korea's early introduction of the VAT enabled the country to grant generous tax incentives geared toward its industrialization and export strategy. In this sense, Korea's VAT played a similar accommodative role as Taiwan's land-based taxes.

Until recently tax incentives had been assumed to have played an important role in Korea's economic development. Embodied in the Tax Exemption and Reduction Control Law (TERCL), they include investment tax credits, special depreciation, tax-free reserves, and liberal expensing from taxable income, in addition to the usual deductions. On the other hand, the rules for foreign direct investment have always been restrictive. Until the mid-1980s, foreign investment was allowed only for "beneficial" activities. Thus, even with a doubling of "arrived" direct foreign investment of U.S. $477 million in 1986 from $236 million in 1985, and reaching $626 million and $894 million in

---

5. Many incentives were aimed at increasing exports. See Kwack (1990).

1987 and 1988, respectively, it still represents only around 3 percent of GDP. The uniqueness of Korea's tax incentives policy, therefore lies in its being tailored toward domestic industrial development, exports, and technology transfer, rather than toward foreign investment.

Recently several Korean studies have begun to question both the effectiveness of those incentives and their equity implications. Several authors have concluded that these tax incentives have been overgenerous, leading to unnecessary revenue loss[6] and have led to inequities (Kim and Lee 1990; Kwack 1990). Lee (1990) strongly condemns the growth-orientation of the economy at a cost to a more balanced development path that would accommodate social objectives. He is of the opinion that "Korea's fiscal policy has played a weak and passive role and thus failed to fulfill necessary social needs" (3). He supports his argument with an international comparison of income distribution.[7] Now that Korea—like Taiwan—has emerged as a "growth tiger," it is beginning to give increasing weight to the objective of equitable income distribution, an objective that had not received a lot of attention in the past. Of course, the overall standard of living of Koreans has improved enormously with the achievement of sustained high rates of growth.

Among the sample countries, Korea may have been the forerunner in recognizing the importance of tax administration. The Office of National Tax Administration (ONTA), created in 1966, appears to have been quite successful in raising the tax/GDP ratio by 4 percentage points between 1966 and 1970. This office has carried a lot of power over the years. Indeed, some researchers are of the opinion that the role of tax administration has been more important than that of tax policy in determining Korea's revenue performance over the past three decades. However, several Korean participants at this conference commented on the increasing incidence of tax evasion and avoidance in Korea in recent years, thereby exacerbating the adverse distributional consequences of the tax system.

Tax Reform

A quotation pertaining to Korea from Asher (1989, 54) seems appropriate: "Tax reform is almost continuous. Major tax reforms were undertaken in 9 out of the 33 years between 1953 and 1986. Choi and Lee (1987) also report that in 7 of those 9 years, the changes were substantial enough to be labeled 'comprehensive.'" Tax policy changes have continued since 1986 with reduction in the top personal income tax rate and in the number of brackets, together with greater relief to lower brackets and wider globalization in the tax structure.

Despite the above changes, the greatest pressure on Korea's future tax re-

---

6. It should be noted that the corporate tax generated only a little more than 2 percent of GDP in 1986–88. Unpublished data indicate that in 1980 tax incentives reduced the corporate income tax base by two-thirds.

7. Kwack's conclusion is that "the tax incentives to promote exports have played only minor roles in Korea's export-oriented development process" (1990, 18).

form reflects its heightened concern toward income redistribution (Sixth Five-Year Plan, 1987–91). Such a concern will inevitably be reflected in higher social spending and in higher taxes. First, to provide nationwide medical insurance and a pension scheme, the payroll tax is slated for increase. Second, a punitive tax on the increased value of land (similar to Taiwan's LVIT) is planned in order to curb speculative forces as well as for reasons of equity. Speculators holding land zoned for housing development will pay a 50 percent tax on the increase in the annual value of the land; urban property in excess of 700 square meters will face high tax rates; and the rating system will be revised to reflect property values rather than the building cost. This is to directly redress to some extent the adverse situation of 70 percent of families in major urban areas that do not own any property. Third, currently allowable false-name stock accounts will be transformed to real-name accounts and made subject to capital gains tax. Similarly, in anticipation of a more advanced society, authors have also cited the need that "fiscal policy should be geared toward establishing medium- and long-term antipollution measures" (Lee 1990, 14).

Korea has extensively used tariff and nontariff barriers to control imports, though with a steady relaxation over recent years that has brought down the average tariff rate. With a burgeoning trade surplus a quicker liberalization of trade would be desirable—as in Taiwan. Interestingly, trade liberalization, so far, has apparently allowed greater luxury imports and, therefore, a notion of ostentatious consumption and at least a perception of increased inequities. Large differences in consumption patterns seem less socially acceptable than large differences in incomes. As a consequence the issue of income distribution has been brought to the forefront. Also, the benefits from export incentives are being questioned. It is likely that these incentives will be reduced if not eliminated in future years.

2.2.4   Singapore

Structural Characteristics

Singapore is the fourth of the sample economies that selected a development strategy based primarily on advanced technology and oriented toward exports. Public revenues have been adequate to meet its expenditure needs; thus revenue increase has not been an explicit concern of tax policy. Instead, tax incentives, fine-tuned for the purpose of generating rapid growth in selected sectors, have played as important a role in Singapore's tax policy as they were intended to play in Taiwan and Korea.

Yet Singapore, like Hong Kong but unlike Taiwan, has continued to draw a major share of its tax revenue—40–45 percent—from income taxes, and two-thirds of this share from the corporate tax. On the other hand, like Taiwan but unlike Hong Kong, it relies relatively heavily on property taxes, which account for 17 percent of tax revenue. Given its relatively heavy reliance on both income and property taxes, the contribution of customs duties and consumption taxes has been limited—about a third of total tax revenue.

Selected Distinguishing Features

Among the distinguishing features of Singapore's tax system is the large number of personal income tax brackets. Thus, Singapore has not followed the current trend toward broad, low-rate taxation with few brackets. Singapore has aimed at as broad a participation as possible by potential taxpayers in an effort to raise their tax consciousness. In 1987, for example, about two-thirds of the taxpayers had assessed income of below S. $15,000 and accounted for only 8 percent of the tax assessed (Asher 1990, 15).

Possibly the most striking feature of Singapore, a feature that sets it apart from the other countries in the sample, is its interventionist policy affecting social security provision. Provident fund contributions that amount to about a third of gross wages, including employer contributions, are tax-exempt. While this narrows the tax base, Singapore's social security needs are being met through a funded rather than a pay-as-you-go principle of social insurance and without resorting to financing through budgetary sources. As Singapore grows into an industrialized economy, the same questions being asked in Korea and Taiwan are being raised in Singapore: Should the government expand its role in providing social insurance through the budget? Does the government have responsibility in this regard as the nation matures? What should not be overlooked, however, is the past management by government in the successful provision of housing to the majority of the population through loans drawn on the Central Provident Fund, an achievement not claimed by Taiwan, Korea, and Hong Kong.

Singapore is not different from Taiwan or Korea in its explicit and forceful use of income tax incentives for promoting industrial policies. As mentioned above, it has used them also as an instrument for its social policies (i.e., deductions of provident fund contributions) as well as for the retention of local and foreign professional work forces. Like Hong Kong, Singapore has used tax incentives to promote its financial policies by exempting capital gains from taxation altogether.

Tax Reform

As Singapore matures further, what role can taxation be expected to play? Perhaps Singapore should move toward a uniform, broader-based system of taxation. While the 1986 Report of the Economic Committee of the Ministry of Trade and Industry recommended phasing out selective fiscal incentives and moving to a uniform, low corporate and personal income tax structure as a long-term goal—a move that would take Singapore in the direction of Hong Kong—it also called for additional incentives in the immediate future, for example, a 30 percent initial allowance for all investment (this would, of course, remove the current promanufacturing bias of tax incentives). Thus, as in Taiwan, Singapore has not effectively questioned the continued role of tax incentives in the near term.

Similarly, while the share of revenue from domestic consumption taxes has increased in the late 1980s, interest in a broad-based VAT remains slight, especially in an environment in which neither private savings nor overall tax revenue are considered low, though Singapore has been studying the advantages of eventually introducing a VAT. In any case, the economy of Singapore is, perhaps, organized enough to render feasible a retail sales tax instead of a VAT.

The primary area where Singapore could seriously consider tax reform, at its present stage of development, is in a reintroduction of the payroll tax for the budgetary financing of social insurance. The Economic Committee's recommendation for a property tax decrease, effective in 1990, would also have a revenue impact and would possibly require some fine-tuning in other tax revenue sources.

2.2.5 Malaysia

Structural Characteristics

Malaysia is the first of the non-NICs in our sample, and its tax history exhibits their common concern regarding revenue generation. Like Indonesia, it is a petroleum exporter and has had a similar problem of trying to raise the share of nonpetroleum revenues in the presence of present or expected reduction in oil revenues. It has experienced large fiscal deficits throughout the 1980s and has accumulated considerable foreign debt. Table 2.3 presents, for available sample countries, the movements over time of tax/GDP ratios. It shows how in the 1980s Malaysia's tax/GDP ratio fell steadily, with the relative decline in nonoil tax revenue being even greater. This fall in revenue has forced a large reduction in public spending in recent years.

Various causes may be cited for the decline in revenue. First, tax incentives have grown to include "investment, export, reinvestment, research and development, labor utilization, manpower training, location, and others" (Asher, Salih, and Salleh 1990, 11). The inevitable result has been a fall in the corporate income tax/GDP ratio. Second, despite a doubling of the sales tax rate from 5 percent to 10 percent in 1983, revenue from this tax has declined slightly in terms of GDP as a result of the progressive erosion of the tax base.[8] Similarly, the excise tax/GDP ratio has stagnated because many of the taxed items have been removed, leaving only traditional excisable items—petroleum, tobacco, alcohol, and motor vehicles. Third, taxes on exports have declined by about 3 percentage points of GDP between 1978 and 1988, while customs duties have declined by 1 percentage point. Finally, despite the use

8. The Malaysian Institute of Economic Research (MIER) has estimated that, up to 1987, 75 percent of domestic manufacturing output was exempt from the tax base. Some of the exemptions were reduced in 1988.

Table 2.3   **Tax GDP Ratio of Sample Asian Countries (time series)**

	1978–80	1979–81	1980–82	1981–83	1982–84	1983–85	1984–86	1985–87	1986–88
Total Tax Revenue									
Singapore	16.81	17.51	18.56	19.20	19.17	18.10	16.16	14.75	13.90
Korea	15.39	15.49	15.56	15.72	15.64	15.40	15.03	15.10	15.53
Malaysia	21.69	22.19	22.46	22.24	21.84	22.28	21.89	20.20	18.27
Thailand	12.42	12.73	12.91	13.44	13.87	14.29	14.22	14.24	14.74
Philippines	11.66	11.25	10.58	10.18	9.83	9.85	9.90	10.86	11.30
Indonesia	19.99	20.82	20.44	19.13	17.99	17.72	16.64	16.03	15.04
Taxes on Income									
Singapore	7.48	8.15	9.25	9.73	9.50	8.59	7.26	6.35	5.79
Korea	4.22	4.16	4.14	4.18	4.12	4.11	4.16	4.48	4.87
Malaysia	8.72	9.30	9.88	10.06	10.03	10.59	11.03	10.22	8.98
Thailand	2.45	2.56	2.73	2.89	3.04	3.15	3.26	3.16	3.18
Philippines	2.81	2.69	2.55	2.40	2.31	2.50	2.76	3.02	3.04
Indonesia	15.48	16.92	16.93	15.87	14.82	14.19	12.09	10.58	9.17
Individual Income Taxes									
Singapore	n.a.	n.a.	n.a.	n.a.	n.a.	n.a.	n.a.	n.a.	n.a.
Korea	2.16	2.14	2.14	2.21	2.18	2.19	2.26	2.44	2.66
Malaysia	2.11	2.05	1.97	2.22	2.42	2.44	2.40	2.33	2.31
Thailand	1.07	1.08	1.17	1.33	1.54	1.71	1.80	1.73	1.63
Philippines	1.52	1.35	1.23	1.13	0.97	0.91	0.89	0.97	1.00
Indonesia	0.45	0.39	0.39	0.44	0.49	0.57	0.61	0.65	0.69
Corporate Taxes									
Singapore	n.a.	n.a.	n.a.	n.a.	n.a.	n.a.	n.a.	n.a.	n.a.
Korea	2.05	2.02	1.99	1.97	1.94	1.92	1.91	2.04	2.21
Malaysia	6.61	7.24	7.91	7.84	7.62	8.15	8.61	7.88	6.66
Thailand	1.38	1.48	1.55	1.56	1.50	1.44	1.46	1.43	1.55
Philippines	1.30	1.36	1.35	1.29	1.31	1.38	1.41	1.55	1.56
Indonesia	14.06	15.61	15.58	14.52	13.62	13.18	11.22	9.68	8.28
Taxes on Income—Other									
Singapore	n.a.	n.a.	n.a.	n.a.	n.a.	n.a.	n.a.	n.a.	n.a.
Korea	0.00	0.00	0.00	0.00	0.00	0.00	0.00	0.00	0.00
Malaysia	0.01	0.00	0.00	0.00	0.00	0.00	0.01	0.02	0.02
Thailand	0.00	0.00	0.00	0.00	0.00	0.00	0.00	0.00	0.00
Philippines	0.00	0.00	0.00	0.00	0.04	0.22	0.45	0.50	0.49
Indonesia	0.96	0.92	0.96	0.91	0.70	0.44	0.26	0.25	0.20
Domestic Taxes on Goods and Services									
Singapore	3.91	3.90	3.87	3.87	3.97	3.93	3.86	4.02	4.12
Korea	7.62	7.89	8.08	8.09	8.00	7.76	7.42	7.08	6.87
Malaysia	4.65	4.38	4.32	4.61	4.79	4.94	4.78	4.59	4.43
Thailand	6.20	6.40	6.60	7.10	7.32	7.46	7.39	7.62	7.84
Philippines	5.35	5.34	4.93	4.61	4.21	4.06	4.24	4.78	5.14
Indonesia	2.22	1.96	1.99	2.02	2.05	2.46	3.39	3.94	4.23

(*continued*)

Table 2.3   (Continued)

	1978–80	1979–81	1980–82	1981–83	1982–84	1983–85	1984–86	1985–87	1986–88
Taxes on General Sales, Turnover, VAT									
Singapore	0.00	0.00	0.00	0.00	0.00	0.00	0.00	0.00	0.00
Korea	3.60	3.71	3.84	3.89	3.86	3.77	3.60	3.49	3.41
Malaysia	1.23	1.25	1.28	1.46	1.59	1.70	1.55	1.45	1.43
Thailand	2.67	2.63	2.64	2.69	2.81	2.88	2.85	2.71	2.81
Philippines	1.79	1.72	1.65	1.56	1.29	1.06	0.97	1.08	1.19
Indonesia	1.19	0.99	1.02	1.04	1.06	1.48	2.07	2.65	2.93
Taxes on Excises									
Singapore	1.47	1.41	1.36	1.37	1.47	1.53	1.47	1.33	1.22
Korea	2.63	2.67	2.55	2.44	2.36	2.32	2.28	2.16	2.11
Malaysia	2.09	1.86	1.71	1.75	1.81	1.85	1.86	1.79	1.73
Thailand	2.56	2.85	3.16	3.57	3.78	3.86	3.92	4.23	4.34
Philippines	2.75	2.60	2.27	2.06	1.99	2.11	2.34	2.70	2.90
Indonesia	1.03	0.97	0.96	0.98	0.99	0.98	0.99	0.96	0.97
Domestic Taxes on Goods and Services—Other									
Singapore	2.44	2.49	2.51	2.50	2.50	2.40	2.39	2.69	2.90
Korea	1.39	1.51	1.69	1.77	1.78	1.66	1.54	1.42	1.34
Malaysia	1.34	1.27	1.32	1.40	1.39	1.39	1.36	1.35	1.27
Thailand	0.97	0.92	0.80	0.83	0.73	0.72	0.62	0.68	0.68
Philippines	0.81	1.01	1.01	1.00	0.93	0.90	0.93	1.00	1.04
Indonesia	0.00	0.00	0.00	0.00	0.00	0.00	0.33	0.33	0.33
Taxes on Foreign Trade									
Singapore	1.86	1.71	1.57	1.45	1.40	1.24	1.05	0.89	0.84
Korea	2.92	2.69	2.53	2.58	2.63	2.62	2.52	2.63	2.67
Malaysia	7.83	7.96	7.63	6.87	6.29	6.01	5.38	4.70	4.20
Thailand	3.49	3.51	3.32	3.18	3.21	3.36	3.27	3.15	3.35
Philippines	3.11	2.92	2.78	2.80	2.97	2.97	2.63	2.75	2.80
Indonesia	1.96	1.67	1.26	0.99	0.84	0.74	0.79	1.11	1.21
Taxes on Imports									
Singapore	1.86	1.71	1.57	1.45	1.40	1.24	1.05	0.89	0.84
Korea	2.92	2.69	2.53	2.58	2.63	2.62	2.52	2.63	2.67
Malaysia	3.56	3.68	3.83	3.77	3.60	3.45	3.18	2.85	2.61
Thailand	2.92	2.84	2.66	2.67	2.79	2.99	2.98	2.92	3.15
Philippines	2.86	2.71	2.65	2.70	2.77	2.66	2.29	2.54	2.70
Indonesia	1.09	0.97	0.91	0.82	0.71	0.64	0.72	0.78	0.90
Taxes on Exports									
Singapore	0.00	0.00	0.00	0.00	0.00	0.00	0.00	0.00	0.00
Korea	0.00	0.00	0.00	0.00	0.00	0.00	0.00	0.00	0.00
Malaysia	4.28	4.28	3.80	3.10	2.69	2.57	2.20	1.85	1.58
Thailand	0.58	0.67	0.66	0.51	0.41	0.34	0.25	0.20	0.17
Philippines	0.25	0.20	0.12	0.09	0.16	0.18	0.20	0.09	0.05
Indonesia	0.87	0.70	0.34	0.16	0.12	0.10	0.08	0.06	0.09

(continued)

Table 2.3   **(Continued)**

	1978–80	1979–81	1980–82	1981–83	1982–84	1983–85	1984–86	1985–87	1986–88
Taxes on Foreign Trade—Other									
Singapore	0.00	0.00	0.00	0.00	0.00	0.00	0.00	0.00	0.00
Korea	0.00	0.00	0.00	0.00	0.00	0.00	0.00	0.00	0.00
Malaysia	0.00	0.00	0.00	0.00	0.00	0.03	0.04	0.03	0.03
Thailand	0.00	0.00	0.00	0.00	0.01	0.03	0.04	0.03	0.03
Philippines	0.01	0.01	0.02	0.01	0.04	0.13	0.14	0.12	0.05
Indonesia	0.00	0.00	0.00	0.00	0.00	0.00	0.00	0.00	0.00
Social Security Contribution									
Singapore	0.00	0.00	0.00	0.00	0.00	0.00	0.00	0.00	0.00
Korea	0.18	0.19	0.19	0.20	0.21	0.23	0.25	0.27	0.41
Malaysia	0.10	0.11	0.13	0.14	0.14	0.14	0.16	0.18	0.18
Thailand	0.00	0.00	0.00	0.00	0.00	0.00	0.00	0.00	0.00
Philippines	0.00	0.00	0.00	0.00	0.00	0.00	0.00	0.00	0.00
Indonesia	0.00	0.00	0.00	0.00	0.00	0.00	0.00	0.00	0.00
Taxes on Wealth and Property									
Singapore	2.96	3.00	3.05	3.29	3.51	3.53	3.10	2.54	2.15
Korea	0.08	0.11	0.15	0.17	0.16	0.13	0.11	0.12	0.20
Malaysia	0.10	0.12	0.14	0.15	0.14	0.12	0.12	0.11	0.10
Thailand	0.18	0.18	0.17	0.19	0.20	0.21	0.20	0.20	0.25
Philippines	0.16	0.10	0.10	0.10	0.09	0.09	0.08	0.07	0.07
Indonesia	0.24	0.20	0.19	0.18	0.19	0.21	0.21	0.21	0.24
Other Taxes									
Singapore	0.60	0.75	0.83	0.86	0.79	0.81	0.89	0.95	1.00
Korea	0.37	0.43	0.47	0.50	0.51	0.55	0.41	0.36	0.35
Malaysia	0.28	0.32	0.37	0.41	0.45	0.46	0.43	0.40	0.39
Thailand	0.09	0.09	0.08	0.09	0.10	0.11	0.11	0.11	0.12
Philippines	0.18	0.20	0.21	0.21	0.20	0.19	0.21	0.23	0.25
Indonesia	0.07	0.06	0.06	0.06	0.06	0.08	0.10	0.10	0.14

Source: Fiscal Affairs Department data base, International Monetary Fund.

of various individual income surtaxes, such as a 5 percent development tax on professional, business, and rental income, as well as a 5 percent excess profits tax, individual income tax in relation to GDP has also declined. Thus, other smaller tax sources and petroleum revenue have increased relative to GDP. Malaysia has been studying the possibility of introducing a VAT at some point. But no decision has yet been made in this direction.

Selected Aspects

In 1986, a 1968 law on tax incentives was replaced by the Promotion of Investment Act on the grounds that the earlier system was difficult to administer, favored capital-intensive and large projects, was too generous, and granted unnecessary protection to domestic industry. However, the incentives do not appear to have been greater than those granted by the NICs. The revised Malaysian act itself, as well as the Malaysia Institute of Economic Research (MIER) tax reform proposals, does not really attempt to reduce the role of tax incentives; MIER, for example, recommends their extension to the service sector and high-risk projects, as well as the widening of their range.

More than the complexity of the incentives themselves, the impact of petroleum as a source of revenue and a lack of resolve toward fundamental tax reform were the primary factors that relegated taxation to a secondary role in Malaysia's development.

Tax Reform

In the future, Malaysia will need to undergo major tax reform. To buttress its future development, it will need to raise substantial additional tax revenue to match its high expenditure needs—for renewed capital expenditure, as well as for maintenance and building infrastructure. These needs have been contained in past years to reduce the large fiscal deficit.[9] The practice of piecemeal tax changes to meet immediate revenue needs will have to be replaced by more structural tax reform.

If Malaysia's experience has demonstrated that it is best to avoid a tax structure made complex by multiple objectives, it should aim at a simpler system. If its system of tax incentives has not worked in the past, it is unlikely that it will work in the future. Instead, it could strive to broaden the base of its sales tax, which already operates on a limited value-added basis. It could consider imposing a property tax such as in Singapore, or introducing taxes on land speculation such as in Taiwan and as proposed in Korea. It should also aim at improvements in the administration of income taxes, together with a broadening of the income tax base.

2.2.6   Indonesia

Much has been written on Indonesia's pre–and post–tax reform experiences (Booth and McCawley 1981, Asher 1989, and Gillis 1990, among others). Here we endeavor to examine the nature of arguments as to why the simplification of Indonesia's tax system is considered successful. In this section, the background for the need for the whole reform effort is considered. Subsequently, the nature as well as the results of the reform is assessed.

Structural Characteristics

Indonesia is the second oil exporter in our sample. Like Malaysia, its tax system lingered in the shadow of revenues from petroleum and gas till 1985 when Indonesia began to implement one of the most comprehensive tax reforms in Asia. The task of reforming the tax system was difficult because the

---

9. Thus, Asher, Salih, and Salleh (1990) point out that government expenditure in relation to GDP fell from 40 percent in 1981–85 to 31 percent in 1986–90.

existing system had become extremely complex, while collection was small (see table 2.3). Direct taxes were a combination of royalties, property, and income taxes, though they were all treated under the "income tax" nomenclature for foreign tax credit purposes. Progressive scales applied to both the personal income tax (5–50 percent) and the corporate income tax (20, 30, and 45 percent) and included exemptions and exclusions that were not implemented efficiently. Incentives, comprising tax holidays and investment tax credits geared toward regional balance, employment promotion, investment in target areas, and the like, abounded. The property tax, dating back to the 1600s and applicable to both urban and rural areas, was collected mainly from the latter and had degenerated to insignificance with ever-growing exemptions. Consumption taxes comprised a turnover tax, selected excises, and customs duties, each accounting for about 1 percent of GDP. The cascading turnover/sales tax was subject to rate differentiation (eight rates between 1 and 20 percent), resulting not only in distortions but also in evasion, and many items were also exempted. In addition, the sales tax element in exports required a complicated export rebate system.

There was a widespread belief that tax administration was very poor while evasion was widespread. Both evasion and corruption were stimulated by the complexity of the tax system. Only a fundamental reform could improve the situation.

A Distinguishing Feature

The most distinguishing characteristic of Indonesia's tax system, as in Malaysia, was its primary dependence on the oil sector for the bulk of its revenue. The benefits of the oil sector allowed a high rate of growth combined with low inflation rates. Thus, spurred on by oil revenues, Indonesia's real annual GDP growth as 7–8 percent in the 1970s up to 1982, and inflation was less than 10 percent except during the 1973 and 1979 oil boom years. This result was achieved despite a "decade of neglect" of physical infrastructure[10] and in the presence of a ratio of nonoil revenue to GDP in the 7–8 percent range throughout the period (see Gillis 1990, table 1). This low ratio was justified in the hope that oil prices would continue to remain strong. Eventually, and as a result of the fall in oil prices in the early 1980s, the authorities came to believe that the excessive dependence on the oil sector should be reduced.

Fundamental Tax Reform

Once Indonesia decided to undertake fundamental tax reform, it made large strides in that direction. The changes made were comprehensive and well planned: the necessary laws were passed in 1983; a unified personal and corporate income tax was introduced in 1984 at rates of 15, 25, and 35 percent; a

---

10. The problem of low expenditure for operation and maintenance remains significant (see Tanzi 1987).

uniform 10 percent VAT (coupled with higher luxury taxes) was introduced in 1985; and a new property tax aimed at urban real estate was introduced in 1986. Income tax–based incentives were abolished.

Indonesia's tax reform experience was clearly influenced by, and in turn it influenced, current world thinking. It was aimed at producing a much simplified system. Such a system would be neutral, that is, as nondistortionary as possible (few and low tax rates with no special incentives); equitable (taxation of urban property and luxuries pari passu, leaving low-income households out of the tax); and revenue-generating (though initially it was revenue-neutral, revenue was expected to rise rapidly from the broader tax base). However, the reform was less successful with respect to import duties. This is a problem that Indonesia will have to face during its next development phase as it attempts to modernize its industries while exposing them to adequate international competition.

It is generally accepted that Indonesia's tax reform has been successful in certain respects at least. First, it has reduced distortions caused by the previous tax structure. Second, its 1983–85 sales tax revenue of 1.5 percent of GDP has been doubled to 3 percent from the VAT (see table 2.3) in 1986–88, while excise revenue has been maintained. Third, administrative reform was a major objective in which initial gains seem to have been made.

2.2.7   Thailand

The last two countries in our sample—Thailand and the Philippines—are neither NICs nor oil exporters.[11] Within a decade, Thailand has increased its tax/GDP ratio by more than 2 percentage points of GDP. On the other hand, the tax/GDP ratio of the Philippines has stagnated in spite of that country's great need for revenue.

Structural Characteristics

Thailand has been a high-growth, low-inflation economy. It has undergone rapid economic transformation, as agriculture's share in GDP has been shrinking rapidly,[12] and as export promotion has replaced import substitution as a development strategy. However, Thailand's tax system has lacked the transparence that is needed to achieve specific objectives. If anything, it has been an obstacle to the achievement of those objectives.

The tax structure itself is complex. It has been characterized by base erosion resulting from many special allowances and high standard deductions (allowed for different sources of income) and by the failure to tax fringe benefits. Also, there are many nonneutralities in the tax treatment of different income sources on different transactions. In the corporate income tax, the differential tax treatment of interest and dividends has led to a bias in favor of

---

11. Given the high growth rate in Thailand in recent years, it may soon establish a claim to be classified as a NIC.

12. For a treatment of sectoral changes in GDP, see Richupan (1990).

debt financing, while asset revaluation formulas, loss carry-forward provisions, and the like do not appear to be internationally competitive.

Selected Distinguishing Features

Heavy Reliance on Domestic Consumption Taxes. Table 2.3 shows that Thailand has historically depended heavily on domestic consumption taxes and continues to do so—obtaining more than half of its tax revenue from a cascading business tax, applied with differentiated and high rates, and from a large number of excises (table 2.1). Customs duties and income taxes yield above a fifth each. Customs tariffs are also very complex, providing a wide range of effective protection to some domestic industries. The overall system of business tax, excises, and customs tariff has formed a complex, distortionary wedge into the production structure of the economy.

The Role of Tax Incentives. Thailand's Board of Investment played a major role in the allocation of the nation's productive resources by encouraging specific sectors and discouraging others through the tax system. The high degree of discretion and selectivity in the granting of incentives for a wide range of objectives, accompanied by little monitoring or follow-up of promoted enterprises, paralleled the experience of Indonesia and the Philippines. Indonesia's solution was to abolish tax incentives altogether. Thailand, like the Philippines, does not appear to have come to that solution.

To conclude, Thailand's tax structure is likely to have generated production distortions, with an adverse impact on production patterns and levels. This has been especially true of its business tax. In this sense, it may have sacrificed some of its potential growth over the years. However, its incentives regime, while complex and distortionary in conception, was even more deficient in implementation.

Tax Reform

Like Malaysia, Thailand has tinkered with its tax system over the years without any major policy reform. In 1989, it introduced further tax changes aimed at simplification, neutrality, and revenue generation. The personal income tax brackets were reduced from eleven to six, while the top rate remains at 55 percent. Also, a greater number of low-income taxpayers were left out of the income tax net. But, to address the revenue objective, a further schedular aspect was introduced with a withholding tax of 15 percent on dividend income. Not much has been done, however, to reduce expense deductions and allowances from business incomes.

The major tax reform under consideration by Thailand is the introduction of a 10 percent VAT to replace the current complex and inefficient business tax with twenty-one rates ranging from 0.10 to 50 percent. While several service activities and agricultural products would be left out of the tax net, this would be a change in the right direction that can only benefit production and growth. While the combined changes in the system of excises and the business tax are to be revenue-neutral, the expectation is that the broad-based VAT would be revenue-enhancing in the medium term. Thailand has been getting ready for the introduction of the VAT. Much of the preparatory work has been done, and an intense campaign to instruct taxpayers has been carried out. However, it appears that some political hurdles must be overcome for the VAT to be introduced in Thailand.

Thailand will need to focus on reducing the wide dispersion of its nominal tariffs—thirty-four rates ranging between 1 and 200 percent—and the excessive rates of effective protection if it wishes to modernize its industrial sector. There is much discussion on this issue and many studies. The next step would be to place it firmly on the tax reform agenda. As in Taiwan and Korea, its current balance-of-payment situation does not justify the continuation of obstacles to import.

Finally, it should be mentioned that there have been major improvements in tax administration in recent years. In this sense, the experience of Thailand is different from that of the Philippines, with the public finances of Thailand having improved considerably in recent years. These improvements have made possible the rise in the tax/GDP ratio and have thus insured that at least the revenue objective was satisfied.

2.2.8   The Philippines

In our discussion of East Asian economies, placing the Philippines at the very end has a certain purpose: it has lagged behind in economic development and has had little success in applying fiscal instruments—both tax and expenditure—to promote its development needs. Furthermore, the quality of its tax administration has been particularly disappointing.

Structural Characteristics

The Philippines' shares of various taxes in total tax revenue parallel those of Thailand. However, while there has been a steady—though slow—increase in Thailand's tax/GDP ratio over the last decade, the Philippines' tax ratio has not increased beyond the low level of 11 percent (table 2.3), which occurred during a period when expenditure increases were significant. The consequence was a continuous fiscal crisis. Despite the recognition, in a number of studies and reports since the mid-1970s, of a need for major tax reform, the period through the first half of the 1980s witnessed only minor ad hoc changes in the tax system.

Changes in excises—especially in petroleum products—sales tax, and trade taxes were among the minor ad hoc revisions made. These changes made the system more complex and the administration more unwieldy. For example, domestic consumption was taxed by a "manufacturers' sales tax" on a value-added basis; a "contractor's tax" on some services while other individual services were taxed at differing rates; "fixed and graduated fixed taxes" on sales establishments, with rates varying according to business; and variously rated sales taxes on imports of domestic consumption goods that were designed to selectively provide protection to domestic production.

Income taxes also went through various revisions. For example, in 1981 the tax base was changed from net to gross income, and separate rates and exemptions were applied to different sources of income. These changes had the objective of improving revenue performance through easier administration. However, their impact on revenue was disappointing. Table 2.3 reveals that the income tax/GDP ratio as well as the individual income tax/GDP ratio both declined steadily in the post-1981 period. The same occurred to other taxes during the first half of the 1980s. This should not be surprising, since fiscal incentives—incorporating a basic 1968 legislation—covered a wide variety of objectives such as import substitution, labor-intensive production, and a well-ranked set—pioneer, nonpioneer (but preferred), and others—of industrial as well as export promotion. Further, instruments used were not just income taxes, but domestic sales taxes as well as customs tariffs.

Selected Distinguishing Features

Behind the stagnancy in the Philippines' tax effort lies a decline in its tax/GDP ratio between 1978 and 1985, and then a steady rise back to the initial level by 1988. The decline followed by the rise is reflected across domestic consumption and income taxes, though not trade taxes. Within these tax groups, the composition has changed: thus general sales taxes have remained at a much lower level than in the 1978–80 era, as has the individual income tax, whose fall has been countered to some extent by selective excises and by the corporate income tax. But the overall pattern that emerges is that, while up to the mid-1980s the tax system had ceased to be buoyant, in the second half of the decade it began to respond somewhat to the reform actions. However, the effort barely brought the tax/GDP ratio back to the level at the beginning of the 1980s.

Despite the large number of studies by international agencies and national bodies, there has been limited action by the authorities to implement serious tax reform. Administrative improvements have also been lacking. The authorities have made frequent use of tax amnesties. Between 1972 and 1981, ten amnesties were declared, yielding substantial revenues and, in effect, validating the failure in tax administration. The 1983–84 economic crisis spurred some action on reforming the tax system and on improving its tax administration.

Tax Reform

Tax reform in the Philippines became a major concern after the 1983–84 economic crisis. That concern accelerated with the 1986 change in government. The new government announced the intention of introducing basic modifications to the tax structure to simplify it, make it more neutral, broaden its base, and raise additional revenue. Several tax measures became effective beginning in 1988.

A uniform 10 percent, consumption-based VAT was adopted. Capital equipment, agricultural inputs, and small businesses are exempt, while certain services such as hotels and insurance are taxed outside the VAT system. However, the performance of the VAT has not been too encouraging, and its revenue in relation to GDP has registered little increase over the pre-VAT years. One reason that has been cited is lack of administrative preparation and poor implementation (Sicat 1990). Unlike Indonesia and Korea, where administrative aspects received careful attention and the revenue response was far more positive, in the Philippines administrative aspects have continued to receive inadequate attention. The excises—mainly tobacco, alcohol, and energy products—have scored better in revenue response.

The Philippines abolished all export taxes—on copper concentrates, sugar, copra, and coconut oil—except those on logs and lumber. While highly desirable from an efficiency and, perhaps, equity perspective, this change led to a loss of a steady source of revenue that the country was not able to replace easily with alternate sources. The schedular income tax system was continued, while the number of individual income tax rates was reduced and the top rate was halved to 35 percent. The base was broadened to a "modified gross"—from the earlier "net"—base system. The top individual and the corporate income tax rates were aligned.

So far the revenue response to these changes has been marginal. This had been expected for the individual income tax—a result exacerbated by the tax exemption of dividend income from 1989—but not for the corporate income tax. For the latter, it had been assumed that tax evasion would be reduced as a result of the introduction of a single corporate tax rate. The tax incentive system was again tinkered with and, possibly, made more ample and unnecessary (Sicat 1990). Finally, a tax amnesty was declared (in 1986), yielding about 3 percent of income tax revenue.

To conclude, the Philippines has introduced various tax reform measures in the late 1980s, comprising income and consumption taxes. Yet the revenue response has so far not been significant. Clearly, the Philippines is one case in which taxation will be ineffective unless major administrative improvements are made.

2.3   Lessons and Conclusions

We have discussed some important features of the tax systems of eight East Asian economies. These eight countries include some very successful economic performers—Hong Kong, Korea, Singapore, Taiwan, and Thailand; some adequate performers—Indonesia and Malaysia; and one that has had substantial and continuous economic problems during the past decade, namely the Philippines. This characterization is made on the basis of growth rates, rates of inflation, balance-of-payments performances, and whether external debt became a major problem.

The question that must be asked now is whether there are any lessons or general conclusions that could be drawn from the experiences of these economies. We will discuss separately conclusions relating to economic performance in general and conclusions derived from the earlier discussion of the tax systems.

2.3.1   Lessons from Economic Performances

Tax policy is only one element of the general economic policy pursued by a country. Other policies, such as fiscal policy in a broader sense, monetary policy, exchange rate policy, price policy, and the various regulations that often greatly influence the allocation of resources, are equally important. It is thus difficult to isolate the effect of tax policy from that of the other policies or to attribute to it economic successes or failures. The countries that performed well generally pursued good policy on many fronts. They did not allow the real exchange rate to become overvalued, they did not allow large and difficult-to-finance fiscal deficits to arise, and they pursued monetary policies that kept inflation under control and real interest rates positive. In fact, in some of these countries, tax policy would not have deserved particularly high marks if assessed in isolation.

By and large, the successful countries avoided difficulties with external debt. They did not borrow to finance consumption or unproductive investment as happened in some other Asian countries (see Tanzi 1987) and in too many countries elsewhere in the world. In Korea and Thailand, the growing size of the external debt became a concern in the early 1980s, and both countries took steps to bring down their ratio of external debt to GDP. In Malaysia, the external debt became a greater concern, having reached a very high ratio of GDP. In more recent years this country has also been attempting to control that problem. In the Philippines, however, the external debt has continued to grow, creating major difficulties for policymakers. In Indonesia, the external debt has been a continuous concern, although it has not created the same difficulties as in the Philippines.

In all of these successful countries, the government has played a major role. Therefore, the hypothesis advanced by some writers, that the success of some of these countries was due to the insignificant role of the public sector, is simply not correct. What is important is that the government's role was limited to its traditional functions, namely, the provision of social and economic infrastructure, the maintenance of a stable economic framework, and the promotion of growth. The signal that the government gave over the years was that increasing the size of the economy, especially through the stimulation of exports, was more important than the redistribution of income or the achievement of special social goals. Public expenditure was mostly of the type that public finance experts sometimes call "exhaustive"—in other words, it directly used goods and services. Education, in particular, received a lot of attention. In this area, these countries outspent most other developing countries. Furthermore, education was oriented toward technical fields. The proportion of transfers in total expenditure was kept small. The role of social security in these countries, with the exception of Singapore, was limited. And welfare transfers were almost nonexistent. Government jobs were generally well paid and carried prestige. Public employees were a powerful group. Clientelism and unemployment reduction did not play any significant role in the selection and hiring of government employees.

In summary, the public sectors in the successful East Asian countries were consistent with the view that public sectors should be small but efficient. In the less successful countries of the sample, some of the above conditions did not exist.

2.3.2   Lessons from the Tax Systems

A few lessons can be derived from the analysis of the tax systems of the sample countries. First, the importance of the *structure* of taxation is directly related to the stability of the macroeconomic framework. The more stable the macroeconomic framework, the more important becomes the tax structure. The tax structure may become largely irrelevant when macroeconomic problems become predominant, and the distortions created by the tax system become of a second order of magnitude. In these situations, it may be preferable to raise the level of taxes through "bad" taxes, in order to reduce the fiscal deficit, than to continue with a low-yielding but "good" tax system that does not generate sufficient revenue to cover expenditure. This conclusion rests on the assumption that raising revenue will necessarily help correct the macroeconomic imbalance by reducing the size of the fiscal deficit. It also implies that a poor tax structure is not itself a major contributor to the macroeconomic problems. However, a country that, for example, attempted to raise a large share of total tax revenue from export taxes might be contributing to its own macroeconomic difficulties by discouraging exports.

Second, there seems to be little relationship between fiscal disequilibrium and the level of taxation. The country with the highest level of taxation (Malaysia) was also the one with the highest fiscal deficit. On the other hand, the two countries with the lowest level of taxation (Hong Kong and the Philippines) included one of the best and the worst economic performers in the group. In this connection it may also be important to ask what countries attempt to achieve with the resources they collect from higher levels of taxation. Why do countries aim for widely different tax levels and expenditure levels? In Malaysia, for example, the level of public spending reached 40 percent of GDP in the early 1980s, while in several of the other countries it was one-third or half that level. Why did Malaysia feel the necessity to bring its public spending to such a high level while, say, Taiwan and Thailand did not? Were there specific objectives (literacy, life expectancy, employment, a better income distribution) that Malaysia was trying to achieve? Was it successful? The experience from developing countries in general also indicates that raising taxes, without controlling nonproductive public spending, often leads to disappointing results.

Third, no clear pattern of tax policy appears among the five most successful countries. None had particularly high tax ratios, and two of them, Singapore and Taiwan, made good use of property taxation, a distinctive feature of these countries. In fact, there is no comparable experience in the developing world. Korea is contemplating following this experience by introducing property taxes to discourage speculative investment in land. The reliance on income taxes was also varied. Some countries had very low income tax rates on both individuals and enterprises, but others did not. In general income tax rates were not particularly low in these countries, except in Hong Kong.

Hong Kong is the classic example of a Reagan-type supply-side economy. It has a small but highly efficient government that has given no role to government bureaucrats in the selection of investments, a decision left essentially to market forces, and has used low tax rates applied to broad bases. Thus, Hong Kong went for the leveling of the playing field long before such an approach became fashionable. In fact, the Hong Kong experience inspired some of the early and influential writers on supply-side economics. Furthermore, the tax environment for investors and decision makers in general was quite stable, since tax rates were kept essentially unchanged over decades and the structure of taxation was left intact over many years. Thus, the playing field was not just leveled across investments at one moment of time but also over time. These low rates were assumed to stimulate high savings and to encourage the use of that saving in the most productive activities. The country did not discriminate between domestic and foreign investment. The government saw its role as that of providing a low-cost and stable environment for potential investors, whether domestic or foreign. This attitude left no role for explicit tax incentives. Given the transparency of the tax system, it probably also left little, if any, role for rent-seeking activities. One would assume that Hong Kong would provide a good model for other countries to imitate. In fact, it has often been considered by supply-siders as the ideal model.

The problem with the above conclusion, however, is that Taiwan followed a very different strategy but achieved similar results. Taiwanese policymakers believed that they could pursue an investment strategy that would second-guess the market and pick winners. As a consequence, Taiwan kept its tax rates much higher than Hong Kong but pushed the investors in the desired direction through the widespread use of tax incentives. These incentives were fine-tuned to a degree rarely seen in other countries. Through tax incentives the government tried to encourage exports as well as investment in high technology industries. At the same time it tried to discourage investment in "unproductive" expenditure through high income tax rates and high land taxes.

This strategy is a challenge to the kind of supply-side economics identified with Hong Kong.

On the basis of the experience of many developing countries, many tax experts are now strongly opposed to the use of tax incentives. These are seen to breed corruption and rent-seeking activities and to negatively affect the quality of the tax system. And often they are also seen to be ineffective. Yet Taiwan has grown at a very high rate and has promoted high technology industries presumably through the use of tax incentives.[13] And, to a large extent, Korea and Singapore have done the same. Was there something peculiar to these countries that made possible for them the productive use of instruments that are largely discredited and ineffective in other countries?

One possible answer is that the effectiveness of the tax incentives may depend less on their own characteristics than on the characteristics of the countries where they are used. In countries where the public bureaucracy is made up of a well-paid, well-trained, powerful, and respected elite and where the population is highly homogeneous and deeply committed to achieving particular social goals, the use of tax incentives will not lead to the same detrimental influences often found in other countries. Korea, Singapore, and Taiwan are clear examples of the former type of countries. There is no doubt that they are highly homogeneous and that their civil servants represent a powerful and efficient elite. In these countries, civil servants can use the incentives and other policy instruments to push economic decisions in directions that give more weight to longer-term results than to immediate results and that may generate important externalities that facilitate the growth process. In other words, the decision-making process of the public bureaucracy may be guided by a lower, implicit, discount rate than the one that guides the private sector.

Private enterprises are likely to make economic decisions on the basis of current relative prices and factor availability. In other words, they tend to focus on immediate and private profits. Or, putting it differently, they make decisions on the basis of a static concept of comparative advantage or efficiency. However, a dynamic society, especially at an earlier stage of development than industrial countries, might be able to pursue policies aimed at changing the current comparative advantage and at exploiting externalities. This line of argument has been developed recently by Murphy, Shleifer, and Vishny (1989), Romer (1989), and others. Government bureaucrats might believe that, with proper policies, including tax incentives, costs of production can be reduced by increasing the factors of production that are now scarce. This is a kind of infant industry argument, but applied to the whole society rather than to a specific firm.

For example, if the incentive legislation favors technologically advanced activities, this (1) will signal to the investors that the government will generate

---

13. Of course, an open question is what would have happened in the absence of those tax incentives.

a desirable habitat in those activities in more ways than just through tax incentives,[14] (2) will stimulate investors to search for and acquire the relevant technology, and (3) will signal to individuals that education in technical fields will be well compensated.[15] In other words, the tax incentives may have a kind of announcement effect that, in time, will change the comparative advantage of the country.

Let us outline a bit more precisely the role of tax incentives and related government policies in Korea, Singapore, and Taiwan. This role can be assessed in the spirit of recent growth theories. The starting point must be the identification of a precise and broadly shared goal of economic policy. In these countries that goal was undoubtedly the stimulation of technologically based export industries. The promotion of that goal was pursued through educational expenditure and the provision of incentives. A sound macroeconomic framework was the essential background. A facilitating factor was a relatively good initial income distribution, which at least for a while reduced social tensions while at the same time enlarging the size of the domestic market for the goods produced.

As already mentioned, public expenditure for education was much higher in these countries than in the majority of developing countries, and education put a lot of emphasis on technological fields, especially on engineering. The brightest students could also get scholarships to do advanced work in foreign schools, especially in foreign engineering schools. The effectiveness of educational spending by the public sector was enhanced by the attitudes of parents. The latter came to believe that the road to success for their children was through education. This promoted an extraordinary competition among the students to get into good schools. Hard scholastic work became the norm.

The widespread technical knowledge among the population created a fertile ground for the transfer of technology from more advanced countries. It also created a fertile ground for the diffusion of that technology within the country. Having started far behind the industrial countries, these countries did not have to generate new technologies themselves but could go a long way by adopting (often with important modifications) technologies that were easily available in advanced countries. They started with simpler technologies (i.e., textiles, shipbuilding, steel) and progressively moved toward more sophisticated ones (electronics, computers).[16]

While education created the ground for the absorption of these technolo-

14. This may signal that that particular habitat will benefit from credit availability, provision of relevant information, and favorable regulations. Furthermore, educational expenditure of the right kind can make that habitat more attractive.

15. This may explain why American engineering schools have been very popular with students from these countries.

16. To quote from Romer (1990, i, 10): "Technological advances generate benefits that are at least partially excludable. . . . This means that . . . nonconvexities matter for growth . . . [and] matter for aggregate level analysis . . . there are large dynamic gains from trade between similar countries."

gies, tax and credit incentives were used to guide investment by specific firms toward particular areas. The assumption was that these were the areas that provided the best chances for future exports. In part the incentives may have compensated the specific firms that benefited from them for the positive externalities that they generated by being the pioneers in some areas. The diffusion of technology may also have been facilitated (especially in Korea) by the financial relations among enterprises (i.e., by the conglomerates).

2.4   Concluding Remarks

In the previous section, we have discussed the (probably) beneficial effects of incentives in Korea, Singapore, and Taiwan. It must be reiterated and emphasized that these were rather unusual experiences. The beneficial effects of incentives will not take place if incompetence, corruption, or various forms of rent-seeking activities become important. In such cases, incentive legislation, especially if based on discretionary decisions, will provide a perfect instrument for enriching some bureaucrats and for permitting some investors to evade paying taxes. The loser would be the public interest. Therefore, the experience of our successful countries is not necessarily transferable to other countries. Even in our successful countries, these incentives will eventually outlive their usefulness. It will become progressively more difficult to pick up winning industries as these countries develop. Furthermore, if the tax incentives are successful, they will make some individuals very rich. If these individuals adjust their consumption standards in line with their incomes, social inequities will become apparent and social tension will rise. This will bring to the forefront the objective of a fair income distribution (see Murphy, Shleifer, and Vishny 1988). The tax system will be seen as an instrument that can be used to achieve this objective. Tax reform should then be aimed at reducing conspicuous spending and high incomes. Wealth taxes and more equitable income taxes can be efficient instruments to achieve these objectives.

References

Asher, Mukul. 1989. Tax Reforms in East Asian Developing Countries: Motivations, Directions, and Implications. *Asian-Pacific Economic Literature* 3 (1): 39–62.

———. 1990. Singapore's Fiscal System in International Perspective. Paper presented at the Conference on the Fiscal System of Singapore, February.

Asher, Mukul, D. K. Salih, and I. M. Salleh. 1990. Directions of Malaysian Tax Reform. Paper presented at the Conference on Tax Policy and Economic Development among Pacific Asian Countries, Taipei, January.

Banque Indosuez. 1990. The Growing Economic Maturity of the Four Asian NICs Reflects in Their Immediate Economic Evolutions. *Index: Quarterly Economic Review*, no. 15 (1): 2–19.

Booth, Anne, and P. McCawley, eds. 1981. *The Indonesia Economy during the Suharto Era*. Kuala Lumpur: Oxford University Press.

Choi, K., and Y. S. Lee. 1987. The Role of Government in Industrialization: The Case of Korea. Paper presented at the Conference on Economic Development of Japan and Korea, Parallel Lessons, East-West Center, University of Hawaii, Honolulu, March 31–April 2, 1987.

Gillis, Malcolm. 1990. The Indonesian Tax Reform after Five Years. Paper presented at the Conference on Tax Policy and Economic Development among Pacific Asian Countries, Taipei, January.

Ho, Henry C.Y. 1989. Public Finance. In *The Economic System of Hong Kong*, ed. H.C.Y. Ho and L.C. Chan, 17–42. Hong Kong: Asia Research Service.

Kim, W., and K. Lee. 1990. The International Dimension of Korean Tax Policy. Paper presented at the Conference on Tax Policy and Economic Development among Pacific Asian Countries, Taipei, January.

Kwack, Taewon. 1990. The Role of Fiscal Incentives in Export-Led Economic Growth: the Korean Experience. In *Fiscal Policy in Open, Developing Economies*, ed. Vito Tanzi. Washington, D.C.: International Monetary Fund.

Lee, Kye-sik. 1990. A New Role of Fiscal Policy and Tax Finance for Social Development in Korea. Paper presented at the Conference on Tax Policy and Economic Development among Pacific Asian Countries, Taipei, January.

Malaysia Institute of Economic Research (MIER). 1989. Malaysia Institute of Economic Research report, part 1. Reprinted in APTIRC Bulletin (February): 56–71.

Murphy, K. M., A. Shleifer, and R. Vishny. 1988. Income Distribution, Market Size, and Industrialization. NBER Working Paper no. 2709. Cambridge, Mass.: National Bureau of Economic Research, September.

———. 1989. Increasing Returns, Durables, and Economic Fluctuations. NBER Working Paper no. 3014. Cambridge, Mass.: National Bureau of Economic Research, June.

Richupan, Somchai. 1990. Tax Policy and Economic Development in Thailand. Paper presented at the Conference on Tax Policy and Economic Development among Pacific Asian Countries, Taipei, January.

Riew, John. 1988. Taxation and Development: The Taiwan Model. Paper presented at the American Economic Association Annual Conference, New York, December.

Romer, Paul. 1989. Increasing Returns and New Developments in the Theory of Growth. NBER Working Paper no. 3098. Cambridge, Mass.: National Bureau of Economic Research, September.

———. 1990. Are Nonconvexities Important for Understanding Growth? NBER Working Paper no. 3271. Cambridge, Mass.: National Bureau of Economic Research, February.

Shome, Parthasarathi, ed. 1986. *Fiscal Issues in South-East Asia: Comparative Studies*. Singapore: Oxford University Press.

Sicat, Gerardo P. 1990. Tax Reform in the Philippines. Paper presented at the Conference on Tax Policy and Economic Development among Pacific Asian Countries, Taipei, January.

Tanzi, Vito. 1987. The Public Sector in the Market Economies of Developing Asia. *Asian Development Review* 5 (3): 31–57.

Comment   Joseph Y. Lim

The paper is a nice summary of the tax policies, experiences, problems, and future prospects and directions of tax reforms in East Asian countries. I particularly like the section on the lessons that can be learned from these countries, and I will concentrate my comments on this part later. However, there is hardly any discussion on the effects of tax policies of East Asian countries on one another, or their interdependence. This is particularly true for the ASEAN countries, since these countries are mainly competitors with respect to exports and foreign investments and they are increasingly dependent on trade relations and foreign investments from Japan, Taiwan, Korea, and Singapore. Yet they desire regional coordination and cooperation. Therefore there is a need to ask if there is room for regional harmonization or mutual cooperation in tax policies. This important aspect seems to have been left out in the paper.

Having said this, let me turn the discussion on the lessons learned from the experience of East Asian countries. What I will say will just be additions to what was said by Vito Tanzi and Parthasarathi Shome. In a way it tries to explain why countries with very different fiscal policies may succeed in an export-oriented path and is also a sort of apology as to why the Philippines is the basket case in the paper's list of countries. In another sense, this is not really an apology, since I will be quite harsh on the Philippines.

At this conference John Whalley posed the question of how issues on tax policies and reforms qualitatively differ between a developed and a developing economy. From the Philippine point of view, this is a very important question indeed. To answer it, we will have to go deeply into the heart of political economy—a most relevant topic for our conference.

It is fortunate that in public finance, especially in recent times, the literature has taken into consideration the hard realities—particularly the importance of the government, the nature of the state, and implicitly the level of social cohesion of the country being analyzed—in tackling fiscal problems.

I remember the old days when I was an undergraduate taking up my basic economic course; fiscal policies were important, not only because they had some effects on the multiplier, but also because all questions pertaining to equity were regulated to the fiscal solution. I simply imagined the Philippine state and was puzzled how this could be done. Would the powerful landlords and monopolists in the executive, legislative, and judicial branches miraculously tax themselves and provide transfer payments to the poor and needy? Surely the realities of our neighbors in Japan, Taiwan, and South Korea have shown that wealth and income redistribution of a backward society like ours was most effectively tackled through a radical agrarian reform, high investments in human capital and education, and other structural transformations rather than through fiscal policies of a rent-seeking state.

Joseph Y. Lim is an associate professor of economics at the University of the Philippines and the director for research for the School of Economics of the university.

Most recently we Filipinos again have been told by textbooks—by way of some pseudo-supply-side arguments—that low tax rates or tax incentives and tax credit should be given to foreign investments without any consideration to the government's responsibility of providing economic and political stability, proper infrastructure, and profitable environment to the investors. Indeed we have given four-to-six-year tax holidays, enormous tax credits (many are distortionary since they exempt capital goods importation in a labor-abundant economy), and even subsidized foreign investments through the debt-to-equity swap scheme (which converted debt papers to equity investments at a 50% discount). Our incentive scheme for foreign investments is (especially if you include the debt-to-equity swap) better than other ASEAN countries. But the foreign investment did not come in a massive scale as it did to our ASEAN neighbors. Much of foreign investment that came in 1986–88 was due to debt-to-equity swaps. Some that came in were fly-by-night investments or investments running away from regulatory restrictions (e.g., strict environmental laws) from other countries. The Philippines lost at least $4 billion of annual revenues from investments that would have come in anyway (the attractive debt-to-equity arrangement saw to it) at a time when we faced extreme fiscal constraint wherein almost 50% of the budget was and is going to debt service (two-thirds of which is domestic debt servicing and the rest foreign debt servicing).

Again we were taught by the textbooks and by the International Monetary Fund and World Bank to practically abolish restrictions on capital outflow as part of the liberalization process, and we did so in the early 80s. But as the paper of Assaf Razin and Efraim Sadka reminds us, this was done without consideration of the country's capability to tax its citizens and firms abroad or to run after runaway capital. So that when economic and political crisis struck in the second half of 1983 (partly caused by the assassination of Benigno Aquino), much evidence showed that capital flight was indeed facilitated by the above scheme.

The Philippines has also done everything a good "boy" should do in the field of tax legislation. The 1986 reform included

1. a movement from schedular to global income taxation,
2. a unification of withholding taxes on interest income and royalties,
3. an elimination of withholding tax on dividends,
4. unification of corporate income tax at 35%,
5. initiation of value-added taxation to replace the cumbersome sales-turnover tax,
6. abolition of export taxes except on logs, and
7. supposed general revision of valuation of real property for tax purposes.

Most of the above (except 3 and 6) were done partly with the goal of increasing government revenue. But now about four years later, our tax/GDP ratio is back only to the prerecession level of the early 1980s, which is around 12%—the lowest in the whole ASEAN region. Because of this poor fiscal showing, Congress has just legislated more taxes on "sin" products (e.g., alcohol and cigarettes). The cabinet has proposed a tax package containing a supposedly progressive scheme on additional taxation of property and nonessentials. The Speaker of the House of Representatives, who (perhaps until this week) is the leading presidential candidate in 1992 representing Aquino's ruling party, opposed the scheme, stating "The rich have to be protected."

Now the IMF is asking us to cut our budget deficit. If we cannot increase tax revenues significantly, which is certain, we will have to cut back on our government expenditures—particularly capital outlays—at a time when the country's infrastructure is deteriorating and the economy is racked by a perennial power shortage.

All of these are related to Tanzi's and Shome's point about the importance of the government and why countries with opposite policies—one using the nonintervention approach (Hong Kong) and others more interventionist (Taiwan, Korea, Singapore)—can all succeed due to the existence of (what I call a) "good" government, i.e., a forward- and long-term-looking, stable, and continuing government with a broad professional bureaucracy serious about attaining a national goal. The Philippines is the other side of the coin; it had a "bad" government epitomized by the Marcos government, which bred corruption and rent seeking (in tax administration, among other areas), combined with various inefficiencies and ineptitude in the bureaucracy. Many critics of Aquino claim that the government has not yet changed. Even the reasonable Aquino supporters admit that the political will and the government's capability to institute radical change is gone. And the social cohesion necessary for a successful transformation to be effected without chaos and anarchy is lacking. The Aquino government also cannot guarantee that whatever policies in effect now will survive 1992 when the Aquino government gives way to its successor.

Implementing fiscal reforms and, as Tanzi and Shome correctly point out, most other economic reforms (trade, industrial, financial) requires a "good" government. This may even accommodate interventionist policies. For the new developments in institutional economics have shown that if there are market imperfections (high transaction costs or market failures), if there is opportunism and asset specificity (to quote Oliver Williamson), then there is need for strong governance. A "good" government, therefore, free of rent seeking, can indeed use interventionist policies to achieve an economic goal, especially if it is supported by the economic agents.

Cooperative and repeated game theories show that, in a prisoner's dilemma type of situation, cooperation rather than individual optimization may yield a higher social utility. Indeed social cohesion and good and responsible government are needed for economic reforms—one of the most obvious being fiscal reform.

It is important then that when talking about fiscal reforms, a concentration on "correct" fiscal policies (which may remain on paper only) without looking at the institutional factors may be misleading and even detrimental, as the Philippines illustrates. It is high time that economists descend from cloud nine and accept that which every man in the street already knows—policy prescriptions and reforms do not exist in a vacuum. Perhaps more important may be the institutional setting and environment wherein these policies and reforms will be undertaken. And I think this is the single most important lesson that we should learn from the Tanzi-Shome paper.

II.

3   Tax Reform in Japan

Masaaki Homma

3.1 Introduction

The tax systems of industrialized countries are changing rapidly and, in some cases, are undergoing major reforms. The ongoing tax reform in Japan is part of this global movement that has been going on since the late 1970s. Although the tax reform plans of other countries differ greatly, they share a number of features with Japan's. In particular, Japan's movement seems to be inspired by a wider introduction of the value-added tax (VAT) in countries such as Korea and to be accelerated by the achievement of the U.S. tax reform, which lowered the income tax rates and broadened the tax base.

More than ten years have passed, however, since the Japanese government took a first step toward tax reform. In 1979 Prime Minister Masayoshi Ohira proposed the plan that includes the VAT and minor revisions of tax preferences. Expanding fiscal deficits were the initial motivation for the tax reform. From the first oil crisis in 1973 to the second in 1979, the Japanese economy experienced unprecedented serious structural changes. The sharp decline in the economic growth rate meant a drop in tax revenues, and new social welfare programs and public investment to stimulate domestic demand drastically increased government spending.

A quick inspection of table 3.1 indicates how much the government budget changed. Up to 1974, the government had a budget surplus or at least a balanced budget. But huge government deficits arose in 1975 from the first oil shock and accelerated due to the second one. As a result, the budget deficits at the general government level amounted to 4.4 percent of the GNP in 1979.

Masaaki Homma is professor of economics at Osaka University.
Comments from Professors Tatsuo Hatta, Hiromitsu Ishi, Takatoshi Ito, and Charles McLure are greatly appreciated.

Table 3.1   Sectoral Saving-Investment Balance as Percentage of GNP, 1970–88

	1970	1971	1972	1973	1974	1975	1976	1977	1978	1979
Public sector	-0.6	-2.3	-2.6	-0.5	-3.8	-7.5	-6.8	-7.3	-7.4	-7.1
General government	1.8	0.5	0.2	2.0	0.0	-3.7	-3.6	-4.2	-4.2	-4.4
Central government	0.0	-1.0	-1.1	0.4	-1.4	-4.0	-4.3	-5.0	-4.8	-5.7
Local government	-0.4	-1.0	-1.1	-1.0	-1.3	-2.1	-1.6	-1.8	-1.7	-1.4
Social security fund	2.2	2.5	2.4	2.6	2.6	2.4	2.3	2.7	2.4	2.6
Public enterprise	-2.4	-2.8	-2.8	-2.5	-3.7	-3.8	-3.2	-3.2	-3.2	-2.7
Private enterprise	-5.5	-4.7	-5.1	-9.4	-8.2	-4.7	-3.4	-1.5	0.1	-2.5
Household	7.9	8.8	10.1	10.6	11.6	11.5	10.9	10.4	8.7	7.6
Domestic	1.8	1.8	2.3	0.7	-0.4	-0.8	0.7	1.6	1.4	-2.0

	1980	1981	1982	1983	1984	1985	1986	1987	1988
Public sector	-6.4	-6.2	-5.7	-5.2	-4.1	-2.9	-2.3	-0.9	
General government	-4.0	-3.7	-3.4	-3.0	-1.8	-0.8	-0.3	0.8	2.9
Central government	-5.4	-5.3	-5.2	-4.9	-4.0	-3.7	-3.1	-2.0	
Local government	-1.3	-1.2	-0.9	-0.8	-0.6	-0.3	-0.4	-0.3	
Social security fund	2.6	2.8	2.7	2.7	2.8	3.2	3.1	3.1	
Public enterprise	-2.3	-2.5	-2.3	-2.2	-2.3	-2.1	-2.0	-1.7	
Private enterprise	-3.3	-3.5	-2.5	-1.7	-2.6	-3.9	-3.1	-4.2	-8.3
Household	9.3	9.8	8.2	9.2	8.9	9.9	9.7	7.8	8.4
Domestic	-0.4	0.2	0.0	2.3	2.1	3.1	4.3	2.7	3.0

Source: Economic Planning Agency, National Economic Accounting, 1989.

Since then, there has been growing concern with how to eliminate government budget deficits.

Unfortunately, strong opposition has emerged to the introduction of the Japanese type of VAT, the "general consumption tax," which is a tax credit type of VAT without invoices. The ruling Liberal Democratic Party (LDP) lost many seats in the lower house in the 1979 general election, mainly due to public resistance to this general consumption tax. This election forced the government to give up plans for the general consumption tax and to change to a strategy of curtailing budget deficits. The only measure that remained was the spending-cut policy.

The government rushed on a campaign for "fiscal reconstruction," which aimed to reduce budget deficits by cutting government expenditures. It adopted the so-called ceiling method, imposing guidelines on the preliminary budget requests from each ministry. This spending cut policy beginning in 1980 was highly successful in that nonentitled central government expenditure remained constant from fiscal 1983 to fiscal 1986. There were two major reasons for this success. One was the reform of social welfare systems such as health insurance in 1984 and social security in 1985. Another was the sharp decline in public investment, which decreased from over 10 percent to 6.5 percent of the GNP.

It should be emphasized that revenues also contributed to the reduction in the budget deficits. The government left the individual income tax untouched except for minor changes after failing to introduce the general consumption tax. This led to automatic increases in income tax burdens, owing to bracket creep from income increases and inflation. Moreover, the corporate income tax rates were raised. For example, in 1984, the basic rate was raised from 42 to 43.3 percent as a temporary measure.

Dramatic recovery from budget deficits started in fiscal 1984. Table 3.1 shows that the budget deficit on the general government level became 0.8 percent of the GNP in 1985, which was better by 3.6 percent than the deficit in 1979. Behind this recovery lay growing criticism of the existing tax system, and the problem of tax reform had become the most important political issue.

The process of tax reform started in September 1985, when Prime Minister Yasuhiro Nakasone appointed the tax advisory commission to review the current tax system and make suggestions for a new one adapted to the challenges of the twenty-first century. Nakasone announced a number of fine-sounding goals, which loosely translated are "equity, fairness, simplicity, freedom of choice, and economic vitality."

3.2   Increased Demand for Tax Reform

Before describing the Nakasone tax reform proposals, I shall analyze why Japan needed the tax reform. The structure of the current tax system was originally based on the recommendations of the Shoup mission in 1949. Although the tax system has been revised occasionally, it has failed to keep up with the big changes in Japanese society and its economy. The tax system and the economy have been badly matched, especially for the last fifteen years.

From 1975 to 1984, the tax burden rose sharply in Japan. Measured in terms of national income, central government taxes were up 4.1 percent and local taxes 2.7 percent. This sort of increase has not been observed in other countries, and both families and businesses feel more heavily and unfairly taxed.

Common dissatisfactions with the present tax system are summarized here.

Tax Burden Differences among Taxpayers. There have been serious complaints about horizontal inequality in Japan, with big differences in tax burden among salaried workers, the self-employed, farmers, and politicians. The popular "10:5:3:1" formulation indicates that labor income of salaried workers is reported in full to the tax authority, while the self-employed can declare only 50 percent of what they earn, farmers 30 percent, and politicians a mere 10 percent.

Differences in tax burden arise partly because the tax collection system for salaried workers is fundamentally different from that for other taxpayers. The former have their taxes withheld by their employers, while the latter pay on the basis of the income they declare in their tax returns. In addition, the self-employed and others filing under the self-assessment system enjoy a far wider variety of tax breaks. The special treatment of unincorporated businesses as quasi-corporations, that is, deemed corporations, is a typical example. This tax preference allows them to deduct all business expenses from taxable earnings and to reclassify much of these earnings as salary payments to themselves and family members. And by making use of the standard deduction for all salaried workers, they further reduce their tax bill.

Differences in the tax collection system and several measures favoring the self-employed and farmers are major causes of the horizontal inequities in the personal income tax. Equity requires elimination of such preferential treatments.

Mismatch between the Wage System and Income Tax Structures. National and local income taxes paid by salaried workers rose from 8.3 percent of their wage earnings in 1970 to 10.6 percent in 1984. This rise has widened a mismatch between the wage system and the individual income tax. Wages in Japan tend to be strongly determined by seniority, and the wage profile rises by age. Yet Japan's income taxes are extremely progressive, placing a pronounced emphasis on the redistribution of income. Between 1970 and 1984, national tax rates ranged from 10.5 to 70 percent in fifteen brackets, local taxes from 4.5 to 18 percent in fourteen brackets.

Such steep graduation does not exist in other countries. Extraordinary progressiveness results in marked unevenness in the distribution of the tax burden among age groups in a society where wages rise with seniority. As workers grow older and earn more money, their tax rates go up steeply, subjecting them to a form of bracket creep.

Figure 3.1 shows the individual income tax burdens at different life stages for the average salaried worker born in 1953. Middle-class or middle-age salaried workers, particularly in their forties and fifties, who are spending a lot for their children's education or for a residence always feel that their tax burden is too heavy. From this point of view, reduction in the progressiveness of the income tax, especially for middle-class salaried workers, has become one of the most important subjects in the tax reform.

Unfairness in Taxation on Capital Income. Tax reform is also aimed at unfair taxation on capital income. Interest income is exempt from income taxation, up to a certain total face value of personal savings. This tax preference is called the "Maruyu system." Moreover, capital gains from selling stock are not taxed in principle, and dividends are preferentially treated under special reduced rates.

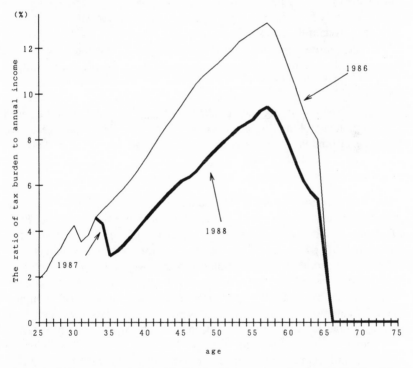

Fig. 3.1   Life-stage tax burden (individual income tax plus local inhabitants' tax)
Source: Basic calculations in Hashimoto et al. 1990.

These special tax measures were initiated to stimulate personal savings and to promote economic growth through capital accumulation. In fact, Japan's high saving rate may have been one of the major factors contributing to the country's rapid growth in the past. But the situation has changed greatly. Preferential tax treatment of personal savings has given rise to especially sharp complaints, not only internally but overseas, as being a source of inequitable tax systems and a factor behind the massive current account surplus. Revising the taxation of income from capital, both to achieve vertical equity and to bring it into line with international standards, is an indispensable part of tax reform.

Complaints about Heavy Corporate Tax Burden. Businessmen often unfavorably compare Japan's corporate income tax to that of other countries. Corporate tax rates have risen several times since 1970, mainly to finance budget deficits. According to Ministry of Finance (MOF) calculations, the effective corporate tax rate, measuring the combined burden of national and local taxes, was 52.92 percent in 1984. This rate is extraordinarily high compared to the United States. As figure 3.2 shows, the marginal U.S. corporate tax rate dropped sharply from 51.55 to 40.34 percent, based on the MOF formula, as a result of Ronald Reagan's tax reform. It has been emphasized in Japan that active corporations might move their place of business to countries where tax burdens are lower, and such a reaction could damage Japanese competitiveness at the international level.

Numerous tax preferences in the corporate income tax, mainly to encourage export and business saving and investment, and a differential rate have added to the complexity of the corporate income tax in Japan. The main objective of corporate income tax reform has been to reduce the tax burden by lowering tax rates and broadening the tax base.

Outdatedness of Indirect Taxes. The outdatedness of Japan's indirect taxes is another problem, because of diversification of consumer spending. From 1970 to 1984, the ratio of indirect tax revenue to final consumer spending shrank from 8.8 percent to 7.7 percent, not because the existing indirect taxes on special categories of consumption had been lowered. On the contrary, the rates had been raised repeatedly, but the tax base was limited to a small number of selected items. Most revenue from excise taxes was collected on purchases of automobiles and home appliances. Many luxuries have never been drawn into the tax base. Services, meanwhile, remained virtually untaxed, even though they accounted for about half of consumption. The failure to update the indirect tax system so as to reflect changing consumption patterns was one of the major reasons indirect taxes had declined in importance relative to direct taxes. A fundamental revision of the indirect tax system is a matter of urgent necessity.

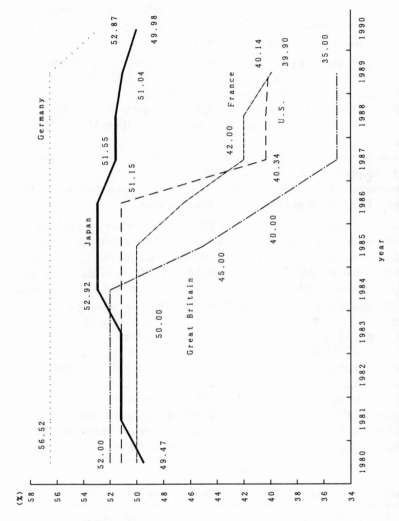

Fig. 3.2 Effective rates of corporate tax (in terms of MOF measure)
Source: Homma and Atoda 1989.

3.3   The Nakasone Tax Reform

Motivated by increased taxpayers' demand for tax reform and inspired by the accomplishment of Reagan's tax reform, Prime Minister Yasuhiro Nakasone took a second step toward tax reform. At his request, the tax advisory commission submitted "The Report on the Overall Review of the Tax System," which constructed a tax reform plan in October 1986. According to the report, the Nakasone administration proposed a fiscal year 1987 tax reform that consisted of the four major recommendations:

1. Reduction of the income tax burden, especially for middle-income salaried workers, mainly through simplification of the tax rates structure and introduction of the special deduction for a spouse.
2. Reduction of the basic tax rate on corporate income to less than 50 percent from the current 52.9 percent, measured in terms of the MOF's effective tax rate.
3. Abolition of tax exemption on interest income for small savers through the adoption of a 20 percent withholding tax.
4. Introduction of the sales tax, which is a variant of the European Community (EC) VAT, in place of the current excise taxes.

Table 3.2 summarizes the reform package of tax increases and reductions. The characteristic feature is that the package was proposed to satisfy "revenue neutrality" in its first year. The concept of revenue neutrality in Japan is slightly different from that in the United States. The U.S. tax reform was designed to be revenue-neutral in the succeeding five years. It should be noted that this mixed reform package results in a shift in the tax mix toward indirect taxes.

As stated above, the basic structure of the Nakasone tax reform would lower the individual and corporate income tax rates by bringing into the tax base income and consumption sources previously excluded, i.e., repeal of the tax exemption for interest income and adoption of a broad-based consumption tax. Thus the Nakasone tax reform avoided the elimination of preferential tax treatment in the individual and corporate income tax, which was strongly resisted by special groups of taxpayers. Instead, it was emphasized that the introduction of a broad-based consumption tax, the sales tax, could contribute

Table 3.2   Tax Bill Proposed in 1987 (in billions of yen)

Tax Reductions		Tax Increases	
Individual income tax	27,000	Introduction of the sales tax	35,000
Corporate income tax	18,000	Repeal of tax exemption for small savers	10,000
Total	45,000	Total	45,000

Source: Ministry of Finance, *Monthly Report of Fiscal and Financial Statistics, Special Issue on Tax,* 1988.

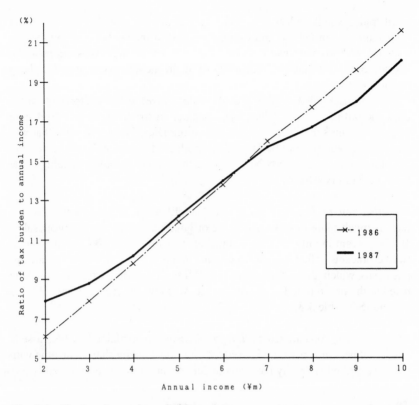

Fig. 3.3   Tax burden on households
Source: Hashimoto et al. 1990.

to horizontal equity because the tax burden would be spread evenly among consumers, irrespective of whether they are salaried workers or self-employed.

Strong opposition to this proposal emerged immediately, for three major reasons. The first was Nakasone's political mistake. During the campaign for the general election in July 1986, he pledged not to introduce a "large-scale" indirect tax. After a landslide victory for the LDP, the tax proposal introduced a large-scale indirect tax, "the sales tax." The general public accused Nakasone of dishonesty.

The second reason was the regressiveness of the package of individual tax reductions and indirect tax increases: the reform was favorable to high-income people rather than to middle- or low-income people. Figure 3.3 shows that those who earned more than ¥6 million annually would benefit from the tax reform, those who earned less would lose.[1] The majority of taxpayers felt betrayed and did not support Nakasone's tax reform.

The third source of opposition was small businesses in the wholesale and

1. See my estimate (1986) for a detailed analysis.

retail trade. Small traders feared that they could not pass the sales tax on at each stage of transactions and would have to bear the tax burden, and that the sales tax with invoices would force them to reveal all their transactions to the tax authority and make it impossible to avoid income tax as they had been doing.

The proposal failed to get approval, and the government was forced to withdraw the bill in May 1987. The Nakasone administration gave up introducing sales taxes and submitted a revised bill to the Diet. The revised bill that was passed in September 1987 was the final product of Nakasone's tax reform.

Let me summarize briefly Nakasone's achievement before proceeding to the next stage of tax reform.

Simplification of Tax Rate Structure. Simplification of the progressive tax rates is much more modest than in the original plan. The original proposal of 10–50 percent in only six income brackets was revised to 10.5–60 percent in twelve brackets. The range of taxable income to which the minimum rate applies was widened, so that about two-thirds of salaried workers would be taxed at the minimum. The maximum rate was lowered from 70 percent to 60 percent. See table 3.3.

Introduction of Special Exemption for Spouse. As explained earlier, a self-employed person is permitted to reduce individual tax by sharing income with a spouse and other family members under special preferences of deemed cor-

Table 3.3   Statutory Rates of Income Taxes

1986		1987	
Taxable Income (millions of Y)	Tax Rates (%)	Taxable Income (millions of Y)	Tax Rates (%)
Under 0.5	10.5	Under 1.5	10.5
0.5–1.2	12	1.5–2.0	12
1.2–2.0	14	2.0–3.0	16
2.0–3.0	17	3.0–5.0	20
3.0–4.0	21	5.0–6.0	25
4.0–6.0	25	6.0–8.0	30
6.0–8.0	30	8.0–10.0	35
8.0–10.0	35	10.0–12.0	40
10.0–12.0	40	12.0–15.0	45
12.0–15.0	45	15.0–30.0	50
15.0–20.0	50		
10.0–30.0	55	30.0–50.0	55
30.0–50.0	60	50.0 and over	60
50.0–80.0	65		
80.0 and over	70		

Source: Ministry of Finance, *Monthly Report of Fiscal and Financial Statistics, Special Issue on Tax,* 1988.

porations. Salaried workers who have no way to split income complain about this preferential treatment, which results in a big tax gap between salaried workers and the self-employed. To lessen this gap, a special exemption of ¥165,000 for spouses of salaried workers is deductable from total income in addition to the ordinary deduction of ¥300,000

Revision of Tax Exemption for Small Savers. As explained earlier, interest income was tax exempt for small savers. This exemption had been abused extensively by rich people because Japan had no adequate enforcement of the limitation on the maximum amount of saving eligible. Since the revision, interest income is taxed in principle by a withholding tax at the uniform rate of 20 percent except for the elderly, fatherless families, and handicapped people.

Minor Reduction of Corporate Tax Rates. The corporate income tax had two split rates, one for retained income (43.3 percent), another for dividends (33.3 percent). In each tax rate, 1.3 percent was temporarily surcharged to help "fiscal reconstruction." This surcharge was abolished by the bill, and the effective corporate tax rate dropped from 52.92 to 51.56 percent in terms of MOF's effective tax rate. See figure 3.2.

3.4   The Takeshita Tax Reform

The Nakasone tax reform ended in September 1987 after he achieved only half of his original plan. But his main ideas of tax reform were adopted by the next cabinet. Nakasone appointed Noboru Takeshita as his successor, asking him to go forward with the tax reform.

When the Takeshita administration relaunched the tax reform in November 1987, great changes were visible in the Japanese economy. Stable and strong economic growth resulted in large tax revenue increases in 1987 and the following years. Thus budget deficits disappeared, and in fact a huge budget surplus at the general government level appeared for the central government, local government, and social security account (see table 3.1).

Taking these changes into consideration, the Takeshita administration abandoned the "revenue-neutral" tax reform approach and offered in 1988 a new tax plan that contained a ¥24,000 billion net tax reduction (see table 3.4). This tax reduction was more attractive to taxpayers and to other countries, for it could increase the domestic market.

Moreover, asset prices such as land and stock soared. This stressed the unfair distribution of asset holdings among the rich and the poor, and revealed that the present tax preferences for income derived from selling land and stock were very inequitable. In addition to the remaining reforms suggested by Nakasone, i.e., introduction of broad-based indirect tax, the Takeshita tax reform plan had to include a new taxation system for capital gains on the sale of stocks.

Table 3.4   **Tax Bill Proposed in 1988 (in billions of yen)**

Tax Reductions		Tax Increases	
Individual income tax	3,100	Introduction of consumption tax (5,400) minus repeal of selective excise tax (3,400)	2,000
Corporate income tax	600		
Inheritance tax	700		
Total	4,400	Total	2,000
	Net reduction 2,400		

Source: Ministry of Finance, *Monthly Report of Fiscal and Financial Statistics, Special Issue on Tax,* 1989.

The four basic features of the tax reform sent to the Diet in July 1988 by the Takeshita administration are summarized here.

Further Reductions of the National Individual Income Tax and the Local In-habitants' Tax. The number of income tax brackets was reduced from fifteen to twelve by the Nakasone tax reform. A flatter tax schedule is proposed by the Takeshita tax reform (see fig. 3.4), ranging from 10 to 50 percent in five income brackets. Also, the progressiveness of the local inhabitants' tax has been reduced to 5–15 percent with three income brackets.

The personal exemption for spouses and the exemption for dependants simultaneously rose from ¥300,000 (¥280,000 for local inhabitants' tax) to ¥330,000 (¥300,000). And two additional measures are expanded or introduced in favor of specific taxpayers. The special exemption for spouses in one-earner couples was introduced at ¥100,000 (¥50,000).

Further Cut and Unification in Corporate Tax Rates. The basic rate for retained income levied on ordinary corporations gradually decreased from 42 percent to 37.5 percent after fiscal 1990, while the reduced rate for dividends rose from 32 percent to 37.5 percent. The two split tax rates are now a single tax rate, simplifying the present corporate income tax. A similar modification applies to tax rates on small and medium-size corporations; the basic rate decreased from 30 to 28 percent, and the reduced rate rose from 24 to 28 percent.

Introduction of the Consumption Tax. The most important issue in the Takeshita tax reform was the new consumption tax, which is a special variant of VAT. The sales tax proposed by the Nakasone tax reform was the invoice-credit method, as used in the EC, but this was clearly rejected by the public. Learning from this experience, the government adopted a VAT that uses no invoices.

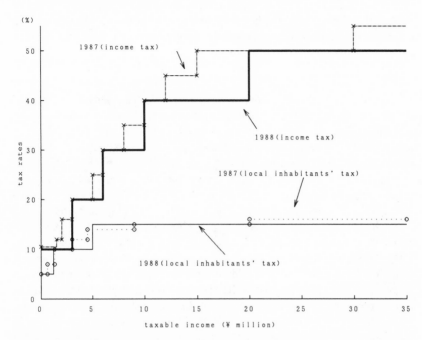

Fig. 3.4   Marginal rates of income tax and local inhabitants' tax for a family of four with a single wage-earner
Source: Basic calculations in Homma et al. (1988).

The consumption tax without invoices depends on the subtraction method of the VAT, which uses bookkeeping to calculate a firm's VAT. In this sense, it is called the account type of VAT. Subtracting total taxable purchases from total taxable sales gives the taxable value added, subject to a 3 percent VAT.

The account type of VAT is useful mainly because it mitigates opposition to the new tax from groups in retail or wholesale businesses. It has several problems, however. First, tracing the transactions from one stage to another is impossible—a strong incentive for cheating, because accurate assessment of the tax base is very difficult for the tax authority.

Second, the account type of VAT cannot make clear distinctions among fully taxed, tax-reduced, and tax-exempt goods and services. This is why the consumption tax covers only a few tax-exempt goods and services, such as some education, medical care, and welfare programs, and abandons multiple tax rates. The broad tax base and single tax rate save compliance costs but appropriately cope with the distributional problem.

Moreover, the consumption tax has a special simplified rule for computing tax that favors smaller firms whose annual sales are less than ¥500 million. This special rule assumes that the total value of purchases from other firms is 80 percent of total sales value for retailers (90 percent for wholesalers). This implies that the value added is 20 percent of total sales, and therefore tax is automatically equal to the total sales value multiplied by 0.6 percent (0.20 of the 3 percent rate). Completely exempt are firms whose annual sales are less than ¥30 million, 68 percent of the total number of firms in 1986.

Taxation on Capital Gains from Selling Stocks. Capital gains on the sale of stocks were to be taxed under the Shoup tax proposals in 1950. But the government decided not to tax these capital gains, partly because they could stimulate domestic savings and promote economic growth and partly because effective enforcement of the tax was very difficult. Since then, capital gains had in principle been tax-exempt except for people who continuously dealt with stocks in large volumes.

Reflecting a sharp rise in stock prices, untaxed capital gains on the sale of stocks had been seriously attacked as a symbol of unfairness. In response the Takeshita administration proposed that taxpayers could choose at each transaction between two tax methods. One was the self-assessed declaration, in which realized capital gains would be taxed separately from other income at 26 percent including local tax. The second was withholding, in which the taxpayers would have to pay 1 percent of the stock sales price, assuming that the capital gain at each transaction is 5 percent of the stock sales prices.

3.5   Effects of the Reform on Households

When a country's tax system is thoroughly overhauled, all taxpayers are affected in one way or another. The Japanese reform, designed to reduce taxes overall, seems basically sound in its thrust. The new consumption tax has a broad revenue-enhancing effect. National and local income taxes are being reduced, mainly through a flatter rate schedule that lowers the maximum rate and raises the minimum amount of income subject to taxation. Other noteworthy changes include a large hike in the special exemption for spouses, which applies only to one-earner couples, and an enhanced exemption for certain dependents aged 16–22.

One basic effect of the reform will be a redistribution of the tax burden on each category of household. Compare, for instance, two-earner couples, in which both spouses work, with one-earner couples. Before the reform a two-earner couple usually paid substantially less taxes than a one-earner couple with the same amount of income, providing an incentive for both spouses to hold jobs. The flattening of the tax schedule reduces this difference, as does the larger exemption for a spouse, which cannot be used by two-earner couples. Introducing a consumption tax will have a similar effect, since it will raise the prices of the domestic services that two-earner couples often hire and the value of those that one-earner couples provide within the home.

Couples living on pensions should see a rise in their tax burden. They will not benefit from the cut in income taxes, and they will be paying more consumption taxes. Neither will the reduction in income taxes help unmarried taxpayers much, unless they happen to earn a lot of money: they generally are big consumers, and the exemption for spouses does not apply.

I have conducted a series of simulations to clarify these and other effects of the tax reform on different household categories. Below I summarize the main findings.

For our study, we used the five-category breakdown of households shown in figure 3.5, drawing on a nationwide survey of consumption. Slightly more than half all Japanese households are in the one-earner couple or single-income category. Less than one-tenth are one-member households—mostly younger men or women living independently. Senior citizens above the pension-entitlement age account for a small fraction of the total. About half of these "old-aged couples," as we label this category, have some employment income; the rest depend almost entirely on pensions. All other households are those in which both husband and wife work.

I have broken this last group into two categories, each of which accounts for about one-sixth of all households. In the "single plus part-time income" category, usually the husband is a full-time worker and the wife supplements the family income with part-time employment, bringing in less than

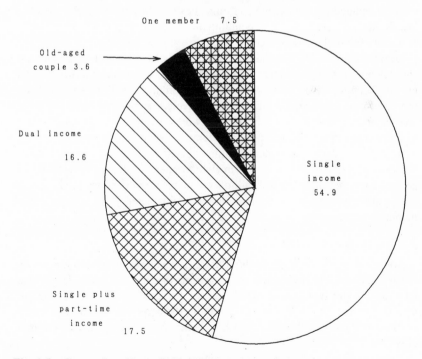

Fig. 3.5   Categories of households (% of total households)
Source: Calculations from Homma et al. (1988).

¥900,000 per year, the threshold beyond which a spouse could not be claimed as a dependent before the reform. The other is the true two-earner couple or dual-income category; it covers all families in which the second worker's income exceeds ¥900,000.

3.5.1   The Rich and the Poor

Next let us consider the typical income profile of these five household categories. On a scale extending from the vicinity of ¥2 million, the earnings of an entry-level employee or lower-class family, to ¥10 million or more for people in upper income brackets, the average family has an annual income of around ¥4 million or ¥5 million.

As shown in figure 3.6, single-income households and younger people living alone account for the majority of low-income families (Homma et al. 1988). At incomes up to ¥2 million, almost 90 percent of all households fall in one of these two categories, and the rest are people living on pensions. On the upper end of the scale, 82 percent of the households earning ¥10 million or more are single-income families, and almost all the rest are dual-income families.

Households of young unmarried people and of old-aged couples are clustered in the lower income brackets; as income reaches the ¥6 million level, their percentage of all households diminishes to a tiny fraction. By contrast, few families with two earners, including the category where the spouse works part time, fall in the lowest income brackets.

Looking more closely at the three categories of households in which both spouses are in their productive years, we can note differentials in their distribution. Thought the one-earner families are prominent in all income brackets, they are most highly represented in the relatively low ¥3 million–¥4 million income range. Families in which the wife works part time are, as noted, infrequent on the upper end. Their distribution rises sharply to a peak in the ¥4 million–¥5 million range and declines almost as sharply. The true dual-income couples naturally have a somewhat richer profile. Their distribution peaks in the ¥5 million–¥7 million range and then declines gradually. A fairly large percentage of the households in this category are in the upper income brackets.

3.5.2   Divided Impact on the Middle Class

Now we can proceed to an analysis of the Takeshita tax reform's impact. As is customary in this sort of analysis, I assume that the "standard" family has two parents and two dependents. What we are looking for is the change in total taxes after the new measures, except for the corporate income tax, are all in place compared with taxes in 1987, before the first measures went into effect.

As noted, one change is a larger special exemption for spouses with no job,

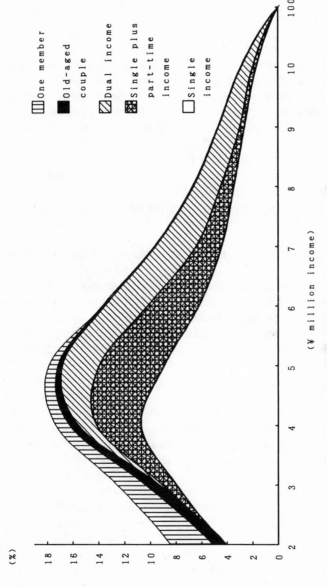

Fig. 3.6 Breakdown of households by annual income

which has been boosted from ¥165,000 annually to ¥350,000. This exemption can be claimed by any one-earner family earning up to ¥10 million a year. Another change is a small ¥20,000 increase in the exemption for each dependent, to ¥350,000, together with a provision enabling families with children between 16 and 22, who have high education expenses, to claim a larger exemption of ¥450,000. These breaks should more than offset the burden of consumption tax for one-earner couples, reducing their total taxes.

Figure 3.7 shows the effects of the reform on middle-class families. Looking first at one-earner couples, we can see that their taxes will decline substantially if they can claim the large exemption for an older child. Slightly smaller but still significant reductions result even when the enhanced exemption cannot be claimed. The biggest savings will be realized by families in the upper-middle class with incomes in the ¥7 million–¥10 million range, who should see a reduction in their taxes of 10 percent or more. For the lower-middle class, which might be defined as families earning between ¥4 million and ¥6 million, the reduction in taxes is slightly lower. A one-earner family earning ¥3 million will benefit only modestly; below that there could be an increase in taxes. Such observations provide clear evidence of the reformers' intention of slanting the benefits in the direction of the middle and upper classes.

Still, even low-income families with one earner will not necessarily bear a heavier tax burden. As long as they have no children or only one, reducing their consumption and thus the burden of consumption tax, I calculate that their taxes should decline slightly even if they are in the ¥2 million–¥3 million bracket. The biggest break is the much larger special exemption for spouses. Families with many children will pay more because of consumption tax; the comparatively small hikes in dependent exemptions will not cancel its effect.

Families in which the wife works part time do not fare as well. They can claim the special exemption only if the second worker brings home ¥570,000 or less. Above that the deduction decreases. Those couples earning less than ¥4 million each year will see a fairly large rise in their tax bills. As I have noted, however, many families in the single plus part-time income category earn more than ¥4 million, and they should all see an average reduction in their taxes of about 5 percent.

The worst off will be the two-earner families who earn less than ¥8 million. They will all have to pay more taxes because consumption tax will more than offset the relatively small cuts in national and local income taxes for their income brackets. Since only a minority of two-earner families earn more than ¥8 million, we can conclude that the reform is not designed to improve the situation of the average family in this category.

Above I noted that families in which both spouses hold regular jobs have been favored in the tax system thus far. By reporting their income separately instead of together, they have been eligible for more breaks. Since many of

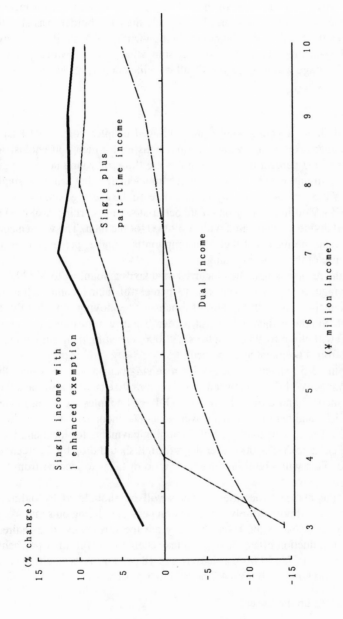

Fig. 3.7 Tax changes for four-member families
Source: Homma et al. (1988).

these two-earner couples will now have a higher tax bill, at least relative to one-earner couples, the reform has moved their taxation closer to the average.

One further point deserves attention. Under the old tax system the two-earner couples came out ahead of the one-earner couples only if their income amounted to ¥5 million or more; below that, their tax burden was slightly higher. Now the breakeven point comes in the vicinity of ¥6 million. Above that, the dual-income family will still pay somewhat less; below that, the size of its disadvantage will grow larger. Of all working couples, these are the ones that are hardest hit.

3.5.3   The Plight of Pensioners

How will Japan's young singles and old-aged couples come out? I have calculated their taxes using average income statistics for their households. As noted earlier, 7.5 percent of all households are those of young people living alone. They divide evenly between males and females, but whereas single men earn ¥2.5 million in employment income on the average, single women earn only ¥1.9 million. The women are better at saving, earning ¥68,000 in interest and dividends compared with ¥39,000 for the men. The women consume less than the men, but their consumption is a higher percentage of income because of their lower earnings.

Before the reform, single men incurred total taxes amounting to ¥329,000 on the average, a level that comes to 13 percent of their income. After the reform their burden will be almost unchanged, moving up slightly to ¥341,000. Single women will be hit harder. Their prereform tax burden of ¥216,000 will climb by 9 percent to ¥235,000, elevating their ratio of taxes to income from 11 percent to 12 percent.

Among the 3.6 percent of households receiving pensions, meanwhile, the reform's impact will differ between those senior citizens who also have employment income and those who do not. Old-aged couples receiving money from both jobs and pensions have an average annual income of ¥4.5 million. Before the reform, their total tax bill, including payments for local and indirect taxes, came to ¥257,000; after the reform it should drop by 7 percent to ¥239,000. This will slightly reduce their ratio of taxes to income from 5.7 percent to 5.3 percent.

One of the heaviest increases in taxes will be shouldered by old-aged couples who are almost entirely dependent on pensions, living on some ¥2.5 million a year. Most of the taxes they pay are the various existing indirect taxes; the introduction of a consumption tax scheme will shift their payments from ¥118,000 to ¥139,000, a sharp rise of 18 percent. As a result, the tax-to-income ratio will climb from 4.7 percent to 5.5 percent.

3.5.4   Adding up the Losers

Having reviewed the tax changes in each household category, we are now in a position to estimate the percentage of households that will be forced to bear a heavier tax burden. Before proceeding, note that my source for the distribution of households in each income bracket is from 1984. Since there has been a rise in income levels since then, the estimates may be somewhat high.

Virtually all one-earner couples will receive tax relief; those that may see an increase in their payments are limited to families earning less than ¥3 million. Even among these, there may still be a slight reduction in taxes depending on their life-style. The families in the ¥2 million–¥3 million bracket with just one child may come out ahead. All in all, I calculate that one-earner couples that will be paying more taxes come to 8.4 percent of all Japanese households.

For families with part-time income from spouses, taxes will increase only for the 4.5 percent of all households that have income of under ¥4 million. Dual-income families in the ¥6 million–¥8 million bracket will still be paying less taxes than single-income families who earn less than ¥6 million. They account for 7.8 percent of all households.

Among old-aged couples, the only beneficiaries are those who have employment income and whose total annual income exceeds ¥4 million. Since most senior citizens do not have that much income, we can add another 3.0 percent share to the households that will be hurt by the tax reform. And the same can be said of the 7.5 percent share of single men and women, almost all of whom will be paying more taxes.

Adding up these shares, we find that slightly over 30 percent of all Japanese households will see a modest to large increase in their taxes. Put another way, the great majority of households should benefit from the reform—or at least not be seriously harmed by it.

3.5.5 The Life-Stage Tax Burden

The Takeshita reform package, switching from direct to indirect taxation, works well in terms of the life-stage tax burden on households. As emphasized in section 3.2, wages in Japan are strongly determined by seniority, and the income tax rate structure of has been extremely progressive. Under this situation, middle-age salaried workers in their forties and fifties have had a heavy tax burden (see fig. 3.1).

As a result of income tax cuts and an increased consumption tax, the tax burden is flattened and averaged over the whole life. Figure 3.8 confirms that this is the case. The combination of income tax cuts and an increased consumption tax will shift the tax burden from the middle-aged stage to the younger or older-aged stage.

3.6 Prospects for Further Reform

I have briefly reviewed the process and contents of tax reform in Japan. Judged from the present achievements, the tax reform unfortunately is far

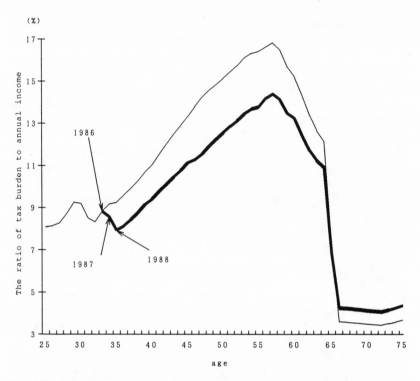

Fig. 3.8   Life-stage tax burden (individual income tax, local inhabitants' tax, and consumption tax)
Source: Homma et al. (1988).

from satisfactory and we still have a lot of work to improve the tax system. Here I shall note prospects for further reform.

The standard procedure for tax reform is to reduce marginal tax rates by broadening the tax base. This is an indispensable step to attain consistent fairness, neutrality, and simplicity. But broadening the tax base is insufficient to substantially reduce individual income tax rates and corporate tax rates.

One approach to broadening the tax base is to repeal special exemptions and deductions for particular groups of taxpayers. Typical examples are the special treatment of the income that medical doctors receive from social insurance programs: the special treatment of unincorporated businesses as deemed corporations; and tax-free reserves, depreciation allowances, and tax credits in corporate tax. These preferences are untouched, except for the elimination of the deductability of corporations' interest payments on land purchases, because the government fears strong political repercussions. In order to secure fair taxation, greater efforts must be made to eliminate these tax preferences.

Another measure to broaden the tax base is to include income sources that were previously excluded. The current tax reform marks a great advance in taxation of capital income. More specifically, the abolition of the tax exemption on interest income for small savers and the repeal of the exemption of capital gains on the sale of stocks have been achieved. But small savers are not very happy about the adoption of a separate withholding tax rate. It is often claimed that the present taxation system on capital income must be changed into a comprehensive tax system. To do so, we must introduce the tax identification number. This has been a most controversial issue in Japan, however, and has not been settled.

The taxation of land has been heatedly discussed. As mentioned earlier, land prices have soared sharply since 1987, accompanied by growing criticism against the present taxation system. The tax base of the real estate tax is extremely undervalued relative to current prices, and therefore the effective real estate tax rates are extraordinarily low. In addition, special treatments for agriculture have induced landholders not to sell their land and have been a major cause of high land prices.

There has been great concern about the revision of consumption tax introduced in the current tax reform. To obtain support from opposing groups in retail and wholesale, the consumption tax has several special measures that are likely to wipe out the possible merits of the usual VAT. The most serious drawback is the subtraction method, which uses bookkeeping without invoices. As explained earlier, there is a strong incentive for cheating, because the chain of transactions from one stage to another cannot be traced. Moreover, the subtraction method is an imprecise way to deal with the export tax credit, compared to the usual type of VAT, i.e., the invoice method.

Special treatment of small or medium-size traders should also be formulated by international standards. Some type of exemption system frees small traders from the VAT in every country. The consumption tax in Japan sets the exemption level of ¥30 million in terms of annual sales, extraordinarily high compared to other countries. In addition, the special simplified procedures for measuring the tax base must be reconsidered, because they include too many taxpayers. Taxable traders with annual sales of less than ¥500 million can apply the simplified procedures, which use fixed percentages. This greatly impairs fairness and distorts economic activity.

References

Hashimoto, K., F. Ohtake, N. Atoda, S. Saito, and M. Homma. 1990. Japan's tax reform: Its effects on the tax burden. *Japanese Economic Studies* 19 (Fall): 31–60.

Homma, M. 1986. A simulation analysis of tax reform proposals: Toward a more desirable tax system (in Japanese). Research Report 4. Tokyo: Forum for Policy Innovation.

————. 1987. Tax money, not people. In *Opinions on Japan's Economic Restructuring*. Reference Reading Series 18, pp. 34–42. Tokyo: Foreign Press Center.

Homma, M., and N. Atoda, eds. 1989. *An empirical analysis of tax reform* (in Japanese). Tokyo: Toyo Keizai Shimposha.

Homma, M., and F. Ohtake. 1990. Japan's tax reform. *Japanese Economic Studies* 18 (Summer): 3–18.

Homma, M., S. Saito, M. Atoda, and K. Hashimoto. 1988. A simulation of the tax reform proposed by the Takeshita administration in 1988 (in Japanese). Research Report 6. Tokyo: Forum for Policy Innovation.

Ishi, H. 1989. *The Japanese tax system*. Oxford: Oxford University Press.

Pechman, J. A. 1988. *World tax reform: A progress report*. Washington, D.C.: Brookings Institution.

Comment   Hiromitsu Ishi

Masaaki Homma has two objectives in his paper on recent tax reforms in Japan: to trace the trends of previous tax reforms and to estimate the distributional effects of the Takeshita tax reform. Both parts are interesting and stimulating and should be of great help to foreign observers. In particular, the first part of this paper is a well-drawn clarification of many issues in the tax reforms attempted by the Japanese government over the past decade.

The facts in this paper are limited to the distributional effects of tax reform. However, Homma does not clearly derive his policy implications from these facts. For instance, he demonstrates that slightly over 30 percent of all Japanese households will see a modest tax increase as a result of the Takeshita reform package. Does this imply a successful tax reform or not? Of course, it is a bit difficult to assess such a complicated reform package, but I'd like to hear Homma's overall judgment of the sweeping tax reforms in Japan.

Second, his argument is restricted to short-term effects of the tax reforms. However, sweeping tax reforms by the Nakasone and Takeshita governments have obvious links to the future performance of the Japanese economy, given Japan's aging population. Consequently, the reform package should be assessed on its long-term policy effect. (Yukio Noguchi puts a positive value on Japan's VAT over the long run [see chapter 9].)

Third, it seems to me that Homma supports a heavier tax burden on capital income, such as interest and capital gains, but does not state his position on comprehensive income tax. I think it is crucial to address taxing of capital income in the controversy over income tax versus expenditure tax.

Even though capital income has been taxed more heavily in recent tax reforms, rates are different from those for other income. Homma does not say whether this tax change on capital income is justifiable. Theoretically, Japan's

Hiromitsu Ishi is professor of economics at Hitotsubashi University.

tax system is still midway between a comprehensive income tax and an expenditure tax.

To continue tax reform, which direction, income tax or expenditure tax, should we take in the future? In view of capital income taxation, should we maintain the current system, levy heavier taxes on capital income, or mitigate its tax burden until it is tax free?

Comment   Charles E. McLure, Jr.

My comments on Masaaki Homma's paper fall into four general categories. They are as much comments on Japanese tax reform as on the paper.

Defects of the Subtraction VAT

Japan has adopted a subtraction-method value-added tax at a time when the defects of such a tax are coming to be widely recognized. Unlike the credit method, the subtraction method involves calculating and taxing "slices" of value added. Thus the tax rate applied at each stage in the production-distribution process actually matters, contrary to the situation under the credit method. Such a tax can operate effectively only if the tax base is comprehensive and there is only one rate. Multiple rates create distortions and make accurate border tax adjustment (taxation of imports and tax rebates on exports) impossible. In the recent Canadian debate this feature of the subtraction method was seen by some to be an asset: politicians would be constrained by the technical features of the tax to avoid legislating multiple rates and exemptions. My own view is that this is naive; legislators will do what they want, whether it makes sense or not. Japanese experience may suggest that those favoring the subtraction method in Canada were right, since there is only one rate in Japan. But one wonders whether the uniqueness of the rate will survive if additional revenues—and higher rates—are required.

The provision of relief for small business is also problematical under the subtraction method. Under the credit method an exemption actually increases tax liability, rather than decreasing it; as a result, no business with substantial purchases of taxed inputs that is capable of compliance with the tax would voluntarily choose to be exempt. By comparison, under the subtraction method, exemption lowers tax liability and is much to be desired. Depending on eligibility requirements for exemption, a small business exemption can encourage fragmentation of business, resulting in inequities, economic distor-

Charles E. McLure, Jr., is a senior fellow at the Hoover Institution at Stanford University and a research associate of the National Bureau of Economic Research. From 1983 to 1985 he was deputy assistant secretary of the U.S. Treasury Department.

tions, and loss of revenue. The potential for mischief is reduced in the Japanese system by an arbitrary assumption that taxed purchases constitute 80 percent of sales. This approach, however, has another disadvantage. It converts the VAT into a turnover tax for businesses that use this provision.

Biting the Bullet

One is struck by the Japanese government's unwillingness to make politically hard choices that would raise taxes on certain segments of society—primarily small business—by introducing commonplace improvements in administrative techniques. The invoice-based credit-method VAT was rejected because taxpayers feared that the audit trail produced by the invoices would facilitate income tax administration. Japan still does not have a comprehensive taxpayer identification number. Those in business are allowed to pay tax-deductible salaries to family members, without regard to whether or not services of equal value are rendered in exchange, a practice that is commonly outlawed in other countries. This kowtowing to small business stands in marked contrast to the increase in the taxation of two-earner families. One wonders whether the lack of a capital gains tax on stock allows the tax on real estate gains to be circumvented by holding assets in corporate form.

Finally, one also wonders why there has been such opposition to the relatively modest 3 percent VAT on the part of housewives. Is it a "foot in the door" phenomenon: the fear that the rate will not remain at 3 percent for long? Are housewives simply fronting for neighborhood merchants who scare them with rumors of tax increases?

Reducing Saving Incentives

Japan, by introducing taxation of interest income, like other countries, has tilted from the consumption tax end of the income-consumption spectrum toward the income tax end. This leads me to make a short comment that may be more relevant for other papers given at this conference than for Homma's paper on Japan.

Economic theory tells us that under certain idealized circumstances, expensing of investment leads to a zero marginal effective tax rate on the income from equity investment. If investment is debt financed, an interest deduction creates a negative marginal effective tax rate at the firm level. This may, however, be compensated if interest income is taxed, though such compensation is sometimes only partial because of differences in tax rates paid by borrowers and lenders. If interest income is exempt, however, the combined marginal effective tax rate paid by firms and their creditors is negative. Even if depreciation allowance (together with whatever investment allowances exist) is less generous than expensing, it is still quite possible to have a negative marginal effective tax rate if interest is exempt or only partially taxed.

This line of reasoning raises interesting questions for the countries represented at this conference. What is the resource allocation effect of a tax policy that implies negative marginal effective tax rates? It is quite common to have theoretical results favoring the exemption of income from capital. It is less common, though not unknown, to have theoretical justifications for negative marginal effective tax rates.

4 The Political Economy of Tax Reforms and Their Implications for Interdependence: United States

Charles E. McLure, Jr.

4.1 Introduction

In 1986 the United States achieved fundamental income tax reform—something that had generally been agreed to be impossible.[1] Among the most important of the changes made in the 1986 reforms were those affecting international economic relations. Because of the growing interdependence of the world economy, the changes in the U.S. income tax that have occurred during the 1980s have affected foreigners as well as Americans.

This paper deals with two topics. After a brief description of the changes made in 1981, section 4.2 describes briefly the salient features of the 1986 act and discusses the political economy of tax reform—how "the impossible became the inevitable."[2] Section 4.3 examines those aspects of recent U.S. tax changes that directly affect foreigners most strongly.[3] These include effects on international flows of trade and capital[4] and induced effects on foreign tax

Charles E. McLure, Jr., is a senior fellow at the Hoover Institution at Stanford University and a research associate of the National Bureau of Economic Research. From 1983 to 1985 he was deputy assistant secretary of the U.S. Treasury Department.

1. Break and Pechman titled their 1975 book *Federal Tax Reform: The Impossible Dream?* Perhaps the most extreme statement of the proposition that tax reform was, indeed, impossible was the following statement from Witte (1985, 380): *"There is nothing, absolutely nothing, in the history or politics of the income tax that indicates that any of these schemes have the slightest hope of being enacted in the forms proposed"* (emphasis in original).

2. Birnbaum and Murray (1987, 6) write, "In the early hours of the morning of May 7, tax reform completed the transformation from the impossible to the inevitable."

3. I use the term "tax changes" rather than "tax reform" advisedly; not all the changes that have occurred qualify as reforms.

4. Jun (1989) distinguishes three ways in which a country's tax policy can affect that country's international direct investment (and the techniques affecting investment): first, by modifying the tax treatment of foreign-source income (tax rates, foreign tax credit, and deferral); second, by altering the relative before-tax profitability of investment at home and abroad (tax rates, investment tax credit, and depreciation allowances); and third, by affecting the relative cost of external financing in various countries (the deductibility of interest and withholding taxes on interest pay-

laws. It does not consider other ways in which changes in U.S. tax law have affected foreigners more indirectly: these include especially the fact that intellectual arguments for reform have been given increased attention and legitimacy by U.S. tax reform.[5] Section 4.4 draws lessons for other countries from the discussion of international issues.

4.2 The 1981 and 1986 Acts and the Political Economy of Reform

4.2.1 The 1981 Act

During the 1970s the United States suffered from historically high levels of inflation and from lagging saving, investment, and economic growth. Some have attributed poor investment performance to the interplay between inflation and an income tax that makes no provisions for inflation adjustment in the calculation of depreciation allowances. Rather than indexing the measurement of income from business and capital, however, Congress enacted an extremely generous system of investment incentives consisting of a 10 percent investment tax credit (ITC) and rapidly accelerated depreciation. In combination these incentives were roughly equivalent in real present value terms to immediate expensing (first-year write-off) of investment, at the rate of inflation prevailing at the time. Together with reductions in marginal tax rates intended to offset the effects of bracket creep resulting from prior inflation, these incentives created enormous budget deficits.

4.2.2 The 1986 Act

The 1986 reform of the U.S. income tax was far-reaching. The individual rate schedule, which had more than a dozen rates and a maximum rate of 50 percent, was reduced to four rates, 15, 28, 33, and 28 percent.[6] The corporate rate was reduced from 46 percent to 34 percent. Rate reduction was paid for by a variety of structural changes: elimination of the investment tax credit, slight deceleration of depreciation allowances, complicated provisions intended to make the timing of the recognition of income and the deduction of expenses track economic reality more closely, taxation of nominal capital gains as ordinary income, repeal of the deductions for state and local sales taxes, and a multifaceted assault on tax shelters, plus many less important

---

ments). For present purposes it might be useful to add a fourth category, changes in the country's tax treatment of domestic-source income attributable to foreigners; this allows us also to consider effects on incoming investment. All of these channels of influence have been active in changes in U.S. tax policy during the 1980s, for portfolio investment as well as for direct investment. In what follows they are noted in footnotes.

5. This aspect of the question is discussed in a variety of places, including the papers in Boskin and McLure (1990), Whalley (1990a), Tanzi (1987), Bossons (1987, 1988), and Pechman (1988). McLure (1989c) discusses lessons for developing countries from U.S. tax reform.

6. The peculiar blip in the rate structure results from provisions taking back the benefits of personal exemptions and the 15 percent rate for upper-middle-income taxpayers.

changes. Interestingly, many of the most important deviations of taxable income from economic income were not touched by tax reform. These include the deductions for interest on owner-occupied housing, the deduction for income and property taxes paid to state and local governments, the tax-free status of health insurance and many other fringe benefits provided by employers, and interest on securities issued by state and local governments. Unlike the provisions that were reformed, these benefit primarily middle-income households and are probably not generally viewed as loopholes.

Notably absent from the 1986 act was any attempt to reduce the federal budget deficit; rather, the 1986 reforms were explicitly intended to be revenue-neutral, that is, to yield neither more nor less revenue than prior law during the first five years after enactment. Given the effects of the 1981 act described above, it is not surprising that many find this to be a major flaw in the 1986 act.[7] The requirement of revenue neutrality is explained by President Ronald Reagan's promise to veto any bill containing a tax increase.

The public policy underpinnings of the 1986 act are fairly straightforward; for the most part they reflect the conventional wisdom of a generation of advocates of income tax reform. As Henry Aaron has written (1989, 9), "The remarkable characteristic of the debate leading up to the Tax Reform Act of 1986 was how much the old concepts of equity and how little recent advances in normative tax theory were invoked not only among politicians but also among economists." The objective of tax reform, as envisaged by the authors of Treasury I, the Department's 1984 report to President Reagan, which set the terms of reference for the ensuing debate, was to tax all real economic income uniformly and consistently, without regard to its source or use.[8] It was believed that this would reduce both inequity and the perception of inequity, allow lower rates, reduce distortions of economic decision making, and even make the system simpler.[9] Contrary to the expectations of some, Treasury I did not contain a proposal to shift from the income tax to a direct tax based on consumption, the recent darling of economists. Such a proposal would almost certainly have been dead on arrival if Reagan had submitted it to Congress.

The decision to scale back investment incentives and reduce statutory tax rates, first advanced in Treasury I, has drawn criticism from some economists; they point out that this policy lowers taxes on old capital and raises taxes on new capital, thereby discouraging investment.[10] They seldom address several

---

7. See, for example, Shoven (1990).

8. I have explained this at length in various places; see, for example, McLure (1986c) and McLure and Zodrow (1987).

9. It should be noted that simplicity goes beyond the complexity of tax rules and the difficulty of complying with them; it includes the question of "transactional simplicity." A tax law that is complex may simplify matters on balance by preventing complicated transactions that are tax-motivated. See McLure (1989a).

10. See, for example, Shoven (1990). Shoven also decries the failure to reduce the favoritism toward owner-occupied housing, an omission that prevents the achievement of a "level playing field." Early in the tax reform process Reagan had declared the sanctity of the deduction for home mortgage interest.

key issues, including the desirability of encouraging increases in investment not matched by increased saving, the complexity and the inequities—both real and perceived—of tax shelters based on investment incentives, and the effects on the tax base of low statutory rates (to be considered below).

A very different line of criticism, associated primarily with Richard Musgrave (1987), objects to the fact that the 1986 act sharply reduces the progressivity of income tax rates paid by individuals.[11] According to this line of reasoning it would have been preferable to combine base broadening with substantially less reduction in the progressivity of rates. It seems, however, that this view is politically unrealistic, since such a proposal would never have seen the light of day if the Treasury Department had submitted it to the White House.

Moreover, the 1986 act did not reduce the progressivity of the income tax; that occurred in 1981. The 1986 act merely restored some of the horizontal equity and economic neutrality that had been lost in 1981 (and before). It did this through a distributionally neutral process of base broadening and rate reduction. The combined effect of the 1981 and 1986 act was, however, to substantially reduce the corporate income tax rate. That has international ramifications to be examined in section 4.3.

4.2.3   The Political Economy of Reform[12]

Luck—the confluence of particular circumstances and personalities—played a large role in the passage of the Tax Reform Act of 1986. First, there was a strong and popular Republican president who detested high tax rates. Whether his understanding of the objectives of tax reform went beyond rate reduction has been widely questioned. What matters is that he made tax reform the number one item on his domestic agenda. It was especially important that Ronald Reagan was a Republican, since tax reform has commonly been a Democratic issue. (See the discussion of horizontal and vertical equity below.) Republicans, especially in the Senate, were called on to support their president's plan for tax reform—and did so—even though they preferred to oppose it.

The role of congressional "brokers" has also been emphasized. Two relatively young members of Congress, Senator Bill Bradley, a Democrat from New Jersey, and Congressman Jack Kemp, a Republican from New York, both former professional athletes who had personal experience with the intricacies and insanity of the U.S. tax code, had both launched independent campaigns for tax reforms. Because of this and their expertise, they played a role in the tax reform process unusual for members of Congress with so little seniority. Moreover, they gave the quest for tax reform a bipartisan character it might have lacked.

---

11. This issue is discussed further in McLure (1990a).

12. On this subject see especially Birnbaum and Murray (1987) and Conlan, Bean, and Wrightson (1990).

Luck also played a role in the staffing of two important positions in the Reagan administration. When the tax reform process began, Donald Regan was secretary of the treasury and James Baker was chief of staff of the White House. Regan was willing to give the tax professionals in the Treasury Department free rein to produce a politically pure proposal that would meet the objectives of tax reform announced in Reagan's 1984 state-of-the-union address. As a result, the Treasury Department proposal set a standard against which subsequent tax reform plans would be judged. It seems unlikely that Baker, the consummate politician, would have done this had he been secretary of the treasury. In early January 1985, after the release of Treasury I, Baker and Regan changed jobs. This put Baker and his deputy secretary Richard Darman in a position to handle the delicate negotiations with Congress, something Regan could never have achieved, and gave Regan ready access to the president where he could champion the cause of tax reform—something he had a psychological interest in doing, given his role in producing Treasury I.

The press, especially the print media, played a crucial role in tax reform. The press reaction to tax reform seems to have gone through three stages. First, for a short period the "liberal Eastern press" seemed unable to believe that something as good as Treasury I could come from the Reagan administration. Then they moved to characterizing the plan as "academic" and "intellectually pure" but "politically naive."

But as the process wore on, the press exhibited a clear if implicit view that tax reform should not die. Through its incessant ridicule of those who attempted to salvage the tax preferences that benefited special interests, the press helped turn politicians into statesmen. This is perhaps most clearly seen in two instances. First, when bank lobbyists cried, "We won! We won!" in response to a vote by the Ways and Means Committee that would have given banking an enormous new tax break, the media excoriated the committee members who had voted for the provision. Second, it began to call Bob Packwood, the chairman of the Senate Finance Committee, Senator Hackwood. Partly because of the press, no one in Congress wanted to find the dead baby of tax reform on their doorstep.

It is awkward for me to speculate on the role of tax experts in explaining the success of tax reform, given my own participation in the process; I would naturally like to believe that tax experts played a significant role.[13] I will simply quote a few statements from a recently published book.

[T]he initial Treasury I plan was an astonishingly pure expression of expert views. Although never formally proposed as legislation, it—rather than the existing law—set the standard against which subsequent proposals were measured. . . . [T]he ideas of tax professionals were less overtly dominant

---

13. One is inevitably reminded of the famous passage from Keynes about the power of ideas. Once while discussing tax reform with Carl Shoup, I referred to myself as an "academic scribbler." Carl said that he thought his generation had been the academic scribblers. That raises the next question: was I one of the "mad men in authority"?

through the remainder of the legislative process. . . . [B]y controlling the critical revenue estimates, the small band of professionals under JTC's David Brockway exercise life-and-death power over countless alternatives considered by decision makers. (Conlan, Bean, and Wrightson, 1990, 243–44)

The international context in which U.S. tax reform occurred played an important role in explaining the early success of the reformers.[14] In early 1984, just as the basic outlines of the Treasury I program were being set, the United Kingdom announced a radical reform in which its corporate income tax rate would be reduced from 52 percent to 35 percent and the expensing of capital goods would be replaced with a return to conventional multiyear depreciation allowances. The reasons given for the British reform—particularly avoiding distortion of investment decisions—were the same as those used to justify similar measures in the United States. These arguments—and especially the fact that Nigel Lawson, the British chancellor of the Exchequer, had found them convincing—were employed to assure Secretary Regan that the Treasury I strategy was sound.

The strategy followed in producing Treasury I probably also contributed to the success of tax reform. First, Treasury I was produced in secret. There is no evidence that anyone outside the Treasury Department knew until the last few weeks before its release what Treasury I would contain. This strategy, which allowed the president to claim truthfully that he did not know what would be in the Treasury proposals, helped assure the independence of the tax experts at Treasury and thus the intellectual purity of the plan. Had the White House known of the contents of Treasury I in advance, it is unlikely that purity could have been maintained; this is especially true since leaks would have brought representatives of special interests to the White House in droves to plead their cause.

The fact that Walter Mondale made the politically unwise decision to announce during the 1984 presidential campaign that he would raise taxes virtually assured that the formulation Treasury I could continue in secret. Had Mondale proposed a tax reform package patterned after that of Senator Bradley, it is likely that the president would have countered and in the process opened the public debate on tax reform before Treasury I became public. That would probably have doomed tax reform.

Historically tax reform has been advocated by Democrats to alter the vertical equity of the tax system—the distribution of taxes across income brackets—by increasing progressivity. Treasury I adopted an entirely different strategy based on horizontal equity. It took as a working hypothesis the proposition that tax reform should be distributionally neutral—that it should not affect the

---

14. This discussion concentrates on the role played by the 1984 reforms in the United Kingdom, which I know to have been important for the reasons stated in the text. It ignores the 1985 Canadian proposals, which were in process before the release of Treasury I but were made more urgent by it. For further discussion, see Whalley (1990b).

distribution across income classes. Thus, rather than pitting rich against poor, it pitted those who paid their fair share of taxes, and more, against those who did not. Whereas it is difficult to argue objectively that the tax system should be either more or less progressive, it is much easier to argue that everyone with a certain real economic income should pay approximately the same tax.

One component of any explanation of the success of tax reform must be the burgeoning of tax shelters that occurred after passage of the 1981 act.[15] The acceleration of depreciation allowances and the ITC provided by the 1981 act, in conjunction with the deduction for nominal interest expense bloated by inflation, created enormous tax shelter activity despite the reduction in tax rates that occurred in 1981. During the years immediately preceding passage of the 1986 act, the news media were full of stories about wealthy individuals and corporations paying little or no tax.[16]

Revenue neutrality—the proposition that tax reform should neither raise nor lower taxes in the aggregate—also proved to be politically important. It helped impose discipline on a Congress that would otherwise have used tax reform as an opportunity to bestow tax breaks, without taking back other breaks of equal value.

Finally, Treasury I exhibited what might be called a whole-hog approach. With only a few exceptions (mortgage interest on owner-occupied housing and the exclusion of interest on municipal bonds) Treasury I took no hostages. That is, it attacked virtually every tax break on the books, including many sacred cows, in order to achieve as much rate reduction as possible and thereby stir the interest of the American public.

In the early stages of their deliberations, both tax writing committees attempted a different and a more traditional approach, preserving some preferences and creating others. Ultimately, however, during a now-famous long lunch, Packwood saw the basic good sense of the Treasury I approach. By being much more ambitious in its base broadening, his committee was able to achieve far more rate reduction that might have been thought possible.[17]

15. Birnbaum and Murray (1987, 10) write, "The phenomenal rise in tax shelters was a central part of the problem." Tax shelters occur when artificial accounting losses in one activity are used to offset income from other activities, such as that from employment or the exercise of a business or profession. Tax shelters result from the combination of accelerated deduction of expenses, postponement of the recognition of income, preferential taxation of income realized as capital gains, deductions of nominal interest expense, and high marginal rates.

16. Birnbaum and Murray (1987, 127) note the concern of Dan Rostenkowski, chairman of the House Ways and Means Committee, that his daughters paid more income tax than some millionaires. According to a U.S. Treasury Department study (1985), in 1983 some thirty thousand taxpayers with incomes (before deduction of tax shelter losses) in excess of $250,000 paid less than 5 percent of such income in taxes.

17. This is not to say that the 1986 act achieved a tax base that approached the comprehensiveness of the Treasury I plan. For example, whereas Treasury I would have eliminated the deduction for all state and local taxes and would have taxed fringe benefits much more heavily, the 1986 act eliminates only the deduction for sales taxes, hardly touches fringe benefits, and makes up the revenue by a truly draconian assault on tax shelters that might accurately be characterized as retroactive.

One extremely important difference between the 1986 act and its 1981 counterpart should be mentioned. In 1981 there were essentially no losers; different industries received larger or smaller tax cuts, but virtually all received some benefit. By comparison, in 1986 there were both winners and losers. Indeed, because there was a large shift in tax liability from individuals to corporations, there were some big losers. Even so, there were enough business winners that it was never possible to put together a "killer coalition" of business interests. Rather, Darman and others put together effective coalitions of industries that would benefit from reform that were strong enough to help assure the passage of tax reform.

Public perceptions about tax reform were interesting, not to say puzzling. Under the Treasury I proposal there would have been two winners for every loser, as measured by changes in individual tax liabilities. This was true in part because there was a large shift in liabilities from individuals to corporations, and the increase in corporate taxes was not attributed to the individuals that would pay them. Yet, throughout the tax reform process a majority of those questioned in surveys consistently thought they would lose from tax reform. At no time was there a public ground swell in favor of tax reform. At best, the public looked on tax reform with indifference; at worst it was hostile. Presumably this reflected some combination of ignorance of the contents of the tax reform program and distrust of Congress; it is unlikely that individuals were factoring in the increase in corporate burdens.

4.3   International Implications of Tax Reform

Most of the remainder of this paper is devoted to examination of the international implications of changes in the U.S. income tax that occurred in 1981 and 1986. The Foreign Investment in Real Property Tax Act of 1980 and the 1984 repeal of the 30 percent withholding tax on most portfolio interest paid to foreigners are discussed more briefly. Finally, I mention briefly an issue that epitomizes the problems created by international economic interdependence, though it does not involve federal tax reform; this is unitary taxation, the method some of the American states use to tax the income of multijurisdictional corporations. I end with speculations about the need for, and the prospects of, international arrangements to reduce the increased tax competition resulting from both increasing economic interdependence and the changes in U.S. tax laws discussed earlier.

4.3.1   International Implications of the 1981 Act

It seems clear in retrospect that those responsible for the 1981 act did not pay adequate attention to the international implications of what they were doing.[18] A bidding war between the Republican and Democrats, rather than

---

18. This argument is developed at greater length in McLure (1990b).

rational analysis, explains the generosity of the investment provisions.[19] Only later was it widely realized that an increase in investment stimulated by tax incentives that is not matched by an equal increase in saving and, indeed, is aggravated by a large increase in public dissaving, would necessarily generate an inflow of foreign capital needed to finance the excess investment.[20] The capital inflow must, of necessity, be mirrored in a deterioration of the U.S. trade balance. This would be achieved by appreciation of the dollar—a development that would make imports more attractive to American consumers and exports less attractive to foreign purchasers. In short, investment incentives would hurt the short-run competitiveness of American industry.[21] Sinn (1991, 1) states the issue as follows:

> An obvious sign of confusion is the popular belief that a policy that makes a country attractive for internationally mobile capital will simultaneously improve this country's competitiveness in international trade. Of course, with flexible exchange rates, this cannot be true since the capital import equals the current account deficit: The investors' attempt to import capital will be successful only to the extent that it leads to a revaluation and thereby to a deterioration of the current account. The confusion is shared by countries that take pride in being world export champions without realizing that they could equally well regard themselves as capital flight champions. Economists have warned of such types of irrationality.

The 1981 act clearly could not affect only the United States. Sinn (1987, 224–25) notes:

> The first half of the eighties was characterized by enormous capital imports into the United States accompanied by a strong dollar and a high world interest rate level. Most countries suffered from this situation. Europe was driven into the worst recession of the post-war period, and the developing countries were shaken by one debt crisis after another. A number of countries were unable to meet their interest obligations, and a collapse of the world banking system was avoided only by strenuous efforts. The United States alone seemed to have benefited: despite the high interest rate it enjoyed a significant consumption and investment boom.

Sinn goes on to observe: "A potential explanation of the development of the world economy that fits all of the facts mentioned could be the Accelerated

---

19. See Rudder (1983, 205–6) and Witte (1985, 221–35). This experience is summarized in McLure (1989a).

20. This case is an example of the second of the channels of influence identified by Jun (1989). It appears that Summers (1988) is one of the first explicit recognitions of this proposition, so obvious in retrospect; see also Bernheim (1988, 3–5). Sinn (1987, 224–31) provides a masterful exposition of this proposition.

21. The concept of competitiveness used here, the ability to compete with imports and to export, is a crude one that does not necessarily make much sense; but it is the one that seems to permeate discussions of public policy. Slemrod (1991), besides noting the faults of this definition, argues for defining competitiveness as the ability to maintain (or increase) a nation's level of real income in the presence of competition from abroad.

Cost Recovery System (ACRS) introduced by the Reagan Administration in 1981." He concludes: "[T]here cannot be much doubt that ACRS caused one of the most severe disturbances of the world economy ever induced by a tax reform."

4.3.2   International Implications of the 1986 Act

Like the 1981 act, the 1986 act has had important effects on international trade and capital flows. Moreover, it has induced foreign governments to alter their tax policies. By eliminating the investment tax credit and reducing the speed with which depreciation allowances can be taken, it has reduced incentives for investment in the United States.[22] This may tend to reverse the excess of investment over saving, capital inflows, depreciation of the dollar, difficulties exporting, and competition from imports noted earlier.

It is interesting to note that discussions of the international effects of tax reform that occurred during the two years preceding passage of the 1986 act reflected only a rudimentary and incomplete understanding of such effects. Those arguing in favor of retention of investment incentives contended that such incentives were necessary to maintain the competitiveness of American industry. They seemed not to understand that, if saving cannot be increased, encouraging investment undermines the competitive position of U.S. industry in the short run, for reasons outlined above, no matter how positive the effects might be in the long run.

Several provisions of the 1986 act, most notably the reduction in corporate rates, the change in "sourcing" rules, and the tighter limitations on the foreign tax credit, can be expected to have extremely important international implications.[23] The reduction in corporate rates has converted the United States into a tax haven in some respects. In particular, multinational firms based in many countries employing the territorial principle will find it attractive to invest in the United States or to manipulate transactions to attribute as much of their income as possible to the United States, in order to have it taxed at the rate of 34 percent, which is one of the lowest in the world. Even corporations based in countries employing residence taxation with foreign tax credit limitations calculated on an overall basis may find it attractive to attribute income to the United States, in order to be able to average low-tax U.S. income with high-tax income earned in other countries.[24]

Multinational corporations may also have an incentive to shift borrowing from the United States to other countries, in order to benefit from interest deductions at the higher rates prevailing there, rather than the lower U.S.

22. This is an example of Jun's second channel of influence.
23. These are examples of Jun's first channel of influence.
24. Slemrod (1991) notes that Japan has enacted provisions intended to restrict the possibility of offsetting high-tax income against low-tax income under its system of overall limitation on the foreign tax credit.

rate.[25] Such a shift could have important effects on the distribution of tax revenues among nations. This has apparently been an important determinant of Canada's decision to reduce its corporate tax rate in response to the American rate reduction.[26]

The United States has long been worried about the incentive effects created by the use of an overall limitation on the foreign tax credit.[27] The overall limitation can create an incentive for corporations to move business to low-tax jurisdictions, in order to offset taxes paid in high-tax jurisdictions. Alternatively, if they have adequate low-tax income, they can invest in high-tax jurisdictions without actually bearing the burden of such higher taxes.[28] Those responsible for U.S. tax reform realized that the proposed rate reductions would aggravate this problem: rate reduction would reduce the ability of U.S. corporations to take full credit for tax paid to foreign countries, and thus increase incentives to shift income to low-tax jurisdictions.[29]

Various approaches have been proposed to deal with this problem. For example, the U.S. Treasury Department (1984, 2:361) and President Reagan's 1985 tax reform proposals to the Congress (p. 389) recommended shifting to a per-country limitation on the foreign tax credit. The 1986 act took a different approach. It retained the overall limitation but expanded the use of separate "baskets." In particular, there are separate baskets for ordinary operating income, for passive income, and for income that is commonly subject to low rates, such as that from financial services and shipping income. Moreover, it provided for a "high-rate kick-out"; interest income subject to high gross withholding taxes cannot be comingled with passive income subject to low tax rates. These rules have greatly increased the complexity of the tax system for U.S. multinational corporations.[30] Most will be forced to classify their income into at least three baskets, operating, passive, and high-tax interest.

The reduction in rates, tighter sourcing rules, and greater use of separate baskets will have important international ramifications. In particular, many more American firms will have excess foreign tax credits—taxes paid to for-

25. This is an example of Jun's third channel of influence. It involves a change in the relative cost of funds resulting from changes in the tax rates at which deductions are taken.

26. This has been emphasized in Bossons (1987, 1988). See also Whalley (1990b).

27. The United States allows U.S. multinationals credit for taxes paid to foreign governments, but only up to the amount of U.S. tax that would be paid on such foreign-source income. It employs an "overall limitation," under which the income earned in all foreign countries and the taxes attributed thereto are combined in calculating the limitation on the credit.

28. See the example in U.S. Department of the Treasury (1984, 2:360–61), and *The President's Tax Proposals* (1985, 387).

29. See *The President's Tax Proposals* (1985, 387). Because the 1986 act contains a 34 percent corporate rate, there is an enormous shift of tax burden from individuals to corporations. Under an alternative reform that would have left corporate liabilities unchanged, the corporate rate might have been reduced to as low as 28 percent. See Birnbaum and Murray (1987, 59). Under such a change excess foreign tax credits would be even more prevalent.

30. On the complexity of the post-1986 U.S. taxation of multinational corporations, see Tillinghast (1990).

eign governments in excess of what can be credited in the United States. As long as the United States had relatively high tax rates and liberal sourcing and averaging rules, foreign governments could operate under an umbrella created by the U.S. foreign tax credit: they could, on average, levy tax rates as high as those in the United States without fear that U.S. taxpayers investing within their jurisdiction would actually bear the burden of local taxes. Now that many more U.S. multinationals are in an excess credit position, the umbrella is shredded; it will be much more common that the investors, rather than the U.S. Treasury, will pay taxes levied by source countries. The result is that conditions now resemble more closely what they would be if the United States employed a territorial system.

One obvious result of this change in U.S. tax policy has been pressure on foreign governments to reduce their own tax rates. Explicit recognition of this is nowhere expressed more clearly than in the Colombian income tax reform passed at the end of 1986. Article 44 of that law provides the government the power to change the tax rates applied to income of foreigners in the light of changes being made in the income taxes of resident countries of foreigners investing in Colombia (the most important of which is the United States); the provision mentions specifically changes in the availability of foreign tax credits. This power has since been exercised; whereas the withholding rate was initially raised from 20 percent to 30 percent when the income tax rate was reduced from 40 percent to 30 percent (producing a combined rate of 51 percent on income distributed to foreigners, compared to 52 percent under prior law), it has since been reduced to 20 percent.

There may be few cases as clear as this one. But there is no doubt that tax rates have been falling around the world. Table 4.1 reports tax rates before

Table 4.1   Tax Rates in Selected Countries, before and after Tax Reform

Country	Top Marginal Rate for Individuals (old/new)	Corporate Rate (old/new)
Australia	60/49	46/39
Canada	34/29	36/28
Colombia	49/30	40/30
Indonesia	50/35	45/35
Israel	60/48[a]	53/48
Japan	70/50	42/37.5
Mexico	55/40	42/36
Sweden	75/50	56/30
United Kingdom	80/40	52/35
United States	70/28 (+ 5)[b]	46/34

Source: Charles E. McLure, Jr., "Appraising Tax Reform," in Boskin and McLure (1990, 282).

[a]Assumes scheduled elimination of surcharge at the end of 1989.

[b]The additional 5 percent represents a surcharge faced by upper-middle-income taxpayers.

and after tax reforms in selected countries. Whalley (1990a) also documents the movement toward lower tax rates.[31] Sinn (1990, 1) writes, "The current world economy seems to be going through a phase of increased tax competition." Of course, it has been necessary to expand tax bases, often by reducing investment incentives, in order to lower rates without sacrificing revenues. Thus it seems that U.S. tax reform has helped encourage the tax reform movement that has swept the world in recent years.

Though this is undoubtedly a welcome development to many of those involved in the process of U.S. tax reform, especially the conservatives in the Reagan White House, there is little reason to believe that worldwide tax reform was a conscious, high-priority objective of those most responsible for advocacy and design of the U.S. reform. They were primarily interested in improving the American system; the reform of other systems is an unexpected if welcome bonus.

4.3.3   Other Tax Changes

The Repeal of Withholding on Interest[32]

During the early 1980s substantial American attention was focused on treaty shopping, the unanticipated and improper use of treaties between the United States and another country to gain the benefits of the treaty for a resident of a third country. Primary attention focused on the Netherlands Antilles, where American corporations would establish finance subsidiaries that would borrow in the Eurodollar market and then relend to their American parents without paying the withholding tax on interest that would be due in the case of direct borrowing from Europe.

The degree of international interdependence is shown by the fact that the United States did not merely repeal its treaty with the Netherlands Antilles or amend it to outlaw this abuse. Rather, the United States repealed its withholding tax on most portfolio interest paid to foreigners.[33] (There had long been no withholding tax on interest on bank accounts.) This route was chosen because of fears that simply repealing the treaty would cause an unacceptable increase the cost of funds to American corporations. This, in turn, is true because there is very little source-based taxation of interest in Europe.[34] Of course, the virtual elimination of source-based taxation of interest by the United States makes it even less likely that any other country will attempt such

31. Whalley (1990a) notes that New Zealand reduced its top individual rate from 66 percent to 33 percent and its corporate rate from 45 to 33 percent.

32. This section draws on McLure (1989d).

33. This is an example of Jun's third channel of influence.

34. When West Germany attempted to introduce a modest withholding tax on interest in 1989 there was such a large exodus of capital to other European countries that the measure had to be repealed. This episode provides evidence that the taxation of interest income is being evaded, since the withholding tax would have been creditable against final liability.

taxation; indeed, it increases the likelihood of further reductions of such taxes by other countries.

Foreign Investment in Real Property Tax Act

American response was quite different in another area, the taxation of capital gains on U.S. real estate. In 1980 the United States enacted the Foreign Investment in Real Property Tax Act (FIRPTA). It modified the normal tax treatment of capital gains realized by foreigners—exemption—to treat gains on real estate as taxable income.[35] This legislation reflected a variety of political pressures, most notably the concern that foreign investors benefiting more from favorable tax treatment than did Americans were bidding up the price of U.S. real estate.

Comparison

It is fascinating to compare the American reaction to greater economic interdependence in these two areas. In the case of interest, source-based taxation was reduced in order to avoid repelling capital inflows or raising the cost of capital to American business. In the case of real estate the stance of public policy was just the opposite; taxes on capital gains were raised in order to prevent capital inflow—or at least make it less attractive. Whether this objective is realized depends on the treatment of such gains and taxes thereon in the country of residence of the foreign investor (territorial, residence with credit, etc.).

Unitary Taxation[36]

The states in the United States employ formulas to apportion the income of multistate corporations among themselves. If several affiliated corporations are deemed to be engaged in a unitary business, their incomes and apportionment factors are "combined" by some states for purposes of determining the income attributable to the state. The idea is that "separate accounting" applied to the activities of the individual corporations cannot adequately determine the division of income between the firms, and thus the geographic source of income. This is true because of the possibility that transfer prices are manipulated and because economic interdependence may be so great that it is conceptually impossible for separate accounting to give an accurate division of income between affiliated firms. In some states this approach is carried to its logical conclusion in "worldwide unitary combination," under which the income and economic activities of all affiliated firms deemed to be engaged in a unitary business are combined, no matter where the firms do business.

This approach has proven to be extremely unpopular with foreign governments, as well as with both domestic and foreign multinational corporations.

---

35. This is an example of the fourth channel of influence added to Jun's list.
36. This section draws on much of my work on unitary taxation, the most important of which is published in McLure (1986a).

There has thus been a general retreat to "water's-edge combination," under which only U.S. source income is apportioned.

This result is somewhat ironic, given the growing interdependence of the world economy. One would expect that as economic integration proceeds in Europe the economic interdependence of affiliated corporations will become so great that formula apportionment will be needed.[37] Of course, there is no reason to expect that worldwide combination would be attempted.

On the other hand, it is entirely possible that the growing economic interdependence of the world will make separate accounting increasingly untenable everywhere. It is said that the determination, defense, and policing of transfer pricing is imposing a rapidly increasing burden on corporations and tax administrators in the United States. While the United States may be able to cope with these problems satisfactorily, many countries cannot; this is especially true of LDCs. It would not be surprising to see a movement to the use of formulas to divide income among nations.[38]

4.4 Lessons

This review of the international implications of U.S. tax policy provides two kinds of lessons. The first are lessons for other countries acting unilaterally and in their own interest. The lessons for individual countries are fairly straightforward and have been anticipated by the foregoing discussion; they are simply stated with little elaboration, except to note that they would be modified if there were greater international tax cooperation. By far the more interesting implications are those for the international community of nations; they involve the need for greater cooperation in tax policy. I deal with them at greater length, but not really satisfactorily.

4.4.1 Lessons for Other Countries

Countries that wish to compete effectively in world markets would do well not to increase investment more rapidly than saving; this is something that economists working in developing countries have known for years, but the United States learned only in the 1980s, if at all.

Countries that want to attract investment from the United States would be well-advised to pay attention to the foreign tax credit position of potential investors. If such firms have excess foreign tax credits, the taxes of the source country will burden the investor, as under a territorial system, and not be borne by the U.S. Treasury. In general, countries would do well to keep their statutory corporate tax rates below the American corporate rate, and that may not even be low enough, due to the working of the overall limitation on the foreign tax credit.

---

37. For a more detailed statement of this position, see McLure (1989b).
38. For discussions of this possibility, see Carlson and Galper (1984) and Kopits and Muten (1984).

The elimination of U.S. taxation on virtually all interest income suggests that other countries may be well advised to reduce their own taxation of income from business and capital, in order to prevent capital outflows. At the very least, it might be appropriate to exempt interest income of residents from tax.[39] A more extreme approach would be to replace the income tax with a direct tax based on consumption.[40] Of course, that policy involves questions that go far beyond the scope of this paper.[41]

Multinational companies have opportunities to chose where to borrow and to manipulate transfer prices in order to minimize their taxes. This also suggests that other countries will do well to avoid statutory rates above the U.S. corporate rate. Moreover, it suggests that they may even want to think of using a form of unitary taxation, both to prevent abuses and to get around the problems inevitably posed by economic interdependence with a group of affiliated firms—problems that will become even more acute for tax administration as international interdependence increases.

4.4.2   Lessons for the Community of Nations

The picture painted above—including the lessons for countries acting unilaterally—is not a pretty one; it is one of intensified tax competition that can be prevented only by international cooperation. As Razin and Sadka (1989, 4) wrote in a recent NBER working paper, "If there is not sufficient coordination with the rest of the world to allow each country to tax its residents on their income from capital in the rest of the world, then tax competition leads to no tax whatsoever on capital income."

Some would find this development to be a positive one; presumably most advocates of consumption-based direct taxes would fall in this camp, as would less-principled advocates of greater capital formation. This is not the place to enter that debate. I will simply take as given the need to prevent wholesale tax competition, for whatever reason, and ask what kinds of cooperation would be needed to achieve this end.[42] The discussion that follows reflects the last three lessons for individual countries given above.[43]

39. I do not consider the possibility that residence countries will adopt the worldwide taxation of interest where it does not now exist; I consider that a futile gesture in the absence of far-reaching international cooperation of the type discussed below.

40. McLure (1989d) suggests this approach. McLure et al. (1990, chap. 9) and McLure (1990a) discuss whether the United States would allow foreign tax credits for such a tax, noting that the development of excess foreign tax credits by many American multinationals reduces the importance of the issue.

41. See, however, McLure et al. (1990, chap. 9) or Zodrow and McLure (forthcoming).

42. On the costs of international tax competition, see Musgrave (1990), Slemrod (1990), and Sinn (1990). The primary reason for favoring the taxation of income from capital is the regressivity of failing to do so. Musgrave relies heavily on the view that source countries are "entitled" to taxes on income, whereas Sinn notes an insurance motive for preventing tax competition. The need to end tax competition is especially grave for LDCs and for countries in the process of emerging from socialism. It may be worth noting explicitly that I have advocated tax competition among subnational governments as a way of assuring that citizens get something of value from their governments; see McLure (1986b).

43. For similar suggestions, see Slemrod (1990, 21–22). Bird (1988) and Bird and McLure (1990) also deal with this issue.

First, it would be appropriate to keep statutory corporate tax rates within a fairly narrow band—or at least above an agreed lower bound. This would protect all countries from destructive tax competition. Second, withholding taxes should be levied on all passive income paid to foreigners. Such taxes could be final taxes, with revenues retained by the source country, or creditable against tax liability in the taxpayer's country of residence (in which case revenues would be remitted to the residence country); alternatively, revenues could be split between source and residence countries. Third, countries not agreeing to the above two rules of the game would be designated as tax havens. Amounts paid to persons residing in them (including "letterbox persons") would be subject to full withholding, without the benefit of crediting. The fourth possible lesson is even more controversial than the above three. It involves the adoption of some variant of unitary taxation, at least within the EC, and perhaps by all countries.

References

Aaron, Henry J. 1989. Politics and the Professors Revisited. *American Economic Review* 79 (2):1–15.

Bernheim, B. Douglas. 1988. Budget Deficits and the Balance of Trade. In *Tax Policy and the Economy,* ed. Lawrence H. Summers, 2:1–31. Cambridge, MA: MIT Press.

Bird, Richard M. 1988. Shaping a New International Tax Order. *Bulletin for International Fiscal Documentation* 42:292–99.

Bird, Richard M., and Charles E. McLure, Jr. 1990. The Personal Income Tax in an Interdependent World. In *The Personal Income Tax: Phoenix from the Ashes?* ed. Sijbren Cnossen and Richard M. Bird, 235–55. Amsterdam: North-Holland.

Birnbaum, Jeffrey, and Alan Murray. 1987. *Showdown at Gucci Gulch.* New York: Random House.

Boskin, Michael J., and Charles E. McLure, Jr., 1990. *World Tax Reform: Case Studies of Developed and Developing Countries.* San Francisco: ICS Press for the International Center for Economic Growth.

Bossons, John. 1987. The Impact of the 1986 Tax Reform Act on Tax Reform in Canada. *National Tax Journal* 40 (3):331–38.

———. 1988. International Tax Competition: The Foreign Government Response in Canada and Other Countries. *National Tax Journal* 41 (September):347–55.

Carlson, George N., and Harvey Galper. 1984. Water's Edge versus Worldwide Unitary Combination. In *The State Corporation Income Tax: Issues in Worldwide Unitary Combination,* ed. Charles E. McLure, Jr., 1–40. Stanford, CA: Hoover Institution Press.

Conlan, Timothy J., David R. Bean, and Margaret T. Wrightson. 1990. *Taxing Choices: The Politics of Tax Reform.* Washington, D.C.: Congressional Quarterly Press.

Jun, Joosung. 1989. Tax Policy and International Direct Investment. NBER Working Paper no. 3048. Cambridge, MA: National Bureau of Economic Research.

Kopits, George, and Leif Muten. 1984. The Relevance of the Unitary Approach for Developing Countries. In *The State Corporation Income Tax: Issues in Worldwide Unitary Combination,* ed. Charles E. McLure, Jr., 269–80. Stanford, CA: Hoover Institution Press.

McLure, Charles E., Jr. 1986a. *Economic Perspectives on State Taxation of Multijurisdictional Corporations.* Arlington, VA: Tax Analysts.
———. 1986b. Tax Competition: Is What's Good for the Private Goose Also Good for the Public Gander?" *National Tax Journal* 39 (3):341–48.
———. 1986c. Where Tax Reform Went Astray. *Villanova Law Review* (6):1619–63.
———. 1989a. The Budget Process and Tax Simplification/Complication. *Tax Law Review* 45 (1):25–95.
———. 1989b. Economic Integration and European Taxation of Corporate Income at Source: Some Lessons from the U.S. Experience. *European Taxation* 29 (8):243–50.
———. 1989c. Lessons for LDCs of U.S. Income Tax Reform. In *Tax Reform in Developing Countries,* ed. Malcolm Gillis, 347–90. Durham, N.C.: Duke University Press.
———. 1989d. U.S. Tax Laws and Capital Flight from Latin America. *InterAmerican Law Review* 20 (2):321–57.
———. 1990a. International Aspects of Tax Policy for the 21st Century. *American Journal of Tax Policy* 8 (2):167–85.
———. 1990b. International Considerations in U.S. Tax Reform. In *Influence of Tax Differentials on International Competitiveness,* 3–23. Deventer, The Netherlands: Kluwer.
McLure, Charles E., Jr., Jack Mutti, Victor Thuronyi, and George R. Zodrow. 1990. *The Taxation of Income from Business and Capital in Colombia.* Durham, N.C.: Duke University Press.
McLure, Charles E., Jr., and George R. Zodrow. 1987. Treasury I and the Tax Reform Act of 1986: The Economics and Politics of Tax Reform. *Journal of Economic Perspectives* 1 (1):37–58.
Musgrave, Peggy B. 1990. Comment on Richard M. Bird and Charles E. McLure, Jr., The Personal Income Tax in an Interdependent World. In *The Personal Income Tax: Phoenix from the Ashes?* ed. Sijbren Cnossen and Richard M. Bird, 256–59. Amsterdam: North-Holland.
Musgrave, Richard A. 1987. Short of Euphoria. *Journal of Economic Perspectives* 1 (1):59–71.
Pechman, Joseph A. 1988. *World Tax Reform: A Progress Report.* Washington, D.C.: Brookings Institution.
The President's Tax Proposals to the Congress for Fairness, Growth, and Simplicity. 1985. Washington, D.C.: U.S. Government Printing Office.
Razin, Assaf and Efraim Sadka. 1989. International Tax Competition and Gains from Tax Harmonization. NBER Working Paper no. 3152. Cambridge, MA: National Bureau of Economic Research.
Rudder, Catherine E. 1983. Tax Policy: Structure and Choice. In *Making Economic Policy in Congress,* ed. Allen Schick, 196–220. Washington, D.C.: American Enterprise Institute for Public Policy Research.
Shoven, John B. 1990. The U.S. Tax Reform of 1986: Is It Worth Copying? In *World Tax Reform: Case Studies of Developed and Developing Countries,* ed. Michael J. Boskin and Charles E. McLure, Jr., 177–85. San Francisco: ICS Press for the International Center for Economic Growth.
Sinn, Hans-Werner. 1987. *Capital Income Taxation and Resource Allocation.* Amsterdam: North-Holland.
———. 1990. Can Direct and Indirect Taxes Be Added for International Comparisons of Competitiveness? In *Reforming Capital Income Taxation,* ed. Horst Siebert, 1–19. Tübingen, Germany: J. C. B. Mohr.
Slemrod, Joel. 1990. Tax Principles in an International Economy. In *World Tax Reform: Case Studies of Developed and Developing Countries,* ed. Michael J. Boskin

and Charles E. McLure, Jr., 11–23. San Francisco: ICS Press for the International Center for Economic Growth.

———. 1991. Competitive Advantage and the Optimal Tax Treatment of the Foreign-Source Income of Multinationals: The Case of the United States and Japan. *American Journal of Tax Policy* 9 (1):113–43.

Summers, Lawrence H. 1988. Tax Policy and International Competitiveness. In *International Aspects of Fiscal Policies,* ed. Jacob A. Frenkel, 349–75. Chicago: University of Chicago Press.

Tanzi, Vito. 1987. The Response of Other Industrial Countries to the U.S. Tax Reform Act. *National Tax Journal* 40 (3):339–55.

Tillinghast, David R. 1990. International Tax Simplification. *American Journal of Tax Policy* 8 (2):187–247.

U.S. Department of the Treasury. 1984. *Tax Reform for Fairness, Simplicity, and Economic Growth.* Washington, D.C.: U.S. Government Printing Office.

———. 1985. Taxes Paid by High-Income Taxpayers and the Growth of Partnerships. Reprinted in *Tax Notes* 28 (August 12):717–20.

Whalley, John. 1990a. Foreign Responses to U.S. Tax Reform. In *Do Taxes Matter: The Impact of the Tax Reform Act of 1986,* ed. Joel Slemrod, 286–314. Cambridge, MA: MIT Press.

———. 1990b. Recent Tax Reform in Canada: Policy Responses to Global and Domestic Pressures. In *World Tax Reform: Case Studies of Developed and Developing Countries,* ed. Michael J. Boskin and Charles E. McLure, Jr., 73–91. San Francisco: ICS Press for the International Center for Economic Growth.

Witte, John F. 1985. *The Politics and Development of the Federal Income Tax.* Madison: University of Wisconsin Press.

Zodrow, George R., and Charles E. McLure, Jr. Forthcoming. Implementing Direct Consumption Taxes in Developing Countries. *Tax Law Review.*

Comment   Toshiaki Tachibanaki

This is a very valuable survey paper on the experience of the U.S. tax reform and its implication for the other countries. Obviously, the United States is the most influential country in the world. Thus, it has a special value for the other countries. One interesting and useful element of this paper is that Charles McLure presents his personal opinions in several cases. This reflects the fact that McLure was at one time an insider of the U.S. tax reform. Therefore, readers can learn some insider stories. My comments are largely addressed to his opinions.

First, McLure attributes the big increase in investment to investment tax credit (ITC) and accelerated depreciation allowances in the 1981 tax reform. In other words, tax reform was quite effective for increasing investment activity in the United States. This opinion was advocated by Hans-Werner Sinn, and McLure supports the opinion to a greater extent. No serious empirical evidence, however, is described in this paper. It is possible to guess that there

Toshiaki Tachibanaki is professor of economics at Kyoto University.

must be some other important reasons for explaining the increase in investment, such as sales increases, profit increases, and others. It would be necessary to report some empirical support of the investment behavior in the United States in view of McLure's emphasis on the increase in investment due to tax policy.

Second, McLure suggests that the big increase in investment is the main cause of the U.S. investment-savings imbalance. I do not deny the effect. It seems to me, however, that excess consumption (or lower saving) of the American people and/or huge government deficits have been more responsible for the U.S. investment-savings imbalance than the increase in investment. This is my personal opinion.

Third, McLure says that tax may affect the degree of competitiveness of the industry. Some people propose that a decrease in the corporate tax rate or an increase in ITC is recommended in order to improve competitiveness. According to the careful international comparison among four countries, namely the United Kingdom, Sweden, West Germany, and the United States, performed by King and Fullerton,[1] the correlation between productivity (or investment activity) and tax burden is inverse. In other words, countries that levy higher taxes have higher productivities or investment activities. Thus, it may be difficult to believe a strong effect of tax on competitiveness. Competitiveness is determined by factors other than the tax factor. This may be again my personal opinion.

Fourth, McLure points out the necessity of international tax coordination particularly in the field of corporate tax rates, the "sourcing" rule, and the limitation of the foreign tax credit. I agree with him because it is important to avoid tax competition or tax war among nations. In other words, a country should learn from the experience of other countries. McLure points out the possibility of broadening the tax base in the United States, namely, a shift to a tax based on consumption rather on income. However, tax reform in the United States failed to have such a shift. In view of the experiences in most of the industrialized nations where a VAT or a tax based on consumption was introduced, the United States may have to learn from the experiences in the other industrialized countries. Otherwise, the United States may be isolated from the world trend. If tax coordination is important as suggested by McLure, the time has come to consider such a tax in the United States.

The comments here were largely my personal reactions to the opinions addressed by McLure. Needless to say, they do not dispute the quality and usefulness of this paper at all.

---

1. Mervyn A. King and Don Fullerton, eds., *The Taxation of Income from Capital* (Chicago: University of Chicago Press, 1984).

5   Tax Reform in Korea

Taewon Kwack and Kye-Sik Lee

5.1 Introduction

In the early stage of Korea's development, the nation's growth depended heavily on strong government leadership because of a lack of both know-how and risk-taking entrepreneurs. The demand of the people for the government to make greater development efforts legitimized an interventionist policy. Thus, the Korean government took the lead in development.

The Korean tax system, which contains a rich assortment of policy tools, has been used in almost all kinds of government development efforts. Tax tools, however, have not been very effective in carrying out the intended goals. First, in the earlier stages of development, the Korean market did not function well enough for price incentives to operate efficiently. The government's extensive intervention was one of the major reasons for this problem. Second, tax administration was inefficient. Third, the level of taxpayer compliance has been very low. For these reasons, despite the extensive and frequent manipulation of the tax system, the Korean government has not depended heavily on these tools in a practical sense. Rather, financial policy has been employed more effectively.

Politically and economically, Korea is now at a crossroads. Many new problems threaten to hinder Korea's economic growth. Korea's successful export-led growth, producing substantial balance-of-payments surpluses, has

Taewon Kwack is professor of economics at Sogang University. Kye-Sik Lee is a research fellow of the Korea Development Institute.

The authors thank the participants of the NBER-KDI conference. The authors would especially like to thank Professors Kun-Young Yun of Yonsei University and Hiromitsu Ishi of Hitotsubashi University for their helpful comments and suggestions. Professor Anne Krueger of Duke University kindly provided long and detailed comments concerning the paper, and the authors really appreciate her deep insights and invaluable suggestions. The authors assume full responsibility for any remaining errors.

elicited friction and growing protectionism from its trading partners. In addition, imbalances in regional, sectoral, and urban and rural development have been exacerbated, which has resulted in increasing income disparities, a major source of discontent and social conflict. With the process of democratization, the pent-up discontent of the past decades has emerged in the form of social conflicts and disorder, thus posing a major obstacle to further development.

Tax policy, as part of the growth-oriented strategies of the past, has been partially responsible for bringing about these problems. In the future, Korea's tax policy should aim not only for sustained economic growth but also for correction of disparities that exist among various economic and social sectors. To redress such imbalances, which arose from the government's long neglect of social development, there is a strong need for redirection of tax policy.

This paper presents an overview of some of the current tax reform issues in Korea. We first briefly review the historical changes in Korean tax policy and the tax structure. Next, we outline the current tax system and structure and identify a few important structural problems with the system. Finally, we discuss current tax reform issues and the tax reforms to be carried out in the coming years.

5.2   A Historical Overview of Korean Tax Policy and Reform

Almost every year since the establishment of the government in 1948, the tax system has changed. The reforms of 1961, 1967, 1971, 1976, and 1982 were carried out on a larger scale than other reforms and were directly linked to Korea's five-year economic development plans. In other words, Korean tax policy has been an integral part of the country's economic development policy. Therefore, in spite of the repeated citation of equity objectives, efficiency objectives have dominated in practically all these reforms. As noted above, only recently have equity issues been seriously discussed in relation to tax reform.

5.2.1   The Preindustrialization Period (1948–61)

The Republic of Korea was formed in 1948, and a set of tax laws were enacted that same year. Previously, the U.S. military regime used a partially revised version of a wartime tax system that had been taken over from the Japanese colonial government. The new system, which was embodied in eighteen tax laws, included income tax, corporate tax, liquor tax, inheritance tax, commodity taxes, and other minor taxes. It was the first modern and democratic tax system introduced in Korea. One of its notable characteristics was the shift in the taxation target from the rural landlord class to the wealthy urban class.

The new system was completely disrupted by the Korean War during 1950–53. By that time, policymakers had also become aware of administrative difficulties in the system. Postwar tax reforms in the 1950s, especially in 1956, can be characterized as reflecting these administrative considerations and as attempting to replace the wartime emergency system with a normalized one. Around the end of the 1950s, the government's policy emphasis partially shifted from rehabilitation and reconstruction to industrialization and economic growth. Tax policy, accordingly, began to emphasize incentive measures to promote capital formation and exports.

5.2.2   The Period of Export-oriented Industrialization (1961–70)

Rapid economic growth in Korea began in the early 1960s, when the military government that came to power in 1961 launched an organized and single-minded policy on industrialization. The new government had to solve several problems before it could promote its ambitious plan to push the economy out of the quagmire of poverty. First, fiscal difficulties arose from the drastic reduction of foreign aid, which had formerly served to meet a considerable portion of the government's fiscal budget. Other financial sources for investment in the Korean economy had to be found. The economy faced the typical problem of a lack of domestic savings to finance investment and a lack of foreign exchange to import capital goods. In addition, the government wanted to carry out its investment projects directly, in order to combat the severe deficiency of social overhead capital. Naturally, the goal of a new tax policy would be to maximize revenue and to encourage savings and foreign exchange earnings.

To maximize revenue, a crucial administrative reform was implemented, the establishment of the Office of National Tax Administration (ONTA) in 1966. The military government diagnosed correctly that the problem was not in the system of taxation as legally defined but in the implementation of the system. Before the establishment of ONTA, some measures were taken to ensure the enforcement of tax laws. These measures included simplifying tax administration, intensifying the punishment for tax delinquency, and providing incentives for bookkeeping and voluntary compliance.[1]

To promote private saving and investment, capital taxation was drastically reduced. In particular, interest income was almost untaxed, a law guaranteeing the anonymity of bank accounts was passed in the early 1960s, and official interest rates for deposits were raised dramatically in the mid-1960s. On the investment side, the definition of "key and strategic industries" in which firms were eligible for quite liberal tax holidays was expanded.

During this period, income generated from foreign exchange–earning activity was taxed at a preferential rate, that is, 50 percent of the normal rate. Previously, the preferential reduction rates were 30 percent for exports and 20

---

1. For example, ONTA introduced a new "green-return system" (so named for the color of the return form) under which firms and individuals file their tax returns on a self-assessment basis rather than having tax officials prepare returns. Taxpayers who kept satisfactory accounting records were selected and brought into the system through certain incentives.

percent for other foreign exchange earnings, such as tourism and sales of goods and services to the foreign military forces stationed in Korea.

Most of the above reforms were made in 1961. In 1967, the urgency of securing tax revenue somewhat relaxed. Hence, more or less "sophisticated" goals were set. A global income tax system with progressive rates was partially introduced, and the exemption level for wage and salary earners increased. An important change in the corporate tax system was the introduction of rates that discriminated between "open" corporations and closely held corporations, to encourage the opening of corporations and to foster the domestic capital market.

5.2.3   The Period of Heavy Industrialization (1971–79)

The first phase of economic development through export-oriented industrialization was extremely successful, and the government ambitiously planned to proceed to the second phase, in which the self-reliance of the economy was to be emphasized. The term "self-reliance" can mean many things. In this case, it meant national security and specifically included self-sufficient production of the main staple crop (rice) and a more balanced and developed industrial structure. Reaching a better balance in the industrial structure required an expansion of the heavy and chemical industries. This expansion was pursued excessively, however, and created many problems toward the end of the 1970s.

From the early 1970s onward, tax reforms reflected an increasing concern for redistribution. This change in tax policy direction seems to have reflected in part the increased capacity of the economy to pursue equity goals and in part a political calculation aimed at pacifying the public, which was growing increasingly restive under the prolonged dictatorship.

Two very important tax reforms were carried out in the mid-1970s. By then, the tax system was in tatters, perhaps due to frequent ad hoc revisions geared to many specific objectives. The dual structure of the personal income tax system, for example, was administratively inefficient and promoted neither horizontal nor vertical equity in distributing the tax burden. The system of indirect taxes was even more complicated. Korea had both excise and turnover taxes with more than fifty rates, ranging from 0.5 to 300 percent. This background led to a strong desire to streamline and simplify the overall tax structure, not only for administrative efficiency but also for greater tax burden equity and neutrality with respect to resource allocation. Specifically, an almost global personal income tax was introduced by the reform in 1974 (implemented in 1975), and a consumption-type value-added tax (VAT) and set of special excise taxes replaced the business tax (a turnover tax) and seven other indirect taxes as a result of the 1976 tax reform (effective in 1977).[2] To compensate for the possible adverse effects of the newly introduced VAT and to

2. The seven taxes included commodities, textile products, petroleum products, electricity and gas, transportation, admission, and entertainment.

soothe political tension due to its introduction, the government introduced additional income tax relief for low- to middle-income workers, certain concessions for taxes on inheritance and land sales, and more generous depreciation allowances. In short, the reforms of 1974 and 1976 determined the basic structure of the current tax system in Korea.

Another significant change in the tax system in the seventies was the introduction of the defense tax, surcharged on various taxes at rates of 0.2 to 30 percent. This tax was introduced as a temporary earmarked levy with an expiry date of 1980, but its expiration was postponed twice, until 1990. It generated a considerable amount of revenue, at the cost of adding a fair number of complications to the tax system.

The essential part of the tax policy in this period, as noted earlier, was unreserved support for heavy and chemical industries. Various types of generous tax incentives were legislated, mainly through the Tax Exemption and Reduction Control Law enacted in 1965. The so-called key industries, which included shipbuilding, machinery, basic metals, petrochemicals, automotive products, electronics, and chemical fertilizers, were extremely favorably treated in terms of corporate or proprietors' income taxation.

From the early 1970s, incentives for heavy industrialization were reinforced, while incentives for export industries were drastically reduced.[3] In 1974, all major incentives for promoting key industries were unified and rearranged under "special tax treatment for key industries" in the Tax Exemption and Reduction Control Law. This "special treatment" included three optional sets of incentives—tax holidays, investment tax credit, and special depreciation—to qualified firms in selected heavy and chemical industries.[4]

A quantitative summary of the incentives extended to key industries during the period from 1963 to 1985 is presented in table 5.1. According to these estimates, during the second half of the 1970s as much as 37 percent of investment at margin was given to investors in eligible key industries in the form of tax privileges.

5.2.4   The Structural Adjustment and Liberalization Period (1980–87)

Dramatic changes in the economic and political environment led to a drastic readjustment of development policy objectives in the early 1980s. The role of the market mechanism in resource allocation was emphasized in order to combat some of the conspicuous structural difficulties in those heavy and chemical industries that had been carefully tended by the government. Hence, liberalization in various areas, such as foreign trade, foreign and overseas investment, and financial markets, was sought. On the other hand, to overcome the macroeconomic crisis of 1980, a series of strong stabilization policy measures

---

3. The 50 percent reduced rate of corporate or proprietors' tax on income from foreign exchange–earning activity was discontinued in 1973 and a couple of tax-free reserve systems, whose incentive effects were much smaller compared with the previous system's, were introduced. See Kwack (1986) for a discussion of the incentive effects of this change.

4. See Choi et al. (1985) for a detailed discussion on the tax incentives for key industries.

Table 5.1   Benefits from Tax Incentives for Investment in Machinery by Firms in Typical Key Industries (Manufacturing) for Selected Years (%)[a]

Year[b]	Discount Rate[c]	Statutory Tax Rate[d]	20% (80%) Spec. Deprec.[e]	Incentives for Key Industries				
				T.H.	Spec. Deprec.	I.R.	I.T.C.	Total[f]
1963	52.5	20	0.8	18.5	—	—	—	18.6
1968	56.0	45	1.7	—	—	—	6.0	7.7
1970	49.8	45	1.8	—	—	—	6.0	7.8
1973	33.3	40	5.6	—	—	—	6.0 (10.0)	11.6 (15.6)
1976	40.5	40	1.7 (5.5)	36.7	6.5	—	8.0 (10.0)	36.9 (37.4)
1982	30.5	38	1.6 (5.3)	—	6.2	3.4	6.0 (10.0)	9.6 (9.6)
1983	25.8	33	1.4	—	5.2	—	3.0 (5.0)	5.2 (5.2)
1985	24.1	33	2.0	—	5.0	—	3.0 (5.0)	5.0 (5.2)

Source: Kwack (1986, 82).

Notes: Figures in parentheses represent the benefit of investment made on domestically produced machinery. Incentives for export promotion are not considered. I.R. = investment reserves; I.T.C. = investment tax credit; Spec. Deprec. = special depreciation; T.H. = tax holidays.

[a]Ratio of tax reduction amount to gross investment. All incentives are converted to investment tax credit equivalent ratio. For example, the total benefit in 1963 is equivalent to having a 18.6 percent investment tax credit. For further details of computation, see Kwack (1986).

[b]The selected years are when major tax reforms were effected.

[c]Curb market interest rate is used as a proxy for discount rate. This rate may be interpreted as an upper limit.

[d]Surtaxes to the corporate tax are not considered.

[e]Assumed asset lifetime for tax purposes is 11 years, and assumed economic depreciation rate is 11 percent.

[f]Interaction and overlapping (some pairs of incentives cannot be adopted at the same time) of incentives were taken into account when the figures in the total column were calculated.

was adopted.[5] Finally, the social aspects of development began to attract public attention, with equity and balance stressed as values to be pursued with a higher priority.

The most significant tax reform in the early 1980s took place in 1982. Though this measure did not involve a major overhaul as did reforms in the mid-1970s, it is particularly important. The reform lowered personal and corporate income tax rates, streamlined the industrial tax incentive system, and moved partway toward the "real-name system" (see sec. 5.4.2) for financial transactions. The intent of these changes was to bring the Korean tax system one step closer to an ideal system of fairness and efficiency. In a practical sense, however, the streamlining of tax incentives was the most significant result of the reform.

Under the announced principle of low taxes and low exemption, the 1982

5. In 1980, for the first time in Korea, a negative growth rate of −4.8 percent was recorded. The wholesale price index jumped by as much as 42 percent, and the current account balance recorded a deficit of U.S $5.3 billion (30.3 percent of the total amount of annual exports).

tax reform revamped the incentive system drastically. Specifically, the liberal tax privileges of key industries were almost completely removed. The effects of this measure can be observed in table 5.1. Incentives for research and development, and investment in small and medium firms were reinforced. In other words, the government adopted a "functional" or "indirect" approach, in contrast to the previous industry-specific or "direct" approach, in providing industrial incentives.

The economy quickly stabilized and showed steady growth through the mid-1980s. Other reform measures for liberalization and structural adjustment were consistently implemented. Tax policy remained largely unchanged during the mid-1980s, however, although the demand for a fundamental tax reform in response to drastically changing internal and external conditions was very strong throughout the 1980s. This increasing demand led the government to establish the Commission on Tax Reform in 1984. The first proposal of the commission was submitted in 1985 and was allegedly reflected in the tax reform of 1988. That reform, however, was not a full embodiment of the commission's proposals but a first response to the rapidly changing political and social environment and its needs. Subsequent tax reform was mainly geared to coping with social and economic needs stemming from the extreme political changes of the past two to three years. Since such reforms are still in progress, we will discuss them separately in section 5.4.

5.3   An Outline of the Current Tax System

5.3.1   The Structure and Characteristics

Currently, Korea has twenty-nine taxes, of which fifteen are national (see the appendix). In terms of revenue, the VAT is the most important national tax, generating more than 20 percent of total tax revenue. Other major taxes are defense tax, personal income tax, corporate tax, and customs duties. Specialized excise taxes (special excise, liquor, and telephone) are also important revenue generators. The revenue from local taxes is only 10 percent of total tax revenue, whereas the taxes on tobacco and on real estate acquisition and registration are significant.[6]

The tax structure in Korea can be characterized by its heavy reliance on indirect taxes. As presented in table 5.2, about 60 percent of total tax revenue is from indirect taxes. The dependence on indirect taxes has been criticized as

6. The distinction between central and local government has relatively little meaning in Korea. Although the country is administratively divided into six special cities and nine provinces, the heads at all levels of local government are directly appointed by the central government. Local autonomy was briefly in effect before the military coup d'état in 1961 but has not been reintroduced. Thus, Korea's local governments have acted merely as agents carrying out the decisions of the central government. They have neither their own kinds of tax nor the power to change tax rates in response to the needs of local residents.

Table 5.2   Direct and Indirect Tax Ratio (% of all taxes)

	Direct	Indirect
1965	42.9	57.1
1970	43.5	56.5
1975	39.5	60.5
1980	36.9	63.1
1985	39.3	60.7
1988	44.9	55.1

Sources: Office of National Tax Administration 1982; Ministry of Finance 1990.

the major source of the regressive nature of the overall tax burden in Korea. This "inequitable" feature of the tax system may be more clearly demonstrated by the relatively insignificant role of the personal income tax (table 5.3). As of 1987, less than 2 percent of GDP was collected as personal income tax, while in most Western countries the level (as of 1985) was around 10 percent. With such a low percentage, it is impossible to significantly affect the distribution of income through tax policies.

There are a few reasons for the poor performance of personal income tax in Korea. First, though the marginal tax rate is very high and progressive, the exemption level is also very high, and only about 40 percent of workers pay income tax. Second, most interest income and about half of dividend income is taxed separately, at a low flat rate (10 percent, plus surcharges and 5 percent education tax). Third, capital gains from financial asset transactions are completely untaxed and those from real asset transactions are undertaxed. Probably most important, the level of income tax compliance and administration is very low. Proprietors' income is especially notorious for escaping taxation.[7]

Revenue from taxes on wealth as a percentage of the total tax revenue of all governments at all levels is about 8.1 percent, which is quite low by international standards.

5.3.2 Taxation on Income

The individual income tax system in Korea is a mixture of global and schedular systems. Not all incomes are included in the global income calcu-

7. It is difficult to construct a statistical proof for this assertion. However, this idea is generally accepted among Koreans, based on their personal experience. Another important indirect argument for the assertion can be found in the following facts: An unincorporated firm whose annual sales are below 36 million won is eligible for the "special taxation" program of the VAT. A firm eligible for this program is not required to keep books, and its VAT liability is 2 percent of total sales. This sales information is also used in estimating the firm's income tax base, by applying the "standard income ratio." If the ratio is 10 percent, monthly taxable income of such a business owner is only 300,000 won, which is even lower than the starting salary of a typical high school–graduate worker. About 70 percent of the unincorporated firms in Korea are covered under the special tax program. As a result, about 65 percent of proprietors belong to the zero bracket even though the personal exemption level for proprietors' income is smaller than that for labor income.

Table 5.3   **Tax Revenue Structure by Type of Taxes, 1985 (% of GDP)**

	Income		Consumption			Social	
	All	Personal	All	General	Property	Security	Total
Canada	15.0	12.0	10.7	4.5	3.2	4.5	33.9
West Germany	13.1	10.8	9.7	6.0	1.1	13.8	37.8
Sweden	21.2	19.5	13.3	7.0	1.2	14.7[a]	50.5
United Kingdom	14.8	9.9	12.0	6.0	4.6	6.7[a]	38.1
United States	12.3	10.3	5.1	2.1	2.9	8.4	28.7
Japan	13.0	7.0	4.0	—	2.7	8.5	23.3
Korea (1987)	3.6	1.9	12.8	4.0	1.6	0.3	18.0

Sources: OECD 1987; Bank of Korea 1989.
[a]Includes taxes on payroll and work force.

lation. Global income comprises interest, dividends, real estate income, business income, and wages and salary and is taxed at a highly progressive rate, ranging from 5 to 50 percent, exclusive of surcharges.[8] There are eight brackets, and the bracket for the top marginal rate is over 50 million won. Currently, almost 100 percent of interest income and more than half of dividend income is taxed separately at 10 percent. (Inclusive of surcharges and 5 percent education tax, the effective rate ranges from 16.75 to 17.75 percent.)[9]

Retirement income, capital gains from sales of real assets, and timber income are taxed under independent schedules. Tax rates for real capital gain from real assets range from 40 to 60 percent according to the size of the capital gain. Capital gains from the financial asset market are simply untaxed. Income from agricultural land is taxed by local governments at progressive rates. As noted previously, liberal deductions and exemptions are stipulated in the income tax law, and, as a result, about 60 percent of workers and 65 percent of proprietors belong to the zero bracket.

Corporate incomes are taxed under the corporate tax. On up to 80 million won, the low rate of 20 percent is applied, and the excess is taxed at 30 percent.[10] For large closed corporations, the high (marginal) rate is 33 percent. Capital gains from real property sales are uniquely treated. First they are taxed as normal corporate income, and then an "additional tax" of 25 to 35 percent is charged. This makes corporate capital gains taxes consistent with the high tax rate on capital gains of individuals.

As previously mentioned, these taxes have been heavily used as policy tools

8. The effective top marginal rate inclusive of defense tax (10–20 percent) and inhabitant tax (7.5 percent) is 63.75 percent.

9. As a means to promote financial savings, income from major financial savings had been almost untaxed until the mid-1970s. The current system of separate taxation of financial income provides incentives for saving and reflects the inability to identify taxable financial income under the system in which fictitious-name financial transactions are allowed.

10. Defense tax (20–25 percent) and inhabitant tax (7.5 percent) are surcharged on the corporate tax amount.

for a variety of purposes. The exemptions and deductions of the personal income and the corporation taxes were considerably reduced by the reform of 1982, but various incentive measures such as accelerated depreciation, investment tax credit, and tax-free reserves are still liberally used in promoting research and development investment, investment in small and medium industries, and relocation of industries away from large metropolitan areas.

The Korean tax system has not yet incorporated serious measures such as the imputation method to handle the problem of double taxation at corporate and personal dividend income levels. A tax credit for dividend income has been adopted for this purpose. More than 50 percent of dividend income, however, is taxed separately at a low rate, and therefore the double taxation problem has not been too serious.

5.3.3 Consumption Taxes

The current structure of the consumption tax system was completed in 1977 when the VAT was introduced. The VAT is the largest consumption tax in Korea. Other consumption taxes are the special excise, liquor, telephone, stamp, and tobacco sales. In terms of revenue, the tobacco sales tax, which is the only local tax among consumption taxes, the special excise tax, and the liquor tax are particularly important.

The Korean VAT is a typical European Community type with a flat rate of 10 percent and zero rating. To the small firms that have difficulty in bookkeeping, the "special taxation" system is applied. Under this system, eligible firms are taxed on a turnover basis; they pay 2 percent of their gross sales amount rather than 10 percent of their value-added amount. Because more than 70 percent of VAT payers are under the special taxation system, the merits of the VAT are not fully exploited.

The special excise tax was first introduced to mitigate the presumed regressivity of the single-rated VAT. Currently thirty-six items (single commodity, groups of similar commodity, or services) are taxed at rates ranging from 10 to 100 percent.[11] Incidence of this tax is estimated to be significantly less regressive, compared with the VAT.[12] Liquor taxes are ad valorem in Korea, ranging from 10 to 300 percent. Tobacco production and sales were monopolized by the government until very recently, when the business unit was changed to a public corporation. Previously, the profit from the government monopoly was included as an indirect tax revenue of the central government, but currently, similar revenue is generated by local government taxation of tobacco consumption.

5.3.4 Taxation on Property Ownership and Transfers

At the national level, the inheritance and gift tax has been the most important tax on property transfers, though the revenue from it has been negligible.

11. Only gasoline and Turkish baths are taxed at 100 percent. Most items are taxed at 10 to 25 percent, and a few items are taxed at 30, 40, or 60 percent.
12. See Lee and Bae (1987) for a comprehensive incidence study of indirect taxes in Korea.

Taxes on capital gains from real property transactions can also be categorized as taxes on property transfers. Capital gains taxes were created to control real estate speculation in the mid-1960s but now are incorporated in the income tax law and corporate tax law as discussed above.[13] Recently, a tax on excess profit from land was introduced. This tax is a selective capital gains tax levied on an accrual basis. We will discuss this tax and related recent legislation in section 5.4.

The inheritance tax in Korea is not a true inheritance tax but an estate tax.[14] Gifts or inter vivos transfers are taxed separately unless such transfers take place within a three-year period before the death of the donor. In such a case, the gift amount is added to the estate tax base. The gift tax base is calculated by accumulating the inter vivos transfers from a donor for three consecutive years. Both taxes have highly progressive rate schemes, ranging from 5 to 55 percent for the inheritance tax and 5 to 60 percent for the gift tax. In addition, a 20 percent defense tax is surcharged on both taxes. Exemption levels are not very high.

These taxes, in spite of such high rates and strictness in other aspects, have generated insignificant revenue. This fact is the most obvious evidence that they have not contributed significantly to redistributing wealth. The most notable reason for such poor performance has been, among other things, the unrealistically low assessment of assets.

Local governments tax property holdings, acquisition, and registration. Currently, the property tax is applied to buildings and construction, mining lots, aircraft, and vessels; the landholdings are taxed under the global landholding tax, which came into effect in 1990. We will discuss this tax in some detail in section 5.4. The acquisition tax and the registration tax have been important revenue sources for local governments.

5.4 Current Tax Reform Issues

5.4.1 Recent Sociopolitical Changes and Emphasis on Equity and Balance

The late 1980s may be considered one of the most important turning points in Korea's modernization. In spite of economic success in the 1980s, the Ko-

---

13. It is not clear why tax measures have been preferred in coping with land speculation in Korea. We guess the following reasons are important. First, Korean financial markets were not working efficiently. Second, land speculation in Korea has been looked at as a social sin, and the policymakers seem to have thought that those who speculate on land deserve a heavy tax as a penalty. Third, as a short term emergency measure to scare away speculators from the overheated real estate market, tax measures sound more powerful than financial measures. Fourth, a financial squeeze not only affects the real estate market but also hampers industrial investment. Policymakers wanted to redirect loanable funds from unproductive real estate speculation to productive industrial investment. In other words, some selective measures were preferred.

14. The legal description of this tax is not perfectly clear, and, indeed, a few scholars claim that the Inheritance and Gift Tax Law is an inheritance tax. But the majority of scholars in this field agree that it is an estate tax as described in the law, which is the official interpretation. For a detailed discussion on this matter, see Choi (1990).

rean citizens' resentment against Chun's dictatorial regime grew rapidly, and in early 1987 it burst out in violent protests. The "June 29 Declaration" of the ruling party, which promised a drastic "democratization" including a direct election of the next president, calmed the protest. The abrupt removal of various controls, however, resulted in social disruption and difficulties of different kinds. Extremely extensive and violent labor unrest hit the economy from the second half of 1987 on. Not only workers but farmers, street vendors, the urban poor, and other groups marched the streets to make their voices heard.

Fortunately, the economy of the country was extremely healthy, with double-digit growth rates, large and unprecedented trade surpluses, and perfect price stability. The Korean public, who had believed that they were personally indebted when the national debt was an economic issue in earlier years, naturally believed that they deserved shares in the large trade surpluses.[15] Specifically, the relatively underprivileged classes began to cry out for equity and balance. They asked the government to secure the awarding of their due shares, which had been suspended until "the pie grew large enough." The presidential election and the general election for representatives of the National Assembly were carried out with severe and confusing competition among four major parties. All the parties and candidates offered fantastic promises, inflating the expectations of the public. Under the new constitution, President Roh Tae Woo was elected and inaugurated in 1988, but the ruling party failed to secure the majority in the National Assembly.

5.4.2   Tax Reform Experiments under a "Democratized" Environment

These social and political changes exercised enormous influence both on policy-making processes and policy objectives themselves. First, popular voices and various interest groups gained much power, whereas the influence of the technocrats and specialists weakened. Public hearings and opinion surveys about policy-making became much more frequent. Second, equity in income and wealth distribution and balance in development among regions and sectors became the prime policy objectives. Recent tax reforms reflect these changes vividly.

Income Taxation and Equity

Income taxation in Korea, in spite of its highly progressive rate structure, has not contributed significantly to distributive equity. Reducing the tax burden of low-income workers, however, seems to make a powerful and attractive political catchphrase at any time. Such tax reform was promised by all competing parties in the elections and was implemented in the 1988 tax reform. Though officially it was the first major reform carried out in response to the proposals that the tax reform committee made in 1985, in effect most of

---

15. Various policy forums had active debates during 1987–88 on how to use the "trade surpluses" to improve social welfare.

the changes were administrative or technical, and few were major. One of the important features of the reform was an increase in the personal exemption level of the income tax. Other major changes were reduction in the number of brackets and the marginal tax rates of the income tax and the inheritance tax, downward adjustment in many excise tax rates, a large-scale upward adjustment of the limit below which the special taxation system of the VAT is applicable, and reduction of some incentives for exports and inducement of foreign capital.

Income tax reform in 1988, ostensibly to help the poor working class, actually undermined the already narrow base of the income tax system and might negatively affect distributive equity in the long run. The majority of the workers were not paying any income tax, and the reform increased the size of this group. By reducing the tax rate without any other compensating measures, the income tax burden of the upper-bracket families was visibly reduced. The tax revenue in general was expected to be reduced, limiting the expansion of welfare-related programs for low-income families.

Ironically, the income tax revenue in 1989 substantially exceeded the budget and the figure predicted by the government.[16] In the event, most newspapers in Seoul printed editorials and columns saying that the "excessive" collected revenue should be refunded. Very hot debates on this matter followed, subsiding after a while without any clear-cut conclusions. Since the "real-name system" is officially suspended, a further reduction of the income tax is being considered by the policy authorities.[17] The income tax base in Korea is thus continually pared down by political motives.

"Public Concept" of Landownership and Land Use

The centerpiece of the recent tax reform issues in Korea is how to control land speculation through tax measures. Land speculation has been a serious economic and social problem in Korea almost from the beginning of industrialization. In the mid-1960s, the land-speculation-control tax was introduced, but land speculation caused various problems throughout the 1970s. After a series of strong stabilization measures in the early 1980s, asset market inflation seemed to be held under control. In recent years, however, speculation in real assets has resumed all over the country. One important reason for this drastic increase is an excessive increase in liquidity supply, due to balance of payment surpluses. Another factor is the elections; they not only contributed to the increase in the liquidity supply but also actively stimulated land

16. There are a few reasons for this excess. The business conditions were extremely good. Nominal wage level increased dramatically as a result of good business conditions and extensive labor unrest. And the budget officers seem to have been too conservative in estimating the revenue implications of the reform.

17. We will say more about the "real-name system" later. Introduction of this system has been associated with a heavier taxation of income from financial assets of high-income-class households. Therefore, to balance the suspension of the introduction of the system, many argued, labor income tax should be further reduced.

speculation when politicians announced blueprints for numerous development projects to be carried out when elected. In addition, industrial investment became extremely unattractive mainly because of the skyrocketing cost of labor, including the psychic cost of violence by workers. As a result, capital owners began to seek a safe and easy way of making money or at least of safely hoarding their wealth. The public, losing confidence in the stability of the value of money, began to escape from financial assets. The real demand for housing was also increasing because of the rapidly rising income level of middle-class workers. The real estate market simply exploded.

Even before this explosion, the government was seriously concerned about the concentration of the distribution of real assets and the severe shortage of urban land for housing and business. Since inflation in the real estate market has been far exceeding that in the commodity markets, the skewed distribution of land and buildings is the single most important source of the ever-widening gap between the haves and the have-nots. The rapidly rising cost of housing, when the supply of urban housing is far short of the desired level, could cause serious social instability. Under these conditions, the government planned to introduce a strong system to fight real estate speculation. In September 1988, an ad hoc committee to study the "public concept" of the ownership of land was established to draft a proposal on various measures to deal with pending land problems. At the same time, the government announced that it would introduce a global landholding tax. The global landholding tax and three other measures proposed by the "public concept" committee were enacted in 1990.

As part of the effort to control land speculation, the government announced a schedule to raise the landholding tax assessment to 60 percent of the actual market price by 1992. One of the major reasons for poor performance of property-related taxes was unrealistically low and extremely uneven assessment of real assets for tax purposes. A survey by the Ministry of Home Affairs reported that the average assessment for property tax was 23 percent of the actual value in Seoul and 46.2 percent in Kyungbuk province as of 1988. The assessment ratio varied among different regions and among different uses or types of land (Lee 1988, 37–39). In addition, several "official" prices of land were assessed by different organizations for different public policy purposes.

As a practical measure to provide a unified and realistic assessment of land to be used for various policy purposes, a new system for assessing land and announcing the results to the public was introduced in 1989. It is expected that the administration of the property-related taxes will be improved and strengthened substantially as a result.

The introduction of the new assessment system and the plan for the upward adjustment of the assessment ratio may be considered complementary measures of the new system on landholding enacted in 1990. A global land tax, under which the property tax operates as a personal tax with a progressive rate system, was introduced.

As early as 1973, a tax measure to deal with speculative holding of real property was introduced. Penalty rates on luxurious real properties and on unused urban land were introduced in the property tax system. A progressive property tax rate scheme ranging from 0.3 to 5 percent (raised to 7 percent later) on houses was introduced in 1974. This system became a partially global personal property tax system in 1988. As an excessive-landholding tax, the system applied progressive tax rates of 1 to 5 percent on the value of a person's local holding of unused urban land. This measure was felt inadequate to control the ever-increasing demand for landholding and to satisfy public demand for equity and social reform. Opinions claiming that public control over landholding and use must be reinforced seemed to gain public support.[18] As a result, a full-fledged global landholding tax and other rather extreme measures to control speculative landholding were introduced.

Under the global landholding tax (the aggregate land tax) system, all land owned by individuals and corporations is classified in three ways: (1) properties to be taxed under the main global scheme, (2) properties to be taxed under the secondary global scheme, and (3) properties to be taxed separately at flat rates.

The first group includes most of the properties previously taxed under the excessive-landholding tax at progressive rates ranging from 0.2 percent for the base which is less than 5 million won, to 5 percent for more than 5 billion won. The second group is mainly composed of commercially used land. In this case, the highest marginal tax rate is 2 percent, and the tax bases are much wider, the maximum base being above 30 billion won. The third group includes properties, owned by a single individual or a corporation, to be taxed at low flat rates (0.1 to 0.3 percent) or at a very high rate (5 percent) depending on the type of use, regardless of the size.

This tax, though a personal tax, is administered as a local tax. The tax liability of each taxpayer is calculated by the Ministry of Home Affairs, but collection is the responsibility of local governments, each of which collects a proportional share from a single individual in case a taxpayer owns land in multiple jurisdictions. This unique feature of the tax may cause significant administrative difficulties in the future. In addition, this tax depends critically on the judgment of the tax administrator in classifying specific properties.

Another important tax measure enacted in 1990 to deal with land speculation is the excessive-land-profit tax. This tax is levied on "excessive" capital gains accrued to landholdings.[19] Under this system, accrued net capital gains (net of capital expenditure on the land) in excess of normal gains, that is, in excess of the national average rate of land price increase, is taxed at a 50

18. Possible reasons for the bias toward tax measures in coping with land speculation are mentioned in footnote 13. Even the "public concept" committee did not propose any financial measure to fight real asset inflation.

19. A similar tax system had been introduced in Korea in the 1967 tax reform but was immediately repealed, mainly because of administrative difficulties.

percent rate every three years. Different percentages (40–80 percent) of the tax may be credited to the existing capital gains tax, depending on the length of time between the levy of the excessive-land-profit tax and the sale of the land. This system critically depends on the accuracy and fairness of the as-sessment of all land as well as on the judgment of the tax authority about the utilization of each piece of land.

Although not exactly a tax issue, the most debated "public concept" issue during the past couple of years was whether a ceiling should be established on the holding of residential land. Those who opposed the introduction of the ceiling emphasized the constitutional right of property ownership and disposal as well as the market system of resource allocation, while those for the ceiling emphasized the public sentiment on land issues, the shortage of housing, and the extreme concentration of landholding. According to the latter group, by sacrificing a handful of large landholders, social justice could be greatly en-hanced, benefiting the majority. A few polls confirmed the public sentiment in favor of the ceiling. The National Assembly eventually passed a bill to establish a ceiling on the holding of residential land in city areas, which was partially enacted in 1990.[20]

The third system proposed by the "public concept" committee and adopted by the National Assembly was the system to retake development profits. Ac-cording to this system, a land developer pays 50 percent of the evaluated profit from the project to the government.

"Real-Name System" of Financial Transactions

Another pillar of the reform debates during recent years has been the so-called real-name system of financial transactions. In fact, it is an "old" issue. In 1961, the capital-hungry military government introduced a system in which financial transactions under fictitious names were allowed, to encourage fi-nancial saving. The anonymity system had long been criticized for generating inequities in the tax burden and providing a safe harbor for curb market activ-ities, the most typical underground economic activity in Korea. It had not been an urgent issue, however, until a national financial scandal was disclosed in 1982. A number of leading corporations were involved in a combination of fraud and curb market financial transactions. The shock of the incident gave strength to the cry for introduction of a forced real-name system. In the same year, the law disallowing fictitious-name financial transactions was passed by the National Assembly, with a proviso that the implementation of the system would be suspended until the economy had gained sufficient strength and the administration was prepared. The authority to implement the system was given to the president.

---

20. Under this system, a household unit cannot hold residential land in excess of 660 square meters in six major city areas. Those who want to hold in excess of the limit must pay annually 7 to 11 percent of the value of the excess land.

Over the past several years, however, the government has failed to launch the system. In the presidential election in 1987, all candidates promised to activate the system when elected. In due course, the government announced the schedule to implement the system and established a working group in the Ministry of Finance. From the second half of 1989 on, in spite of the scheduled introduction of the "public concept" systems, real asset prices skyrocketed and the stock market slid steeply down. In particular, price increases in the housing market were formidable. In addition, the real economy was performing very poorly in 1989 and did not improve in 1990. Facing such conditions, the government cancelled the scheduled activation of the system early in 1990 and instead is concentrating on the fight against real asset inflation.

5.5   Pending Issues and Prospects

A number of important issues are oppressing the Korean economy. The industrial sector is in the midst of a drastic structural adjustment. The leading export sectors are rapidly losing their competitiveness in international markets, due mainly to dramatically increasing labor cost. The agricultural sector, which includes about one-fifth of the population, cannot be easily restructured. At the same time, the public's inflated expectations must be taken care of somehow. Macroeconomic stability is very seriously threatened.

All these problems are important and urgent, but politically the public demand for justice and equity or a "social reform" seems to be the top policy concern. The government and the ruling party try to show their willingness to "reform" by proposing tax reforms. There is little likelihood of achieving this goal through reform of income taxation unless the real-name system is implemented in the near future. Even if the system is enacted successfully, however, it is clear that it will not immediately bring equitable income taxation.

Equity and balance may be pursued by increasing transfer expenditures and other social programs. This approach, however, requires increased government revenue. Over the past several years, government plans to raise the tax/ GNP ratio moderately have not been successful. It is not likely that the government will reform the tax system to raise revenue substantially in the near future, mainly because it is not politically rewarding. To the contrary, outspoken political pressure is forcing the government to further cut taxes on labor income. In addition, industries are demanding tax cuts to facilitate smooth structural adjustment.

The demand for reform can be satisfied in large part by stabilizing the real estate market and eliminating speculation. Currently, the government is both persuading and threatening large corporations to dispose of their excessive real properties. This is only a stopgap, and permanent and truly effective policies should be introduced. As noted above, radical tax measures have already been introduced in recent years. The real problem is that land and housing prices increased even more rapidly after strong antispeculation measures were announced. It is quite clear that the public either do not believe in the consistency of the government in pursuing certain policy goals or do not understand the effects of the new systems.

The most challenging and important issues in the area of tax policy in the coming years, we believe, will be to operate the property-related tax systems effectively and smoothly and to reinforce them, rather than introducing new systems.

Appendix

Table 5A.1   **The Tax Structure in Korea (%)**

	1980	1985	1990 (budget)
NATIONAL TAXES	88.3	87.7	82.2
Domestic	855.6	54.8	60.9
Personal income	10.2	11.1	11.3
Corporate	7.5	8.5	11.7
Inheritance and gift	0.1	0.3	0.5
Assets revaluation	0.3	0.1	0.2
Excess profit	0.0	0.0	0.0
Value-added	22.7	21.8	26.2
Special excise	8.9	7.4	4.7
Liquor	4.6	3.8	3.1
Telephone	0.8	1.3	0.8
Stamp	0.5	0.6	0.6
Securities transaction	0.0	0.1	1.8
Customs duties	11.8	11.8	7.1
Surcharges	13.1	14.9	14.2
Defense tax	13.1	12.5	12.5
Education tax	—	2.4	1.7
Monopoly profits	7.8	6.2	—
LOCAL TAXES	11.7	12.3	17.8
Ordinary taxes	10.2	10.6	16.3
Acquisition	2.4	2.6	2.6
Registration	1.9	2.7	3.3
License	0.3	0.2	0.2
Inhabitant	1.8	1.5	1.8
Property	1.8	1.8	0.7
Automobile	0.9	0.9	1.3
Global land	—	—	1.2
Farmland income	1.0	0.1	0.0
Butchery	0.1	0.1	0.1
Horse race	0.0	0.1	0.1
Tobacco	—	0.6	5.0
Earmarked taxes	1.5	1.7	1.5
City planning	0.8	0.9	0.7
Fire service facilities	0.2	0.3	0.3
Workshop	0.5	0.5	0.5
TOTAL	100.0	100.0	100.0

Sources: Economic Planning Board 1989, 1990.

References

Bank of Korea. 1989. *Economic Statistics Yearbook.*

Choi, K., T. Ito, T. Kwack, E. Tajika, and Y. Yui. 1985. *Public Policy, Corporate Finance, and Investment.* Tokyo: Institute of Developing Economies.

Choi, M. 1990. A Study on the Taxation of Intergenerational Wealth Transfers in Korea. Ph.D. thesis, Kyung-Hee University, Seoul.

Economic Planning Board. 1989. *Korean Statistical Yearbook.* Seoul: Economic Planning Board.

————. 1990. *Summary of Budget for Fiscal Year.* Seoul: Economic Planning Board.

Kwack, T. 1986. Business Taxation and Industrial Policy in Korea. *Korea Development Review* (Spring): 77–97.

Lee, J. H. 1988. *Management of Local Tax Base under the Public Assessment System of Land Prices.* Seoul: Korea Local Administration Research Institute.

Lee, K. S., and J. H. Bae. 1987. Incidence of Indirect Taxes in Korea. *Korean Journal of Public Finance* (March): 111–46.

Ministry of Finance. 1987. *Korean Taxation 1990.* Seoul: Ministry of Finance.

————. 1990. *Fiscal and Financial Statistics.* Seoul: Ministry of Finance.

OECD. 1987. *Revenue Statistics of OECD Member Countries 1965–1985.* Paris: OECD.

The Office of National Tax Administration. 1982. *Statistical Yearbook of National Tax.* Seoul: ONTA.

6   An Appraisal of Business Tax Reform in Taiwan: The Case of Value-Added Taxation

Chuan Lin

6.1 Introduction

After more than seventeen years of debate, contemplation, and preparation, the government in Taiwan finally incorporated value-added taxation into the tax system on April 1, 1986, in a move toward the establishment of a complete value-added tax (VAT) system in Taiwan.

The earliest reference to the adoption of the VAT can be traced back to a suggestion made by the Tax Reform Commission of the Executive Yuan in 1969. The proposed VAT, to a large extent, was to be substituted for the existing system of indirect taxes. It was to be a sales tax (the business tax) supplemented by a tax to finance education, the stamp tax, and the commodity tax.

The main reason the VAT was not implemented in Taiwan was fear of the inflation that many countries have experienced after adopting a VAT. The Taiwan government, however, recognized that it needed to reform the indirect tax system because it was economically distortionary and socially inequitable. In 1985, the Economic Reform Commission was established for a six-month period under the Executive Yuan and functioned as a temporary policy-consulting body. The implementation of the VAT was recommended by the council and finally realized in 1986.

The indirect taxation of business enterprises, prior to the tax reform of April 1986, consisted of a turnover tax on sales (the "old" business tax) by all business entities (corporations, partnerships, and sole proprietorships), and a stamp tax on certain activities that required the drawing up of contracts, deeds, documents, and/or monetary receipts. The stamp tax required that a

Chuan Lin is professor of economics at National Chengchi University, Taipei, Taiwan.

The author would like to thank Ching-huei Chang, Kwang Choi, Takatoshi Ito, and the other participants of the conference for their helpful comments on an earlier version of this paper.

stamp be bought and affixed to the taxable articles. Both the business tax and the stamp tax were provincial (municipal) taxes. Revenues collected in Taipei and Kao-hsiung, however, were shared equally with the central government in accordance with the Central and Local Public Revenues and Expenditures Determination Law. Revenues from the business tax constituted 11.4% of total tax revenues in fiscal year 1986, and the stamp tax accounted for 3.8% of total tax revenues during the same period. In the tax reform of 1986, the VAT was incorporated into the business tax. The reformed business tax's contribution to total tax revenues increased to 13.5% in 1987, while the stamp tax's contribution decreased to 0.6%.

The commodity tax is a national excise tax assessed on an ad valorem basis. Taxable commodities include tobacco, liquor, sugar, beverages, cosmetics, oil and gas, electric appliances, vehicles, etc. Many commodities were exempt or had their rates reduced after the adoption of the VAT; therefore, revenues from the commodity tax dropped from 12.3% of total tax revenues in fiscal year 1986 to 11.2% in 1987.

The goals of the tax reform of 1986 were, first, to reduce the importance of the stamp tax and the commodity tax within the indirect tax system by reducing either tax rates or tax base. Second, the new tax system subdivides the business tax (sales tax) into two categories: the ordinary business category having a 5% VAT rate, and the special business category, mainly consisting of small entrepreneurial businesses, specialty restaurants and nightclubs, and financial institutions, to whom turnover tax rates of 1%, 15–25%, and 5% are applied, respectively.[1] The administration emphasized that the reform was primarily aimed at alleviating the objectionable features of turnover taxation, and not at generating more tax revenues.[2]

According to the administration, the 1986 tax reform is only the initial stage of the VAT implementation process in Taiwan. The ultimate goal of the reform is to integrate the stamp tax and a majority of the items covered under the commodity tax into the sales tax system, i.e., into the VAT system. The threats of revenue imbalance and of inflation were the main reason the government did not implement wide-ranging tax reform all at once. They hoped that the experience gained from the 1986 tax reform would be helpful in reaching the goal of establishing a complete VAT system. Therefore, it is worthwhile to review the impact of the 1986 tax reform from both theoretical and policy points of view.

1. As in most countries, the small entrepreneurial business is excluded from the VAT system becuase of concern over compliance costs. Furthermore, specialty restaurants and nightclubs are subject to a high turnover tax instead of a VAT, mainly for the purpose of discouraging these types of businesses. The VAT is not applied to financial institutions, since their original turnover tax rate is 5 percent. Taxing financial institutions using a 5 percent VAT rate would result in a loss of revenue.

2. For example, see Public Finance Training Institute (1988, 3).

6.2   Administration

Entities subject to the business tax are divided into two categories: i.e., ordinary businesses are subject to a uniform 5% VAT rate, and special businesses are subject to various turnover tax rates. In 1988, there were 865,000 businesses in Taiwan; more than half of these (456,000) were classified as special businesses (99.3% being small entrepreneurial businesses[3]) and were excluded from the VAT. Business entities with average monthly sales of less than N.T. $200,000 (about U.S. $7,700) are considered small entrepreneurial businesses and pay a lump-sum tax to the tax authorities. Since bookkeeping is not required of small entrepreneurial businesses, the tax administration has had difficulty identifying their actual income. In fact, the monthly sales of many of these small entrepreneurial businesses greatly exceed N.T. $200,000, although their average reported monthly taxable sales are only around N.T. $60,000, according to government statistics. The total monthly taxable sales of small entrepreneurial businesses constitute only 15.2% of total sales in Taiwan.[4] Thus, the small entrepreneurial business category is considered a tax shelter by many taxpayers. It also gives businesses further incentive to stay small—to reduce their tax burden. Since the adoption of the VAT, small businesses have been entitled to declare 10% of their total tax as a tax credit. However, small entrepreneurial businesses with actual monthly sales exceeding N.T. $200,000 would rather underreport their income than receive the credit. In order to take full advantage of the tax credit, the businesses would have to reveal their actual income and lose their status as small entrepreneurial businesses. Therefore, the 10% tax credit is seldom used by them. This dilemma hinders the so-called built-in self-enforcement function of the VAT by making impossible the matching of tax credits of small businesses with the payable tax of other businesses under the VAT system.

A problem in tax administration surfaced as a result of the uniform invoice system established in the 1960s. Because of the popularity of "artificial" bookkeeping, the tax authorities have required all businesses, except for small entrepreneurial businesses, to use uniform invoices that are issued by the tax administration. After a sale, the duplicate copy of the uniform invoice must be returned by the taxpayer to the administration so that the transaction can be recorded. There is, however, a well-established black market for uniform invoices. Businesses can falsify expenses on their tax form by buying blank invoices and filling in any purchase amount, thereby reducing their income tax liability. Meanwhile, the owners of the businesses selling the blank in-

3. See "Annual Report of Data Processing Center of the Ministry of Finance, 1988" (in Chinese), Table 26-1.
4. Data are estimated from *Monthly Report of Business Tax Resources in Taiwan Area,* March 1990, unpublished.

voices close up shop and run away without ever having paid any income tax. Under the VAT, other incentives lead businesses to use forged invoices to reduce their tax liability by overreporting their deductible expenses; i.e., the practice of using forged invoices reduces not only their business income tax liability but also their business tax liability. In an attempt to close this loophole, the administration has established a computerized cross-checking system, which requires businesses to report their monthly sales as the sum of the amounts indicated on their copies of the uniform invoices. The reported sales data together with the tax identification numbers of both the seller and the buyer are then matched by the computer, against the data from the original copy of the uniform invoice submitted by the buyer for tax deduction purposes.

To simplify the administrative work, there are now two types of uniform invoices. One is used in the sale of intermediate goods or services. A duplicate of the invoice is sent to the Tax Administration, and its data are entered into the computer data system. The original invoice is held by the buyer, and the other duplicate is held by the seller for its records. When the buyer applies for a credit, the sales data from the original invoice (held by the buyer) and the duplicate (submitted to the Tax Administration) corresponding to each sale of intermediate goods and services are cross-checked to verify the accuracy of the data. The other type of invoice, having only one duplicate, is used in the final sale of goods and services and is not entered into the computer data system, since the final buyer (the consumer) cannot claim this purchase as a tax credit.

The computerization of uniform invoices, however, is costly. First, the local tax administration must key in the information on each invoice. This results in very high labor costs. For example, Taipei hired 210 full-time employees to key in the invoice information in 1986—a direct result of the adoption of the VAT in that year. The average monthly number of invoices that were processed at that time was around 4.6 million. Recently, the number of computer key-in employees has increased to 336, and the average monthly number of processed invoices is more than 8 million.[5] The second cost involves the matching of data and the cross-checking of the invoices, done by the Data Processing Center at the Ministry of Finance. Table 6.1 shows the amount that was budgeted for the Data Processing Center from fiscal year 1984 to fiscal year 1989. The data processing cost associated with the business tax has increased from N.T. $1 million in fiscal year 1986 (July 1985 to June 1986) to N.T. $102 million in fiscal year 1987. In 1989, the business tax became the most expensive tax to administer, mainly because of its high data processing cost.[6] Computerization, meanwhile, significantly helped to reduce the size of the black market for uniform invoices—between July 1986 and

5. Data are provided by the Bureau of Tax Administration, Taipei City Government.
6. It is interesting to note that, while the administrative cost of the business tax increased in 1987, the administrative cost of the business income tax fell moderately and the administrative

Table 6.1   **The Cost Incurred in Tax Administration for Data Processing (N.T. $1,000)**

Fiscal Year	Total Cost	Business Tax	Business Income Tax	Individual Income Tax	Commodity Tax	Other Taxes
1984	254,050	9,840	3,778	182,120	913	57,399
(July 1983–June 1984)						
1985	247,723	4,434	3,566	220,250	323	19,150
(July 1984–June 1985)						
1986	373,025	1,025	36,534	305,640	350	29,476
(July 1985–June 1986)						
1987	410,959	102,450	35,438	250,330	2,540	20,201
(July 1986–June 1987)						
1988	417,662	104,121	36,016	254,413	2,581	20,531
(July 1987–June 1988)						
1989	369,785	142,768	69,724	109,151	5,395	42,747
(July 1988–June 1989)						

Source: Department of Statistics (1989, table 132).

June 1987, 224 firms were found guilty of selling blank invoices; between March 1988 and February 1989, the number dropped to just 16.[7]

6.3   Revenue Impacts

6.3.1   Revenue Redistribution among Regions

The business tax is a provincial (and municipal) tax. Given the lack of local autonomy in Taiwan, however, the Business Tax Law, like all other laws, was legislated at the central government level. Business tax reforms, therefore, have to be initiated at the central government level. Local governments in Taiwan have no choice but to accept changes in the tax system. Handling the VAT at the central government level is suitable, since tax payments from one jurisdiction can be taken as tax credits in other jurisdictions. The adoption of the VAT, therefore, changes the tax base of local governments from gross sales to value added and redistributes business tax revenues. Table 6.2 summarizes the impacts of changes in revenue. I found that business tax revenues collected in Taipei dropped from 48% of total business tax revenues in fiscal

---

cost of the individual income tax declined substantially. This result could be explained either by a crowding-out effect under the budget constraint of the Data Processing Center or by the fact that an increase in the administrative cost of the business tax indirectly reduced the administration cost of income taxes. To prove the existence of such effects, further empirical studies would be needed. These studies, however, are not needed to draw the above-mentioned conclusion, since changes in the administrative cost of the business tax after fiscal year 1986 are much higher; therefore, the 1986 tax reform must have played a large role.

    7. Statistics are provided by the Data Processing Center, Ministry of Finance, ROC.

Table 6.2   Business Taxation Revenue Changes of the Different Jurisdictions in Taiwan
                   (millions of N.T. dollars)

	Taipei			Kao-hsiung			Taiwan Province		
Fiscal Year[a]	Business Tax Revenue	Gross Sales	Business Income Tax Revenue	Business Tax Revenue	Gross Sales	Business Income Tax Revenue	Business Tax Revenue	Gross Sales	Business Income Tax Revenue
1983	12,306	2,234,812	16,564	2,235	327,398	2,448	10,747	2,069,699	9,982
	(48.7)	(48.2)	(57.1)	(8.8)	(7.1)	(8.5)	(42.5)	(44.7)	(34.4)
1984	13,713	2,066,485	19,157	2,515	474,310	2,951	12,568	2,421,754	11,742
	(47.6)	(41.6)	(56.6)	(8.7)	(9.6)	(8.7)	(43.7)	(48.8)	(34.7)
1985	14,687	2,199,284	19,212	2,533	481,497	3,137	13,434	2,638,336	14,338
	(47.9)	(41.3)	(52.4)	(8.3)	(9.1)	(8.5)	(43.8)	(49.6)	(39.1)
1986	18,733	2,329,675	20,070	3,342	434,321	3,159	16,935	2,900,533	14,029
	(48.0)	(41.1)	(53.9)	(8.6)	(7.7)	(8.5)	(43.4)	(51.2)	(37.6)
1987	27,042	2,763,777	23,456	7,448	515,601	3,554	27,730	3,546,755	17,809
	(43.5)	(40.5)	(52.3)	(12.0)	(7.6)	(7.9)	(44.5)	(52.0)	(39.8)
1988	33,328	3,250,777	34,571	8,105	664,324	4,713	32,288	4,124,464	21,779
	(45.2)	(40.4)	(56.6)	(11.0)	(8.3)	(7.7)	(43.8)	(51.3)	(35.7)

Source: Department of Statistics (1984–89, tables 59, 64, and 113)

Note: Numbers in parentheses indicate the percentage share of the total corresponding values.

[a]Fiscal year starts on July 1 and ends on June 30 of the next year.

year 1986 to 43.5% and 45.2% in fiscal years 1987 and 1988, the two years immediately following the introduction of the VAT; these figures are much lower than the average percentage that prevailed before 1986. During the same period, both reported gross sales and business income tax revenues in Taipei stayed practically at the same percentage, as shown in the table, even with the introduction of tax reform. These figures imply that the decline of business tax revenue in Taipei should not be attributed to declines in either sales or profits.

One possible explanation for the relative decline of business tax revenue in Taipei is that commodities sold there are usually produced outside of the city. Therefore, the change in the tax base from gross sales (under the turnover tax) to value added increases the amount of tax credits that can be taken and results in a reduction of the tax base in Taipei, more so than in other areas in Taiwan. Furthermore, it is interesting to note, as can be seen from table 6.2, that such a redistribution of revenue makes Kao-hsiung, instead of Taiwan province, the leading beneficiary of tax revenues from business tax reform. After fiscal year 1986, the shares of business tax revenues of Kao-hsiung increased from 8.6% to 12.0% and 11.0% in fiscal years 1987 and 1988.

6.3.2 Total Revenue Changes

Three factors affect the level of business tax revenues: the tax rate, the tax base, and tax compliance. The Business Tax Law lists thirty-one exempt categories of the sale of goods or services; however, the purchase of these goods cannot be used as a tax credit in the VAT system. Exempt items mainly include land; the inputs and outputs of agricultural production; medical services; textbooks approved by government authorities; newspapers; goods and services made in or provided by prisons; public-monopoly goods; postage stamps; fish caught and sold by fishers; government-promoted insurance, bonds, and securities; military supplies; interest on the flow of funds among the head and branch offices of banks; gold; and research services provided by nonprofit organizations (art. 8). In addition, there is a zero-rate category. The purchase of goods in this category, however, may be used as a tax credit. The zero-rate category mainly includes exports, export transactions, and international transportation services (art. 7).[8]

The tax authorities had expected that, with a 5% VAT rate, tax exemptions, and the zero-rate treatment mentioned above, the revised business tax system would generate the same level of tax revenue as before. It turns out, however, that they were a bit optimistic. Lin and Lin (1989) estimated the amount of revenue that would have been collected from the business tax, the stamp tax, and the commodity tax for the years 1986 and 1987, had the 1986 tax reform not been adopted. Their findings indicate that, although the business tax revenues increased significantly after the tax reform, when economic growth and the revenue losses of the commodity tax, the stamp tax, and the education surcharge are taken into consideration, the new business tax did not collect as much revenue as the old one would have. The loss has been estimated at approximately N.T. $11,444 million in fiscal year 1986 and N.T. $13,801 million in fiscal year 1987—about 20% of the total business tax revenue collected during those two years.

The overestimation of the new business tax revenue by the tax authorities probably was a result of two factors. One was pointed to by Lin and Lin (1989): the 5% VAT rate, which was supposed to generate a level of tax revenue equal to that before the tax reform, was too low. They furthermore suggested that, in order to maintain the same revenue-generating capacity, the VAT rate should have been fixed at around 6.1% or 6.2% (42).

Their suggestion, however, overlooks the other factor that plays a very important role in revenue changes under tax reform, i.e., the change in tax compliance.[9] Before April 1986 the business tax liability incurred at the time of sale, under the turnover rate system, was included in the list price of the commodities (tax-included pricing). After the adoption of the VAT, however, the government required that the list price be taxed, for the convenience of calculating the tax credit. This tax-excluded pricing policy has hindered the functioning of the uniform invoice system and has resulted in a high level of tax evasion.

8. For details, see Public Finance Training Institute (1988, 16–17).

9. Lin and Lin (1989) did mention that better tax compliance is one method that could result in better collection of the business tax. Their estimation, however, indicates that changes in tax compliance after the tax reform were insignificant.

The uniform invoice system was established on the proviso that firms voluntarily issue invoices at the time of every sale. In fact, this has not happened. Firms tend to underreport sales by not issuing an invoice at the time of sale. As a result, the tax authorities have been trying to induce consumers to ask for invoices with every purchase. The most important device being used to induce this kind of behavior is the uniform-invoice lottery. Consumers have a chance to win N.T. $2 million just by obtaining an invoice at the time of purchase.

Before the adoption of the VAT, under a tax-included pricing policy, whether invoices were issued or not, consumers paid one price, because the tax was already included in the sale price. Because of the VAT and because tax payments were now based on the list price of commodities, the tax shifted to those consumers who were issued invoices. Under this kind of tax-excluded pricing policy, consumers can pay a lower "price" for products, that is, they do not pay the tax if they do not ask for an invoice. If they request an invoice, they pay an amount equal to the noninvoice price plus the amount of the tax. Consumers, therefore, are discouraged from asking for an invoice. In short, under both pricing policies, firms end up receiving hidden income from sales if no invoices are issued (no revenues recorded) at the time of sale. Consumers and firms found it in their best interest to cooperate with each other to escape the business tax and the business income tax, respectively.

In order to encourage consumers to demand invoices, the tax authorities finally decided to change the pricing rules that are applied to firms; the change requires that the list price of final goods include the amount of the business tax (tax-included pricing). This was put into effect in July 1988, and as a result, tax revenues increased significantly starting in fiscal year 1989. Table 6.3 summarizes the changes in the tax revenue of the various taxes before and after the tax reform.

Column (3) of the table shows total annual business tax revenues before and after the introduction of tax reform. The integration into the business tax of the education surcharge and items covered formerly by the commodity tax and the stamp tax has increased the average business tax rate from 0.58 cents per dollar of sales in 1985 to 0.90 cents in 1986, as shown in column (4). Column (10) indicates the revenue difference between the current business tax and that of the pre-1986 tax system. It is interesting to note that the tax-excluded pricing policy in effect between 1986 and 1988 seems to have been the main cause of the differences in revenues during the period. When the pricing policy was changed to include the amount of the business tax in fiscal year 1989, the revenue from the business tax increased by about 25%, as indicated in column (11).

Table 6.3   Comparison of Revenues between the "Old" and the "New" Business Tax (millions of N.T. dollars)

Fiscal Year	Taxable Sales Tax Included (1)	Taxable Sales Tax Excluded (2)	Average Business Tax Revenue (3)	Business Tax per Dollar Sales (4)[a]	Estimated Tax Revenue without 1986's Tax Reform Business Tax (5)	Education Surcharge (6)	Stamp Tax (7)	Commodity Tax (8)	Total (9)[b]	Revenue Difference (10)[c]	Revenue Difference (%) of "New" Tax Revenue (11)[d]
1978	1,895,122	1,871,211	10,955	0.5876							
1979	265,031	2,620,658	14,348	0.5475							
1980	3,213,108	3,174,781	18,880	0.5947							
1981	4,480,565	4,435,867	23,222	0.5235							
1982	4,652,202	4,605,579	24,686	0.5360							
1983	4,611,614	4,560,023	26,831	0.5884							
1984	5,313,484	5,256,418	30,188	0.5743							
1985	5,324,748	5,268,559	30,568	0.5802							
1986	6,004,306	5,950,597	53,709	0.9026	34,573	8,470	15,105	7,005	65,153	11,444	21.31
1987	7,647,957	7,579,741	68,216	0.9000	44,038	10,789	19,240	7,950	82,017	13,801	20.23
1988	8,431,170	8,360,834	70,336	0.8413	48,576	11,901	21,226	8,157	89,857	19,521	27.75
1989	9,780,273	9,679,566	100,707	1.0404	56,236	13,778	24,569	8,165	102,745	2,038	2.02

Sources: Data for columns 1 and 3 are from the Department of Statisitcs (1984–89, 1990).

Note: Columns 2 and 4–11 are estimated using the method in Lin and Lin (1989).

[a](4) = [(3)/(2)]/100.

[b](9) = (5) + (6) + (7) + (8).

[c](10) = (9) − (3).

[d](11) = [(10)/(3)]/100.

6.4 Economic Impacts

6.4.1 Price Effects

The economic impacts of the 1986 tax reform are wide-ranging, and it is hard to identify each of them individually. One beneficial effect often mentioned by the supporters of the VAT is encouragement of exports. To analyze the effect is difficult, since the observation period is too short for empirical tests. Nevertheless, some impacts are discussed in the following paragraphs.

Before the adoption of the VAT, inflation caused by tax changes was an issue of debate within Taiwan society. Projections on the price effects resulting from tax reform were made using input-output analysis—widely practiced at that time by many researchers such as Lin (1984) and Lin (1986). They concluded that there would be a mild price increase with the adoption of the VAT in Taiwan. In fact, the adoption of the VAT in 1986 has not brought on inflation; the consumer price index and the wholesale price index dropped in the months immediately following the implementation of tax reform.

The stability of the price level, given the adoption of the VAT, could be attributed to the following facts:

1. Persistent wholesale-price decline since 1982 is believed to be closely related to relatively low economic growth in Taiwan and the decline in the price of energy on the international market. Inflation expectations in 1986, therefore, were very weak.

2. The government took several preventive measures to stabilize the price level, including the reduction or elimination of the tariff rates on more than eight hundred imported items in February 1986; the abolition of valuation provisions that required a 5% increase in the value of imported goods above the CIF value of imports for tax purposes; the reduction in the price of public utility services, especially of petroleum products and electricity, before and after the introduction of the VAT; zero-rating public businesses and enterprises such as the Taiwan Fertilizer Company, Taiwan Sugar Corporation, Taiwan Salt Works, China Steel Corporation, and the Taiwan Railway Administration, which would have borne an extra tax burden as a result of the adoption of the VAT.[10]

3. The government chose 151 commodities including items of food, clothing, housing, transportation, communications, medicine, and education, calculated their "rational" prices, and then informed the general public so that businesses would have to reset their retail prices. In addition, the government oversaw the price changes in department stores, supermarkets, and restaurants to be sure that there was no "irrational" pricing of goods, i.e., to be sure that the reduction in prices was passed on to the consumer. Business entities refusing to cooperate with the government took the risk of being boycotted as a

10. For details, see Public Finance Training Institute (1988, 8–9).

result of mass-media coverage or of being harassed by the tax authorities and having their tax returns audited by the tax bureau.

4. The introduction of the 5% VAT rate, which replaced the old tax system for many businesses, did not result in any significant change in the business cost of production.

6.4.2 Distribution

It has become controversial as to which consumption items should be exempt from the VAT and which items should be subject to the higher turnover tax rates. The controversy arises mainly from concern over income distribution and social equity. Like all sales taxes (business taxes), Taiwan's is also regressive (Davies 1959, 70)—the average propensity to consume declines as income rises. The regressivity of the tax, however, can be reduced through the use of tax exemptions or multiple tax rates on various consumption items with different income elasticities. To determine the degree of regressivity of the business tax, therefore, an empirical analysis of the income elasticities of various final goods and services is needed.

My empirical analysis of business tax regressivity in Taiwan was conducted with two sets of cross-sectional data on household expenditures and income: the entire sample composed off 3,881 households and the random subset, 515 households. The data on households were taken from a survey conducted by the Directorate-General of the Budget, Accounting, and Statistics, Executive Yuan, 1986. A random sample of 500 was deemed sufficient for the regression analysis. The data on the 3,881 households were further divided into twenty-four income brackets. The year, 1986, was selected because it is the year tax reform was introduced in Taiwan. Finally, all the variables in the regression analysis were transformed into logarithms, so that the estimated income elasticity of each tax base could be regarded as a regressivity (or progressivity) index.

The Schaefer (1969) model was used to estimate the regressivity of the business tax. Since comprehensive income data were not readily available, I used the best approximations that could be obtained from the available information. Total monetary income was employed; it is assumed to be a good measure of ability to pay taxes. The model is succinctly delineated as follows:

$$(1) \qquad \sum_{j=1}^{n} w_j \log \bar{t}_{ij} = \log a_i + b_i \sum_{j=1}^{n} w_j \log \bar{y}_j + \sum w_j \log e_{ij},$$

where $\bar{t}_{ij}$ = mean ith business tax base for the jth income group, $\bar{y}_j$ = mean income for the jth income group, b_i = progressivity index for the ith business tax base, a_i = a constant, e_{ij} = error term for the ith business tax base for the jth income group, and w_j = the population weight of the jth income group. The regressivity or progressivity of the business tax depends on its tax coefficient, b_i. If the income elasticity of the ith tax base is unitary ($b_i = 1$), this implies that the effective tax rate remains constant as income increases, so that the business tax is considered proportional. If $b_i < 1$, the tax rate decreases as income increases; the tax is considered regressive. Similarly, if $b_i > 1$, the tax rate increases as income increases, and the tax is considered progressive.

All estimates reported in table 6.4 were obtained by the ordinary least squares estimation method, which assumes a constant variance in the error terms among income groups. According to the criteria described earlier, it is apparent that business taxes on most items are regressive except for the taxes on recreation and education, as well as those on financial services, which are progressive. Most of the coefficients are statistically significant at the 1% level.

Using the average data from the complete sample site of 3,881 households, the business tax on financial services is the most progressive, and the business tax on recreation and education is proportional or slightly progressive. The results change moderately when the data of the randomly selected subset of 515 households are used. It should be noted that, while the tax on financial services was progressive for the complete set of data, it was found to be regressive for the subset data.

Table 6.4   **Progressivity Indexes for Various Business Tax Bases, Using Aggregate and Disaggregate Data**

Business Tax Base (dependent variable)	3881 Households	Random Sample of 515 Households
Food consumption	0.305*	0.323*
	(0.013)	(0.024)
Beverage expenditures	0.514*	0.589*
	(0.046)	(0.089)
Tobacco expenditures	0.244*	−0.451
	(0.083)	(0.403)
Clothing expenditures	0.821*	0.841*
	(0.033)	(0.050)
Utility expenditures	0.821*	0.841*
	(0.023)	(0.033)
Medical expenditures	0.098	0.502*
	(0.097)	(0.084)
Recreational and educational expenditures	1.083*	1.329*
	(0.057)	(0.085)
Financing services expenditures	1.603*	0.642*
	(0.194)	(0.202)
Total consumption	0.666*	0.668*
	(0.022)	(0.024)
Total consumption excluding food and medicine	0.838*	0.863*
	(0.031)	(0.032)

Notes: Standard errors are in parentheses. All variables are in log form.
*Significance at 1% level.

Since the business tax on food and on medicine is highly regressive regardless of the data type, one can expect that the exemption of these items from taxation might reduce the regressivity or increase the progressivity of the business tax. The bottom row in table 6.4 shows that both food and medicine exemptions improve the progressivity index from 0.666 to 0.838 when using the complete set of data. To test the robustness of the result, the smaller data set was used to measure the impact of these exemptions. A very similar result was found—the progressivity index increased from 0.668 to 0.863.

Tax exemptions on agricultural products and medical services have been in effect since the revision of the 1986 Business Tax Law that came along with the adoption of the VAT. However, financial organizations are subject to a 5% turnover tax. The tax also may not be credited. Based on my estimation, therefore, I conclude that the current business tax, which includes the VAT, has improved the progressivity of the tax system—the result of tax reform. In order to further improve the progressivity of the business tax, the tax authorities in Taiwan might need to grant more exemptions on the sale of food items and on utility expenditures. Furthermore, since the introduction of the VAT in 1986 is considered only one step of the indirect tax reform in Taiwan, changes on other indirect taxes, such as the commodity tax, the stamp tax, and even the monopoly profits from tobacco and wine, could be involved in future tax reforms. Therefore, the results found in table 6.4 provide information on how to improve the progressivity of the indirect tax system.

6.5   The Importance of the 1986 Tax Reform

According to the government, the introduction of the VAT in 1986 emphasized not the generation of more tax revenues but improvements in the economic efficiency and social equity of the tax system. It is puzzling, however, that the government has not yet made any effort to evaluate or improve the tax system with a view either to economic efficiency or social equity since the adoption of the VAT. The Business Tax Law was revised in May 1988 to provide for more tax exemptions, mainly for convenience of tax administration. There are no data available with which to empirically investigate the impacts of the tax reform on investment or international trade.

Nevertheless, the 1986 business tax reform could be considered an important building block for other tax reforms in Taiwan in the future. As a result of tax exemptions and widespread tax evasion, income taxation in Taiwan has played a very limited role in the generation of government revenue, in comparison to other countries. Currently, high income tax rates are applied to relatively narrow tax bases. For example, in 1988, there were 4.65 million households in Taiwan, but only 2.66 million filed individual income tax reports and paid taxes. Among these, only 1,919 households' adjusted gross income was reported to be in the highest income bracket (income above N.T. $3.50 million or about U.S. $125,000) and was taxed at a 50% marginal rate.

The aggregate adjusted gross income of all taxpayers constituted only 33.32% of total national income. As for the business income tax, there were 834,416 business entities in Taiwan in 1987. Even with an effective business income tax rate of around 25%,[11] the average business income tax payment for each business entity was only N.T. $63,798 (about U.S. $2,300) for 1987. The seriousness of income tax evasion implies that income tax reforms that reduce tax rates are needed to expand the tax base. In fact, tax rate reduction has already taken place; the government revised the Income Tax Laws in 1990. As a result, there might be more losses in tax revenue.

In addition to income taxes, commodity taxes at relatively high rates are being levied on a few selected items and have been regarded as very distortionary. One of the reasons for the adoption of the VAT was to curtail the rise in the commodity tax rates. The revenue lost as a result of the 1990 income tax reform, therefore, should not be made up by increasing the commodity tax rates. Furthermore, revenues from custom duties declined dramatically from 17.2% of total tax revenues in 1986 to 11.8% in 1989 as a result of recent U.S. political pressure demanding tariff reductions. The Taiwan government must find a way to compensate for the revenue losses due to the income tax rate, tariff rate reductions, and abolition of some commodity taxes. One viable way to do this is to raise the business tax rates, since the VAT in Taiwan is only 5%, which is lower than the rates adopted by other countries. Currently, the business tax generates approximately 14% of total tax revenue at all levels of government, which is higher than either the business income tax (12.3%) or the individual income tax (11.9%). The shifting of the major source of tax revenue from income taxes to the business tax would further encourage business entities to honestly report their sales revenues, since sales taxes are easier to shift onto consumers than income taxes are. This would improve the tax evasion problem, not only in income taxation but also in business tax, and would generate more revenue.

6.6 Conclusion

Before the 1986 tax reform, the tax system and tax structure in Taiwan, as in most developing countries, were poor. Income taxes were constantly being evaded, and high tax rates could not generate very much tax revenue. The main revenue sources were tariffs, commodity taxes, and business taxes (sales taxes). High tariff rates hindered international trade, the high rates of the commodity tax distorted resource allocation, and the business tax that used turnover rates was considered the worst type of sales tax in the world (Due and Friedlaender 1981, 414–16). The introduction of the VAT in 1986 was the

---

11. There is a 15% tax rate applied to business entities with an initial income less than N.T. $100,000. There is also a tax ceiling for qualified businesses under the Statute for Encouragement of Investment.

first step in reforming the indirect tax system in Taiwan and was, therefore, very important.

Unlike the experiences of Japan and the United States, the introduction of the VAT in Taiwan did not encounter too much resistance from the public. This is because the VAT was introduced not as a new tax but as a replacement for the business tax based on turnover rates, which had been widely condemned by the public in Taiwan. Since the VAT rate was very low and the government promised the public that total tax revenues would not increase under the tax reform, the impacts of the VAT were accepted by the public. In fact, the government successfully stabilized price levels and improved the distributional function of the business tax under the tax reform. After a trial-and-error process, the government further avoided possible loss of revenue by changing the pricing policy, from one of tax-excluded to tax-included, for business entities.

Some problems remain, however. One is that the business tax is a local tax, and economic development and democratization will sooner or later give rise to demands for decentralization and local autonomy in Taiwan. Once this comes to pass, decisions concerning the tax rate or the tax base of the business tax will be made by the provincial or municipal governments. Operating the VAT system would become infeasible. Swapping the business tax at the provincial (and municipal) level for a national tax, therefore, was necessary. A tax-sharing or intergovernment-grant system is further needed in order to keep the level of revenue of the provincial and municipal governments the same.

The second difficulty is how to reduce the increasing administration costs of keying in each piece of data from the uniform invoices. The uniform invoice system cannot effectively eliminate the people's widespread evasion of the income and business taxes, and it results in an enormous administrative burden on both the tax administration and the taxpayers. In fact, business entities have the incentive not to issue an invoice at the time of sale, since they would prefer to escape their business income tax liability even more than their business tax liability: although neither tax would be paid if invoices are not issued, the business tax is easier to shift to consumers. Reducing the business income tax liability, therefore, would reduce the incentive for business entities not to issue invoices. Besides, given the predominance of small entrepreneurs in Taiwan, it is difficult for the tax administration to trace those who evade payment of business income tax and to collect the income tax. A more realistic solution, therefore, would be to reduce the current income tax rate (and tax liability). This would help eliminate the widespread problem of tax evasion. To reduce the business income tax liability, another tax reform is necessary, involving the integration of the income taxes (the business income tax and the individual income tax) or lowering the income tax rate to expand the tax base. Income tax reform together with a further reduction in commodity tax rates and custom duties definitely would reduce tax revenues. On the other hand, the VAT tax rate could be increased, thereby increasing tax revenue; the increased revenue could then be used to reduce other taxes. The prerequisite of such an arrangement would be to enlarge the VAT system and diminish the size of the small entrepreneur category.

Finally, the tax authorities might need to give tax exemption status to several new food and unprocessed agricultural products categories and to all medicines, in order to improve tax regressivity. This would guarantee that the shifting of tax burden from income taxes to the business tax would not hurt social justice or equity.

References

Davies, D. G. 1959. An empirical test of sales tax regressivity. *Journal of Political Economy* 67:72–78.

Department of Statistics. 1984–89. *Yearbook of tax statistics, ROC*. Taipei: Ministry of Finance.

———. 1990. *The ROC Monthly of Financial Statistics*. Taipei: Ministry of Finance, March.

Due, John, and Ann F. Friedlaender. 1981. *Government finance: Economics of public sector*. 7th edition. Homewood: Irwin.

Lin, An-loh. 1986. The price and distribution effects under the new business tax (in Chinese). *Public Finance Review* 18(2): 10–36.

Lin, An-loh, and Chuan Lin. 1989. The revenue and price effects resulting from the adjustment of the business tax rate (in Chinese). *Public Finance Review* 21(5): 34–46.

Lin, Hua-Te. 1984. The price effects and tax redistribution of the VAT in Taiwan (in Chinese). *Monthly Journal of Taipei City Bank* 15(9): 1–29.

Public Finance Training Institute. 1988. *An introduction to the value-added tax in the Republic of China*. Taipei: Ministry of Finance.

Schaefer, J. M. 1969. Sales tax regressivity under alternative tax bases and income concepts. *National Tax Journal* 22:516–27.

Comment   Ching-huei Chang

In this paper Chuan Lin attempts to evaluate the recent business tax reform in Taiwan. In 1986 the old system of multistage turnover tax was replaced by the value-added tax, which imposes a flat rate of 5 percent on almost all goods and services sold except those subject to the commodity tax. The tax reform is considered by Taiwan's government to be a great success in the sense that the new business tax has brought in more revenue each year than the old one. Also, the general price level, which it was thought might be pushed up by the tax substitution, turned out to be quite stable after reform. The experience in

Ching-huei Chang is a research fellow of Sun Yat-sen Institute for Social Sciences and Philosophy, Academia Sinica, Taiwan.

Taiwan has attracted the attention of some Southeast Asian countries, which are also interested in adopting the VAT.

However, Lin is not so optimistic about Taiwan's result. He argues that the introduction of the VAT has increased administrative costs and does not solve some serious problems that arise mainly from preferential treatment of small firms. In fact, the VAT aggravates the difficulty by its use of the uniform invoice. He also points out that the VAT in fact does not produce substantially more tax revenues than would be produced under the old system of turnover tax. Judging from the equity goal of taxation, the VAT in Taiwan is found to be regressive; the tax burden on the poor may be higher than that on the rich. In view of the defects of the current VAT system, Lin suggests that consumption of food and other necessities should be exempt from taxation. The loss in tax revenue could be compensated by raising the current rate form 5 percent to 6 percent. He expects that in this way the VAT can be made less regressive and the amount of tax revenue can be maintained or even increased.

I agree with most of Lin's points, but I have some general observations to make. First, when measuring the revenue impact of this tax reform, Lin compares the amount of revenue the VAT generates with what the old turnover tax might have produced. When measuring the effect on administrative cost, however, he does not make such a comparison. Thus, the case may be that, even without the tax reform in 1986, administrative costs would have increased to the level shown in table 6.1 or even higher. In other words, the increase in the costs should not be attributed solely to the new business tax. Table 6.1 also shows that, although the cost of administration for business tax increased in 1987, the cost for business income tax fell moderately and that for individual income tax fell substantially. Is this just a coincidence or does a negative correlation exist between the two? Further empirical studies must be done.

Second, at least in theory, one of the major arguments in favor of the VAT is that a uniform VAT rate applied to a wide range of goods and services would correct the serious distortions associated with the old turnover tax. However, the tax alone may work against distributional objectives, since it is proved that the tax burden is regressive. Thus, as is often suggested, this tax should be supplemented by the commodity tax, which is in essence an excise tax and imposes differential rates on certain luxury goods. In this way the indirect tax system, rather than the business tax alone, can take care of both efficiency and equity goals. If this argument of the "policy mix" is accepted, I think an appropriate approach to evaluating the impact on income distribution is to measure the combined effect of business tax, commodity tax, and possibly monopoly revenue, which in a sense is also an excise tax.

Third, another consideration of introducing the VAT into Taiwan was its beneficial effect on export. No further elaboration is needed because the argument is quite straightforward. But an empirical estimation must be done of how much of the recent trade expansion in Taiwan can be attributed to the tax substitution.

Comment   Kwang Choi

The paper by Chuan Lin provides an excellent appraisal of business taxes (value-added tax) reform in Taiwan. Though short, the paper covers all important issues raised in the introduction of the VAT, including administrative problems, revenue impacts, price effects, and distributive implications.

I have little to say in criticism of the paper itself. Though this is not a good place to raise theoretical questions of a general nature, I would like to ask the rather fundamental question of whether the VAT is a consumption tax (borne by consumers) or an income tax (borne by owners of businesses). I would like to point out that, in almost all writings on the VAT, authors have been applying double standards on the incidence of the VAT or on who really pays the VAT.

On one hand, when we talk about the regressivity of the VAT, we always assume that the tax is shifted to consumers and that the burden is borne by the consumers. On the other hand, when we exempt small businesses from the VAT or when special treatments of no bookkeeping or lower tax rates are provided to small businesses, we take it for granted that small businesses bear all the tax burden, or that the VAT is not shifted to consumers. Needless to say, special treatment is provided to small businesses, not to reduce the tax burden but to expedite administration.

A more or less similar argument applies to the "exemption" system of the VAT. Exemption takes two forms: exemption of certain taxpayers and exemption of certain goods and services. Small businesses are exempt from the VAT since the government can reduce administrative and compliance problems by excluding taxpayers with small turnovers. For social, political, and administrative reasons, exemptions are granted on basic necessities such as unprocessed food stuffs, on hard-to-tax services such as banking and insurance, on social and cultural goods such as medical service, education, books, newspapers, and on goods and services supplied by public enterprises.

The purpose of exemption is not to reduce the VAT burden but to facilitate the administration of the VAT. Exempt supplies are outside the scope of the VAT altogether. In contrast to the zero rate, exempt transactions bear some VAT on the value of transactions. The reason for the exemption scheme in the VAT structure lies not in the reduction of regressivity but in the simplification of administration and compliance. The moderation of the VAT's regressivity or improvement in the progressivity of the VAT burden can be achieved more effectively through the zero rating rather than through the exemption scheme. This simple but important point has not yet caught the attention of the VAT policymakers in Korea and Taiwan, as well as in many other countries.

It is very important to emphasize why small businesses want to stay small

Kwang Choi is professor of public economics at the Hankuk University of Foreign Studies.

and why they seldom use the 10% tax credit. Small traders cheat on their sales, not to evade the VAT but to evade personal or corporate income taxes. It must be emphasized that an effective VAT greatly aids income tax administration and that the operation of a VAT resembles that of the income tax more than that of other taxes.

In this regard it is quite interesting to see that, although the data processing costs for the VAT increased sharply after its introduction in Taiwan, the total cost of tax administration for the VAT, corporate income tax, and personal income tax remained more or less the same as before.

I would like to see Lin describe the rather long history of preparation leading to the introduction of the VAT in Taiwan and elaborate on the political economy aspects of the VAT's introduction.

Lin should be congratulated for his successful efforts at elucidating the reform of business tax in Taiwan.

III.

7　The Dynamic Efficiency Effect of a Change in the Marginal Capital Income Tax Rate: The Nakasone-Takeshita Tax Reform

Tatsuo Hatta and Hideki Nishioka

The Nakasone-Takeshita tax reform, which took place during 1987–89 in Japan, is best known for making a deep wage tax reduction and establishing a new value-added tax. Less attention has been paid to the reform's restructuring of capital income taxation.[1]

1. The corporate income tax rate was reduced. In particular, the top statutory rate for the national corporate tax was reduced from 42% to 37.5%.[2]
2. A flat interest tax of 20% was introduced, changing the interest tax in two ways:
   a. The maximum tax rate on interest income was reduced from 35% to 20%.
   b. Before the reform, various exemptions entitled each individual to have savings of ¥9 million with their interest free of tax. The reform eliminated these exemptions. We will call the eliminated exemptions "the maruyu system" after its principal exemption program, maruyu.[3]

Tatsuo Hatta is professor of economics at Osaka University. Hideki Nishioka is assistant professor of economics at University of Osaka Prefecture.

The authors would like to thank Kanemi Ban, Takatoshi Ito, Yasushi Iwamoto, Joosung Jun, Masahiro Kuroda, Leslie Papke, Shinji Nakazawa, and Larry Summers for their helpful comments on earlier drafts. Maria Gochoco, Medhi Krongkaew, and Kun-Young Yun gave useful suggestions at the conference. Hatta is grateful to the Twenty-first Century Foundation for financially supporting this research.

1. See Yukio Noguchi's and Masaaki Homma's papers in this volume for details of the Nakasone-Takeshita tax reform.

2. The combined national and local effective tax rate as defined by the Ministry of Finance was reduced from 52.92% to 49.98%. See Ministry of Finance (1990).

3. The maruyu system consists of three programs, maruyu, tokuyu, and yucho. They allowed each individual to have ¥3 million of bank deposits, government bonds, and postal savings, respectively, with their interest free of tax. Exclusion of interest income from the tax base remains

Japan does not have a social security number system; hence a person can open several bank accounts, each with different false names, without being detected by the tax authority. By doing so a wealthy person was able to get around the maximum individual exemption level and evade the interest tax payments completely. Although it is difficult to tell exactly how much evasion was taking place, circumstantial evidence indicate that it was pervasive. For example, there were more maruyu savings accounts than the population of Japan in 1983, and the Tax Administration Agency estimated illegal maruyu savings to be at least ¥5 trillion (" 'Maruyu' Akuyo 5600 Oku Yen" 1983). Thus the primary purpose of abolishing the maruyu system was to make interest taxation more equitable between honest savers and tax evaders.

The effects on efficiency of abolishing the maruyu system, however, were mixed. For those honest savers who paid the interest tax at rates between 21% and 35%, the reform lowered the marginal interest tax rate, reducing tax distortion, while for those whose interest tax rates were below 20%, the reform raised the interest tax rate, increasing distortion. In all likelihood, abolishing the maruyu system increased the marginal interest tax rate for the median taxpayer, since 73% of interest income was exempted from income tax.[4] Indeed some economists, including Noguchi (1987, 99), criticized the abolition of the maruyu system for increasing tax distortion.

The aim of reducing the corporate income tax rate, on the other hand, was to reduce tax distortion. The tax cut was intended to stimulate capital formation by lowering the effective marginal capital income tax rate.[5] The resulting revenue reduction was roughly similar to the increased revenue from the abolition of the maruyu system.[6]

---

after the reform for those with minimal income-earning capabilities, such as the aged, fatherless families, and the handicapped.

The maruyu system was applicable to every taxpayer. In addition, each employee was entitled to have additional savings of ¥5 million with tax-free interest. This privilege, called zaikei, was retained after the reform.

4. In 1987, untaxable interest income from nonpostal savings was ¥9.8 trillion, according to Ministry of Finance (1991) and that from postal savings was ¥6.7 trillion, according to unpublished data obtained from the Saving Bureau of Ministry of Post and Telecommunications. These figures imply that 73% of the interest income was nontaxable in 1987.

5. See Nakatani, Inoue, Iwamoto, and Fukushige (1986) and Economic Federation of Japan (1984) for the argument for reducing the corporate tax to stimulate capital formation.

6. We estimate the hypothetical revenue increase in the interest income tax and revenue decrease in the corporate income tax in 1986, assuming the entire Nakasone-Takeshita reform had taken place at the beginning of that year.

Although the average interest tax rate from 1977 through 1986 was 7.8%, the rate jumped to 14% in 1989 when the abolition of the maruyu system was fully implemented. If we assume that the difference, i.e., 6.2%, is due to the abolition of the maruyu system, we can estimate that the abolition would have reduced the government revenue by $0.062 \times 24.1 = ¥1.5$ trillion in 1986, when ¥24.1 trillion was the personal interest income.

In computing average interest tax rates, we obtain the data on tax revenue and on interest income from different sources. First, we obtain tax revenue from the Ministry of Finance (1991). Second, we obtain personal interest income from Economic Planning Agency (1990b). This is

Therefore, the Nakasone-Takeshita package of capital income tax changes was a reform to eliminate the maruyu-related tax evasion accompanied by a revenue-neutralizing measure that mitigates the possible increase in the effective marginal tax rate. Yet the reform may have increased intertemporal dynamic efficiency cost.

Intertemporal efficiency cost could be unequivocally reduced without reducing the revenue, by making the capital income tax proportional. This could be attained, for example, by abolishing the corporate income tax while making the tax rates flat on interests, dividends, and capital gains.[7] The Nakasone-Takeshita package can be viewed as the first step of such reforms, since it reduced tax rates on corporate capital income and installed a flat tax on interest income.[8] It would be of interest to estimate the size of the efficiency gain that would have been caused by an alternative reform of making the capital income tax proportional.

Moreover, the intertemporal efficiency cost would be eliminated if the capital income tax were abolished, with the revenue loss compensated with an increased tax on wage or consumption, even if it would reduce equity. Clearly, the Nakasone-Takeshita reform did not change the tax system in this direction.[9] But this would be the policy of choice for those who opposed the abolition of the maruyu system on efficiency grounds. In order to determine whether or not future reforms should be carried out in the direction of no capital income tax, it is essential to estimate the efficiency gain from abolishing the capital income tax so that it can be compared with the subjective cost of lost equity.

---

because the Ministry of Finance figures before the reform do not contain interest from postal savings.

It should be noted that the interest income figures of the Ministry of Finance cited above contain corporate interest receipt as well. The reform must have reduced interest tax payment by corporations, since the corporate income tax rate was reduced, while the abolition of the maruyu system did not affect corporations. Thus the above estimate of the reduction in the personal income tax payment as the result of the reform, i.e., ¥1.5 trillion, is likely to be an underestimation.

On the other hand, Ministry of Finance (1988, 1991) and Local Tax Association (1987, 1989) estimate that the Nakasone-Takeshita tax reform reduced the revenue from the national corporate income tax by ¥0.45 trillion in 1987 and ¥1.20 trillion in 1988, while it reduced the local corporate income tax by ¥0.08 trillion in 1987 and ¥0.15 trillion in 1988. We can estimate the loss in tax revenue in 1986 under our hypothetical tax reform by scaling down these figures in proportion to the corporate income of the respective years. Since the corporate income was ¥34.48 trillion in 1986, ¥36.28 trillion in 1987, and ¥40.64 trillion in 1988, we estimate that the revenue loss from the corporate income tax reform would have been ¥1.66 trillion in the 1986 base.

See Nishioka (1991) for more detail on the estimation of average tax rates.

7. Capital gains can be taxed at realization, as if they have been taxed actuarially. See Vickrey (1939), Hatta (1987, 1988), and Auerbach (1991).

8. If we take this view, the logical next step has to be the establishment of substantive capital gains tax on stocks and bonds, coupled with deeper reductions in corporate income tax rates.

9. After all, the flat interest tax was introduced to roughly offset the revenue loss from the reduced corporate tax. On the other hand, the cut in the wage tax rate was so drastic that the resulting revenue loss exceeded the revenue gain from the indirect taxes.

The principal aim of the present paper is to estimate the dynamic efficiency effect of the Nakasone-Takeshita package of the capital income tax reform. To this end, we will estimate the effective marginal tax rates before and after the reform. From these estimates, we will derive the lower and upper bounds of the dynamic efficiency effect of the reform.

We will also estimate the dynamic efficiency effects of two hypothetical reforms: (1) making the capital income tax rate proportional to the level of the prereform average capital income tax rate, and (2) abolishing the capital income tax while raising the wage tax to make the reform revenue-neutral. This will enable us to examine alternatives to the actual Nakasone-Takeshita reform that are consistent with eliminating the maruyu system.

We will assume that the prereform equilibrium was in a steady state and that the reform brings the economy to an adjustment path that takes it to the new steady state in the long run. The equivalent variation associated with the consumption stream in the prereform steady state and that along the adjustment path is the dynamic efficiency effect of the tax reform.

In his pioneering work, Chamley (1981) estimates dynamic efficiency effects of reductions in the capital income tax rate. Chamley as well as Judd (1987) and Nishioka (1989) is concerned with the efficiency gains of a *marginal* reduction in the marginal tax rate. Efficiency gains of *global* reductions in the capital income tax rate are studied through simulations. Auerbach, Kotlikoff, and Skinner (1983) and Auerbach and Kotlikoff (1987) construct overlapping generation models where the bequest motive is assumed away. They estimate welfare effects of changing average tax rates. Jorgenson and Yun (1986a, 1986b), on the other hand, use a multisector multi-capital-good dynasty model to perform a global simulation analysis of various hypothetical tax reforms that narrow capital income tax rates among different capital goods. Fullerton, Henderson, and Mackie (1987), Jorgenson and Yun (1990), and Goulder and Thalmann (1990) apply such models to the U.S. Tax Reform Act of 1986. For the Japanese economy, Hatta and Nishioka (1989, 1990) estimate the dynamic efficiency effects of abolishing the capital income tax, using one-sector, one-capital-good dynasty models.

Unlike the 1986 Reagan tax reform, the Nakasone-Takeshita reform hardly changed relative tax rates among different capital goods. Hence little will be sacrificed by using a one-capital-good model in examining its efficiency effect. Since the reform kept the average capital income tax rate constant, however, the average tax rate models of Hatta and Nishioka (1989, 1990) are inadequate for examining this reform. In the present paper, we will extend the model of Hatta and Nishioka (1990) by allowing the discrepancy between the marginal and the average capital income tax rates.

Section 7.1 presents our model and a measure of the efficiency change a tax reform causes. Simulation analyses of tax reforms are discussed in section 7.2, where an adjustment path comparison is presented. Section 7.3 compares our results with those of the literature. Concluding remarks are given in section 7.4. The effective marginal capital income tax rate is estimated in appendix A, and the production function is estimated in appendix B.

7.1 The Model

We present a simple neoclassical dynasty model for which the efficiency effect of a change in the marginal tax rate can be examined. For this purpose we modify the model of Hatta and Nishioka (1990) by allowing the capital income tax rate structure to be nonproportional.[10] We deliberately preserve the same notation and a similar order of presentation to facilitate the comparison of the two models.

7.1.1 Production Sector

We assume that the production function obeys Harrod neutral technical progress and is linear homogeneous with respect to labor (measured in efficiency units) and capital. The production function is written as

$$Y(t) = F(K(t), N(t)),$$

where $Y(t)$ denotes gross output, $K(t)$ the capital stock, and $N(t)$ labor input measured in efficiency units at time t. Letting small letters denote the variables per efficiency unit of labor, we can rewrite the production function

$$y(t) = f(k(t)).$$

The following relationship holds between the labor inputs measured in efficiency units and in man-hour units:

$$N(t) = L(t)e^{\mu t},$$

where $L(t)$ is the labor input measured in man-hour units and μ is the constant exogenous rate of technical progress.

We assume that the rate of depreciation is constant at δ, so that net output is $Y(t) - \delta K(t)$. We define the marginal productivity of capital net of depreciation, $r(t)$, by

(1) $$r(t) \equiv f'(k(t)) - \delta,$$

and the marginal productivity of labor, $w(t)$, by

(2) $$w(t) \equiv f(k(t)) - k(t)f'(k(t)).$$

These are equal to the before-tax rate of return of investment and the before-tax wage rate, respectively.

---

10. Hatta and Nishioka (1990) assume that the capital income tax is proportional at the prereform situation. This model gives useful information for the purpose of designing a desirable mix of tax base but is unsuitable for examining the efficiency effects of the Nakasone-Takeshita reform, which changed the marginal capital income tax rate but kept the average rate roughly constant.

7.1.2 Government Sector

Government expenditure is financed through the capital income tax and the wage tax. A proportional wage tax rate of $\theta_w(t)$ is imposed, so that the total revenue from wage tax in year t is $\theta_w(t)w(t)N(t)$.

Since the focus of the present paper is to examine reforms of the marginal and average capital income tax rates, we assume that, after the reform, the marginal tax rate θ_r^m and the average tax rate θ_r are fixed over time, while the lump-sum tax rate $\theta_r^\ell(t)$ is variable. Thus total government revenue from the capital tax is $\theta_r^\ell(t) + \theta_r^m r(t)K(t)$. The average tax rate on capital income θ_r satisfies

$$\theta_r r(t)K(t) \equiv \theta_r^\ell(t) + \theta_r^m r(t)K(t).$$

Let $G(t)$ denote government expenditures at t. Then a balanced budget in each period implies

(3) $\qquad G(t) = \theta_r^\ell(t) + \theta_r^m r(t)K(t) + \theta_w(t)w(t)N(t) \quad$ for all t.

Hence

(4) $\qquad\qquad G(t) = \theta_r^m r(t)K(t) + \theta^\ell(t)N(t) \quad$ for all t,

where

$$\theta^\ell(t) \equiv \theta_r^\ell(t)\frac{1}{N(t)} + \theta_w(t)w(t).$$

The term $\theta^\ell(t)$ denotes the lump-sum portion of the taxes per efficiency unit of labor in year t.

We assume that the government increases the supply of public goods at a constant rate $n + \mu$, so that its level per efficiency unit of labor is maintained constant at g. Thus we have

$$G(t) \equiv g \cdot N(t).$$

This and (4) yield

(5) $\qquad\qquad g = \theta_r^m r(t)k(t) + \theta^\ell(t), \quad$ for all t.

We further assume that the government constantly adjusts the lump-sum tax $\theta^\ell(t)$ so that equality (5) always holds for given g and θ_r^m. This can be carried out by adjusting $\theta_w(t)$, $\theta_r^\ell(t)$, or both.

7.1.3 Household Sector

We assume that the consumer has an infinite horizon. The consumer's labor supply, $L(t)$, grows at a given constant rate n. There is no leisure-labor substitution.

We define the instantaneous utility function by

$$u\,(\tilde{c}(t)) \;=\; \frac{1}{1-1/\sigma}\,\tilde{c}(t)^{1-1/\sigma} \text{ if } \sigma \neq 1,$$

(6)

$$= \ln \tilde{c}(t) \text{ if } \sigma = 1,$$

where σ is the elasticity of intertemporal substitution. The intertemporal utility function is then represented by

(7)
$$U = \int_0^\infty e^{-(\rho-n)t}\, u\,(\tilde{c}(t))dt,$$

where $\tilde{c}(t)$ is consumption per man-hour at time t and ρ is the rate of time preference.

Define the after-tax net return on capital at time t by

(8)
$$s(t) = (1 - \theta_r^m)r(t).$$

This is the rate of return that consumers face at time t. The after-tax net return on capital between time 0 and t is defined by

(9)
$$s(t) \equiv \int_0^t s(\tau)d\tau.$$

Then the household's intertemporal budget equation is

(10)
$$\int_0^\infty e^{-s(t)+nt}\,\tilde{c}(t)dt = \int_0^\infty e^{-s(t)+nt}\,(\tilde{w}(t) - \tilde{\theta}^\ell(t))dt + \bar{k}^0,$$

where $\tilde{w}(t)$ is the per-man-hour wage rate, $\tilde{\theta}^\ell(t)$ is the per-man-hour lump-sum tax rate, i.e.,

$$\tilde{\theta}^\ell(t) \equiv \theta_w(t)\tilde{w}(t) + \frac{\theta_r^\ell(t)}{L(t)}$$

at time t, and $\bar{k}^0$ is the per-man-hour capital endowment at the initial equilibrium. We assume that the household with perfect foresight maximizes (7) subject to (10), given a time path of future prices.

Since technical progress is Harrod neutral, the following relationships hold between per-man-hour variables and per-efficiency-unit variables:

(11) $\tilde{c}(t) = c(t)e^{\mu t},\ \tilde{w}(t) = w(t)e^{\mu t},\ \bar{k}(t) = k(t)e^{\mu t},\ \tilde{\theta}^\ell(t) = \theta^\ell(t)e^{\mu t}$.

From (6) and (11), we can rewrite (7) as

(12)
$$U = \int_0^\infty e^{-(\rho^* -n-\mu)t}\, u(c(t))dt,$$

where

$$\rho^* \equiv \rho + \mu/\sigma.$$

Similarly, applying (11), we can rewrite the intertemporal budget equation as

(13) $$\int_0^\infty e^{-s(t)+(n+\mu)t}(c(t) + \theta^\ell(t) - w(t))dt = k^0,$$

where k^0 is the per-efficiency-unit capital endowment. The original con-strained utility maximization problem is equivalent to the problem of maximizing (12) subject to (13). The household chooses the optimal consumption path, $c(t)$, taking the price profiles $s(t)$ and $w(t) - \theta^\ell(t)$ as given.

The first-order conditions for this problem are

(14) $$\dot{c} = (\sigma c) [r(k) (1 - \theta_r^m) - \rho^*]$$

and

(15) $$\lim_{t \to \infty} k(t)\, e^{-s(t)+(n+\mu)t} = 0,$$

which is the transversality condition.

7.1.4 Market Equilibrium

The market equilibrium condition for output is

$$C + G + (\dot{K} + \delta K) = F(K, N),$$

where C denotes consumption expenditures. We thus obtain

(16) $$\dot{k} = f(k) - c - g - (n + \mu + \delta)k.$$

We may rewrite this and (14) as

(17) $$\dot{k} = \dot{k}(k, c)$$

and

(18) $$\dot{c} = \dot{c}(k, c; \theta_r^m),$$

respectively. These two equations yield the time path of (k, c), given the initial condition $k(0) = k^0$ and the value of the parameter θ_r^m. Figure 7.1 is the phase diagram of the system (17) and (18). Dark arrows depict saddle paths, which are the only stable paths of the model. If the initial level of k is at k^0, away from the steady-state level for the given θ_r^m, the economy under perfect fore-sight will choose $c(0)$ on the saddle path. From (5) and the path of $k(t)$ and $c(t)$ thus determined, the time paths of $\theta^\ell(t)$ and of $\theta_w(t)$ are derived.

7.1.5 Evaluating the Efficiency Effect of Tax Reform along the Adjustment Path

In the present paper, we consider the long-term efficiency effect of an un-expected, permanent change in the marginal capital income tax rate. We as-sume that the change in the capital income tax rates is accompanied by a revenue-offsetting adjustment in the lump-sum tax stream.

Economic adjustment following such a tax reform is depicted in figure 7.1.

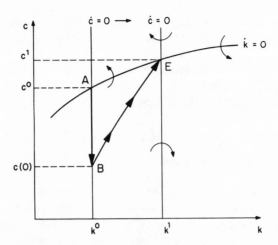

Fig. 7.1   Phase diagram

Let A be the initial steady state, and imagine that the $\dot{c} = 0$ line is a vertical line passing through point A with coordinate (k^0, c^0) rather than through point E. Now assume that the marginal capital income tax rate θ_r^m is reduced, shifting the $\dot{c} = 0$ line to the right so that it passes through point E. Since this does not affect the $\dot{k} = 0$ curve, the new steady-state equilibrium is obtained at point E.

Immediately after the reform, however, the economy will jump from point A to point B, which is on the saddle path leading to the new steady state, by lowering the consumption level to $c(0)$. It will then gradually move along the saddle path toward the new steady state E by adjusting the stock variable k.

We now compare the welfare level along the initial steady state with that along the adjustment path after the reform. As the measure of the efficiency change caused by the tax reform, we adopt the equivalent variations as a percentage of the initial consumption wealth.[11] It is formally defined as

$$(19) \qquad \frac{\displaystyle\int_0^\infty e^{-s0(t)}\, C^1(t)dt - \int_0^\infty e^{-s0(t)}\, C^0(t)dt}{\displaystyle\int_0^\infty e^{-s0(t)}\, C^0(t)dt} \times 100,$$

11. The present value of the consumption stream $C(t)$ discounted by the private rate-of-return stream $s(t)$, i.e.,

$$\int_0^\infty e^{-s(t)}\, C(t)dt,$$

is called *consumption wealth* of $C(t)$ discounted by the rate-of-return stream $s(t)$.

where $C^0(t)$ and $s^0(t)$ are the prereform consumption and rate-of-return streams, respectively, while $C^1(t)$ is the consumption stream that minimizes consumption wealth evaluated by $s^0(t)$ among all the consumption streams that attain the postreform utility level. The numerator of (19) compares the values of $C^0(t)$ and $C^1(t)$ under the constant price stream corresponding to $C^0(t)$, and hence is the equivalent variation of the tax change.[12]

7.2 Numerical Evaluation of the Efficiency Effects of the Tax Reform

We now numerically estimate the efficiency effect of the changes in the capital income tax rate in the Nakasone-Takeshita tax reforms as well as the reforms that the government could have carried out. Since the Nakasone-Takeshita reform took place between 1987 and 1989, the last year for which the reform did not affect the data is 1986. Thus we choose 1986 to be the base year of our simulation analysis. We assume that the economy was in a steady state under the prevailing tax mix in 1986, that the entire Nakasone-Takeshita reform took place at the end of 1986, and that the tax reform immediately brought the economy to the adjustment path.

7.2.1 Specification of the Model

We specify the various parameter values of the model, by setting time 0 to be 1986. First, we choose the functional form of the production function to be Cobb-Douglas,

$$(20) \qquad\qquad Y = AK^\alpha (Le^{\mu t})^{1-\alpha},$$

and set the parameter values as

$$(21) \qquad A = 148.16,\ \alpha = 0.31,\ \mu = 0.03,\ \text{and}\ \delta = 0.1513,$$

based on the estimation procedure described in appendix B.

Second, we set

$$\rho^* = 0.046\ (\text{when}\ \theta_r^m = 0.5434),$$
$$= 0.055\ (\text{when}\ \theta_r^m = 0.4465).$$

These parameter values are derived from the assumption that the economy is in a steady-state equilibrium in the base year of 1986. Since $\dot{c} = 0$ at the initial equilibrium, (14), (20), and (21) yield

12. In the present study, we can directly compute cardinal utility levels of the economy both before and after reforms. Thus we could directly examine the rate of change in the utility level caused by the relevant reform instead of comparing consumption wealth. Under our specification of the utility function, however, doubling the budget under a fixed stream of prices will not necessarily double the expenditure minimizing utility level. The specification of σ in the utility function crucially affects the degree of cardinality. Use of equivalent variations may be viewed as a way to avoid this arbitrariness. When the sensitivity analysis is carried out with respect to σ as in Hatta and Nishioka (1990), this becomes particularly important. Note, however, we will specify σ to be one in the main part of our paper, and hence the utility function becomes linear homogeneous. For this particular case, the rates of change in the equivalent variations and in utility levels are equivalent.

$$\rho^* = r(k(0))\,(1 - \theta_r^m)$$
$$= (0.31y(0)/k(0) - \delta)\,(1 - \theta_r^m).$$

The value of ρ^* is obtained by substituting the 1986 values of $y(0)/k(0)$, δ, and θ_r^m. Estimation of θ_r^m is explained in section 7.2.2 as well as in appendix A. Note that, in view of the definition of ρ^*, the corresponding values of ρ are 0.016 and 0.025 when the values of ρ^* are 0.046 and 0.055, respectively.

Third, we set the elasticity of intertemporal substitution equal to $\sigma = 1$. This value is within the range of the estimates (0.3–1.0) of Ogawa (1986) for the Japanese economy. The estimates by Summers (1987) for the U.S. economy are also similar. Moreover, this value was assumed in Jorgenson and Yun (1986a, 1986b) and Hatta and Nishioka (1990) in their simulations. A sensitivity analysis for this parameter for the average tax changes by Hatta and Nishioka (1990) shows that the welfare effect increases monotonically with respect to the value of σ, but it is insensitive when σ takes a value higher than 1.

Fourth, other parameter values and the initial conditions $y(0)/k(0)$ are set as displayed in table 7.1. The data sources of these parameter values are given in the documents published by the Japanese government cited in the list of references. For the data of capital stock, see appendix B. Our estimation of tax rates is discussed in section 7.2.2

Since the rate of return on land is considerably different from that on nonland physical capital in Japan, and since tax structure on land is different from that on nonland physical capital, we exclude land from the definition of capital in the above numerical specifications. Also in calculating capital tax rates below, we ignore land taxes for the same reason.

7.2.2 Tax Rates

Average Tax Rates

The average capital income tax rate θ_r is obtained by dividing the tax revenue by its base. The capital income tax is defined as the sum of interest taxes, dividend taxes, and corporate income tax. The property tax is excluded, since housing and land are excluded from the definition of K in the present model.

Table 7.1   **Parameter Values**

Parameter	Symbol	Value
Elasticity of intertemporal substitution	σ	1
Rate of population growth	n	0.005
Wage tax rate	θ_w	0.23
Average capital income tax rate	θ_r	0.327
Marginal capital income tax rate	θ_r^m	0.4465
		0.5434
Government revenue/GNP ratio	g/y	0.20
Initial value of Y/K	$y(0)/k(0)$	0.81

The base for the capital income tax is the sum of income from interest and dividends, entrepreneurial income (corporate, public), and a part of noncorporate entrepreneurial income. Noncorporate entrepreneurial income is divided into capital and labor income in proportion to the economy-wide share excluding this income. This yields $\theta_r = 0.327$.

The wage tax rate is computed on the assumption that all the tax revenue other than the capital income tax is the wage income tax. Thus this revenue includes excise taxes and others that are not classified as a part of the income tax in the tax code. In our model, however, taxes other than the capital income tax are nondistortional and hence can be treated in the same category as the wage tax. The base for the wage tax is the sum of the compensation for employees and three-fourths of noncorporate entrepreneurial income. Since the revenue-GNP ratio (g/y) is 20.0% according to the Japanese Ministry of Finance (1990, 8), these definitions and the above estimates of θ_r yield $\theta_w = 0.23$.

Effective Marginal Capital Income Tax Rates

In the Nakasone-Takeshita reform of 1987–89 the effective marginal capital income tax rate was changed in three major ways: (1) the corporate income tax rate was reduced, (2) the maximum tax rate on interest income was reduced from 35% to 20%, and (3) the minimum tax rate on interest was increased from 0% to 20%

In appendix A, we estimate the effective marginal capital income tax rate before and after the reform. This estimation shows that the effective marginal capital income tax rate is 46.58% after the reform. For a person who formally faced the 35% marginal interest tax rate, the effective marginal capital income tax rate was 54.34%, and the reform reduced the rate. For a person who formally faced zero marginal interest rate because of the maruyu system, the initial effective marginal capital income tax rate was 44.65%, and the reform increased the rate. In view of the widespread evasion of the interest income tax, it is not possible to determine the percentage of the people for each marginal rate of interest. Rather than attempt to estimate the "representative" marginal capital income tax rate, we will estimate the efficiency effects of the tax reform for the case in which everyone faces the maximum interest tax rate and for the case in which everyone faces the minimum rate. The efficiency effects of the tax reform are bound by these two extreme cases.

7.2.3   Dynamic Efficiency Effects

Estimates of the dynamic efficiency effects of tax reforms are presented in table 7.2 and illustrated in figure 7.2.

The Nakasone-Takeshita Reform

The heavy line in figure 7.2 depicts the value of (19) corresponding to various changes in the effective marginal capital income tax rate when the initial

Table 7.2   **Sensitivity Analysis with Respect to *g/y*: Efficiency Gains from Tax Reforms (%)**

	Marginal Tax Rates after the Reform (θ_r^m)			
	46.58%	32.70%	0%	
(g/y)				
(A)	(B)	(C)	(D)	(D–C)
Initial Marginal Tax Rate 54.34%				
20.00	0.87	1.69	2.15	0.46
30.00	1.05	2.05	2.61	0.56
40.00	1.33	2.61	3.31	0.70
Initial Marginal Tax Rate 44.65%				
20.00	−0.18	0.77	1.31	0.54
30.00	−0.22	0.92	1.58	0.65
40.00	−0.27	1.15	1.97	0.82

Note: The figures show the percentage increase in consumption wealth caused by the respective reforms for the respective initial conditions.

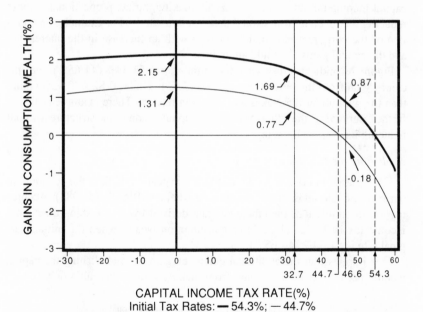

CAPITAL INCOME TAX RATE(%)
Initial Tax Rates: — 54.3%; — 44.7%

Fig. 7.2   Efficiency gains from changes in the capital income tax rate

rate is 54.34%.[13] It indicates that tax reform reduced the effective marginal rate from 54.34% to 46.58% and improved efficiency by 0.87% of consumption wealth in the economy.

The light line in figure 7.2 depicts the value of (19) corresponding to the various changes in the effective rate when the initial rate is 44.65%. It indicates that a tax increase in the effective marginal rate from 44.65% to 46.58% reduces efficiency by 0.18% of consumption wealth in the economy.

Thus the efficiency effect of the changes in the capital income tax rate in the Nakasone-Takeshita reform was in the range between −0.18% and 0.87%. To put it differently, the efficiency cost of eliminating widespread tax evasion through the illegal use of the maruyu system was at most 0.18% of consumption wealth. Since the amount of interest income for which the tax rate was reduced was at least one-third of that for which the tax rate was raised,[14] however, the elimination is likely to have yielded a small efficiency gain.

Making the Capital Income Tax Rate Proportional

The marginal tax rate could be lowered to the level of the initial average capital income tax rate, i.e., 32.7%, by making the tax proportional without reducing the revenue from capital taxation as a whole. For example, an abolition of the corporate income tax coupled with an increase in the interest tax and the capital gains tax could attain this.

Figure 7.2 indicates that when the initial rate is 54.34% (44.65%), the efficiency gain from this reform is 1.69% (0.77%). This is 0.82% (0.95%) more than the gain under the Nakasone-Takeshita reform. There is ample room for further improving the efficiency of the capital income tax structure without reducing its average tax rate.

Abolishing the Capital Income Tax

If the marginal tax rate is reduced to 0% instead of 32.7%, the economy in our model could attain the optimum (see Abel and Blanchard 1983). According to our simulation, the efficiency gain derived from abolishing the capital income tax is 2.15% (1.31%) of consumption wealth when the initial marginal rate is 54.34% (44.65%).

This implies that the additional efficiency gain from abolishing the capital income tax in excess of the gain from making it proportional is only 0.46%

---

13. See Hatta and Nishioka (1990, nn. 10, 12) for the computational method.

14. According to Ministry of Finance (1989), interest income that was taxed 20% or higher was ¥ 3.3 trillion, while untaxable interest income was ¥ 16.5 trillion in 1987. If we assume that only 60% of the formally untaxed interest income is now taxed, the amount of interest income for which the tax rate was reduced was one-third of that for which the tax rate was raised.

Note that the above figure of untaxable interest income contains interests on zaikei savings, but the balance of zaikei savings is only 7% of maruyu savings, as is reported by the Bank of Japan (1987, 160). Thus our assumption that 40% of the formally untaxed interest income is still untaxed implies that we are assuming that the balance of the savings by the elderly is substantial.

(0.54%), i.e., approximately 0.5% of the consumption wealth. Thus a large portion of the efficiency gain obtained from abolishing the capital income tax could be attained simply by making the capital income tax proportional without reducing the revenue from the capital income tax.

Since the present study assumes a fixed labor supply, our estimate of additional efficiency gains ignores the efficiency loss due to the revenue-compensating increase in the wage rate. Hence even 0.5% is an overestimation of the efficiency gain obtainable from eliminating capital income tax as a tax base. This implies that eliminating capital income as a tax base hardly gives additional efficiency gains.

7.2.4   Sensitivity Analysis

The sensitivity analysis with respect to σ for reductions of average tax rates in Hatta and Nishioka (1990) showed that assuming a value higher than 1 hardly changes the efficiency effect but that assuming a lower value makes the effect smaller. This implies that our estimates above are the upper bounds of these effects.

Iwata, Suzuki, and Yoshida (1987) estimated the rates of depreciation of various types of capital for Japan in 1983. Our estimate of the rate of depreciation, which is 15.13%, is obtained as an aggregate of these rates weighted by the capital stock of each type. This estimate of depreciation rate is much higher than that of the United States, presumably because of a higher Japanese growth rate. A lower depreciation rate would reduce effective marginal capital income tax rates, as can be seen from the comparison between the estimate of Kikutani and Tachibanaki and those of others in table 7A.2. Thus lower depreciation rates would further reduce our estimate of the efficiency effect of the Nakasone-Takeshita reform, reinforcing our qualitative conclusion.

The sensitivity analysis with respect to the share of government spending is presented in tables 7.2 for the two initial marginal tax rates; the range of the efficiency effect of the Nakasone-Takeshita reform would be −0.22% and 1.05% if g/y were 30%, while it would be −0.27% and 1.33% if g/y were 40%. Thus the change in g/y has rather mild impacts on the efficiency effect of a given tax reform.

The tables also indicate that the additional efficiency gain brought about by abolishing the capital income tax in excess of making it simply proportional is approximately 0.6% of consumption wealth when g/y is 30% or less.

7.3   Notes on the Literature

Different measures of efficiency gains have been employed in the literature. In equation (19) we are concerned with the "rate of increase in consumption wealth" as defined in that equation. Goulder and Thalmann (1990), however, examine "the rate of increase in full wealth," where full wealth is the sum of consumption wealth and the present value of leisure time. Jorgenson and Yun

(1990), on the other hand, use a measure whose numerator is the same as that of Goulder and Thalmann and whose denominator is "private national wealth," which is full wealth minus human wealth (i.e., the present value of leisure and the wage income streams). Thus their percentage figures overestimate the rate of increase either in full wealth or in private wealth. (See their footnote 27.) Although the ratio of private national wealth to full wealth is not available in Jorgenson and Yun (1986a, 1986b, 1990), it is 5.6% in Goulder and Thalmann (1990).[15] We will thus transform Jorgenson and Yun's percentage figures into the rate of increase in full wealth by multiplying by 0.056.

We are now in a position to compare our simulation results with those of the literature.

First, Fullerton, Henderson, and Mackie (1987), Jorgenson and Yun (1990), and Goulder and Thalmann (1990) estimate the dynamic efficiency effects of the U.S. Tax Reform Act of 1986. While the Nakasone-Takeshita reform simply reduced the statutory rate of corporate tax across the board, the U.S. reform reduced intratemporal tax wedges among different capital goods. Thus these articles use large-scale simulation models that allow different marginal tax rates on heterogeneous capital goods. Fullerton, Henderson, and Mackie (1987) and Jorgenson and Yun (1990) show that the efficiency improvement caused by the reduced intratemporal tax wedges outweigh the efficiency loss caused by the increased intertemporal tax wedge, while Goulder and Thalmann (1990) show the opposite. The former models may yield higher efficiency gains from reductions of intratemporal distortions than the latter, because the former assume an instantaneous shift of capital assets between different types and sectors, while the latter does not.

Second, Jorgenson and Yun (1990) show that elimination of all intratemporal wedges increases full wealth by 16.7% of private national wealth, or by 0.96% of full wealth. Goulder and Thalmann (1990, 29) show that a hypothetical, revenue-neutral reform that "combines housing integration with a 30 percent reduction (on average) of marginal effective tax rates" increases full wealth by 0.5%.

These estimates of the gains are smaller than our estimate of the gains from making the capital income tax rate proportional for Japan, which is between 0.77% and 1.69%. This may be caused by the fact that the prereform effective marginal tax rate is higher in Japan than in the United States.

Third, Jorgenson and Yun (1986a, 1986b) study the dynamic efficiency effect of making all the marginal tax rates of heterogeneous capital goods zero. They show that expensing investment expenditure increases full wealth by 26–27% of private national wealth, or 1.5% of full wealth, if the resulting

15. According to Goulder and Thalmann (1990, 45), the private national wealth (financial wealth in their terminology) is 20/355 = 0.056 of full wealth (present value of full consumption). See page 43 n. 1, for their terminology.

revenue loss is financed by an increase in the wage tax. Jorgenson and Yun (1990) also estimate an almost identical percentage increase in efficiency gain from a reform that removes "intertemporal tax wedges on all assets."[16]

These efficiency gains are in the same order of magnitude as our estimate of the gain from abolishing the capital income tax, which is between 1.31% and 2.15% of consumption wealth. The closeness is purely accidental, however. The prereform Japanese effective marginal tax rate is higher than that of the United States, but intrasectoral distortions, especially between business capital and housing, are greater in the United States.[17] It appears that these two factors offset each other to yield similar total efficiency effects.

Fourth, several authors study the dynamic efficiency effect of abolishing the capital income tax in a single-capital-good model where the capital income tax is assumed to be already proportional in the prereform equilibrium. Employing an overlapping generation model with endogenous labor supply, Auerbach, Kotlikoff, and Skinner (1983) and Auerbach and Kotlikoff (1987) estimate a *negative* efficiency gain associated with the abolition of the capital income tax accompanied by a revenue-offsetting increase in the wage tax rate. This implies that the efficiency gain obtained from reducing intertemporal distortions is smaller than the efficiency loss from increasing the distortion in the labor-consumption choice. Employing a dynasty model with an endogenous labor supply for the Japanese economy, Hatta and Nishioka (1989) estimate that the dynamic efficiency gain from abolishing the capital income tax would be 0.08% of the consumption wealth.

Employing a similar model with fixed labor supply, Hatta and Nishioka (1990) estimate that this gain is around 0.43% of consumption wealth. This number is remarkably similar to our estimate in the present paper that the difference between the efficiency gain from abolishing the capital income tax in excess of the gain from making the tax proportional is just about 0.5% of consumption wealth. This suggests that average tax rate models, as simple as they are, are sufficiently powerful for the purpose of analyzing the relative efficiency of different tax bases.

7.4   Concluding Remarks

We have evaluated the efficiency effects of changing the effective marginal capital income tax rate by simulating the Nakasone-Takeshita reform and a few alternative reforms.

16. Their estimate of the efficiency gain is $3,853.9 billion, while the nominal value of the U.S. private national wealth at the beginning of 1987 was $15,920.2 billion (Jorgenson and Yun 1990, S189, S182). The rate of increase in the full wealth is obtained from footnote 17.

17. In particular, the large discrepancies between the marginal tax rate between housing and other capital goods in the United States, which do not exist in Japan, appear a major cause of inefficiencies in the U.S. tax system. See Jorgenson and Yun (1990), Goulder and Thalmann (1990), and Skinner (1990) on the importance of the wedge between the housing sector and the business sector.

The revenue-neutral changes in the capital income tax rates in the Nakasone-Takeshita reform eliminated a source of major tax evasion—the maruyu system. Our estimates show that this reform was accompanied by an efficiency gain of between -0.18% and 0.87% of consumption wealth. We may conclude, therefore, that the Nakasone-Takeshita reform eliminated a major source of tax evasion with relatively little efficiency cost, if any.

Our simulation also indicates that the marginal capital income tax rate could have been reduced to the level of the average tax rate to yield an efficiency gain of between 0.77% and 1.69% of consumption wealth, while maintaining a constant level of revenue from the capital income tax. The additional efficiency gain that could be brought about from abolishing the capital income tax is 0.5% of consumption wealth, and even this is likely to be an overestimation of the gain. This implies that eliminating capital income as a tax base yields relatively small additional efficiency gains.

Appendix A
Estimation of Effective Marginal Capital Income Tax Rates

In this appendix, we estimate the aggregate effective marginal capital income tax rates for the 1986 Japanese economy. In this estimation, the marginal interest rate that firms face are not given exogenously, but will be derived from the data on production function and tax rates.

Marginal Capital Income Tax Rate and Interest Rate

From equation (8), the effective marginal capital income tax rate can be expressed as

$$(A1) \qquad \theta^m_r = \frac{r - s}{r},$$

where r is the before-tax real rate of return on marginal investment and s is the after-tax real rate of return that savers face.[18] At the initial equilibrium, the value of r is derived from the production function. Once s is determined, then θ^m_r at the initial equilibrium can be estimated.

The relationship between s and the marginal nominal interest rate i is given by

$$(A2) \qquad s = (1 - \theta_i)i - \pi,$$

18. The basic reference for the concept of the effective marginal capital income tax is King and Fullerton (1984).

where θ_i is the marginal personal tax rate on interest income and π the rate of inflation. Statistical data are amply available for average interest rates but not for marginal rates; hence we have to estimate the value of i.

The profit maximization condition requires the real rate of return, r, to be equal to the capital cost:

(A3)
$$r = \frac{(1 - A(\iota))(\iota + \delta - \pi)}{1 - \theta_c} - \delta,$$

where ι is the nominal discount rate that investing firms face, θ_c is the marginal corporate tax rate, and $A(\iota)$ is the present value of grants and tax allowances per unit of investment (the functional form of which is to be defined later).

The nominal discount rate is different for each source of finance. In 1983 (Iwata, Suzuki, and Yoshida 1987), 49% of corporate investment was financed by retained earnings, 48% by debt, and 3% by newly issued shares. Thus we approximate the nominal discount rate by

$$\iota = 0.49 \, \iota_e + 0.48 \, \iota_b + 0.03 \, \iota_n,$$

where ι_e is the nominal discount rate for retained earnings, ι_b is that for debt financing, and ι_n is that for new share issues. In turn, ι_e, ι_b, and ι_n may be defined as

$$\iota_e = \frac{i \, (1 - \theta_i)}{(1 - \theta_z)},$$

$$\iota_b = i \, (1 - \theta_c),$$

and

$$\iota_n = \frac{i(1 - \theta_i)}{\lambda \, (1 - \theta_d)},$$

where λ is the opportunity cost of retained earnings in terms of gross dividends foregone, while θ_i, θ_d, θ_c, and θ_z are the tax rates on interests, dividends, corporate income, and accrued capital gains, respectively. Combining the above three equations, we obtain the following:

(A4) $\iota = i\{0.49 \, \dfrac{1 - \theta_i}{(1 - \theta_z)} + 0.48 \, (1 - \theta_c) + 0.03 \, \dfrac{1 - \theta_i}{\lambda \, (1 - \theta_d)}\}$.

We are now in a position to estimate i at the initial equilibrium. Since r is known, we can solve for ι from (A3) once the functional form of $A(\iota)$ and other parameters are given. By substituting this solution for ι in (A4), we can solve for i from (A4). In view of (A1) and (A2), we thus find the value of the marginal capital income tax rate at the initial equilibrium.

A tax reform will not change r immediately because K and L do not shift instantaneously. By changing the tax parameters but not r in equation (A3), we get a new ι. This and (A4) together yield the new interest rate after the tax reform. The new marginal capital income tax rate is similarly obtained as above.

Definition of the Function $A(\iota)$

Let us now define the function $A(\iota)$ for Japan by simplifying the formulation of Kikutani and Tachibanaki (1987). Let ω_1, ω_2, and ω_3 be the shares of the cost of assets that are depreciated by declining balance, by straight line, and by the first year write-off, respectively. Let $\theta_c A_1$, $\theta_c A_2$, and $\theta_c A_3$ be the present values of tax saving from the respective depreciation methods. Then the present value of all tax allowances, denoted by A, satisfies

$$A \equiv \theta_c \{\omega_1 A_1 + \omega_2 A_2 + \omega_3 (A_3 + \xi)\} \,,$$

where ξ is the proportion of special depreciation. In turn, A_1, A_2, and A_3 may be defined as follows:

$$A_1 = \frac{a (1 - e^{-(a + \iota)T})}{a + \iota} \,,$$

$$A_2 = \frac{(1 - v) (1 - e^{-\iota T})}{\iota T} \,,$$

$$A_3 = \frac{(1 - v) (1 - e^{-\iota T*})}{\iota T*} \,,$$

where a is the rate of tax depreciation on an exponential basis, v the rate of residual value of the asset, T the tax lifetime, and $T*$ a depreciable period after the first-year special write-off($T* \equiv T(1 - \xi - v)/(1 - v)$). From the last four equations A can be expressed as a function of ι, and this defines the function $A(\iota)$.

Parameters ω_3, ξ, a, v, T, and λ are aggregated from the data provided in Iwata, Suzuki, and Yoshida (1987) by taking a weighted average of the capital stock share. Parameters ω_1 and ω_2 are obtained by combining the data provided by Iwata et al. and by Kikutani and Tachibanaki (1987). These parameter values are presented in table 7A.1.

Estimates

Our estimates of the marginal capital income tax rates for 1986 are presented in table 7A.2 along with the estimates of Iwata, Suzuki, and Yoshida (1987) for 1983 and Kikutani and Tachibanaki (1987) for 1980. Our estimate is very close to that of Iwata et al. As Iwamoto (1989) reveals, different specifications of δ and π explain most of the difference between the estimates of Iwata et al. and Kikutani and Tachibanaki. Similar specification of these two key parameters in Iwata et al. and ours, therefore, explains the similarity of the estimates of the marginal tax rates between these two articles.[19]

Table 7A.1 **Parameter Values for Computing Marginal Tax Rates**

Parameter	Value	Parameter	Value
θ_d	0.20	ξ	0.3499
θ_z	0.00	a	0.1564
π	0.014	T	19.28
ω_1	0.72	ν	0.1
ω_2	0.18	λ	1.1
ω_3	0.099		

Table 7A.2 **Estimates of the Effective Marginal Capital Income Tax Rates (%)**

	Present Paper			Iwata, Suzuki, Yoshida 1983	Kikutani, Tachibanaki 1980
	1986	1986	1986 (after reform)		
θ_i	0	35	20	20.02	18.85
π	1.4	1.4	1.4	0.6	8.25
δ	15.13	15.13	15.13	15.13	5.38
θ_c	52.92	52.92	49.98	56.83	52.61
θ_r^m	44.65	54.34	46.58	47.19	9.6

Appendix B
Estimation of the Production Function

Parameter values (21) are based on the following maximum likelihood estimation of (20) obtained under the assumption that the error term obeys the first order autoregressive model:

$$\ln (Y/L) = 4.9983 + 0.31353 \ln (K/L) + 0.019669 \, t,$$
$$(6.4504) \quad (2.7653) \quad\quad\quad (2.2414)$$

$$R^2 = 0.998262, \bar{R}^2 = 0.998058,$$

$$F = 4450.25, SER = 0.0230643, DW = 1.4580.$$

From this we obtain $\alpha = 0.31$, $A = 148.16$, and $\mu = 0.03$.

19. The cited estimate of Iwata, Suzuki, and Yoshida in table 7A.2 is based on their assumption that the capital cost is 10%. By accident, this is close to our value, 9.98%, which is derived from our estimated parameter values of the production function. This gives an additional reason for the similarity of the estimates θ_m of the two articles. Note that Iwamoto (1991) shows that the marginal capital income tax rate is lower than the estimate of Iwata, Suzuki, and Yoshida (1987) when land is included in capital.

In the above estimate, fiscal year data from 1968 to 1987 are used. The data sources are as follows: Y is from Economic Planning Agency, *Annual Report on National Accounts*, L is obtained by multiplying the employed labor force from *Monthly Report on the Labor Force Survey* and hours of labor from *Monthly Labor Survey* (both Ministry of Labor), and K is obtained by multiplying the capital stock data from Economic Planning Agency, *Capital Stock of Private Enterprises,* and the utilization ratio obtained from Ministry of International Trade and Industry, *Industrial Statistics Monthly.*

References

Abel, A. B., and O. J. Blanchard. 1983. An Intertemporal Model of Saving and Investment. *Econometrica* 51(3): 675–92.

Auerbach, A. J. 1991. Retrospective Capital Gains Taxation. *American Economic Review* 81 (1): 167–78.

Auerbach, A. J., and L. J. Kotlikoff. 1987. *Dynamic Fiscal Policy.* Cambridge: Cambridge University Press.

Auerbach, A. J., L. J. Kotlikoff, and J. Skinner. 1983. The Efficiency Gains from Dynamic Tax Reform. *International Economic Review* 24 (2): 81–100.

Bank of Japan. 1987. *Economic Statistics Annual.* Tokyo.

Chamley, C. 1981. The Welfare Cost of Capital Income Taxation in a Growing Economy. *Journal of Political Economy* 89(3): 468–96.

Economic Federation of Japan (Keidanren). 1984. Senshin Kakkoku no Kigyo Zeisei to Zei Futan (The corporate tax system and tax burdens of advanced countries). *Keizai Shiryo* 350, Tokyo.

Economic Planning Agency. 1987. *Keizai Youran.* Tokyo.

———. 1990a. *Capital Stock of Private Enterprises.* Tokyo.

———. 1990b. *Annual Report on National Accounts.* Tokyo.

Fullerton, D., Y. Henderson, and J. Mackie. 1987. Investment Allocation and Growth under the Tax Reform Act of 1986. Washington, D.C.: Office of Tax Analysis, U.S. Department of Treasury, Compendium of Tax Research.

Goulder, L., and P. Thalmann. 1990. Approaches to Efficient Capital Taxation: Leveling the Playing Field vs. Living by the Golden Rule. NBER Working Paper no. 3559. Cambridge, Mass.: National Bureau of Economic Research.

Hatta, T. 1987. Zen Shisan Shotoku no Ichiritsu Bunri Kazei (Flat tax on capital income). *Ekonomisuto* (September 15): 36–43.

———. 1988. *Chokusetsuzei Kaikaku* (Reform of direct taxation). Tokyo: Nihon Keizai Shimbun Sha.

Hatta, T., and H. Nishioka. 1989. Saiteki Shisan Shotokuzeika no Keizai Kousei to Shihon Chikuseki (Economic welfare and capital accumulation under optimum capital income tax). *Nichizeiken Ronshu* 10 (December): 183–237.

———. 1990. Efficiency Gains from Reducing the Average Capital Income Tax Rate in Japan. Paper presented at the NBER Conference on Japanese Corporate Financial Behavior, Cambridge, August 3.

Iwamoto, Y. 1989. Shihon Shotoku eno Kokusai Kazei no Shomondai (Issues in international taxation on capital income). Manuscript, Osaka University.

———. 1991. The Japanese Tax Reform and the Cost of Capital. Kyoto Institute of Economic Research, Discussion Paper no. 327.

Iwata, K., I., Suzuki, and A. Yoshida. 1987. Setsubitoshi no Shihon Kosuto to Zeisei (Capital cost of investment and taxation). *Keizaibunseki* 105: 1–72.

Jorgenson, D. W., and K.-Y. Yun. 1986a. The Efficiency of Capital Allocation. *Scandinavian Journal of Economics* 88 (1): 85–107.

———. 1986b. Tax Policy and Capital Allocation. *Scandinavian Journal of Economics* 88 (2): 355–77.

———. 1990. Tax Reform and U.S. Economic Growth. *Journal of Political Economy* 98 (5): S151–93.

Judd, K. L. 1987. The Welfare Cost of Factor Taxation in a Perfect Foresight Model. *Journal of Political Economy* 95(4): 675–709.

Kikutani, T., and T. Tachibanaki. 1987. The Taxation of Income from Capital in Japan: Historical Perspectives and Policy Implications. Kyoto Institute of Economic Research, Discussion Paper no. 242.

King, M. A., and D. Fullerton, eds. 1984. *The Taxation of Income from Capital: A Comparative Study of the United States, the United Kingdom, Sweden, and West Germany.* Chicago: University of Chicago Press.

Local Tax Association (Chiho Zeimu Kyokai). 1987, 1989. *Kaisei Chiho Zeisei Shokai* (Detailed explanations of the local tax reform). Tokyo.

"Maruyu" Akuyo 5600 Oku Yen (Tax evasion through "maruyu" reaches ¥560 billion). 1983. *Nihon Keizai Shimbun* (Tokyo), October 8.

Ministry of Finance. 1988. *Showa 63nen Kaisei Zeiho no Subete* (The tax reform act of 1988). Tokyo: Printing Office.

———. 1989. *Zei no Hanashi* (A tale of tax). Tokyo: Printing Office.

———. 1990, 1991. *Zaisei Kinyuu Toukei Geppou, Sozei Tokusyu* (Public finance statistics monthly, special tax issue). Tokyo.

Ministry of International Trade and Industry. *Industrial Statistics Monthly.* Tokyo.

Ministry of Labor. *Monthly Report on the Labor Force Survey.* Tokyo.

———. *Monthly Labor Survey.* Tokyo.

Nakatani, I., T. Inoue, Y. Iwamoto, and M. Fukushige. 1986. *Wagakuni Kigyo Zeisei no Hyoka to Kadai* (Evaluation and problem of Japan's corporate tax system). Tokyo: Kigyo Katsuryoku Kenkyusho.

Nishioka, H. 1989. An Efficiency Evaluation of the Japanese Tax System. *Economic Studies Quarterly* 40(3): 264–75.

———. 1991. Nakasone-Takeshita Zeisei Kaikaku no Shisan Shotoku ni Kansuru Zeishu Koka (Effects of the Nakasone-Takeshita tax reform on revenue from capital income taxes). Manuscript, University of Osaka Prefecture.

Noguchi, Y. 1987. Koreika Shakai dewa "Zozei" mo Hituyo (Tax should be increased in the high average age society). *Seiron* (September); 96–101.

Ogawa, Kazuo. 1986. Nihon ni Okeru Kojo Shotoku Kasetsu no Kensyo (A test of permanent income hypothesis in Japan). *Kokumin Keizai Zasshi* (Kobe University) 154 (3): 63–85.

Skinner, J. 1990. The Dynamic Efficiency Cost of Not Taxing Housing. NBER Working Paper no. 3454. Cambridge, Mass.: National Bureau of Economic Research.

Summers, L. H. 1987. Tax Policy, the Rate of Return, and Private Savings. Manuscript, January.

Vickrey, W. 1939. Averaging Income for Income Tax Purposes. *Journal of Political Economy* 49: 379–97.

Comment   Medhi Krongkaew

I have to start by saying that I am not a practitioner of neoclassical economic modeling. I rarely need to depend on it in my work in Thailand. This is not to say that it is not useful or relevant. It's just that we can find a better way to explain to the public at large or convince policymakers than using neoclassical modeling.

But perhaps this neoclassic paper by Tatsuo Hatta and Hideki Nishioka is different. It addresses a very pertinent issue, how much the economy gained from the reduction of distortions associated with capital income taxation.

This paper is concise yet comprehensive. It explains the steps involved and procedures used clearly and carefully. It is a very neat paper, and the authors should be congratulated for this.

I have several comments that might help to improve the paper. I will separate my comments into two parts: those on the technical aspects of the paper and those on the political economic aspects of the paper.

I don't find anything unusual about the model itself, but I know that for practitioners of neoclassical modeling the realism of assumptions is unimportant as long as the model's predictive power is assured. A general reader would find that the assumptions here are unacceptable: the consumer is an infinitely long-lived representative agent; the consumer has no leisure-commodity substitution; the household has perfect foresight; and the time path for future prices is freely visible. Of course some could try to relax some of the restrictive assumptions to make them more realistic, or put in more scenarios that might effect the outcomes of the study—and this is what Hatta and Nishioka might attempt to do. But since some parameter values are not actual but estimated, the more adjustments you make, the more estimations for parameter values you have to make. That may lead you farther from the true picture of the situation rather than nearer to it. I don't know whether we could call this the second-best theorem applied to model estimations.

The second comment has to do with the estimation techniques used in the study. In the neoclassical model where the economy is divided into two sectors, labor and capital, the measurement problems can become acute without a good statistical data base. Measuring labor is easy enough, but measuring capital may be a little tricky. I am not quite sure how reliable the statistics used by Hatta and Nishioka to measure capital inputs are. There seem to be several roundabout ways to get to the size of K. You used the sampled survey data from *Capital Stock of Private Enterprises* and the *National Wealth Survey of Japan* and multiply that by survey data on utilization ratio from *Industrial Statistics Monthly*. How reliable are these data and your method? If my understanding of your technique is correct, you have to work backward through the estimated depreciation rate.

Medhi Krongkaew is a lecturer on the Faculty of Economics, Thammasat University, Bangkok.

Third, the use of 1985 as the base year begs the question whether it is a typical or representative year that will not unnecessarily distort the final findings of the study. I don't know what happened in Japan during that year, but for countries in Southeast Asia, 1985 was an unusually bad year. Recession had hit many countries in the area. We have high growth economies such as Singapore and Malaysia experiencing negative growth rates for the first time in their modern history. In Thailand we still had positive growth rate but very small. In an unusual situation such as this, I don't know whether using 1985 as a base year in this study would affect the result so much that the use of another year's data is called for.

Fourth, most estimated values of parameters look reasonable. The rate of population growth in Japan is OK; the wage tax rate of 12% is OK; the import and capital income tax of 25% is OK; but the ratio of government revenue (from both wage and capital income) to GNP of 11.7% is too small. This should be explained.

Finally, the difference in the magnitude of the efficiency gains from the reduction in capital income tax between this study and the studies by other researchers, especially that of Jorgenson and Yun, requires further investigation. I tend to agree with the findings by Hatta and Nishioka that the efficiency gain from capital income tax abolishment is only 0.5% of the net present of future private consumption. But since this contrasts fantastically with the finding by Jorgenson and Yun that a similar tax change would lead to an increase of 25% of the national private wealth, there must be something wrong somewhere, if not in the modeling, then in the statistical data. This point should be considered more carefully.

This leads me to a comment on the political economics aspects of capital income tax change. Hatta and Nishioka confirms my existing belief that tax on capital income does not much affect the investment capital accumulation, because the capital owners can always find ways to shift the burden somewhere else. Therefore his finding that the efficiency gain from capital income abolition is only 0.5% of future consumption may lend support to a policy position against giving additional incentives to capital owners at the expense of wage earners. Perhaps the finding of John Whalley that taxes have little contribution to growth could also be used to support said position, although in a reverse fashion: if tax doesn't help, it doesn't hurt either.

The suggestion that the capital income tax be abolished and the revenues foregone recouped through increase in wage tax may be casually made in this paper or similar papers. But we all know that in actual practice this is a very difficult undertaking indeed. On many occasions we may find that a partial reform or revision of existing tax may not lead to the desired result, but that only partial reform is politically feasible. The question is whether you should wait until the situation and timing are right for a total reform or be content with piecemeal changes that are slow and ineffective. This kind of problem is not considered in most neoclassical papers.

The political economic issues governing capital income and wage income may be more sensitive than what the paper such as Hatta's and Nishioka's would indicate. In a country where the growth is good but the distribution is quite unequal, such as Thailand, the capital sector obviously benefits more from growth than does the wage sector. And wealth begets political power to protect and increase wealth. Any drastic, or I could even say blatant, effort to cut capital income tax and substitute the revenue loss by wage tax for the sake of efficiency would certainly lead to protest and political upheaval. So one needs to be very careful in coming to a conclusion that may lead to unintended revolution.

Despite these comments I still think that Hatta and Nishioka have done a very good job. They will have to continue to fight with other scholars such as Yuan, who has done similar studies with quite different results.

Comment   Assaf Razin

The paper by Tatsuo Hatta and Hideki Nishioka provides estimates for the macroeconomic effects of a permanent change in the tax rate on capital income within the framework of a neoclassical growth model. The authors calibrate the basic parameters of the model and initial values to fit Japan's economic structure, based on 1985 figures. In their model the optimal capital income tax is zero, as in Chamley.[1] They estimate that the efficiency gain of a decline in the capital income tax from 50 percent to 25 percent, while adjusting the wage tax rate so as to maintain a balanced government budget, is at most less than one-half of a percent of consumption. This low estimate is in the spirit of the low estimate for the gains from consumption smoothing in Lucas.[2]

Two potentially important mechanisms, which could augment the gains from such a reform, are missing, however. First, the model abstracts from investment in *human capital*. Evidently, a tax on capital income discriminates against capital accumulation in human as well as physical form, because of the double taxation of saving, and against investment in physical capital in particular due to a substitution of human for physical capital. The wage tax on the other hand distorts the incentives to invest in human capital.[3] Both the

Assaf Razin is the Daniel Ross Professor of International Economics at Tel Aviv University and a research associate of the National Bureau of Economic Research.

1. Christopher Chamley, "The Welfare Cost of Capital Income Taxation in a Growing Economy," *Journal of Political Economy* 89(3)(1981): 468–96.

2. Robert E. Lucas, *Models of Business Cycles* (New York: Basil Blackwell, 1987).

3. Marc Nerlove, Assaf Razin, Efraim Sadka, and Robert K. von Weizsacker, "Tax Policy, Investments in Human and Physical Capital and Productivity," NBER Working Paper no. 3531 (Cambridge, Mass.: National Bureau of Economic Research, 1990).

volume and the mix of capital accumulations are affected by a revenue-neutral shift from capital income to labor income tax in ways that may significantly change the welfare implications of the tax reform. It is not a priori clear whether the welfare-improving reform should require such a tax shift at all. Second, it is commonplace that investments in human and physical capital augment not only the individual investor's earning capacity but also the economy's stock of knowledge. Incorporating this *externality* into the model tends to enlarge the gains from tax restructurings such as the ones considered in the paper.

8   The Role of Tax Policy in Korea's Economic Growth

Irene Trela and John Whalley

8.1 Introduction

This paper both summarizes and expands on our earlier work (Trela and Whalley 1991), which seeks to investigate the contribution of outward-oriented policies to Korean growth, through induced intersectoral resource transfers and impacts on effort and labor supply in both the agricultural (rural) and manufacturing (urban) sectors. Our earlier paper focused on the role tax policies played in Korean growth in stimulating intersectoral resource transfers toward export-oriented industries in a general equilibrium model with endogenous effort determination. The expansion described here involves disaggregating the manufacturing sector into two subindustries—import substituting and export promoting. This allows us to capture the resource reallocation effects not only between agriculture and manufacturing but also between import-substituting and export-oriented manufacturing.

The themes that emerge from the model calculations are similar to those from earlier work—that one should look beyond tax policy for the main factors underlying strong Korean growth. Model calculations portray the tax component of outward-oriented policies as accounting for 3.0 to 4.2 percent of Korean growth between 1962 and 1982, and only 3.6 percent between 1962 and 1972. These are less than half of those reported from the earlier model. The divergence stems from the additional resource reallocation effects within

Irene Trela is a research associate at the University of Western Ontario. John Whalley is professor of economics at the University of Western Ontario and a research associate of the National Bureau of Economic Research.

This paper draws heavily on an earlier paper first presented at a World Bank Conference on Taxation and Development, Washington, D.C., March 28–30, 1990, and reprinted in *Tax Policy in Developing Countries,* ed. J. Khalilzadeh-Shirazi and A. Shah (Washington, D.C.: World Bank, 1991). We are both grateful to organizers of the World Bank Conference for permission to draw on the earlier work here, and to Anne Krueger and other NBER/KDI conference participants for helpful comments.

manufacturing that are captured in the expanded model. Since marginal product pricing is used in both manufacturing sectors, this generates a common effort level in the two sectors. A reallocation of labor within manufacturing and from agriculture to manufacturing, encouraged through the promotion of export-oriented manufactures, thereby has a less stimulative effect on growth than if labor were transferred only from the low-effort agricultural sector to the high-effort manufacturing sector, as is the case in the two-sector model.

The relatively modest role for taxes in Korean growth our model projects mirrors what we portray as the robustness of Korean growth performance to various policy regime switches, including tax policy. High savings rates (amounting to almost 38 percent of GDP in 1988 [Park 1989, table 3]) and high investment rates have both been central to Korean growth performance, as have significant transfers of labor from rural to urban sectors, especially in the early phases of growth. What the paper suggests, therefore, is that tax policy in Korea should be seen as accommodating high growth in Korea, rather than being one of the key factors driving it.

8.2   Korean Policy Regimes and Their Incentive Effects for Exports

Existing literature attributes much of the success of Korea's economic growth to a policy shift in the 1960s away from import substitution toward export promotion.[1] This is not to say that Korea's growth rates can be explained solely by changes in trade policy. In fact, the policy structure in Korea is substantially more complex than this, and there have been three distinct regime switches since the early 1960s. Growth in Korea has been remarkably resilient to these switches in policy regime and the changes in tax policy that were part of them.

Taxes played their role as part of the early outward-oriented phase of economic expansion (1961–72) through the rebating of cascading sales and excise taxes, and the rebating of a portion of corporate taxes to export industries. In the second phase (1973–79), when the growth of heavy and chemical industries (primary metals, shipbuilding, machinery, chemicals, and electronics) was being promoted, the tax system was used to facilitate sector-specific capital accumulation. As protection has come down in the trade liberalization and structural adjustment phase (1979 onward), duty remissions have become progressively less important. A number of the tax rebate schemes linked to exports have also been eliminated over the last ten to fifteen years. In the process, the Korean tax system has matured from a relatively narrowly based system, focused on traditional excisables, trade, and other taxes, to a system

---

1. See Brown (1973), Hasan and Rao (1979), Krueger (1979), Kwack (1988), and Scitovsky (1985). The results from Chenery, Robinson, and Syrquin (1986, table 11–3) are opposite to the conclusions from these studies and seem to indicate that outward-oriented policies have been relatively unimportant to Korean growth.

with a broadly based value-added tax (VAT) accounting for a major portion of revenues, along with income and corporate taxes with much wider coverage and more sophisticated administration than in most other developing countries.[2]

Establishing the effects of these measures and how they have changed over time is difficult. For the model analyses we report here, we draw heavily on a recent study by Kim (1988) that estimated the export subsidy effect of a range of tax and nontax policies in Korea over the period 1958–83 (see table 8.1). We use these estimates in our subsequent model calculations of the effects of Korean tax policies on outward orientation and growth. Kim includes only those policies for which consistent time-series data were available and which are quantitatively significant. These include direct cash subsidies, exchange rate premiums, interest subsidies, indirect tax exemptions, tariff exemptions, and direct tax reductions (exclusive of accelerated depreciation provisions and reserve funds both for developing export markets and for covering export losses).

The export subsidy effect of direct tax exemptions is the difference between tax liabilities in the absence of any such exemptions and actual direct tax payments. The incentive effect of different interest rates can be determined in an analogous fashion. The interest subsidy is the difference between the interest rate paid at the nonpreferential commercial bank lending rate and the interest actually paid. Similar calculations can be made for the various other tax and nontax export incentives.

Several interesting observations flow from table 8.1. Exchange rate policy, via the foreign exchange premiums, played an important role in stimulating exports during the late 1950s and early 1960s, before being changed in 1965. Furthermore, the largest export incentives were during the 1960s and early 1970s, during which time the effects of export promotion schemes notably increased. Beginning in the early 1970s, however, the government tried to reduce the scope of export incentives. Kim's estimates clearly show fluctuations in these subsidies from 29.6 percent in 1971 to a low of 16.7 percent in 1975 and, with subsequent rises, to a high of 21.3 percent in 1980. Gross export subsidies in this data declined from 136.2 percent of the official exchange rate in 1960 to 18.1 percent in 1961, mainly because of the substantial depreciation of the won and the resulting rapid increase in exports. Net export subsidies per U.S. dollar declined from 23 percent of the official exchange rate in 1964 to about 4–7 percent during 1965–67, mainly because of the abolition of the export-import link system.

Table 8.1 also clearly indicates the growing importance of tax policy as part of the outward-oriented strategy of the 1970s. Direct tax reductions for exporters were consistently small and had disappeared by the early 1970s. But indirect tax exemptions for exporters grew from approximately one-third of

---

2. See the discussion in Han (1986).

Table 8.1   Estimates of Net and Gross Exports Subsidies per Dollar of Export for Korea, 1958–83 (annual averages)

Year	Official Exchange Rate (won/$) (1)	Various Export Subsidies Calculated per U.S. Dollar of Export (won)								Ratio to Exchange Rate (%)	
		Direct Cash Subsidies (2)	Export Dollar Premium (3)	Direct Tax Reductions for Exporters (4)	Interest Rate Preference for Exporters (5)	Net Export Subsidies[a] (6 = 2+3+4+5)	Indirect Tax Exemptions for Exporters (7)	Tariff Rebates for Exporters (8)	Gross Export Subsidies[a] (9 = 6+7+8)	Net Export Subsidies (10 = 6/1)	Gross Export Subsidies (11 = 9/1)
1958	50.0	0.0	64.0	—	1.2	65.2	—	—	65.2	130.4	130.4
1959	50.0	0.0	84.7	—	1.3	86.0	—	—	86.0	172.0	172.0
1960	62.5	0.0	83.9	—	1.2	85.1	—	—	85.1	136.2	136.2
1961	127.5	7.5	14.6	—	1.0	23.1	—	—	23.1	18.1	18.1
1962	130.0	10.3	—	0.6	0.9	11.8	5.1	4.7	21.6	9.1	16.6
1963	130.0	4.1	39.8	0.8	2.9	47.6	5.3	6.6	59.5	36.6	48.8
1964	214.3	2.9	39.7	0.7	6.0	49.3	7.6	10.1	67.0	23.0	31.3
1965	265.4	—	—	2.3	7.6	9.9	13.9	15.4	39.2	3.7	14.8
1966	271.3	—	—	2.3	10.3	12.5	17.8	21.3	51.6	4.6	19.0
1967	270.7	—	—	5.2	14.7	20.0	17.8	24.6	62.4	7.4	23.1
1968	276.6	—	—	3.0	15.2	18.2	19.9	39.6	77.7	6.6	28.1
1969	288.2	—	—	3.7	14.7	18.4	27.4	34.3	80.1	6.4	27.8
1970	310.7	—	—	3.5	17.3	20.8	27.0	40.4	88.1	6.7	28.4
1971	347.7	—	—	4.8	18.1	22.8	32.2	48.0	103.0	6.6	29.6
1972	391.8	—	—	1.9	10.5	12.5	26.4	66.3	105.2	3.2	26.9
1973	398.3	—	—	1.4	7.4	8.7	21.0	64.4	94.2	2.2	23.7
1974	407.0	—	—	—	8.6	8.6	22.5	55.1	86.3	2.1	21.2
1975	484.0	—	—	—	12.9	12.9	33.8	34.3	81.0	2.7	16.7
1976	484.0	—	—	—	12.3	12.3	33.6	35.9	81.8	2.5	16.9
1977	484.0	—	—	—	9.4	9.4	53.1	30.6	93.1	1.9	19.2
1978	484.0	—	—	—	11.0	11.0	53.6	30.0	94.6	2.3	19.5
1979	484.0	—	—	—	11.0	11.0	56.6	30.3	97.9	2.3	20.2
1980	618.5	—	—	—	20.6	20.6	74.6	36.4	131.6	3.3	21.3
1981	686.0	—	—	—	15.0	15.0	n.a.	n.a.	n.a.	2.2	n.a.
1982	737.7	—	—	—	3.0	3.0	n.a.	n.a.	n.a.	0.4	n.a.
1983	781.2	—	—	—	0.0	0.0	n.a.	n.a.	n.a.	0.0	n.a.

Source: Kim (1988, table 3.1).

Note: n.a. = not available.

[a]Totals may not add up due to rounding errors.

gross export subsidies in 1965 to approximately one-half by 1980. Adoption of the destination basis VAT system in 1977, under which exports are zero rated, which increased the border tax rebates on exports is included by Kim (1988) as part of his export subsidy measure.

8.3 Using a General Equilibrium Model to Evaluate the Tax Contribution to Outward Orientation and Growth in the Early Growth Phase

Evaluating the effects of the tax policy component of outward-oriented policy on Korean growth over the last three decades in a single consistent model framework is difficult, because of the regime switches and the changes that have occurred in the economy. Savings rates have risen sharply, there has been substantial human capital accumulation, resources have transferred from the rural to the urban sector, and so on. Therefore, the incentive effects of the various tax schemes used over the years have come into play on several different margins, all of which ought ideally to be captured in any assessment of the contribution of taxes to growth. These include the effects of tax changes on export performance, savings, investment, and sectoral structure, among others.

Our approach has been to expand on a model we developed earlier (Trela and Whalley 1991) to analyze the contribution made by intersectoral resource transfers and by tax incentives to outward orientation and to growth in the early growth phase in Korea. The structure of the new model is basically the same as the earlier one except there are now three sectors rather than two. This three-sector model, like its two-sector counterpart, does not include the effects of such general factors as savings and human capital, but it does capture the effects of export promotion on manufacturing, the effect of tax policies on rural/urban migration, and, importantly, the endogenous determination of effort in both manufacturing and nonmanufacturing sectors.

In contrast to other multisectoral modeling efforts that have looked at growth in Korea and other Asian NICs (see Chenery, Robinson, and Syrquin 1986), this model uses average product pricing of labor in agriculture, reflecting traditional family farming arrangements. Decisions regarding effort in all sectors are endogenously determined through utility-maximizing behavior. Average product pricing of labor in agriculture, in contrast to marginal product pricing in manufacturing sectors, generates lower effort in agriculture than in manufacturing, which is matched by a correspondingly lower wage rate in agriculture. Promoting manufacturing through exports thus transfers labor both from the low-effort agricultural sector to the high-effort manufacturing sector, and from import-substituting to export-oriented manufacturing, thereby fueling growth.

We have used this model here to assess the importance of tax polices for Korean growth, especially in the earlier phase (1962–72). As we emphasize above, the second and third phases of this growth sharply curtailed some of the key features of the outward-oriented policies of the early years. In addition, many of the features that fostered high Korean growth are not captured by the model, such as high savings rates and rapid human capital accumulation, to mention but two.

Our modeling strategy is to construct a microconsistent data set for a given base year to which the model is calibrated. We then compute counterfactuals, in which a new equilibrium for the model is found in which outward-oriented policies (including tax elements of outward orientation) are removed. Comparing the two equilibria gives an assessment of the contribution of outward-oriented policies to GDP during the year. Because of the work involved in constructing base year data sets for each of a series of years, we use two alternative base years and sequentially introduce the policy variable characteristics of earlier or later years for comparison to the policy neutral equilibrium.

Thus, using what we term the 1962 base year model, we compute a policy neutral equilibrium and then compare sequentially the 1962 model with 1962 policies, with 1963 policies, 1964 policies, and so on. The policy contribution to GDP from each year's policy regime is assessed and the combined effect over ten (or twenty) years evaluated. We also use a 1982 base year model in which earlier year policies (1981, 1980, . . .) can be sequentially introduced in the same way. This procedure allows us to evaluate the contribution of the tax component of outward-oriented policies to growth through induced intersectoral resource transfers. We are also able to evaluate the contribution of outward-oriented policies in general, the specific indirect tax component of policies, and the specific direct tax component of policies.

In the model, Korea is treated as a small, open, price-taking economy. The resource endowment of the economy comprises three primary factors—capital, labor, and land. Only two of these appear as inputs for any sector. The rural sector uses only land and labor, while the urban sector uses capital and labor. The supply of workers is endogenous; rural/urban and urban/urban migration proceeds in response to differences in worker utility across sectors.

Utility is assumed to be a positive function of consumption and a negative function of effort, with individuals trading off differences in effort against differences in income. We induce both rural/urban and urban/urban migration in the model by introducing policy incentives to promote exports, including tax policies.

8.3.1 Production

The three production sectors that appear in the model are distinguished by the types of goods they produce. The rural sector specializes in the production of a single agricultural good (sector/good 1), while the urban sector produces two types of manufactured goods—import-substituting (sector/good 2) and export-oriented (sector/good 3). The output of each good is produced according to a constant elasticity of substitution (CES) production function:

$$(1) \quad Q_j = F \, \gamma_j \left[\alpha_j L^{(\sigma_j - 1)/\sigma_j} + (1 - \alpha_j) (\sum_{q=1}^{N_j} \varepsilon_j^q)^{(\sigma_j - 1)/\sigma_j} \right]^{\sigma_j/(\sigma_j - 1)}, \quad j = 1;$$

$$(2) \quad Q_j = \gamma_j \left[\alpha_j K_j^{(\sigma_j - 1)/\sigma_j} + (1 - \alpha_j) (\sum_{q=1}^{N_j} \varepsilon_j^q)^{(\sigma_j - 1)/\sigma_j} \right]^{\sigma_j/(\sigma_j - 1)}, \quad j = 2, 3,$$

where Q_j represents the output of sector j, γ_j is a constant defining units of measurement, α_j is a share parameter, F denotes the number of farms, ε_j^q is the effort of a typical worker in sector j, L denotes land used per farm in agriculture, K_j and N_j are capital and labor,[3] and σ_j is the elasticity of substitution between factor inputs.

On the factor side, land and capital are assumed to be sector specific while labor is intersectorally mobile, although because of the differential effort decision across rural/urban sectors, wage rates are not equalized across these sectors. In equilibrium factors are fully employed:

$$(3) \qquad\qquad \bar{L} = L,$$
$$(4) \qquad\qquad \bar{K} = K_2 + K_3,$$

and

$$(5) \qquad\qquad \bar{N} = FN_1 + N_2 + N_3,$$

where $\bar{L}$, $\bar{K}$, and $\bar{N}$ define the economy's fixed factor endowments.

Assuming that urban producers in both the import-substituting and export-oriented industries wish to minimize their costs and given that capital supply is fixed, producers in each urban sector choose the labor input that minimizes their costs:

$$(6) \quad \min \mathcal{L} = w_j \sum_{q=1}^{N_j} \varepsilon_j^q + \lambda_j \left[Q_j - \gamma_j \left[\alpha_j K_j^{(\sigma_j - 1)/\sigma_j} + (1 - \alpha_j) (\sum_{q=1}^{N_j} \varepsilon_j^q)^{(\sigma_j - 1)/\sigma_j} \right]^{\sigma_j/(\sigma_j - 1)} \right], \quad j = 2, 3,$$

where w_j is the price of labor in urban sector j measured in efficiency units. This leads to the first-order condition

$$(7) \quad w_j = \frac{P_j \, \gamma_j \left[\alpha_j K_j^{(\sigma_j - 1)/\sigma_j} + (1 - \alpha_j) (\sum_{q=1}^{N_j} \varepsilon_j^q)^{\sigma_j/(\sigma_j - 1)} \right]^{1/(\sigma_j - 1)} (1 - \alpha_j)}{(\sum_{q=1}^{N_j} \varepsilon_j^q)^{1/\sigma_j}},$$
$$j = 2, 3,$$

where P_j is the price of good j produced in urban sector j.

The optimal amount of labor in the rural sector is determined using the average product pricing rule for labor:

3. In the agricultural sector, N_j is labor per farm.

$$(8) \quad w_j = \frac{P_j \gamma_j \left[\alpha_j K^{(\sigma_j - 1)/\sigma_j} + (1 - \alpha_j)(\sum_{q=1}^{N_j} \varepsilon_j^q)^{\sigma_j/(\sigma_j - 1)} \right]^{\sigma_j/(\sigma_j - 1)}}{N_j}, \quad j = 1,$$

where w_j is the return to labor in the rural sector.

The return to capital in each urban sector is derived by residual:

$$(9) \quad r_j = \frac{P_j \gamma_j \left[\alpha_j K_j^{(\sigma_j - 1)/\sigma_j} + (1 - \alpha_j)(\sum_{q=1}^{N_j} \varepsilon_j^q)^{(\sigma_j - 1)/\sigma_j} \right]^{\sigma_j/(\sigma_j - 1)} - w_j \sum_{q=1}^{N_j} \varepsilon_j^q}{K_j}$$

$$j = 2, 3.$$

8.3.2 Consumption

Consumers are differentiated according to their sector of residence, although their utility functions defined over goods and effort (leisure) are the same. We assume an augmented CES form:

$$(10) \quad U = \left[\sum_{j=1}^{3} \beta_j X_j^{(\theta - 1)/\theta} \right]^{\theta/(\theta - 1)} - \frac{\varepsilon^z}{z\delta},$$

where X_j defines consumption of good j, β_j is a share parameter, θ is an elasticity parameter, and $z > 1$ and $\delta > 0$ are constants, with z measuring the curvature of the disutility of effort function and δ defined as a units term in this subfunction.

Each consumer owns labor and an equal proportion of the economy's capital endowment which, along with transfers, yields consumer incomes. If T^q denotes transfers (recycled tax revenues) received by individual $q(\sum_{q=1}^{N} T^q = T)$, $\bar{K}^q$ denotes capital owned by individual $q(\sum_{q=1}^{N} \bar{K}^q = \bar{K})$, and X_j^q are purchases of good j by individual q, then individual budget constraints can be written as follows:

for workers in the rural sector

$$(11) \quad \sum_{j=1}^{3} P_j X_j^q = w_1 + r\bar{K}^q + T^q;$$

for workers in the urban import-substituting sector

$$(12) \quad \sum_{j=1}^{3} P_j X_j^q = w_2 \varepsilon_2 + r\bar{K}^q + T^q;$$

and for workers in the urban outward-oriented sector

(13)
$$\sum_{j=1}^{3} P_j X_j^q = w_3 \varepsilon_3 + r \bar{K}^q + T^q.$$

Maximizing (10) subject to (11), (12), and (13) yields the demand functions:

(14)
$$X_j^q = \frac{I_j^q \beta_j^\theta}{P_j^\theta \left[\sum_{j=1}^{3} P_j^{1-\theta} \beta_j^\theta \right]}, \quad j = 1, \ldots 3,$$

where I represents consumer income.

Substituting (14) into (10) yields the indirect utility function

(15)
$$U = IC - \frac{\varepsilon^z}{z\delta},$$

where

(16)
$$C = \left[\sum_{j=1}^{3} \left(\frac{\beta_j^\theta}{P_j^{\theta_j - 1} \left(\sum_{k=1}^{3} P_k^{1-\theta} \beta_k^\theta \right)^{(\theta-1)/\theta}} \right) \right]^{\theta/(\theta-1)}$$

Substituting (7) and (12) into (15), and (7) and (13) into (15), and optimizing with respect to ε_2 and ε_3, respectively, implies the optimal effort of a typical individual in the urban sector satisfies

(17)
$$\varepsilon_j = [w_j C \delta]^{1/z - 1}, \quad j = 2, 3.$$

Substituting (8) and (11) into (15) and optimizing with respect to ε_1 implies that the optimal effort of a typical individual in the rural sector satisfies

(18)
$$\gamma P_1 (1 - \alpha_1) \delta C = \frac{\varepsilon_1^{z-1} + (1/\theta) N_1^{(\theta+1)/\theta}}{\left[\alpha_j L^{(\theta-1)/\theta} + (1 - \alpha_1)(\sum_{q=1}^{N_j} \varepsilon_1^q)^{(\theta-1)/\theta} \right]^{1/(\theta-1)}}.$$

8.3.3 Government

Government interventions in taxes, subsidies, and transfers are also incorporated in the model. The government collects net revenues from the tax subsidy system and is assumed to distribute them on an equal per capita basis. In the model, we only capture those components of government revenues that are affected by taxing imports and subsidizing exports.

Revenue raised is thus given by

(19)
$$R = \sum_{j=1}^{3} t_j P_j^w \max(X_j - Q_j, 0),$$

where X_j and Q_j are consumption and production, respectively, and t_j is the ad valorem tariff rate applied to imports of good j evaluated at world prices P_j^w. Subsidies paid are thus given by

$$(20) \qquad S = \sum_{j=1}^{3} \frac{s_j}{(1 - s_j)} P_j^w Q_j ,$$

where s_j is the subsidy rate applied to production of good j.

In setting the parameters of the model, we use estimates of effective subsidy rates in Korea. Thus rebates of indirect or direct taxes on exports and import duty remissions on exports are not directly modeled but are captured through the parameter values used to represent trade taxes and export subsidies. These are modeled in ad valorem form.

The government net revenue T is, therefore, given by

$$(21) \qquad T = R - S.$$

The expenditure side of the government budget consists only of transfers to households, as the government makes no real expenditures on goods. The government collects tariff revenues, pays export subsidies, and transfers its net revenues to individuals such that in equilibrium its budget is balanced. If transfers are made in lump-sum form and are distributed on an equal per capita basis, then transfers received by each individual are

$$(22) \qquad T^q = \frac{T}{\bar{N}}, \quad q = 1, \ldots, \bar{N}.$$

8.3.4 Foreign Sector

A specification of the external sector (rest of the world, ROW) completes our model. The ROW produces the same number of goods as the domestic Korean economy and both imports and exports so that, in equilibrium, it meets Korean desired net trades. Foreign and domestically produced goods are treated in the model as homogeneous commodities; commodities are treated as importables if net imports by Korea are positive, and as exportables if net imports are negative.

The model incorporates an external balance condition which requires that the value of imports equal the value of exports, evaluated at world prices:

$$(23) \qquad \sum_{j=1}^{3} P_j^w (X_j - Q_i) = 0.$$

Korea is modeled as a taker of prices on world markets for all tradeables where P_j^w denotes the fixed world prices. The relationship between Korean domestic producer prices and world prices for importables is

$$(24) \qquad P_j = P_j^w (1 + t_j), \quad j = 1, 2,$$

and for exportables is

$$(25) \qquad P_j = \frac{P_j^w}{(1 - s_j)}, \quad j = 3.$$

8.3.5 Equilibrium

We use an iterative search procedure to solve for the equilibrium combination of rural to urban employment in the model. From this, commodity demand and supplies are determined as well as net trades. Because of the small, open economy assumption, equilibrium in the model involves factor market clearing and government budget balance, with trade balance a property of such an equilibrium. We begin by making an initial estimate of a common wage rate in the two urban sectors and of the return to labor in the rural sector. We then vary the parameters until an equilibrium is found that produces a set of factor prices that clears goods and factor markets, holds external balance conditions, and equalizes utility across the three sectors.

8.4 Using the General Equilibrium Model to Analyze the Role of Tax Policies in Korea's Outward-oriented Growth Strategy

We have used the model described above in counterfactual equilibrium analysis to assess the contribution of tax policy to growth in Korea. As indicated above, we calibrate the model to a microconsistent data set for a given base year incorporating a number of outward-oriented growth policies, including tax policies. Because of data difficulties, we have built data sets for two years only, 1962 and 1982, representing early and recent years in Korea's growth process. This yields two alternative models, a 1962 and a 1982 base year model.

Using each base year model, we perform a series of counterfactual equilibrium calculations. First we remove the export subsidy component of the policy mix used in the base year, yielding what we term an "export policy neutral equilibrium" (in other words, tariffs remain present). This enables us to assess the contribution to Korean growth of policies pursued in the base year. The contribution to growth of policies pursued in other years is evaluated by introducing the policies of the alternative year into the model in place of the base year policies and computing a new equilibrium in the presence of each. Comparison between each of the equilibria and the policy neutral equilibrium then provides the model estimate of the year's policy contribution to growth in the year. The effects of policies over a number of years are evaluated as the sum of the individual year's effects.

We have performed these calculations using both the 1962 and 1982 base year models; different results are obtained in each case, depending on the choice of base year model. We also perform calculations for different types of policy evaluation, for a removal of all export subsidies, for the tax component alone and for the direct (or indirect) tax component.

Parameter values for the production and demand functions in the model are determined using calibration techniques. Calibration procedures widely used in other applied general equilibrium models are followed (see Mansur and Whalley 1984). The requirement set for parameter values chosen in this way is that they be capable of replicating the base year microconsistent data set as an equilibrium solution to the model, given extraneous estimates of elasticities of substitution, policy parameters, endowments, and other data.

The first step in calibration is to break down the base year microconsistent data, constructed in value terms, into separate price and quantity data. For this purpose, a unit's convention is adopted (also see Mansur and Whalley 1984) that defines physical units for commodities as those amounts that sell for one currency unit (U.S. $1.00).[4] For factors, base year equilibrium data on the price of capital, labor employment, and rural/urban wage differentials are used to decompose capital and labor payments into separate price and quantity observations.

The share parameters for the demand and production functions can then be determined by calibration, dependent on the choice of elasticity values for the production and utility functions in the model. In the rural sector, the values of the share parameter α_j are taken from the average product pricing rule for labor and from the first-order condition from producer cost minimization in the urban sector. These are

$$(26) \quad \alpha_j = \frac{\left((w_j N_j)/(\gamma_j P_j)\right)^{(\sigma_j - 1)/\sigma_j} - (\sum_{q=1}^{N_j} \varepsilon_j^q)^{(\sigma_j - 1)/\sigma_j}}{L_j^{(\sigma_j - 1)/\sigma_j} - \left(\sum_{q=1}^{N_j} \varepsilon_j^q\right)^{(\sigma_j - 1)/\sigma_j}}, \quad j = 1;$$

$$(27) \quad \alpha_j = \frac{1}{1 + \frac{w_j}{r_j}\left(\dfrac{\sum_{q=1}^{N_j} \varepsilon_j^q}{K_j}\right)^{1/\sigma_j}}, \quad j = 2, 3.$$

γ_1, the units term in the production function, is arbitrarily set equal to 1, allowing equation (26) to be solved for α_1. The values for γ_2 and γ_3 are then derived by residual, using equation (9), given the units' definition for output.

Demand-side parameters are determined in an analogous fashion using calibration techniques, except that first-order conditions for utility maximization are used. Taking the derivative of (10) with respect to X_j yields

---

4. The 1962 and 1982 benchmark data on production and labor income in won are converted into U.S. dollars using official exchange rates from Economic Planning Board (1964, 1984). Trade data for both years are reported in U.S. dollars.

(28) $$\frac{\beta_j}{\beta_k} = \frac{P_j}{P_k}\left(\frac{X_j}{X_k}\right)^{1/\theta}, \quad j = 1, \ldots, 3; k = 1, \ldots, 3.$$

Normalizing so that $\sum\limits_{j=1}^{3} \beta_j = 1$, individual β_j values can be obtained. Because ε_2 and ε_3 can be arbitrarily set equal to 1 in the base case data, the value for δ can be derived from (17). ε_1 can then be determined directly from the equal utility condition linking the manufacturing and agricultural sectors.

The microconsistent data sets to which we calibrate our model are built for the two years of 1962 and 1982, each chosen to reflect different stages of Korean growth. One is largely pre–outward orientation, the other post–outward orientation and for a more recent year. In constructing these data sets, different basic data sources have been used and various incompatibilities between source materials have had to be dealt with. Adjustments have been made to the data, both to resolve incompatibilities (differences in definition, and measurement differences) and to ensure that the equilibrium conditions of the model are satisfied in the data.

Data on the aggregate income of urban wage earners are from the Economic Planning Board (1964, 1984). These data are dissaggregated in order to provide estimates of labor income in the two manufacturing industries in the model using the ratios of value of production for the individual manufactured goods to total manufacturing production. The common urban wage rate (in terms of efficiency units) is calculated by dividing the aggregate urban wage bill by the product of the number of employed persons in the urban sector and the effort level of a typical worker in this sector, which is arbitrarily set equal to 1.0 in the base case equilibrium data. Data on urban employment in aggregate for both years are from the Economic Planning Board (1964, 1984). The average farm income per worker is estimated using data on urban/rural differences in earnings taken from Hong (1979). Since the data from Hong are only available up to 1976, we use the 1976 data and assume they reflect urban/rural differences in earnings in 1982. The rural wage bill is estimated as the product of average farm income per worker and the number of persons employed in the rural sector. Data on rural employment in each year are from Economic Planning Board (1982, 1986).

The income return to capital in each urban sector is estimated as the residual of the value of production less labor income in that sector. To translate these into observations on the physical quantity of capital used in determining parameters in the model, an estimate of the rate of return on capital in each manufacturing sector is needed. Assuming a common value between sectors in the base case equilibrium data, we use estimates on rates of return on capital during 1954–61 and 1972–75 (the latest period available to us) and assume them to be roughly equivalent to the rates in 1962 and 1982.

Trade in the urban import-substituting good is estimated using data on the value of imports of manufacturers, while trade in the export-oriented good is estimated using data on the value of manufacturing exports. Trade in the agricultural good, on the other hand, is estimated using data on net trade in this good. Data on the value of trade by commodity for each year are from the Economic Planning Board (1964, 1984).

Data on the value of production by commodity for each year are also from the Economic Planning Board (1964, 1984), except for data on agricultural production, which from our model definition is equal to labor income from employment in the rural sector. For each commodity, the value of consumption is determined as the residual between the value of production and trade. The value of trade evaluated at world prices must, for general equilibrium consistency, satisfy trade balance, and a scaling procedure incorporating the import data is used to ensure that condition holds.

The model also requires elasticity values for production and demand functions. We use values of 1.5 and -1.5. The unobservable parameter z, which measures the curvature of the utility function, we assume to be 1.5. Because of the potentially crucial nature of these values for model behavior, we use these values as our central set of values around which sensitivity analyses are performed.

To incorporate outward-oriented growth policies into the model, data are also required on tariffs and export subsidies. Since agriculture and import-oriented manufactures are the two goods that are imported in our model, we need tariff rates on these products. We use weighted average tariff rates on primary and manufactured products (adjusted for rebates) in 1968 (the earliest period available to us) from Westphal and Kim (1977) and assume them to be roughly equivalent to the tariff rates on these products in 1962. For tariff rates in 1982, we use simple average tariff rates on live animals and vegetable products and manufactures in 1982 from World Bank (1987).

Data on subsidy rates are taken from table 8.1, which we reproduced from Kim (1988). Since 1980 is the most recent year for which detailed information on subsidy rates from this source is available, we use the 1980 data and assume it to be roughly equivalent to the rates in both 1981 and 1982.

Table 8.2 reports some summary statistics from the two data sets we have constructed. The rapid expansion in the economy between 1962 and 1982 is evident, as is the change in the industrial composition of employment and output, and the changes in importance of trade to the economy. What remains to be established is how significant tax policies were in promoting outward orientation and how great a contribution they made to Korea's strong growth performance.

8.5 Results

We have used the general equilibrium model described above to assess the contribution of tax policies to Korean growth as part of the outward-oriented growth strategies used in recent decades. The counterfactual policy exercises

Table 8.2   Summary Features of 1962 and 1982 Microconsistent Data Sets Used
                   to Evaluate Inputs of Tax Policies in Korea's Outward-Oriented
                   Growth Strategy

	1962 Microconsistent Data Set	1982 Microconsistent Data Set
Value of GDP (in millions of U.S. dollars)	1,935.59	92,587.56
Ratio of employment in manufacturing to agriculture	1:15	1:2
Percentage of GDP		
Agricultural imports	0.18	0.81
Manufactured exports	2.39	23.60
Manufactured imports	2.21	22.79
Manufactured exports as percentage of total exports[a]	27.0	93.7
Average tariff rate		
Agricultural imports (%)	7.1	13.4
Manufactured imports (%)	11.6	14.7
Average export subsidy rate (%)	16.6	21.3

[a]These figures are based on actual data. In the model Korea exports only one good.

we have performed involved a series of counterfactual experiments in which the base year (1962 or 1982) policies are removed, and a new equilibrium for the model computed and compared to the benchmark equilibrium. This comparison yields estimates of quantitative changes in all the endogenous model variables under the policy change. Further counterfactual experiments are then performed, in which outward-oriented tax policies during each year of the specified time periods (1963–82, 1963–72, or 1981–62) are sequentially introduced. For each of these policy changes, a new counterfactual equilibrium is computed and compared with the same no policy equilibrium.

Before exploring the results that have been produced from the counterfactual experiments described above, it may help if we first restate the results from our earlier work. These are reported in tables 8.3 and 8.4.

Table 8.3 reports results for the model experiment on which the tax component (direct tax reductions and indirect tax exemptions) of outward orientation is introduced. Results indicate that the average annual increase in GDP over this period attributable to tax policies is small, only 0.54 percent using the 1982 base year model or less than 10 percent of actual average annual Korean growth in real GDP. A similar result is reached with each of the other model experiments, which use the 1962 base year model. These results suggest that tax policies played only a minor role in Korea's outward-oriented developmental process, even in the early phases of Korean growth (1962–72). These policies also clearly had the effect of inducing migration from the rural to the urban sector. The effect of removing 1982 tax policies using the 1982 base year model shows the share of labor in agriculture as increasing to 70.63

Table 8.3   General Equilibrium Estimates of Effects of Korean Tax Policies 1962–82 (%)

	Contribution over 20 Years of Outward-oriented Tax Policies Using 1982 Base Model	Contribution over 20 Years of Outward-oriented Tax Policies Using 1962 Base Model	Contribution over 10 Years of Outward-oriented Tax Policies Using 1962 Base Model	Actual Average Annual Growth Rate	
				1962–82	1962–72
ANNUAL AVERAGE GROWTH RATE					
GDP	0.54	0.68	0.62	8.65	9.25
Exports of manufactures using 1982 base model[a]	1.07	—[a]	—[a]	35.37	55.66
Imports of agriculture using 1982 base model[a]	1.10	—[a]	—[a]	11.94[b]	21.58[b]

	1982 Base Year Model with 1982 Policies	1982 Base Year Model with Tax Policy Neutral Mix	1962 Base Year Model with 1962 Policies	1962 Base Year Model with Tax Policy Neutral Mix	Actual Distribution[c]		
					1962[d]	1972	1982
DISTRIBUTION OF EMPLOYMENT							
Agriculture	67.35	70.63	93.73	94.16	63.1	50.6	32.1
Manufacturing	32.67	29.37	6.21	5.84	36.9	49.4	67.9

Source: Trela and Whalley (1991).

[a]Trade growth using the 1962 base model is unrealistically high because of the small manufactured export base involved, and is not reported.

[b]Figures are based on imports of food and live animals.

[c]The distribution is between agriculture and nonagriculture.

[d]Based on the 1963 distribution.

Table 8.4 Assessing the Effects of Tax Policies on Korean Growth Using the 1982 Base Model (%)

	Contribution of Indirect Tax Component of Outward-oriented Korean Growth Strategy	Contribution of Direct Tax Component of Outward-oriented Korean Growth Strategy	Contribution of Combined Tax Component of Outward-oriented Korean Growth Strategy	Contribution of Both Tax and Nontax Components of Outward-oriented Korean Growth Strategy	Actual Average Annual Growth Rate
ANNUAL AVERAGE GROWTH RATE					
GDP	0.51	0.03	0.54	1.40	8.65
Exports of manufactures	1.01	0.07	1.07	2.64	35.37
Imports of agriculture	1.04	0.07	1.10	2.66	11.94[a]

	1982 Base Year Model with 1982 Policies	1982 Base Year Model without 1982 Indirect Tax Policies	1982 Base Year Model without 1982 Direct Tax Policies	1982 Base Year Model with Tax Policy Neutral Mix	1982 Base Year Model with Export Policy Neutral Mix	Actual Distribution[b]	
						1962[c]	1982
DISTRIBUTION OF EMPLOYMENT							
Agriculture	67.35	70.63	67.32	70.63	73.27	63.1	50.6
Manufacturing	32.67	29.37	32.68	29.37	26.73	36.9	49.4

Source: Trela and Whalley (1991).

[a]Figure is based on imports of food and live animals.

[b]The distribution is between agriculture and nonagriculture.

[c]Based on the 1963 distribution.

percent from its 1982 benchmark level of 67.35 percent, while the share of labor employed in manufacturing fell from 32.67 percent to 29.37 percent. Also, these policies caused exports of manufactures to expand by 1.07 percent on an annual basis over the twenty-year period.

Using the same modeling approach, the relatively small contribution of tax policies to growth can also be broken down into two separate effects—direct tax reductions (mainly corporate tax rebates for exporters) and indirect tax exemptions (rebates of sales and excise taxes on exports). These results are reported in table 8.4. Results indicate that indirect tax exemptions have contributed far more to Korean growth than have direct tax measures, which have been relatively inconsequential.

Table 8.4 also reports results for a model experiment in which both tax and nontax components of outward-oriented Korean growth strategies are sequentially introduced. The quantitative magnitudes involved emphasize the dominant role that nontax components (direct cash subsidies, export premiums, interest preferences, and tariff rebates) have played in Korea's development process. Overall, however, the results seem to imply that outward-oriented policies in Korea have little significance in driving growth.[5]

Results produced by the three-sector model can now be compared to those from the earlier model. Results in table 8.5 from the three-sector model portray the tax component of outward-oriented policies as accounting for 3.0 to 4.2 percent of Korean growth between 1962 and 1982, and 3.6 percent between 1962 and 1972. These results are less than half of those reported from the two-sector model. The difference stems from the additional resource reallocation effects within the urban sector that are captured in the three-sector model. In this model, labor in both import-substituting and export-oriented manufacturing sectors is paid their marginal product. This generates a common effort level in the two sectors, which is matched by a correspondingly common wage in the two sectors. A reallocation of labor within the urban sector and from the rural to urban sector, encouraged through export-oriented promotion policies, thereby fuels lower growth than if labor were only transferred from the low-effort agricultural sector to the high-effort manufacturing sector, as is the case in the two-sector model.

8.6   Conclusion

This paper both discusses and evaluates the role of tax policy in the Korean growth process from the early 1960s to the late 1980s. As such, it seeks to do

5. A recent study, Chenery, Robinson, and Syrquin (1986), also uses a multisectoral general equilibrium model for analyzing the contribution of trade policy to growth in Korea. Results of their model simulations indicate outward-oriented policies account for as much as 1 percent of output growth in Korea. Our results indicate a somewhat larger contribution to growth. However, our model provides only a very partial view of the Korean growth process, since savings, investment, human capital formation, and many other factors are missing.

Table 8.5   Impact on Results in Table 8.3 of a Change in Model Structure From Two to Three Sectors (%)

	Two-Sector Model			Three-Sector Model		
	Contribution over 20 Years of Outward-oriented Tax Policies Using 1982 Base Model	Contribution over 20 Years of Outward-oriented Tax Policies Using 1962 Base Model	Contribution over 10 Years of Outward-oriented Tax Policies Using 1962 Base Model	Contribution over 20 Years of Outward-oriented Tax Policies Using 1982 Base Model	Contribution over 20 Years of Outward-oriented Tax Policies Using 1962 Base Model	Contribution over 10 Years of Outward-oriented Tax Policies Using 1962 Base Model
ANNUAL AVERAGE GROWTH RATE						
GDP	0.54	0.68	0.62	0.26	0.36	0.33
Exports of manufactures using 1982 base model[a]	1.07	—[a]	—[a]	0.96	—[a]	—[a]
Imports of manufactures using 1982 base model[a]	n.a.	n.a.	n.a.	0.92	—[a]	—[a]
Imports of agriculture using 1982 base model[a]	1.10	—[a]	—[a]	2.84	—[a]	—[a]

n.a.: not applicable.

[a]Trade growth using the 1962 base model is unrealistically high because of the small manufactured export based involved, and is not reported.

two things: (1) to describe briefly the evolution of Korean tax policies over this developmental sequence, and (2) to use and expand on a general equilibrium model developed earlier by the authors to provide a comparative assessment of the role that tax policies may have played in this growth.

What emerges from the first section of the paper is a picture of a tax system in Korea that has evolved over nearly thirty years from a system raising small amounts of revenue from a series of narrowly based taxes to a more broadly based, mature system raising more revenue that relies heavily on a broadly based VAT. Throughout this period, the Korean tax system has also been remarkably adept in responding to the various swings in Korean growth policies. In the outward-oriented phase (1961–72), rebates of direct and indirect taxes on exports were used; in the heavy industry and chemical industry phase (1973–79), investment tax credits, tax holidays, and other incentives for these industries were used; and in the most recent trade liberalization and structural adjustment phase (1980–89), neutrality in tax policy has been the approach. The GDP growth rate in each of these phases has been consistently high, which implies that the changing tax system in Korea has probably facilitated rather than fueled high growth.

In the second part of the paper, we have modified a general equilibrium model (Trela and Whalley 1991) we used earlier to investigate the contribution of tax policy to Korean growth, by extending it to a three-sector model with two manufacturing industries. This model, like its two-sector counterpart, provides only a very partial view of the Korean growth process, as savings, investment, human capital formulation, and many other key factors are missing. But unlike the earlier model, this captures resource reallocation effects from import-substituting to export-oriented manufacturing. As a result, export promotion policies, which stimulate manufacturing, move labor not only from the low-efficiency rural sector to the high-efficiency urban sector but also within manufacturing, thereby fueling growth that is lower than if labor moved only from the rural to urban sector, as is the case in the two-sector model.

Using these models to examine the contribution of tax-oriented policies in the earlier years of Korean growth seems to indicate a relatively modest role for taxes, accounting for less than 10 percent of actual Korean growth over the period 1962–82 and over the intensive outward-oriented phase of 1962–72.

References

Brown, G. T. 1973. *Korean Pricing Policies and Economic Development in the 1960s.* Baltimore: Johns Hopkins University Press.
Chenery, Hollis, Sherman Robinson, and Moshe Syrquin. 1986. *Industrialization and Growth: A Comparative Study.* Oxford: Oxford University Press for the World Bank.

Economic Planning Board. 1964. *Korea Statistical Yearbook: 1964.* Seoul: Economic Planning Board.
————. 1982. *Major Statistics of Korean Economy: 1982.*
————. 1984. *Korea Statistical Yearbook: 1984.*
————. 1986. *Major Statistics of Korean Economy: 1986.*
Han, Seung-Soo. 1986. Korea's Recent Tax Reform Effort: Personal Observation of Reform Effort in 1984–85. Provisional Papers in Public Economics no. 85–32. Washington, D.C.: World Bank.
Hasan, Parvez, and D. C. Rao. 1979. *Korea: Policy Issues for Long-Term Development.* Baltimore: Johns Hopkins University Press for the World Bank.
Hong, Won-tack, 1979. *Trade, Distortions, and Employment Growth in Korea.* Seoul: Korea Development Institute.
Kim, Kwang Suk. 1988. The Timing and Sequencing of a Trade Liberalization Policy: The Case of Korea. World Bank. Manuscript.
Krueger, A. 1979. *Studies in the Modernization of the Republic of Korea, 1945–75: The Developmental Role of the Foreign Sector and Aid.* Cambridge, Mass.: Harvard University Press.
Kwack, Taewon. 1988. Public Finance, Trade, and Economic Development: The Role of Fiscal Incentives in Korea's Export-Led Economic Growth. Paper presented at the 44th Congress of the International Institute of Public Finance, Istanbul, August.
Mansur, A., and J. Whalley. 1984. Numerical Specification of Applied General Equilibrium Models: Estimation, Calibration, and Data. In *Applied General Equilibrium Analysis,* ed. H. Scarf and J. Shoven. Cambridge: Cambridge University Press.
Park, Won-Am. 1989. Korea's Macroeconomics Adjustment and Outlook. Paper presented at the KDI/IIE Policy Conference, Washington, D.C., December 12.
Scitovsky, Tibor. 1985. Economic Development in Taiwan and South Korea: 1965–81. *Food Research Institute Studies* 14 (3): 215–64.
Trela, I., and J. Whalley. 1991. Taxes, Outward Orientation, and Growth Performance in the Republic of Korea. In *Tax Policy in Developing Countries,* ed. J. Khalilzadeh-Shirazi and A. Shah. Washington, D.C.: World Bank.
Westphal, L. E., and K. S. Kim. 1977. Industrial Policy and Development in Korea. World Bank Staff Working Paper no. 263. Washington, D.C.
World Bank, 1987. *Korea: Managing the Industrial Transition.* Vol. 1, *The Conduct of Industrial Policy.* Washington, DC: World Bank. Reprinted 1988.

Comment   Anne O. Krueger

Korea's growth performance has been either the best, or one of the two best (with Taiwan), in the world over the past thirty years. Because of that spectacular performance, there is great interest in assessing the contributions of various factors to it.

Irene Trela and John Whalley have made an interesting and important contribution to that discussion by focusing on the role of tax policy and its importance in affecting the rate of growth. Although the overall role of government

Anne O. Krueger is Arts and Sciences Professor of Economics at Duke University and a research associate of the National Bureau of Economic Research.

and the effect of the trade regime in leading to Korea's success have been extensively analyzed, there has been little analysis of other policies. The Trela-Whalley contribution is therefore greatly to be welcomed.

To estimate the role of changes in the tax structure, Trela and Whalley construct a computable general equilibrium model and then analyze the changes in output that occur over the longer term under alternative tax structures.

The analysis is thoroughly professional, and their findings are clear: tax policy contributed probably around 0.54 percentage points to the growth rate over the period covered by them. They therefore conclude that the Korean growth rate was relatively impervious to individual policies, and especially to reforms in taxes that rendered the system more efficient.

I have two quarrels with the paper: (1) the treatment of the import-competing and exportable sectors and (2) the interpretation of their results.

Turning first to the computable general equilibrium (CGE) model's structure, there are two questions. An issue arises with regard to the prices that are used to evaluate growth rates. It is not clear from the paper which prices are used and whether it makes a difference.

The second question concerns the model's treatment of all manufacturing as an exportable industry and all agriculture as an import-competing industry. Especially given Korea's strong comparative disadvantage in agriculture, a question arises as to where resources would have gone had there not been an export-oriented trade policy. The evident answer would appear to be, into import-competing manufacturing industries. To be sure, the rate at which out-migration from agriculture would have occurred would have been lower, but the most plausible scenario is that the import-substitution drive of the 1950s would have continued, and that there would have been high walls of protection for domestic manufacturing industries. As such, I do not believe that the Trela-Whalley model provides a valid basis on which to measure the alternative uses of resources under other policies.

Turning to interpretation of the model, there are serious questions as to whether the finding that 0.54 percent points implies that the contribution was small, and whether the Korean growth performance was as robust as indicated, or whether instead it was attention to *many* policy parameters, each of which was altered to the extent possible to achieve economic efficiency, that gave Korea its excellent growth performance.

We should not regard 0.54 percentage points as small, even when the overall growth rate averages around 10 percent. For many countries (such as India over the past thirty years, or most Latin American countries over the past decade), half a percentage point on the growth rate would be a major achievement. Moreover, if one observes all developing countries, the average real rate of economic growth over the period 1965 to the early 1980s ranged from about 3 percent to Korea's 10 percent. It is a reasonable inference that a rate of growth of 3–4 percent would have been achieved with a very poor policy stance, and that it is the responsibility of the authorities to establish economic policies conducive to attaining higher levels of economic growth and welfare than the minimum. If so, the range for policy improvement is from 3–4 percent to 10 percent. On that reading, reforms in tax policy might account for as much as one-tenth of the difference between a mediocre and a spectacular growth performance. Surely, that is nothing to be dismissed as "small"!

This always seems to be a problem with estimating the impact of policies: each one alone provides a "small" estimate. Yet it must be asked, in light of the number of policies set by governments (labor market interventions, agricultural pricing policies, investment and maintenance of infrastructure, macroeconomic environment, trade policy, monetary policy, controls over the credit market, etc.) how much significance one would expect to be attached to any one of these alone.

In the Korean case, most policies appear to have been established and executed in a highly inefficient manner in the 1950s: inflation was rampant, there was rigid credit rationing at strongly negative real rates of interest, the government was incurring large fiscal deficits, the exchange rate was greatly overvalued, imports were subject to quantitative restrictions, exchange controls were in place to prevent capital flight, and infrastructure investment was often inefficient and ineffective. In this regard, it may be significant that policies had already shifted markedly away from import substitution by 1962, the year that Trela and Whalley use as their base.

Starting in 1960, policies were reformed on many fronts. Until the late 1980s, there was a fairly strong social consensus for rapid economic growth, and technocrats within the government were given a fairly free hand in establishing economic policies. The result was a concerted effort to find means of achieving more rapid growth. Not surprisingly, policies were reformed when it was deemed feasible to do so. The process of increasing the efficiency of economic activity through policy reform (and increased incentives for factor accumulation) has gone in waves since that time and still continues (although there is some question as to whether the current political structure will provide an environment conducive to "tight" economic policy as did the earlier regime).

In this environment, it is not surprising that tax policy could account for "only" 0.54 percentage points of growth. If similar analyses could be done for the effects of shifting to positive real interest rates, of unifying the exchange rate, reducing the levels of protection to import-competing industries, increasing the rate of utilization of infrastructure, and reducing the budget deficit and the rate of inflation, the total would surely be substantial. It is too much to expect, however, that any one policy instrument alone could have sufficient impact on its own to account for a major portion of Korea's growth performance.

Indeed, the relevant lesson may be that almost all policies need to be reasonably conducive to efficiency in order for rapid economic growth to occur. Governments that undertake policy reforms in the field of taxation in order to enhance economic efficiency and growth are also likely to put into place other policy reforms. Without these complementarities among policies, none of the reforms would have quite the impact they otherwise could.

9 Aging of Population, Social Security, and Tax Reform

Yukio Noguchi

9.1 Introduction

The basic structure of the Japanese tax system since the Shoup reform of 1949 can be characterized by two factors: heavy reliance on direct taxes, especially on individual and corporate income taxes at the national level, and the absence of a broad-based indirect tax such as the value-added tax (VAT) in European countries. A significant change has been brought about by the reform bill that passed the Diet in December 1988. This bill introduced a new indirect tax called *shohi-zei* (consumption tax) while reducing the burden of both individual and corporate income taxes.

Opinions concerning the consumption tax were sharply divided. Not only opposition parties but also some members of the ruling Liberal Democratic Party (LDP) opposed the government's proposal. Major arguments against the consumption tax can be summarized as follows:[1]

1. The most common complaint against the consumption tax was that it is regressive. Thus critics, especially opposition parties, argued that the reform was relatively favorable for middle- and upper-class incomes.

2. There was an argument, also from the opposition parties, that a consumption tax (or indirect taxes in general), which people are relatively unconscious of paying, would make it possible to finance the growth of a big government.

3. A more specific complaint about the consumption tax was voiced by small business owners, important supporters of the LDP. These people main-

Yukio Noguchi is professor of economics at Hitotsubashi University.

The author deeply appreciates useful comments given by the participants of the conference, especially by Professors Anne Krueger, Takatoshi Ito, Hiromitsu Ishi, Charles McLure, Tatsuo Hatta, and Maria Gochoco.

1. Details of the tax reform debates is reviewed in Noguchi (1990). See also Ishi (1989) and Nagano (1988).

tained that in practice it would be difficult for them to shift the burden, so that they must bear it themselves. They also argued that the costs involved in complying with tax collection, such as the cost of making new forms, revising accounting slips, and modifying computer software, would impose an undue burden on businesses.[2]

The government argued two major points in defending the consumption tax. One was the necessity of reforming the indirect tax system. It was argued that the former system of individual commodity taxes was full of problems. The other was related to the horizontal equity issue. It has long been pointed out that the most serious problem of the Japanese tax system is that the income tax burden of salaried workers is heavier than that of small business owners and farmers of the same income. While opposition parties argued that a solution must be found within the framework of the income tax system, the government argued that the introduction of a consumption tax, which distributes tax burden evenly among people of different occupations, was a more realistic solution to the problem.

Although the importance of these issues cannot be denied, they fail to capture the most important implication of the consumption tax, namely, its potential role in the economy to finance increased social security expenditures. Although the need for financing the future welfare society was pointed out by the government as one of the reasons for the reform, the discussion was quite unsatisfactory in that it was made only in vague and abstract terms and the reforms of tax system and social security system were not treated simultaneously. In this paper I will concentrate on this issue and consider long-term implications of tax reform.

I review trends in tax burden and social security payments in section 9.2 and population trends in section 9.3. Based on the population forecast, I examine projected increases in social security payments and the tax burden in section 9.4. Section 9.5 is an analysis of relative well-being of workers and retired people in a future society. My basic conclusion is that the role a consumption tax plays in spreading the burden evenly among different generations will become very important in a society in which the burden on workers is bound to rise.

9.2   Trends in National Burden and Social Security Payments

9.2.1   Tax and Social Security Burden

Table 9.1 shows the trend in tax revenue and social security contributions. Tax burden measured by the ratio to national income was quite stable until the early 1970s at about 19 percent. The ratio rose in FY 1973 but fell sharply in FY 1975 due to a recession caused by the oil shock. It recovered at the end of

---

2. This argument was somewhat superficial. Their true apprehension was that the tax authority would be able to obtain detailed records of transactions (especially if the invoice system were used), so that their transactions would become transparent to the tax authority.

Table 9.1   **Trends in Government Revenues in Japan, FY 1960–90 (%)**

FY	RNB	RSOC	RTAX	RDIR
1960	22.5	3.3	19.2	53.4
1961	23.3	3.4	19.9	55.1
1962	23.4	4.0	19.4	57.8
1963	22.9	3.8	19.1	58.0
1964	23.4	3.9	19.5	58.5
1965	23.0	4.7	18.3	59.2
1966	22.3	4.8	17.5	59.3
1967	22.5	4.7	17.8	60.6
1968	23.2	4.9	18.3	61.7
1969	23.4	4.6	18.8	63.8
1970	24.3	5.4	18.9	66.1
1971	25.1	5.8	19.3	67.0
1972	25.7	5.8	19.9	67.7
1973	27.3	5.8	21.5	72.3
1974	28.3	6.9	21.4	73.9
1975	25.8	7.4	18.4	69.3
1976	26.6	7.6	19.0	67.6
1977	27.2	7.9	19.3	67.8
1978	29.1	7.8	21.3	69.3
1979	30.2	8.4	21.8	68.4
1980	31.3	8.5	22.8	71.1
1981	32.8	9.3	23.5	70.1
1982	33.4	9.5	23.9	70.8
1983	33.9	10.0	23.9	71.1
1984	34.5	10.2	24.3	71.5
1985	35.3	10.8	24.6	72.8
1986	36.4	10.9	25.5	73.1
1987	38.5	11.0	27.5	73.3
1988	39.7	11.5	28.2	73.2
1989	39.9	11.6	28.3	73.5
1990	40.4	12.1	28.3	70.9

Source: Ministry of Finance, *Fiscal and Monetary Statistics* (Tokyo: Government Printing Bureau, 1960–90).

Notes: Figures are those of the settlement basis, except for FY 1989 (revised budget base) and FY 1990 (initial budget base). RNB = national burden; RSOC = social security contribution; RTAX = tax. These are ratios to national income. RDIR = share of direct taxes in national tax.

the 1970s and is now much higher than the pre-oil-shock level. Social security contributions have also increased dramatically. Their ratio to national income was only 3.3 percent and far smaller than that of tax in FY 1960. By FY 1987, it had risen to 11.0 percent, which is about one-half of tax. The sum of tax and social security contributions is usually called the "national burden." Its ratio to national income rose from 24.3 percent in FY 1970 to 38.5 percent in FY 1987.[3] In FY 1990, it is estimated to be 40.4 percent.

3. In the case of social security contributions, the increase in the burden was a result of explicit revisions in the system. For example, the rate of contribution to the Employees' Pension (Kosei Nenkin) was raised (in several stages) from 6.4 percent in FY 1970 to 12.4 percent in FY 1986

The composition of taxes has also changed significantly. While the ratio of indirect taxes to national income in recent years has been about the same as that in the 1960s, that of direct taxes has increased considerably during the past decade. As a result, the share of direct taxes, which was about one-half in 1960s, has risen to about 60 percent in recent years. A more distinct trend can be observed in national taxes. In FY 1970, the share of direct taxes in national taxes was 66.1 percent. In FY 1988, it had risen to 73.2 percent. Among the national taxes, income tax has increased the most sharply. In FY 1970, the ratio of income tax revenue to national income was 4.0 percent, whereas in FY 1986, it had risen to 6.4 percent.

9.2.2 Social Security

Table 9.2 shows the trend in social security payments. Their ratio to national income was stable at about 6 percent during the 1960s. Significant improvements in social security programs were made during FY 1972 and 1973. Improvements in FY 1973 were so dramatic that this year was called "the first year of the welfare era." Reflecting these improvements, the ratio rose significantly during the late 1970s. During the 1980s, however, the ratio was stable at about 14 percent, due to the tight budget policy.

Public pension payments and medical expenses account for most of the social security payments. Increase in public pension is very dramatic. Its ratio to national income was only about 1.3 percent during the 1960s. Due to the significant improvements in the payment level and to the increase in the number of recipients, the ratio has risen to the present level of over 7 percent. Medical expenses also increased significantly during the 1970s. During the 1980s, however, the ratio has become rather stable at about 5.6 percent.

9.2.3 International Comparison

In spite of the recent increase, the tax burden in Japan is still low compared to that in European countries. The main reason is that the share of social security expenditures in national income remains small in Japan. This is clearly seen in the international data (table 9.3). This does not, however, imply that social security programs in Japan are insufficient. On the contrary, improvements undertaken during the early 1970s made the Japanese social security system comparable, and in some respects even superior, to those of European countries.[4]

(including the employees' share) as shown in table 9.2. In the case of income tax, however, the increase in the burden in recent years was not the result of explicit revisions in the income tax law. Rather, it was "bracket creep," which occurs when a progressive tax structure is not indexed to offset inflation or economic growth. Until the early 1970s, the income tax law was amended almost every year in order to prevent this mechanism from operating. A significant change in this trend came after the first oil shock. Adjustments to the income tax law were not undertaken for seven full years between FY 1977 and 1984.

4. For example, average per capita old age pension benefit in Japan is 1.9 times higher than that in the United Kingdom and 1.6 times higher than that in Germany. For a detailed discussion, see Noguchi (1986).

Table 9.2   **Trends in Social Security in Japan, FY 1965–87 (%)**

FY	RSOP	RPEN	RMED	RCON	R65
1965	6.03	1.30	3.50	3.50	6.29
1966	6.00	1.30	3.50	5.50	6.48
1967	5.88	1.30	3.40	5.50	6.65
1968	5.82	1.40	3.40	5.50	6.80
1969	5.65	1.30	3.30	6.20	6.93
1970	5.79	1.34	3.50	6.40	7.06
1971	6.02	1.47	3.42	6.40	7.16
1972	6.31	1.51	3.60	6.40	7.34
1973	6.40	1.68	3.53	7.60	7.51
1974	7.93	2.31	4.19	7.60	7.68
1975	9.48	3.06	4.62	7.60	7.92
1976	10.46	3.76	4.90	9.10	8.14
1977	11.03	4.19	4.96	9.10	8.37
1978	11.82	4.57	5.32	9.10	8.61
1979	12.26	4.89	5.43	9.10	8.88
1980	12.70	5.26	5.50	10.60	9.10
1981	13.51	5.81	5.65	10.60	9.34
1982	14.13	6.17	5.69	10.60	9.56
1983	14.00	6.35	5.70	10.60	9.77
1984	14.00	6.49	5.60	10.60	9.94
1985	14.01	6.68	5.56	12.40	10.30
1986	14.59	7.14	5.70	12.40	10.58
1987	14.83	7.35	5.79	12.40	10.86

Source: Secretariat of the Social Security System Council, *Yearbook of Social Security* (Tokyo: Shakai, Hoken Hoki, Kenkyukai, 1989).

Notes: RSOP = social security payment; RPEN = public pension; RMED = medical expenses. These are ratios to national income. RCON = rate of welfare pension contribution; R65 = ratio of people over age 65.

Table 9.3   **Social Security Payments and Demographic Condition, International Comparison**

Country	RSOC	RNB	R65
Japan	12.1	40.4	12.0
United States	9.9	36.3	11.9
United Kingdom	11.4	53.3	15.1
Germany	22.4	52.3	14.7
France	28.2	62.3	13.0
Sweden	18.9	77.0	17.9

Source: Yoshio Nakajima, *Anatano Chojushai Dokuhon* (Handbook for the aged society) (Tokyo: Daiamondo Sha, 1990).

Notes: RSOC = social security contribution; RNB = national burden. These are ratios to national income. R65 = ratio of people over age 65. RSOC and RNB are those for 1987 (Japan's figures are for FY 1990 budget; United Kingdom figures are for 1986). R65 is for 1985 (Japan's figure is for 1990).

The essential reason for the relatively low level of social security expenditure is that the percentage of elderly people in the Japanese population is low and Japan's public pension system has not reached "maturity," meaning that as yet relatively few people have become entitled to full pension benefits.

As the years go by, this situation will inevitably change, and the public pension programs will automatically mature. Moreover, the aging of the population is expected to take place rapidly in the future, as reviewed in section 9.3. These factors would increase social security expenditures considerably even if no improvements were made in the system.

9.3   Changes in Population Structure

Let us review changes in population structure (table 9.4).[5] Japan's population will experience dramatic aging in the coming decades. The number of people over age 65, which was about 5 million in 1960 and is now about 15 million, is expected to increase to about 30 million by 2015. The ratio of this age group to the total population was about 5 percent for many years. It began to rise in the latter half of the 1960s and is now about 10 percent. The number is expected to rise to about 15 percent at the end of this century, which is about the same level as that of the European countries presently, and to 23.6 percent in 2020. At that time, Japan will have one of the most aged populations in the world (table 9.5).

A significant change is also observed in the number of people of working age, which I define as 20 through 64. Population in this age group doubled from 34 million in 1945 to 70 million in 1980. The rate of growth of population in this age group showed a significant decline around 1980. A more dramatic change is expected in the future. The absolute number of people in this age group will decrease during the period from about 2000 through 2020.

As a result, the dependency ratio, which I define as the number of people over 65 per person of working age and which is shown by C/B in table 9.4, will undergo an even more dramatic change. The ratio, which remained at a relatively stable level of about 10 percent until about 1975, will rise to 22.9 percent in 1995 and to as high as 44.1 percent in 2020.[6]

In general, aging of population is caused by two factors: a decline in the birth rate and an increase in longevity. Both factors have contributed and will continue to contribute to aging in Japan. The total fertility rate has fallen from 2.37 in 1955 to 1.76 in 1985. The average male life expectancy at birth has increased from 63.6 years in 1955 to 74.8 years in 1985.

In the case of Japan, another factor causes the above change. It is the exis-

5. The future figures are the projections (the "middle series") by the Institute of Population Problem of the Ministry of Health and Welfare (1987).

6. In terms of the dependency ratio including children, which is shown by (A + C)/B in table 9.4, the change is not so dramatic. The figure is now at the historic minimum and will gradually rise.

Table 9.4   **Trends in Japan's Population Structure**

	Population by Age Groups (in thousands)				Annual Growth Rate	
Year	A 0–19	B 20–64	C 65–	D Total	B	D
1925	27,809	28,906	3,021	59,737	0.0123	0.0131
1930	30,119	31,268	3,064	64.450	0.0158	0.0153
1935	32,186	33,844	3,225	69,254	0,0160	0.0145
1940	33,778	35,842	3,453	73,075	0.0115	0.0108
1945	34,297	34,000	3,700	71,998	−0.0105	−0.0030
1950	37,996	41,091	4,110	83,200	0.0386	0.0293
1955	38,425	45,103	4,748	89,276	0.0188	0.0142
1960	37,376	50,693	5,350	93,419	0.0236	0.0091
1965	36,017	56,076	6,181	98,275	0.0204	0.0102
1970	33,887	62,502	7,332	103,720	0.0219	0.0108
1975	35,170	67,860	7,866	111,940	0.0166	0.0154
1980	35,779	70,381	10,648	117,060	0.0073	0.0090
1985	35,012	73,526	12,467	121,005	0.0088	0.0067
1990	33,100	76,200	14,800	124,100	0.0072	0.0051
1995	30,900	78,600	18,000	127,500	0.0062	0.0054
2000	31,000	78,800	21,400	131,200	0..0005	0.0057
2005	32,200	77,800	24,100	134,100	−0.0026	0.0044
2010	33,000	75,700	27,100	135,800	−0.0055	0.0025
2015	32,400	72,900	30,700	136,000	−0.0075	0.0003
2020	31,000	72,400	31,900	135,300	−0.0014	−0.0010
2025	30,000	73,000	31,500	134,500	0.0017	−0.0012

	Share of Age Groups			Dependency Ratio	
	A/D	B/D	C/D	C/B	(A + C)/B
1925	0.466	0.484	0.051	0.105	1.067
1930	0.467	0.485	0.048	0.098	1.061
1935	0.465	0.489	0.047	0.095	1.046
1940	0.462	0.490	0.047	0.096	1.039
1945	0.476	0.472	0.051	0.109	1.118
1950	0.457	0.494	0.049	0.100	1.025
1955	0.430	0.505	0.053	0.105	0.957
1960	0.400	0.543	0.057	0.106	0.843
1965	0.366	0.571	0.063	0.110	0.753
1970	0.327	0.603	0.071	0.117	0.659
1975	0.314	0.606	0.070	0.116	0.634
1980	0.306	0.601	0.091	0.151	0.660
1985	0.289	0.608	0.103	0.170	0.646
1990	0.267	0.614	0.119	0.194	0.629
1995	0.242	0.616	0.141	0.229	0.622
2000	0.236	0.601	0.163	0.272	0.665
2005	0.240	0.580	0.180	0.310	0.724
2010	0.243	0.557	0.200	0.358	0.794
2015	0.238	0.536	0.226	0.421	0.866

(*continued*)

Table 9.4   (continued)

	Share of Age Groups			Dependency Ratio	
	A/D	B/D	C/D	C/B	(A+C)/B
2020	0.229	0.535	0.236	0.441	0.869
2025	0.223	0.543	0.234	0.432	0.842

Source: Past figures are from the National Census Statistics Bureau, *Japan Statistical Yearbook* (Tokyo: Japan Statistical Association, 1990) Future figures are projections by the Institute of Population Problems (1987).

tence of the "bulge generation" (*dankai no sedai*), or the baby-boom genera-tion, which consists of about 8 million people born during 1947–49. During this period, the number of births was about 2.7 million a year, about 1 million more than that since then.[7] This generation made the age group 0–19 increase during the period 1950 through 1965. Since the late sixties, this generation has shifted to the 20–64 age group. They will shift to the group over age 65 around 2005, increasing the population of this age group sharply and at the same time decreasing the working-age population.

9.4   Increase in Social Security Payments and National Burden: Projections

9.4.1   Social Security Payments

The above mentioned change in population, together with "maturing" of public pension programs, will cause dramatic increases in social security pay-ments. I first review several projections prepared by the government and other organizations (table 9.6).

The Economic Council Projection. The most comprehensive projection is from the Economic Council in 1982 (A in table 9.6). According to this projec-tion, the ratio of social security payments to national income will increase to 21.6 percent in the year 2000 and to 31.2 percent in 2020. Most of the in-crease will result from the growth of public pension payments: their share in national income will rise to 19.2 percent in 2020.[8]

It may be argued that this projection has an overestimation bias due to two factors. First, this was made before the significant reform of the public pen-sion system in 1986, in which measures were taken to mitigate the effects of maturing. Second, this projection does not take into account effects of various

7. The second wave (or the "echo effect") of the baby boom occurred during the 1970s. But the echo was much more gradual than the initial wave.
8. The basic assumption for estimating future benefits is that the present formula for calculating benefits will remain unchanged.

Table 9.5   **Percentage of People over Age 60**

	1950	1980	1990	2000	2025
Germany	14.0	19.3	20.7	23.9	31.1
Belgium	16.0	18.3	19.9	20.9	26.9
Denmark	13.4	19.4	20.2	20.5	29.7
Spain	10.9	14.9	16.8	18.5	21.9
France	16.2	17.2	18.3	19.4	25.9
Greece	10.0	17.4	19.3	21.7	23.8
Ireland	14.8	14.8	13.6	12.3	17.0
Luxembourg	14.5	17.6	18.8	1.1	28.6
Italy	12.2	17.2	19.8	21.9	26.8
Holland	11.5	15.7	17.2	18.6	30.1
Portugal	10.5	14.6	15.9	16.6	22.1
United Kingdom	15.5	20.1	20.7	20.3	25.7
Japan	4.9	9.1	17.3	22.1	29.0

Source: Genevieve Reday-Mulvey, "Work and Retirement: Future Prospects for the Baby-Boom Generation," *Geneva Papers on Risk and Insurance* 15(55)(April 1990):100–113.

Table 9.6   **Projections of Social Security Payments (% of national income)**

	2000	2010	2020
A. Japan in the year 2000			
Social security payments	21.6	26.8	31.2
Public pension	13.5	16.8	19.2
Medical expenses	7.1	9.1	11.0
B. Ministry of Welfare,			
Ministry of Finance			
Social security	21.5–23	26–29	
C. Rengo			
Social security	19.8–21.3	26–27	
Public pension	10.4–10.7	13.1–13.9	
Medical expenses	7.0–7.5	8.5–9.0	

Sources: For A, Economic Planning Agency, *2000 nen no Nihon* (Japan in the year 2000) (Tokyo: Government Printing Bureau, 1982). For B, an estimate submitted to the Budget Committee of the House of Representatives on March 10, 1988. For C, Rengo (Japan Federation of Labor Unions), *Towards a Welfare Society* (Tokyo: November 1989).

reforms made in the medical insurance system during the 1980s to hold down medical expenses.

The MOF-MOW Projection. The most recent official projection was made jointly by the Ministry of Finance and the Ministry of Welfare in 1988 (B in table 9.6). The ratio of social security expenditure to national income will rise 26 to 29 percent in 2010, according to this projection. Note that the Economic Council projection falls within this range, in spite of the above-mentioned reforms in the social security system.

Unfortunately, this projection does not go beyond 2010.

The Rengo Projection. Another projection was made by the Rengo (Japan Federation of Labor Unions) in 1989. According to this projection, social security payments will be 19.8 to 21.3 percent of national income in 2000 and 26 to 27 percent in 2020. This is considerably lower than the government projection; the major reason is fairly low estimates of public pension payments.

To check the above projections, I first examine public pension. The total amount of public pension payments is determined by the number of recipients and per capita benefit. The former is represented by the number of elderly people and the latter can be represented by a trend. Thus, I estimated an equation in which the ratio of public pension payments to national income (RPEN) is correlated to the ratio of people over age 65.[9] Using this equation, I calculated future values of RPEN as column (A) in table 9.7. Compared with the projections reviewed above, this result seems somewhat high; it does not contain effects of possible policy changes, in particular the effect of raising the eligible age. If this is taken into account, the result becomes smaller, as shown in column (B) in table 9.7.[10] In 2020, public pension payments will be about 21 percent of national income. This is still higher than the government projection reviewed above (table 9.6, column [A]). However, compared to the projections for other countries shown in table 9.8, this seems reasonable.

Some remarks are necessary on the implications of firms' retirement policies on the above estimates. There are arguments that, if retirement age can be raised, social security payments can be reduced. While this is not deniable in principle, it is hard to expect that the effect will be significant. At present,

9. The equation used for the projection is

$$RPEN = -6.688 + 1.309 \, R65 - 0.971 \, DUMMY,$$
$$(0.337) \quad (0.107) \quad (0.279)$$

where RPEN is the ratio of public pension payments to national income, R65 is the ratio of people over age 65, and DUMMY is a dummy variable that equals 1 before 1974. The 1965–86 data are used. The numbers in parentheses are standard errors. The adjusted R^2 is 0.979.

As mentioned above, remarkable improvements in the social security programs were made during 1972 and 1973. That the coefficient of the dummy variable is significant indicates that the effect of the reforms is well captured by the DUMMY variable.

The coefficient of the R65 variable indicates that the increase in RPEN is greater than the change in population structure. This is due to the fact that the number of years in which average workers have contributed always increases, and, as a result, per capita benefit increases. This effect is usually called "maturing of the pension system."

10. According to the government plan, the age at which one becomes eligible for the benefit will be raised gradually as follows: birth years 1938–39, eligible age 61; 1940–41, 62; 1942–43, 63; 1944–45, 64; 1946–, 65. Thus after 2010, all recipients will be over age 65.

According to the government calculation, the rate of contribution for the Employees' Pension can be lowered by this measure from 31.5 percent to 26.1 percent in 2020. Since the system is virtually pay-as-you-go at this time, we may suppose that the total payment of the Employees' Pension is reduced by the same percentage, i.e., by 17.1 percent. On the other hand, total payment of the Employees' Pension will be about 76 percent of the total public pension payment when the system matures. Therefore, total public pension payment will be reduced by 13 percent ($= 0.17 \times 0.76$).

In 2000, the rate of reduction will be about 19 percent of the steady state. Thus, the reduction in payment will be about 2.5 percent ($= 0.13 \times 0.19$).

Table 9.7   **Projections of Social Security Payments (% of national income)**

| | RPEN | | | |
Year	(A)	(B)	RMED	RSOP
1985	6.7	—	5.6	14.0
2000	14.6	14.2	6.5	22.5
2010	19.4	16.9	7.2	25.8
2020	24.1	21.0	7.8	30.5

Notes: RPEN = public pension; RMED = medical expenditure; RSOP = social security payments; A = no change in the eligible age; B = eligible age gradually raised to 65 (RSOP is for case B).

Table 9.8   **Share of Pension in National Income (%)**

	1983	2000	2010	2020	2030
Germany	14.0	16.4	19.8	21.7	28.2
Belgium	14.1	13.9	14.9	17.0	21.1
Denmark	9.1	10.1	11.4	14.4	17.2
Spain	9.6	11.1	11.7	12.9	15.8
France	14.2	16.5	17.4	21.7	25.4
Greece	10.2	12.3	13.9	14.9	16.7
Ireland	6.6	6.1	5.8	6.7	8.1
Italy	16.6	19.4	22.0	25.1	30.2
Holland	12.6	13.5	15.2	19.8	26.0
Portugal	8.2	10.9	11.2	12.4	15.0
United Kingdom	8.3	7.6	7.7	8.8	10.7

Source: Genevieve Reday-Mulvey, "Work and Retirement: Future Prospects for the Baby-Boom Generation," *Geneva Papers on Risk and Insurance* 15(55)(April 1990):100–113.

some firms still set their retirement age earlier than 60. This means that for some people even the present eligible age of 60 is troublesome. It is therefore probable that the difficulty of further raising the retirement age deters the realization of the government's proposal of raising the eligible age to 65.

In regard to medical expenses, use of the past trend will cause an overestimation bias, because significant reforms have been undertaken to curb medical expenses. Therefore, I use the fact that per capita medical expenses for the elderly is about 5.2 times higher than that for younger people and estimate future values using the population forecasts.[11] The result is shown as RMED in table 9.7.

11. Note the following definitions:

• M, M_y, and M_o: total medical expenses, those for people under age 65, and those for people 65 and over, respectively.

• m_y and m_o: per capita values of M_y and M_o.

• N, N_y, and N_o: total population, that of people under age 65, and that of people age 65 and over, respectively.

If we suppose that the ratio of other social security expenditures to national income (about 1.8 percent in FY 1985) will remain unchanged, the trend in social security payments can be calculated as RSOP in table 9.7. It will increase by about 16 percentage points from 1985 to 2020.[12] This figure will be used in the following analysis.

9.4.2   National Burden

Since Japan's public pension programs are managed essentially according to the pay-as-you-go method, national burden must increase to finance the increased expenditure. We may suppose that the necessary increment in national burden is about the same magnitude as that in social security payments, because it is difficult to expect savings of this magnitude by cutting other expenditures.

Some people argue that since the number of children will decrease in the future, education-related expenditures can be reduced. However, the total amount of these expenditures is presently only about 3.8 percent of national income, including those by local governments. Thus, saving from this source is quite limited. Others argue that defense expenditures should be cut. Again, the magnitude is very small, since total defense expenditure is only about 1.26 percent of national income. Still others argue that if the amount of national debt is reduced by further pushing the "fiscal reconstruction," interest payment could be reduced. Unfortunately, saving from this source is also quite marginal.[13]

In its final report (March 1983), the Rinji Gyosei Chosakai (Ad Hoc Council on Administrative Reform) set a long-term objective of maintaining the

---

• Y: National income.

Then,

$$M/Y = (M_y + M_o)/Y = (m_y N_y + m_o N_o) / Y$$
$$= (m_y N/Y) [N_y/N + (m_o/m_y) (N_o/N)].$$

Using the present values, $M/Y = 0.0556$, $n_y/N = 0.897$, $N_o/N = 0.103$, and $m_o/m_y = 5.22$. $m_y N/Y$ is calculated as 0.0388. Using this value and assuming that the value of m_o/m_y remains unchanged, the future value of M/Y is calculated from the population data.

12. In this examination, I chose 1985 as the base year since the increase in tax burden thereafter contains some short-term effects.

13. Let us suppose that the so called "deficit financing bond" (*akaji kosai*) of the general account budget is totally eliminated. Since the total outstanding amount of this bond (¥69 trillion at the end of 1988) is 25.7 percent of the total outstanding debt of the general government (¥268 trillion), interest payment by the general government would be reduced from the present level of 5.4 percent of national income to 4.0 percent. The saving is therefore only 1.4 percent of national income.

The condition may even deteriorate, since the social security fund will be considerably reduced. Suppose that the fund of the Employees' Pension (¥72 trillion at the end of 1988) vanishes in the future, as predicted by the Ministry of Welfare. Since this amounts to 35.5 percent of the total financial assets of the general government (¥203 trillion at the end of 1988), interest receipts of the general government will fall from the present level of 4.3 percent of national income to 2.7 percent. The reduction will therefore be greater than the savings calculated above.

nation burden at a significantly lower level than the present European level of about 50 percent of national income. Recently, the Rinji Gyosei Kaikaku Suishin Shingikai (Council for Promoting Administrative Reform) revised the objective and recommended that the ratio of national burden to national income must be about 45 percent at the beginning of the next century and below 50 percent in 2020. The above analysis indicates that it would be very difficult to achieve these objectives.

9.5 The Role of the Consumption Tax

The question, then, is what tax should be used to collect the additional revenue required. In order to examine this issue, I undertook a simple simulation analysis (tables 9.9 and 9.10).

I first distinguish between working people and retired people. I assume that all wage income and business income are earned by the former and that interest income is distributed according to the ratio of population. As for transfer payments from the government, I assume that working people receive one-half of medical expenses. I further assume that all direct taxes on household and social security contributions are borne by working people (i.e., I neglect tax on interest income).

Then, figures for a through i in table 9.9 are obtained for 1985 from the National Account Statistics (the figures in the table are ratios to national income). Note that in these statistics, social security contribution paid by employers is included in both wage income and social security contribution. In defining disposable income, I neglect transfer receipts other than pension payments (i.e., "disposable income" in the tables is disposable pecuniary income).

Figures for k, l, and n in the table are per capita values. These are expressed in terms of the ratio to per capita national income and are calculated using the ratio of population.[14] Thus in 1985, the ratio of per capita pension to per capita gross income, which I call "gross replacement ratio," is 0.418. The ratio of per capita pension to per capita disposable income, which I call "net replacement ratio," is 0.525.

In estimating the figures for 2020, I note that in the present fiscal system about two-thirds of social security payments are financed by social security contributions and the rest by taxes. Assuming that national burden increases by 16 percentage points from 1985 to 2020, the ratio of social security contri-

---

14. Let N, N_w, and N_r be total population and the number of working and retired people, respectively. Let Y and y be national income and per capita national income. Then, for example, letting P denote total pension payment, per capita pension in terms of the ratio to per capita national income is calculated by

$$P/N_r)/y = P*N / (N_r*Y) = (P / Y)/[N_r/N] = f/j.$$

Here I define N_w as the population of age 20–64, and N_r as the population of age 65 and over.

Table 9.9   **Effects of Increased Burden (increase in direct tax)**

	1985		2020	
	Working	Retired	Working	Retired
Macro				
a. Wage income	0.689	0.000	0.689	0.000
b. Business income	0.151	0.000	0.151	0.000
c. Interest income	0.107	0.018	0.085	0.038
d. Income = a + b + c	0.947	0.018	0.925	0.038
e. Transfer	0.027	0.121	0.027	0.281
f. (Pension)		(0.067)		(0.207)
g. Direct tax	0.087	0.0	0.140	0.0
h. Social security contribution	0.107	0.0	0.214	0.0
i. Disposable income =				
d + f − (g + h)	0.754	0.085	0.572	0.245
j. Population share	0.608	0.103	0.535	0.236
Per capita				
k. Income = d/j	1.557	0.176	1.729	0.161
l. Pension = f/j		0.650		0.877
m. Gross replacement ratio =				
l/k(w)		(0.418)		(0.507)
n. Disposal income = i/j	1.239	0.826	1.068	1.038
o. Net replacement				
ratio = l/n(w)		(0.525)		(0.821)

Source: 1985 figures are from the National Account Statistics, Economic Planning Agency, *Yearbook of National Account Statistics* (Tokyo: Government Printing Bureau, 1991).

Notes: Figures for a–i are in terms of the ratio to national income. Figures for k, l, and n are in terms of the ratio to per capita national income; k(w) and n(w) are those of working people. Working people are age 20–64. Retired people are over 65.

Assumptions: National burden increases by 16 percentage points. All increments in tax take the form of direct tax on working people.

butions to national income will rise by 10.7 percentage points and that of taxes will rise by about 5.3 percentage points if the present system remains unchanged.

9.5.1   Increase in Direct Tax

Let us first assume that all the increment in taxes takes the form of direct tax on working people (i.e., individual income tax). Then, in 2020 tax on working people and social security contribution will be 14.0 percent and 21.4 percent of national income, respectively. I further assume that public pension payments will increase by 14 percentage points in terms of the ratio to national income and that the shares of factor incomes will remain unchanged from those in 1985.[15] Then, by the same procedure as before, figures k through o can be calculated for 2020 as shown in table 9.9.

15. This is true if the production function is Cobb-Douglas (unitary elasticity of substitution) and income distribution is determined according to the marginal product principle.

Table 9.10   **Effects of Increased Burden, Alternative policies, 2020**

	Consumption Tax		Plus Tax on Pension	
	Working	Retired	Working	Retired
d. Income	0.925	0.038	0.925	0.038
f. Pension		0.207		0.207
g'. Direct tax	0.087	0.0	0.087	0.019
h'. Social security contribution	0.214	0.0	0.195	0.0
i'. Disposable				
income = d + f − (g + h)	0.624	0.245	0.643	0.226
p. Consumption tax	0.037	0.016	0.037	0.016
q. Adjusted income = d − p	0.888	0.022	0.888	0.022
r. Adjusted disposable income = i − p	0.587	0.229	0.606	0.210
Per capita				
s. Adjusted income = q/j	1.660	0.093	1.660	0.093
l. Pension		0.877		0.797
m'. Gross replacement ratio = l/s(w)		(0.528)		(0.480)
t. Adjusted disposable income = r/j	1.097	0.970	1.133	0.890
o'. Net replacement ratio = l/t(w)		(0.799)		(0.785)

Notes: See notes to table 9.9. The assumptions are: In the "consumption tax" case, all increments in tax burden are financed by the consumption tax. In the "plus tax on pension" case, pension benefit is taxed at 9 percent, and the revenue is used to reduce social security contribution.

Note first that disposable income of working people (in terms of the ratio to national income) falls significantly due to increases in tax and social security contribution. In per capita terms, income grows due to decrease in the relative number of working people. Disposable income falls even in per capita terms.

Per capita pension receipts will grow from 65 percent of per capita national income in 1985 to 87.7 percent in 2020. The gross replacement ratio will rise from 0.418 in 1985 to 0.507 in 2020. This change may appear fairly mild. However, the distinction between gross and net replacement ratios becomes very important. In fact, a dramatic change occurs in the net replacement ratio: it will rise from 0.525 in 1985 to 0.821 in 2020. Namely, per capita pension receipt will become as high as 82.1 percent of per capita disposable income of working people. Since this is an average of the Employees' Pension and the People's Pension, and since payment level of the former is much higher than the latter, it is probable that pension receipts will become greater than disposable income of average workers for most recipients of the former. In terms of disposable income (i.e., including interest income of retired people), that of retired people will become almost the same as that of workers even in average values. If transfer payments other than public pension are included in the definition of disposable income, that of retired people would become significantly greater than that of working people. This is clearly absurd, since people

---

It is quite possible that the share of interest income will rise because a significant part of the national asset will be held in the form of overseas assets, whose rate of return is exogenously given.

of working age need more income than do the retired. Considering the difference in the number of household members, it can be argued that per capita disposable income of working-age people should be about 50 percent greater than that of the retired.

9.5.2   Alternative Policies

What measures should be taken to remedy the above situation? Of course, the most direct measure is to lower the payment level of public pensions. This, however, is politically very difficult. Hence I will examine whether tax policies can alter the situation.

First, let us consider the case in which consumption tax alone is used to finance the necessary increment in tax revenue, which is 5.3 percent of national income.[16] I assume that the burden will be distributed among working and retired people in proportion to population, i.e., by ratios of 0.69 and 0.31.[17] Then the burden of the former will be 3.7 percent of national income and that of the latter will be 1.6 percent of national income.

The resulting situation is equivalent to the one in which income and disposable income (except for pension) of working and retired people are reduced with unchanged price levels by 3.7 and 1.6 percent of national income, respectively.[18] These are shown as "adjusted income" and "adjusted disposable income" in table 9.10.

On the other hand, the real value of a pension will be unchanged if pension payments are fully indexed. Thus, replacement ratios can be obtained by dividing pension payments by adjusted income and adjusted disposable income. The results are shown on the left-hand side of table 9.10. Net replacement ratio will fall to 0.799. Disposable income of a retired person will become smaller than that of a worker.

Next, let us suppose that pension receipts are taxed at the same rate as workers' income in 1985 (about 9 percent).[19] I assume that the revenue is used to reduce social security payment. In this case, the gross replacement ratio will fall to 0.480 and the net replacement ratio will become 0.785 (table 9.10). Although the relative disposable income of the retired seems to be still higher, the situation is considerably improved.

Politically, the easiest way to increase the burden is to rely on increases of the income tax revenue, which would automatically happen if the income tax

16. In FY 1990, expected consumption tax revenue is 1.63 percent of national income. In order to obtain the necessary revenue in 2020 (6.93 percent of national income), the tax rate would have to be raised from the present 3 percent to 12.3 percent, assuming that the statutory tax base is unchanged and that the amount of tax base (in terms of the ratio to national income) is unaffected by increased tax rate.

17. Here I neglect the possibility that per capita consumption of the working people is in general greater than that of the retired because of expenses for children.

18. In the original paper, I failed to take this effect into account. The necessity of considering this was pointed out by Tatsuo Hatta.

19. Under the present tax law, pension receipts are taxable income. In practice, however, they are virtually exempt due to a very generous deduction.

law remained unchanged. The above analysis shows a serious problem in this scenario. It can be argued that raising the consumption tax rate is necessary to spread the high tax burden as evenly as possible in a society in which tax burden is growing.

It has been pointed out that there is a transition effect of tax reform: namely, if the consumption tax rate is raised, the present working generation bears a heavier lifetime burden than that of other generations because they presently bear the major burden of income tax. The analysis presented above shows that the intergenerational transfer caused by the public pension system is greater than the transition effect of the tax reform.

9.6   Undiscussed Issues and Concluding Remarks

Several important issues were not discussed in this paper.

The first issue is the reexamination of the social security system. In this paper, I assumed that the present system will be maintained. It is of course conceivable to fundamentally modify the system and reduce benefit levels. In fact, this issue should be the starting point of the debate on tax reform. If we choose to keep the present social security system intact and go the route of the European welfare state, the goal of a tax reform should be to create a system capable of raising taxes to the European level. If we abandon the idea of a welfare state and decide to reform the system, assigning only limited functions to the government, tax reforms would naturally have different goals; in particular, it would be necessary to offer incentives for people to save for retirement. Since the present tax treatments of different types of saving devices are quite unsystematic and inequitable, this issue is very important.

The second issue is the long-term effect on saving and external performance of the economy. In the analysis in section 9.5, I assume that macroeconomic conditions are unaffected by the choice of taxes to finance social security expenditures. Needless to say, this is not warranted. Whether consumption tax or income tax is used to finance increased social security expenditures would have significant impacts on the long-term performance of the economy, especially on the saving rate.

In principle, there are two possible effects, substitution and distributional. Since a consumption tax exempts saving, it would increase saving relative to when the income tax is used, unless elasticity of substitution is very small. Since a consumption tax imposes a relatively smaller burden on those who are in the process of saving, it would increase macroeconomic saving relative to when the income tax is used.

I have examined this issue elsewhere by using an overlapping-generations simulation model originally developed by Auerbach and Kotlikoff (Noguchi 1987b). My basic conclusion was that Japan's current external surplus will become a deficit in 2015 and will enlarge to as much as -7.5 percent of GDP in 2020 if the income tax alone is used to finance increases in social security expenditures. On the other hand, it will remain positive in 2015 and will be − 3.4 percent of GDP if a consumption tax is used instead. In this way, the use of a consumption tax will alleviate Japan's external deficit problem in the future.

Needless to say, the use of a consumption tax would enlarge Japan's external surplus in the near future. It must be noted that the difference is small, however, since the amount to be financed is still small. When the need for financing social security expenditures becomes large, Japan's saving rate would become considerably lower than the present level. Preventing Japan's saving rate from falling too much would therefore be desirable from the international viewpoint also.

Although the consumption tax was introduced in April 1989, the issue has not yet been settled. In the 1989 upper house election, the opposition parties chose the abolition of the consumption tax as the main political issue and obtained a "landslide victory." The political discussions were very myopic, however, in the sense that most of them were concerned with the details of the consumption tax. Very few discussions were held on long-term problems such as the ones discussed in this paper.

If these problems are seriously considered, discussion must focus on revising the present tax so that it can finance the increased fiscal needs. From this standpoint, the following points are important:

1. Reexamination of the "simplified taxation method," which allows deduction of a certain percentage of sales regardless of the actual purchase.
2. Reform from the present subtraction method with no invoices to a tax credit method with invoices.
3. Reexamination of the exemption level, which is presently too generous.
4. Earmarking the consumption tax revenue for social security expenditures.

Another round of tax reform will be necessary in the near future to deal with these issues.

Appendix
An Outline of Japanese Social Security and Private Pensions

The Japanese social security system consists of three major components: public assistance, social insurance, and other welfare programs. The social insurance system, which consists of health insurance, public pensions, and unemployment compensation, is the most important of the three, especially from the fiscal viewpoint.

The social insurance system in Japan is complex because people of different employment statuses belong to different programs. The basic distinction made in the system is among employees of private firms, government employees, and the self-employed. In the case of public pensions, employees of private firms belong to the Employees' Pension (Kosei Nenkin), the self-employed to the People's Pension (Kokumin Nenkin), and government employees to the Cooperative Pension (Kyosai Nenkin).

Contributions to the Employees' Pension are determined in terms of their ratio to "regular earning," which is wage earnings minus bonuses. For the People's Pension, contributions are set at fixed amounts.

Administrative arrangements vary as well. Health insurance for the self-employed is operated by local governments, that for employees of large private firms is operated by cooperatives in each firm, and all other programs are operated by special accounts of the national government. For most programs, subsidies are provided from the general account budget; that is, the programs are financed by both social security contributions and taxes.

In Japan, the phrase *social security* is used in a different way from that in the United States: it includes not only public pension programs but also medical insurance programs and various welfare programs. In this paper, I use the words in this broader sense.

Private pensions play certain roles in supplementing the public pension programs. The most important schemes are the Employees' Pension Fund (Kosei Nenkin Kikin) and the Tax-Qualified Pension (Zeisei Tekikaku Nenkin). The former is similar to the British contracting-out system, while the latter is similar to the U.S. corporate pension system.

Tax treatments of private pension programs are similar to those of public pensions. The number of workers covered was about 7.9 million for the former and about 7.3 million for the latter in 1986. Together they amount to more than half of the workers covered by the government's Employees' Pension, which is about 27 million (there are some duplications in these numbers). Accumulated funds were ¥14.5 trillion for the former and ¥8.3 trillion for the latter at the end of FY 1986. They amount to more than one-third of the funds of the Employees' Pension, which were about ¥55 trillion at the end of FY 1986.

Private pension plans for individuals are sold by insurance companies and the post offices. However, their importance is not so large (the accumulated fund was about ¥3 trillion at the end of FY 1986).

References

Homma, Masaaki. 1986. *Zeisei Kaikaku no Simulation* (A simulation of tax reform). Tokyo: Seisaku Koso Forum.

Institute of Population Problems. Ministry of Health and Welfare. 1987. *Population Projections for Japan: 1985–2085* (in Japanese). Tokyo: Health and Welfare Statistics Association.

Ishi, Hiromitsu. 1989. *The Japanese Tax System.* Oxford: Clarendon Press.

Nagano, Atsushi. 1988. Japan. In *World Tax Reform: A Progress Report,* ed. Joseph A. Pechman. Washington, D.C.: Brookings Institution.

Noguchi, Yukio. 1986. Overcommitment in Pensions: The Japanese Experience. In *The Welfare State East and West,* ed. Richard Rose and Rei Shiratori. Oxford: Oxford University Press.

————. 1987a. Koteki Nenkin no Shorai to Nihon Keizai no Taigai Performance (Future of public pensions and external performance of the Japanese economy). *Financial Review* (5) (June): 8–19.

————. 1987b. Public Finance. In *The Political Economy of Japan,* vol. 1, *The Domestic Transformation,* ed. Kozo Yamamura and Yasukichi Yasuba. Stanford: Stanford University Press.

————. 1990. Tax Reform Debates in Japan. In *World Tax Reform,* ed. M. Boskin and Charles E. McLure, Jr. San Francisco: International Center for Economic Growth.

Tachibanaki, Toshiaki, and Osamu Ichioka. 1988. Public Investment, Aging Trend, and Financing: General Equilibrium Evaluations. In *Papers and Proceedings of the Fourth EPA International Symposium, Global and Domestic Policy Implications of Correcting External Imbalances,* Tokyo, March 15–17.

Comment   Hiromitsu Ishi

I find Yukio Noguchi's paper very suggestive and instructive. If we admit his assumptions and basic framework, this paper will automatically lead us to his results, although some assumptions look very heroic. It is difficult to find any serious defects in the paper. His argument is very robust. Most remarkably, he clarifies the apparent effects of two tax structures, direct tax and VAT, on each age group, working or retired, in an aging population.

Many people in Japan have discussed predictions of tax effects on different age groups under different tax schemes, but no one has so far tried to quantify future tax burdens in relation to the demographic change. In this sense, Noguchi's results should be considered when deciding whether to introduce the VAT to Japan.

Let me raise a couple of points. First, what kind of policy implications does Noguchi derive from his estimated results? Needless to say, estimated results are extreme cases and merely serve as reference points for further discussion. In order to reach more practical or realistic conclusions, he might consider some combination of restricted tax increase and reductions of social security benefits.

Second, related to the first point, all estimates are based on the assumption that the present social security system will remain unchanged. As Noguchi fully understands, however, this assumption is quite unrealistic. Many people

Hiromitsu Ishi is professor of economics at Hitotsubashi University.

agree that further reforms in the social security system must cut benefits in the future. We need ideas for reform of the present social security system. In particular, Japan's demographic changes will increase the relative share of the group over age 85, as compared with less-old retirees. Will this special feature be important in the reconstruction of the social security system?

Third, Noguchi mentioned the emergence of the "bulge generation" (dankai sedai) in the demographic structure, caused by the baby boom immediately following the war. Toward 2020, this generation will play a vital role in maintaining Japan's social security system. This generation may wish to choose their own self-supporting scheme apart from the public pension, although in practice it's almost impossible. At least they will have reason to complain about the big gap between their contribution and benefits over a life-cycle period. If possible, they may get out of the public pension scheme and move to a private pension, mainly because the private scheme could benefit them more. How will the bulge generation influence improvements to social security?

Comment   Maria S. Gochoco

Yukio Noguchi's paper documents the changing demographic structure in Japan, particularly the aging of the population, and the need to find sources of revenue to finance projected increases in pension payments. It proposes the use of an indirect tax, namely, the consumption tax, as an alternative to the current use of direct taxes in the form of income taxes and social security contributions. The author contends that the use of the consumption tax achieves a greater degree of intergenerational equity in terms of tax burden.

I have two sets of comments: one takes issue with some of the technical aspects of the paper and the other consists of suggestions regarding the overall framework of the study.

In footnote 9, Noguchi presents the equation he uses to forecast the ratio of public pension payments to national income (RPEN) as a function of the ratio of people over age 65 to total population (R65) and a dummy variable. It is the following estimated over the period 1965–86:

$$RPEN = -6.7 + 1.3\,R65 - 0.9\,DUMMY$$

The estimated values of RPEN are presented in column (A) of table 9.7, which I reproduce here and compare with R65, or C/D taken from table 9.4.

First of all, table 9C.1 implies that in the years to come the formula for calculating benefits will change as an increasing proportion of the population

Maria S. Gochoco is associate professor of economics at the University of the Philippines.

Table 9C.1

Year	RPEN (%)	R65 (%)
1985	6.7	10.3
2000	14.6	16.3
2010	19.4	20.0
2020	24.1	23.6

composed of those age 65 and over receive an increasing share of national income in the form of pension payments.

It is important to ask, therefore, whether the author's forecasting equation for RPEN is appropriate. The equation for RPEN implies that a 1% increase in R65 gives rise to a 1.3% increase in RPEN. This is why the author obtains the result that pension receipts become larger than the disposable income of workers. However, one may take issue with the author's estimating the RPEN equation over the 1965–85 period. A look at the trend in RPEN in table 9.2 strongly suggests a structural break between 1973 and 1974. This structural break may not be adequately accounted for by the DUMMY variable in the RPEN equation. Furthermore, there appears to be a decelerating rate of increase in RPEN between 1974 and 1979 and between 1980 and 1987, for example, which means that a linear function fitted for these years will tend to overestimate RPEN. My suggestion is for the author to reestimate RPEN from 1974 onward with the appropriate functional form.

More generally, while it is clear that the consumption tax is preferable to direct taxation on equity grounds, the problem is that it hits the working people as well. While the consumption tax can be used to reduce the income tax burden on the working group, a scheme that subjects the old to global income taxation would be superior to simply using the consumption tax. Global taxation of old people's incomes would allow for smaller increases in the consumption tax, a point that should not be taken lightly, since a mere 3% consumption tax almost cost the ruling LDP the last election. The author suggests that cutting pension payments is politically infeasible. In addition, it is also unfair because all pensioners are taxed regardless of where their income comes from. A reduction in pension payments taxes the old who have little or no other source of income besides pension payments and the old who have a lot of interest income. Again, global taxation of old people's incomes leads to greater equity.

Finally, Japan might consider a change in its employment/retirement policy in the direction of lengthening the working years. Such a policy change would alter the dimensions of the problem addressed in this paper.

Comment   Charles E. McLure, Jr.

Yukio Noguchi makes a convincing case that the social security system of Japan is in serious trouble. This is shown by his statistics on the national burden, dependency ratios, and the ratio of social security cost to national income. This may come as a surprise to those who believe that social security is inadequate in Japan. Noguchi argues that demographics, and not inadequate benefits, explains this perception. Replacement ratios are actually quite generous by international standards, but the covered population is still young. As the social security system matures, its finance will become increasingly burdensome.

Every means of dealing with the anticipated fiscal implications has political problems. Reducing benefits directly or reducing them indirectly, by taxing benefits, are both said to be politically unacceptable. Financing currently scheduled benefits through increases in payroll taxes would impose unacceptable tax rates on the working population. Noguchi suggests an alternative, using increased consumption tax revenues to finance social security expenditures. One wonders whether this is any more likely to be politically acceptable than the other solutions. After all, increasing consumption taxes is tantamount to imposing a capital levy on existing wealth. If Noguchi's scheme were implemented, pensioners would join housewives in opposition to the VAT. Moreover, if pensions are indexed for inflation, increasing consumption taxation will not reduce the real income of pensioners, as required for financial soundness.

Charles E. McLure, Jr., is a senior fellow at the Hoover Institution at Stanford University and a research associate of the National Bureau of Economic Research. From 1983 to 1985 he was deputy assistant secretary of the U.S. Treasury Department.

10 Bequest Taxes and Accumulation of Household Wealth: U.S.-Japan Comparison

Thomas A. Barthold and Takatoshi Ito

10.1 Introduction

The objective of this paper is twofold. First, we describe and compare the gift and bequest (estate) tax systems in the United States and Japan. Second, we use tax data to estimate the magnitude of intergenerational transfers.

From the description of the bequest and gift tax systems in the two countries, we discuss distortions and incentives of those systems. Our findings of the economic significance of bequests in household assets hold important implications for the controversy regarding how much outstanding wealth is the result of intergenerational transfers. In Japan and the United States, a substantial portion of wealth, and especially of land in Japan, is bequeathed from one generation to the next. The study of the transfer tax system is also timely, because in both countries significant revisions have recently been made or have been proposed.

In the macroeconomic literature of saving, studies have suggested the existence of a bequest motive in Japan (Hayashi 1986; Hayashi, Ito, and Slemrod 1988; Hayashi, Ando, and Ferris 1988; Ishikawa ᵃ1988; Noguchi, Uemura, and Kitoh 1989). Other studies have estimated the magnitude of intergenerational transfers in the United States (Cox 1990; Hurd 1987; David and Menchik 1979; Menchik and David 1983; Bernheim, Shleifer, and Summers 1985). In particular, Kotlikoff and Summers (1981, 707) pointed out that be-

Thomas A. Barthold is a staff economist for the Joint Committee on Taxation of the U.S. Congress. Takatoshi Ito is professor of economics at Hitotsubashi University and a research associate of the National Bureau of Economic Research.
An earlier version of this paper was presented at the macroeconomics workshop of the University of Tokyo, Comments from Professors Ching-huei Chang, Tatsuo Hatta, Patric Hendershott, Hiromitsu Ishi, Tsuneo Ishikawa, Anne O. Krueger, Minoru Nakazato, Yukio Noguchi, Assaf Razin, and John Whalley are greatly appreciated. This paper does not represent the views of the staff of the Joint Committee on Taxation or any member of the U.S. Congress.

quests play an important role in capital accumulation: "American capital accumulation results primarily from intergenerational transfers." However, a consensus does not exist about the size and importance of intergenerational transfers as opposed to life-cycle saving in determining outstanding wealth (Modigliani 1988 and Kotlikoff 1988 offer opposing views).

Despite proliferating studies on bequests in the United States, few studies have examined the effect of the transfer tax system on bequest behavior in Japan. (Notable exceptions are Dekle 1989a, 1989b.) If the Kotlikoff-Summers effect is strong and universal, is the high saving rate in Japan a result of a strong bequest motive combined with its transfer tax system? This paper presents an estimate of the amount of wealth transferred by bequest in Japan. Although the estimate is sensitive to assumptions about behavior in nontaxable deaths, the estimate takes a first step toward an understanding of the significance of bequests in Japan.

To our best knowledge, this paper is the first to analyze bequest taxation time-series data (collected by tax agencies) of the two countries in a comparative perspective, and to estimate bequeathed assets in proportion to outstanding assets from tax data. The approach used in this paper may be contrasted with the survey method (Noguchi, Uemura, and Kitoh 1989, for example) or the method of estimating lifetime income and consumption (Kotlikoff and Summers 1981, for example).

The rest of this paper is organized as follows. Section 10.2 highlights the differences and similarities between the intergenerational transfer tax systems of Japan and the United States. (Detailed descriptions of the two tax systems are in the appendices. For the Japanese system, the tax reform of 1988 will be discussed as much as possible.) Section 10.3 shows the compositions of bequeathed properties in the two countries. Section 10.4 is devoted to analyzing the effects of tax distortions on portfolio behavior in Japan. Section 10.5 and 10.6 give estimates of the proportion of assets obtained by intergenerational transfers in Japan and the United States, respectively.

10.2   Intergenerational Transfer Taxes in Japan and the United States

This section highlights the similarities and differences of the bequest tax and gift tax systems of Japan and the United States (the inheritance tax in Japan and the estate tax in the United States). (Detailed legal descriptions will be found in the appendices and in Ishi 1989, chap. 11.) All property of a decedent is subject to the inheritance tax in Japan and to the estate tax in the United States. The gift tax in both countries is a tax on the transfer of wealth during life.

10.2.1   Overview

The basic difference between the inheritance tax in Japan and the estate tax in the United States is that the tax is imposed on recipients (beneficiaries) of bequest in Japan, while it is imposed on the estate of the decedent (benefactor) in the United States. One may think that this is a superficial difference. However, the structure of bequest taxation is affected by this philosophical difference. In Japan, a progressive rate schedule is applied to each statutory heir and then aggregated to calculate the total tax liability. More (statutory) heirs for a given estate lessens the total tax liability on the estate. (This was a known loophole for the wealthy in Japan prior to 1988. The term "statutory heir" and the tax-saving scheme will be explained later.) In the United States, the number of heirs is irrelevant in the calculation of the estate tax. The tax is assessed progressively on the value of the estate, regardless of its distribution. In both countries, agricultural land and family business properties benefit from special provisions to lessen their assessment value. In Japan, however, land generally is assessed significantly below its market value, partly due to a special assessment rate reduction and partly due to assessment in practice. There is no such provision in the United States. Such undervaluation of land should create some tax-induced portfolio shifting among bequest-minded elderly Japanese. This point will be examined later in this section.

The basic philosophies of the gift tax in relation to the bequest tax are rather different between Japan and the United States. The gift tax in Japan is defined as complementary to the bequest tax, with the intent to prevent inter vivos transfers that are meant to lessen the bequest tax. In the United States, the gift and estate taxes are, in principle, a unified transfer tax system in that one progressive tax is imposed on the cumulative transfers during the lifetime and at death. In sum, the gift tax in Japan discourages inter vivos transfers, while the gift tax in the United States is integrated in a unified tax schedule on intergenerational transfers, not discriminating, in theory, inter vivos and postmortem transfers.

In both countries, it is possible to take advantage of a basic deduction per transfer in the gift tax system, by making a small gift each year for many years in order to reduce bequest (inheritance or estate) tax liability. However, the extent of this loophole is more limited in Japan than in the United States. In Japan, this basic deduction for a tax-free gift is ¥600,000 ($4,000) per recipient, while in the United States, an individual can make annual gifts of $10,000 to any other individual without being subject to tax. Couples jointly can make $20,000 of tax-free gifts to each recipient. In both countries, gifts within three years prior to death are recaptured as inheritance or part of the estate and are subject to the bequest or estate tax. (See details in appendices.) In the United States, the difference in calculating tax liability on a tax-inclusive or tax-exclusive basis makes the gift tax liability less than the estate tax liability. (See details in appendix B.)

In both countries, the bequest and gift taxes are presumed, in principle, to be taxes on intergenerational transfers. There are various credits on transfers within the generation and penalties on transfers to recipients other than lineal descendants. However, the manner in which this principle is reflected in the tax code is different in the two countries. In Japan, the Civil Code guarantees a spouse, a son, or a daughter a minimum share of the bequest (50 percent of the "statutory" share, explained in appendix A). This is a direct intervention, rather than a tax incentive, on the composition of intergenerational transfers. In the United States, there is no legal provision designating to whom or how much of a bequest is to be given.

From the principle of taxing intergenerational transfers, the United States' estate and gift tax system makes any transfers, inter vivos or upon death, to a spouse tax-exempt. In Japan, there is a limit on the size of a tax-free bequest or gift to a spouse. A relatively large tax credit is available for a bequest to a spouse. In effect, the greater of half of the decedent's property, regardless of size, and ¥80 million ($533,333) may be bequeathed to a spouse tax-free. In the case of gifts, a gift of (own) residential housing valued up to ¥20 million ($133,333) may be transferred to a "longtime spouse" (once per marriage of twenty years or more). Beyond this amount, theoretically even between spouses, gifts are taxable.

In theory, transfer taxes should apply to a family's wealth once per generation. Transfer of wealth from a grandfather to a grandchild would be taxed twice in a normal succession of bequests. Hence, there is a penalty for skipping generations in transfers in both countries. In Japan, if an asset is bequeathed to a grandchild, a 20 percent surcharge over the normal tax liability is imposed. No such penalty exists for gift taxation. In the United States, a flat rate of tax equal to the highest rate of the estate tax (55 percent) after allowing a $1 million exemption per taxpayer would be imposed on a generation-skipping transfer (bequest or gift) in addition to payment of gift or estate tax. In both countries, if the grandchild's parent has predeceased the grandparent, the generation-skipping tax does not apply.

10.2.2 "Statutory Heirs" and "Statutory Shares" in Japan

The Japanese civil law concept of "statutory heir" is critical to an understanding of the Japanese inheritance tax. We concentrate on the case where there are surviving children. (For other cases, see appendix A.)

Suppose that a spouse and two children survive the decedent. They constitute three statutory heirs, and the spouse has a statutory share of one-half and each child has a statutory share of one-fourth. In the case of a spouse and three children, that is, four statutory heirs, each child has a statutory share of one-sixth. If the spouse predeceased and three children are alive, each child has a statutory share of one-third.

It is presumed in the civil law that, unless otherwise designated, one-half of the estate goes to the spouse and each child receives an equal share of the remainder. Moreover, one-half of the statutory share is a guaranteed bequest. For example, assume a spouse and two children survive the decedent; the spouse is entitled to no less than one-quarter and each child is entitled to no less than one-eighth of the property. Even if the decedent leaves a will designating a sole recipient for the entire estate, statutory heirs may sue for their automatic entitlement. More important, regardless of the actual distribution of property, the number of statutory heirs and statutory shares determine the total inheritance tax liability. (See appendix A for details.)

10.2.3 Bequest Taxable Property, Exemption, and Tax Base

In principle, a decedent's gross estate (property value) is the market value of all the decedent's assets. (A notable deviation, which we will explain in detail shortly, involves the assessment of land in Japan.) We note several provisions that define what constitutes a decedent's assets and how to value assets. In Japan, a decedent's property includes a portion of his or her lump-sum severance (retirement) payment in excess of ¥5 million times the number of statutory heirs. (Severance payments, prevalent among all corporations, have been traditional in lieu of pension or annuity plans, and are on the order of two or three times annual salary.) In Japan, any gifts within three years prior to death are deemed to be bequeathed property.

Conditions under which proceeds from a decedent's life insurance policy are included are different between the two countries. In Japan, if premiums had been paid by the decedent, the policy is bequeathed property. In general, if a daughter pays a share of the premiums of her father's life insurance, that share of the proceeds is exempted from bequeathed property. However, the amount of ¥5 million times the number of statutory heirs is deductible from the property value calculation for life insurance.

In the United States, a decedent's gross estate includes the proceeds of a life insurance policy on the decedent's life if either (1) the proceeds are receivable by the executor or administrator or payable to the estate; or (2) the decedent at his or her death (or within three years of death) possessed any "incidents of ownership" in the policy. Incidents of ownership include the power to change the beneficiary of the policy, to assign the policy, to borrow against its cash surrender value, and to surrender or cancel it.

The gross estate does not include the proceeds of a life insurance policy if the decedent, at least three years prior to death, irrevocably designates beneficiaries of the policy and transfers all other incidents of ownership to another person. This exclusion holds even if the decedent pays all policy premiums. In Japan, such a policy would be included in decedent's bequeathed property.

Both in the United States and in Japan, there is substantially favorable treatment for farm property and the assets of family businesses. This provides a tax benefit to small family businesses. In the United States, an executor may elect to have certain real property used in farming and other closely held businesses valued at its current use, rather than at fair market value, for estate tax purposes. In Japan, only agriculture qualifies for this special provision, but land value of family business properties may benefit from the underassessment of land to be explained below.

In the United States, the benefit operates by permitting the estate to value qualifying property based on the present discounted value of its current cash flow, rather than at its highest and best use. For example, the value of a farm on the outskirts of an urban area may be based on the present discounted value of the current cash flow generated by its crops, rather than on the land's value to a developer who would build suburban housing.

This provision is virtually the same in Japan. The difference comes in the qualification for this special treatment. In the United States, the decedent or a member of the family must have used the property in its qualifying use (farming or family business) in at least five of the eight years prior to death. The property must be bequeathed to a member of the decedent's family, and that beneficiary must use the property in its current use in each of the succeeding ten years. The beneficiary must actively participate in the property's use and cannot be an absentee landlord. In Japan, the qualification is that the decedent was engaged in agriculture at the time of death and the successor in family agriculture must be engaged in farming by the time of inheritance tax filing (within six months after death) and continue farming for twenty years. Failure to comply with the posttransfer requirements triggers a recapture of the benefit of the special valuation in both countries.

There are several deductions and exemptions. First, in the United States, the law permits an unlimited deduction for transfers between spouses. (In Japan, the favorable treatment of transfers to the spouse is technically done via tax credit, not deduction.) In addition, transfers and bequests to charities (to organizations certified by the Internal Revenue Service in the United States, and organizations specially defined as public welfare (interest) corporations in Japan) are deductible. Funeral and burial (or cremation) expenses and any liabilities are deductible in both countries. Expenses of administration of the estate are also deductible in the United States.

A minimum bequest amount escapes taxation regardless of other exemptions and deductions. Currently, in Japan the amount of ¥40 million plus ¥8 million times the number of statutory heirs is deducted from the property value. If a spouse and two children survived the decedent, bequests valued up to ¥64 million ($426,666) are tax free. A similar arrangement is done through a tax credit in the United States. In effect, bequests valued up to about $600,000 are tax free.

10.2.4   Tax Rate Schedule, Tax Credit, and Surcharge in Japan

In Japan, the total amount of inheritance tax owed by all heirs is determined as follows. First, assign the total tax base (property values after all deductions and exemptions) to each statutory heir by the statutory share (defined above). Then apply the tax schedule shown in table 10.1 to the assigned amount for each heir (that is, the total tax base times statutory share) to calculate a tax amount for each heir. Deduct any tax credit (to be explained shortly) from this individual tax amount. Then sum the individual tax amounts to arrive at the total inheritance tax liability. The total tax liability is independent of the actual

Table 10.1   Inheritance Tax Table in Japan (in millions of yen)

Old Schedule, 1975–87				New Schedule, 1988–present			
Taxable Transfer More Than	But Less Than	Tax	Plus MTR on Excess (%)	Taxable Transfer More Than	But Less Than	Tax	Plus MTR on Excess (%)
0	2	0	10	0	4	0	10
2	5	0.2	15	4	8	0.4	15
5	9	0.65	20	8	14	1.0	20
9	15	1.45	25	14	23	2.20	25
15	23	2.95	30	23	35	4.45	30
23	33	5.35	35	35	50	8.05	35
33	48	8.85	40	50	70	13.30	40
48	70	14.85	45	70	100	21.30	45
70	100	24.75	50	100	150	34.80	50
100	140	39.75	55	150	200	59.80	55
140	180	61.75	60	200	250	87.30	60
180	250	85.75	65	250	500	117.30	65
250	500	131.25	70	500	—	279.80	70
500	—	306.25	75				

Note: MTR = marginal tax rate.

division of property, and the actual inheritance may differ from that which the statutory shares presume. Then actual tax liabilities are adjusted in proportion. (Appendix A gives an example of how to calculate and distribute inheritance tax liability.)

The tax rate schedule starts at 10 percent for the first ¥4 million ($26,000). The marginal rate goes up to 70 percent at ¥500 million ($3.3 million). However, note again that this rate schedule is applied to a property value divided by statutory share.

In Japan the surviving spouse, minors, and the handicapped receive a tax credit. First, the surviving spouse receives a special tax credit. If a surviving spouse inherits property, she or he may deduct from the inheritance tax liability the following amount:

$$\frac{\text{Tax credit}}{\text{for spouse}} = \frac{\text{Total}}{\text{inheritance}} \times \frac{\text{Min (max [¥80 million, spouse's statutory share times taxable property value], value of property actually given to spouse)}}{\text{Total taxable property value}}$$

To understand the formula with respect to the spouse's tax liability, it is instructive to consider several examples. Assume a spouse and two children survive the decedent. If the spouse actually inherits less than the estate statutory share (one-half), the inherited amount is free from inheritance tax, however large the property is. Even if the spouse actually inherits more than the statutory share, if the bequest to the spouse is less than ¥80 million, however large a share of estate it may constitute, it is free from inheritance tax.

Second, minors and the handicapped receive a tax credit. (See appendix A for details.) Third, any gifts that were made within three years of death are deemed inheritance. In order to avoid double taxation, the gift tax paid for such gifts is credited against the inheritance tax. Fourth, if the decedent was a beneficiary of an inheritance within the ten years prior to death, an additional tax credit applies.[1]

If a beneficiary is not a child (or a grandchild if there are no children), a parent, or a spouse of a child (or a grandchild if there are no children), then there is a 20 percent surcharge on the amount of tax calculated above. So marginal rates for unrelated beneficiaries can exceed 80 percent. As explained above, this provision works to the disadvantage of generation-skipping bequests and lucky strangers.

10.2.5 Tax Rate Schedule, Tax Credit, and Surcharge in the United States

Under present law in the United States, the gift and estate tax rates begin at 18 percent on the first $10,000 of taxable transfers and reach 55 percent on transfers over $3 million (table 10.2). In addition, for transfers between $10 million and $21.04 million, the benefits of the lower rates and the unified schedule are phased out at a rate of 5 percent, creating an effective marginal tax rate of 60 percent. This schedule is applied to the estate, unlike the case of Japan, so that a direct comparison of tables 10.1 and 10.2 is meaningless.

The cumulative amount of any gift or estate tax is reduced by a unified credit. The gift or estate tax is computed without any exemption, and then the unified credit is subtracted to determine the amount of gift or estate tax payable before the allowance of other credits. The present amount of the credit is $192,800, which has the effect of exempting the first $600,000 of transfers from gift and estate tax. As a consequence, the first dollar of a taxable estate faces a 37 percent marginal tax rate. The unified credit is not indexed for inflation. Tax liability accounts for any prior gift taxes paid or unified credit claimed.

A limited credit is available for any state death or inheritance taxes paid. The state credit works as revenue sharing with the states, encouraging them to establish a death tax at least to soak up the benefit of the dollars that the federal government would otherwise tax. In Japan, there are no additional inheritance taxes at the prefecture (local) level.

While the credit is unified, the rate structure is not. The estate tax is calculated on a tax inclusive basis while the gift tax is calculated on a tax exclusive basis. This implies that the effective tax rate on gifts may be significantly lower than the effective tax rate on bequests, when the same amount of gift or

1. The formula is complicated. The interested reader is referred to a detailed tax book (Ministry of Finance 1989).

Table 10.2   **Unified Estate and Gift Tax Rate for U.S. Citizens and Residents (in dollars)**

Taxable Transfer More Than	But Less Than	Tax	Plus MTR on Excess (%)
0	10,000	0	18
10,000	20,000	1,800	20
20,000	40,000	3,800	22
40,000	60,000	8,200	24
60,000	80,000	13,000	26
80,000	100,000	18,200	28
100,000	150,000	23,800	30
150,000	250,000	38,800	32
250,000	500,000	70,800	34
500,000	750,000	155,800	37
750,000	1,000,000	248,300	39
1,000,000	1,250,000	345,800	41
1,250,000	1,500,000	448,300	43
1,500,000	2,000,000	555,800	45
2,000,000	2,500,000	780,800	49
2,500,000	3,000,000	1,025,800	53
3,000,000	—	1,290,800	55

bequest inclusive of tax liabilities is transferred. (See appendix B for an example.)

10.3   Composition of Bequest: Japan versus the United States

10.3.1   Composition of Wealth of Decedents in Japan

Table 10.3 shows property values, various exemptions, credits, and surcharges in 1977, 1987, and 1988 in Japan. Significant revision of the rate schedule, basic exemption, and tax credits occurred between 1987 and 1988 (detailed in appendix A). Bequeathed property values (equivalent to the gross estate in the United States) changed significantly from 1977 to 1987, under the same rate structure. This reflects both bracket creep due to inflation and wealth accumulation among the wealthy, in particular a rapid inflation in land prices. (See section 10.4.2 for an analysis of the composition of bequeathed property.)

Table 10.4 shows the time series of outstanding assets and liabilities of the household sector at year end. The value of landholdings and land's share of total assets also are shown. Land accounts for about one-half of the value of outstanding household assets in Japan. The ratio fluctuates according to land's price relative to other prices. The relative land price was much higher in 1973 and 1987 than in other years.

Table 10.5 shows the composition of bequeathed assets from data of the

Table 10.3   **Inheritance Tax Record (in billions of yen)**

	1977	1987	1988
Property value	2,002.220	8,990.381	10,488.777
Minus liability and funeral	128.691	774.323	891.776
Plus gifts within three years	10.724	34.843	41.054
Tax base	1,884.253	8,250.859	9,637.996
(Basic exemption)	(661.307)	(2,107.261)	(2,550.032)
Inheritance tax before sur-charge and credit	337.843	2,371.289	2,773.637
Plus 20% surcharge	2.658	6.178	19.552
Gift tax (credit)	1.620	4.996	7.444
Spouse provision (credit)	74.456	675.342	934.865
Minors (credit)	0.549	2.256	2.593
Handicapped (credit)	0.519	1.782	1.760
Two in ten years (credit)	3.099	11.874	12.733
Net inheritance tax	300.259	1,681.209	1,833.788

Source: Ministry of Finance, Tax Bureau, *Tax Bureau Statistics Annual* (1977, 1988, 1989).

Notes: Years apply to those who died in that year (and whose filings were done by the end of June, the deadline for those who died on December 31 of the preceding year). Only those who were required to file are reported. Corrections in filing included.

Tax Bureau. Only those bequeathed assets belonging to a decedent whose heirs were subject to nonzero inheritance tax are reported here, as "taxable deaths." In Japan, those who do not pay the inheritance tax are not required to report to the Tax Bureau's office, except for a spouse who benefits from the special spouse tax credit to become nontaxable.

Among bequeathed assets, land predominates. Its share fluctuates between 65 and 69 percent. Securities account for only 10 to 13 percent. This table is an underestimation of what was really transferred from the decedents of 1976–88 to the next generation. First, only taxable deaths are covered. There are many decedents whose heirs did not have to pay inheritance taxes either because bequests were small or because the number of heirs was large. Second, land value reported in this table grossly underestimates the true market value. As explained in section 10.4.2, the assessed value is in practice one-half to two-thirds of the market value. There is also a special provision for an additional 50 percent exemption for small residential lots. In fact, this incentive makes land a favorite vehicle of bequest in Japan.

10.3.2   United States

Table 10.6 shows the composition of wealth reported on U.S. estate tax returns filed in 1985. In the majority of cases these returns represent wealth transfers resulting from deaths in 1984. The nearly 68,000 federal estate tax returns filed in 1985 represent less than 3.5 percent of total deaths in the United States in 1984. Those estates subject to tax represented less than 1.5

Table 10.4   **Household Outstanding Assets and Liability at the End of Year**
                        (in billions of yen)

	Assets (1)	Land (% of assets) (part of 1)	Liability (2)	Net Assets (3) = (1) − (2)
1973	442,449.4	235,962.6 (53.33)	48,405.0	394,044.4
1974	469,683.8	233,825.4 (49.78)	54,175.3	415,508.5
1975	517,504.4	247,229.5 (47.77)	67,151.6	450,352.8
1976	583,453.4	263,566.8 (45.17)	78,002.6	505,450.8
1977	642,486.6	284,566.6 (44.29)	87,469.0	555,017.6
1978	738,848.3	326,573.8 (44.20)	102,381.0	636,467.3
1979	864,851.9	393,556.6 (45.50)	114,412.5	750,439.4
1980	984,954.3	467,210.9 (47.43)	129,168.7	855,785.6
1981	1,104,237.9	537,526.9 (48.67)	142,661.0	961,576.9
1982	1,182,808.1	574,418.3 (48.56)	154,977.9	1,027,830.2
1983	1,252,943.4	595,207.7 (47.50)	167,369.6	1,085,573.8
1984	1,340,621.0	627,389.4 (46.79)	181,583.3	1,159,037.7
1985	1,438,991.6	672,882.2 (46.76)	194,538.1	1,244,453.3
1986	1,674,186.7	831,247.4 (49.65)	209,501.5	1,464,685.2
1987	2,027,702.3	1,089,883.8 (53.74)	236,998.7	1,790,703.6
1988	2,249,380.3	1,198,149.0 (53.26)	264,287.0	1,985,093.3
Average		(48.3)		

Source: Economic Planning Agency (1990 and various issues)

percent of total deaths in the United States in 1984. The table is largely self-explanatory. The unified nature of the U.S. transfer tax system is exhibited by the inclusion of taxable lifetime transfers (gifts) in the gross estate. These represent 11.4 percent of the gross estate. The importance of the marital deduction is seen in that one-third of the value of gross estates for which returns were filed was exempted from tax by the marital deduction. Appendix B contains similar data for returns filed in 1977, 1982, 1983, 1984, 1986, 1987, and 1988.

For comparison purposes, table 10.7 presents estimates of aggregate net

Table 10.5   Composition of Bequeathed Assets, Japan Taxable Death Only (in billions of yen; shares of total in parentheses)

Year	Land[a]	Structures[b]	Business[c]	Securities[d]	Cash[e]	Miscellaneous	Total Assets	Liabilities	Funeral Expenses	Bequest Tax
1973	1,220.5 (70.95)	53.0 (3.08)	20.4 (1.19)	179.4 (8.93)	149.9 (6.97)	97.1 (4.83)	1,720.3	116.5		375.4
1974	1,437.8 (71.53)	63.3 (3.15)	24.8 (1.23)	182.2 (9.06)	169.2 (8.42)	132.6 (6.60)	2,010.0	133.3		437.7
Tax reform										
1975	1,121.0 (70.38)	44.4 (2.79)	15.2 (0.76)	169.8 (8.45)	138.4 (6.89)	104.0 (6.53)	1,592.8	74.5	16.7	241.0
1976	1,205.6 (68.28)	53.5 (3.03)	18.5 (1.04)	198.9 (11.26)	158.8 (8.99)	130.4 (7.38)	1,765.6	90.9	20.1	264.4
1977	1,349.1 (67.78)	64.7 (3.25)	21.4 (1.07)	219.9 (11.04)	175.7 (8.82)	158.5 (7.96)	1,990.4	102.2	24.3	300.3
1978	1,538.8 (67.04)	79.3 (3.45)	28.1 (1.22)	244.9 (10.67)	207.6 (9.04)	196.3 (8.55)	2,295.1	120.9	29.2	349.4
1979	1,728.8 (66.33)	88.0 (3.37)	35.3 (1.35)	273.7 (10.50)	236.5 (9.07)	243.7 (9.35)	2,606.1	153.1	34.8	398.1
1980	2,144.0 (66.91)	106.0 (3.30)	37.9 (1.18)	343.9 (10.73)	277.2 (8.65)	295.0 (9.20)	3,204.0	169.6	44.3	525.6
1981	2,773.5 (68.38)	129.5 (3.19)	39.8 (0.98)	401.0 (9.88)	331.4 (8.17)	380.7 (9.38)	4,056.0	211.1	54.0	672.0

1982	3,331.0	150.9	45.6	417.3	371.0	430.6	4,746.4	247.9	63.2	809.6
	(70.17)	(3.17)	(0.96)	(8.79)	(7.81)	(9.07)				
1983	3,656.0	170.8	48.7	501.6	425.9	496.6	5,299.6	269.7	71.6	914.6
	(68.98)	(3.22)	(0.91)	(9.46)	(8.03)	(9.37)				
1984	3,918.8	202.2	64.9	563.7	483.0	570.4	5,803.1	350.6	79.9	979.1
	(67.52)	(3.48)	(1.11)	(9.71)	(8.32)	(9.82)				
1985	4,437.4	233.9	54.9	703.3	576.3	653.3	6,659.2	382.0	92.8	1,158.4
	(66.63)	(3.51)	(0.82)	(10.56)	(8.65)	(9.81)				
1986	4,682.6	272.6	61.9	868.4	664.4	715.1	7.265.0	465.4	101.3	1,277.4
	(64.45)	(3.75)	(0.85)	(11.95)	(9.14)	(9.84)				
1987	5,747.3	326.9	68.2	1,152.3	811.1	850.6	8,956.6	653.1	120.6	1,681.2
	(64.16)	(3.64)	(0.76)	(12.86)	(9.05)	(9.49)				
Tax reform										
1988	7,411.5	358.7	59.0	1,220.9	911.3	737.7	10,699.3	755.8	113.3	1,833.8
	(69.27)	(3.35)	(0.55)	(11.41)	(8.51)	(6.89)				

Source: Ministry of Finance, Tax Bureau, *Tax Bureau Statistics Annual* (various issues).

[a]Including residential, rice paddy, field, and forest.
[b]Including houses.
[c]Family business property.
[d]Including bonds and stocks.
[e]Cash and deposits.

Table 10.6　　　　**U.S. Estate Tax Returns Filed in 1985**

	Returns		Value	
	Number	%	Millions of $	%
Gross estate	67,961	100.0	62,805.4	100.0
Real estate	47,795	70.3	13,948.4	22.2
Bonds (total)	28,656	42.2	4,894.9	7.8
Federal savings	9,507	14.0	368.9	0.6
Federal other	10,118	14.9	1,409.7	2.2
State and local	16,073	23.7	2,761.9	4.4
Corporate and foreign	11,100	16.3	354.5	0.6
Corporate stock	45,126	66.4	15,001.2	23.9
Noncorporate business	16,721	24.6	1,981.4	3.2
Cash	58,036	85.4	8,439.7	13.4
Notes and mortgages	20,499	30.2	2,386.2	3.8
Life insurance	36,805	54.2	2,108.7	3.4
Annuities	12,131	17.8	1,011.0	1.6
Household goods	53,437	78.6	2,614.5	4.2
Lifetime transfers	8,777	12.9	7,181.8	11.4
Deductions (total)	67,961	100.0	31,364.4	49.9
Funeral expenses	63,820	93.9	378.7	0.6
Administrative expenses (total)	43,688	64.3	1,506.7	2.4
Executors' commission	19,488	28.7	524.5	0.8
Attorneys	35,429	52.1	624.8	1.0
Other	42,355	62.3	357.4	0.6
Debts and mortgages	56,005	82.4	3,608.4	5.7
Charity	11,713	17.2	4,543.1	7.2
Marital	31,823	46.8	21,327.5	34.0
Taxable estate	59,459	87.5	31,644.9	50.4
Adjusted taxable gifts	3,566	5.2	208.2	0.3
Adjusted taxable estate	59,459	87.5	31,925.1	50.8
Estate tax before credits	59,459	87.5	11,247.6	17.9
Credits (total)	59,459	87.5	6,212.2	9.9
Unified	59,459	87.5	5,038.9	8.0
State death taxes	33,060	48.6	1,077.6	1.7
Other	—[a]	—	95.7	0.2
Estate tax	30,518	44.9	5,035.4	8.0

Source: Internal Revenue Service, Statistics of Income Division.
[a]Number not disclosed to retain taxpayer confidentiality.

worth by major components for the United States based on the Survey of Consumer Finance (SCF, 1983 data), the Panel Study in Income Dynamics (PSID, 1984 data) and the Survey of Income and Program Participation (SIPP, 1984 data). Note that in the table secured debt is netted from the reported asset. By these data, bequeathable wealth reported on estate tax returns made up between 0.6 and 1.0 percent of private national wealth. This, of course, is an

Table 10.7   **Estimates of Aggregate Net Worth and Major Components (in billions of dollars)**

	SCF	PSID	SIPP
Vehicle equity	308	503	410
House equity	2,904	2,573	2,683
Other real estate equity	1,640	1,170	783
Liquid assets	1,032	1,204	965[a]
IRAs, Keoghs	149	—[b]	125
Common stock mutual funds	1,056	709	466
Farm/business equity	2,391	1,436	843
Other assets	1,260	820	365
Other debt	227	159	240
Net worth	10,505	8,254	6,401

Note: PSID = Panel Study in Income Dynamics (1984 data), SCF = Survey of Consumer Finance (1983 data), SIPP = Survey of Income and Program Participation (1984 data).

[a]Includes corporate, municipal, and tradable federal debt, which are included in "Other assets" in the SCF and PSID data. The SCF total for such bonds is $314 billion.

[b]Included partly in liquid assets, partly in common stock.

underestimate. Those who file estate tax returns represent a small percentage of all decedents, albeit the wealthiest of all decedents. At this aggregate level, bequeathable wealth appears to represent a larger fraction of total national wealth in the United States than in Japan.

10.4   Distortions in the Japanese Inheritance Tax

10.4.1   Token Adoption

It is apparent from the calculation of the inheritance tax that the number of statutory heirs plays an important role. The number of statutory heirs need not equal the true number of heirs. Having more statutory heirs reduces total inheritance taxes imposed upon actual heirs. This is independent of how the decedent actually divides his or her property. Three features of the inheritance tax produce this result. First, the basic exemption depends on the number of statutory heirs. Second, the total property value after exemptions is divided by the number of statutory heirs before a progressive tax schedule is applied. Third, a tax credit for life insurance payment and severance payment depends on the number of statutory heirs.

Hence, a family may reduce inheritance tax liability by adopting children to increase the number of statutory heirs, with an understanding that the adopted children receive only a nominal compensation for this service. (By being adopted by someone else, one does not forfeit the legal right of being the statutory heir to one's biological parents.) This loophole was widely recognized and exploited by wealthy families. Table 10.8 reveals a strong correlation between the size of the estate and the number of statutory heirs.

Table 10.8   Number of Statutory Heirs in Relation to Property Values, 1988

Tax Base (in millions of yen)	Number of Statutory Heirs											
	0	1	2	3	4	5	6	7	8	9	10	11+
0–30	39	257	158									
30 < 40	10	597	798	495	264							
40 < 50	11	604	1,124	904	586	710	70	57				
50 < 100	12	913	4,630	4,472	3,233	3,170	603	279	121	70	27	112
100 < 200	14	545	2,780	3,644	3,305	2,563	864	467	244	113	61	141
200 < 300	11	123	726	1,105	1,143	842	347	226	136	54	33	71
300 < 500	19	94	435	779	854	582	327	155	113	60	32	49
500 <	2	67	305	568	799	559	335	261	136	83	42	85

Source: Ministry of Finance, Tax Bureau, *Tax Bureau Statistics Annual* (various issues).

Note: The median number of statutory heirs for each bequeathed taxable income bracket was 1 for 0–30 (million yen); 2 for 30–40; 3 for 40–50; 3 for 50–100; 4 for each of 100–200, 200–300, 300–500, and over 500.

To close this loophole, the 1988 revision included a cap on the number of adopted children counted as statutory heirs. The effective date for this change was not until December 31, 1988, unlike most other changes, which became effective on January 1, 1988. Hence, we have to wait one more year to see the difference in this kind of table. We conjecture that when we compute table 10.8 for 1989, the number of statutory heirs among the wealthy will be significantly reduced. That would prove that adopted children, real or token, have been significantly lowering the tax liability of wealthy families.

10.4.2   Land Assessment

All bequeathed assets, securities, and real estate are, in principle, valued at their fair market value. In practice, two deviations from this principle exist. Real estate, such as residential land, and land and structures for family business, are assessed at less than their market value. This results partly because assessments for inheritance purpose are underestimated and partly because there is a special provision for small property.

The first factor results from administrative practice. Land, which is a major portion of real property in Japan, is assessed for inheritance tax according to a valuation map (known as Rosen Ka) in the Tax Bureau's office. This is different from the land price survey (known as Koji Kakaku) done by the Land Agency of the Japanese government, or the land valuation for real estate taxes (imposed by municipal governments). Each of these three government assessments (Koji Kakaku, Rosen Ka, and real estate tax assessment) is below the market value of property.

Experts widely follow a rule of thumb. The Koji Kakaku, polled once a year, is approximately 70 to 80 percent of the market value. The Rosen Ka, for bequest evaluation, is approximately 50 to 70 percent of the Koji Kakaku. Homma and Atoda (1989, 134–35) investigated the gap between the Koji

Kakaku and Rosen Ka at the places of highest Rosen Ka in the capital cities of prefectures. They found that in 1988 the gap ranged from 33.5 percent in Kyoto to 94.1 percent in Kōfu, with an average of 56.4 percent. Hence, the ratio of Rosen Ka, the assessment of land for bequest, to the market value is anywhere between 25 and 80 percent, but more likely around 40 to 50 percent.

The second factor for underassessment is a provision for small sites for residences such as rental housing or for business. The assessment for the 200 square meters of residential property is reduced by 50 percent and for business sites by 60 percent. If the property is partly residential and partly business, the business portion is reduced by 60 percent, and the residential portion is reduced by 40 percent, providing that the average rate is above 50 percent.

In sum, a bequest carried in the form of real estate is subject to less inheritance tax than that carried in the form of securities. Moreover, since the amount of debt is deductible in full, an effective way to reduce inheritance tax is to borrow a large sum of money to purchase real property, preferably shortly before death, so that the property is still highly levered at the time of intergenerational transfer.

To curtail such tax planning, the 1988 tax reform mandated that any real estate (land and structures, excluding the decedent's personal residence) purchased within three years of the date of death is assessed at its purchase price. (This is evidence that the tax authority admits that assessed values are in practice less than the market value.) This rule still permits a tax advantage in periods of high land inflation.

We expect that this favorable assessment induces the elderly with a bequest motive to shift their portfolio into real estate. The evidence suggests that is the case. First, the share of land in tax-filing bequeathed property value is higher than the share of land in outstanding property value of households. In 1988, the former was 69 percent, while the latter was 53 percent. Second, the share of land in bequest property value is higher in Japan than in the United States. In Japan about 65 percent of bequests are in the form of land, while in the United States, only about 20 percent are in land. Even under the most generous interpretation, which would accept the SIPP data as the most accurate and count none of the farm and business property as real estate, and at the same time attribute no debt to the real estate claimed on the estate tax returns, the percentage of real estate in decedent's estates is barely 0.4 percent of U.S. wealth represented by real estate. This figure is less than half of the comparable figure for Japan. This may reflect the substantial benefit in Japan to the decedent holding his or her wealth in real estate at the time of death.

However, some cautious notes to the above conclusion are due. There may be some reasons that the land component in bequests may become larger, even in the absence of underassessment for bequest purposes. First, unrealized capital gains on the land of the elderly may avoid capital gains tax if bequeathed instead of sold. Second, one might argue that the relatively high land component in Japan may not reflect a bequest motive and rational tax saving strategy, but may result from unexpected capital gains on land and premature death. Put differently, if precautionary saving in imputed housing services is prevalent, unexpected land price increases, as in Japan, create a large proportion of land value in bequests. In fact, in Japan the land proportion has increased at times of land price increases.

Both arguments stress that land prices have increased faster in Japan than the United States. The ratio of land to total bequest has been consistently higher in Japan than in the United States, by a large margin. Moreover, if the (intended) bequest motive is weak, financial borrowing (second mortgage) among the elderly against unrealized capital gains should increase as unexpected land price inflation takes place. Existing data do not reveal commensurate increases in second mortgages.

10.5   Estimating Bequeathed Assets in Outstanding Assets in Japan

10.5.1   Simulation

In this section, we make an attempt to estimate how much assets are transferred from one generation to another. This is a relevant question in the controversy of Modigliani (1988) and Kotlikoff (1988). If intergenerationally transferred assets constitute only a minor share of outstanding assets, then asset accumulation can be regarded mostly as a life-cycle phenomenon. However, if intergenerational transfers are large compared to outstanding assets, this suggests intended and unintended bequests play an important role in asset accumulation, and life-cycle saving theory has to be revised as such.

Our method of inference is to measure the amount of bequest from deaths as a proportion of the outstanding household assets, and then multiply by 25 to obtain the generational transfer. (For other methods of inference, see Modigliani 1988.)

In estimating intergenerational transfers from bequest tax data, there are several stumbling blocks on the way from bequest taxation data to bequeathed assets. We identify several key problems below and make explicit assumptions to surmount them. When possible, the reasonable lower and upper bound will be provided. When we have to make judgmental assumptions, we try to estimate the lower bound of intergenerational transfers.

First, we concentrate on intergenerational transfers upon the deaths of couples, ignoring inter vivos transfers altogether. As mentioned in section 10.2, one may transfer a significant amount to heirs as gifts without taxes if transfers were planned for many years. In this sense, our estimates constructed solely from bequest data constitute the lower bound of intergenerational transfers.

Second, bequest taxation covers only those we call "taxable deaths." We have to assume how much wealth is transferred by those who are not required to file the bequest tax form, that is, nontaxable deaths. This is a problem common to both Japan and the United States. At the lower bound, nontaxable death can be assumed to leave zero wealth, and as a reasonable upper bound, nontaxable death may be assumed to leave a full deductible amount (that is the basic deductible amount, 40 + (3 × the number of statutory heirs) million yen in Japan and $600,000 (the unified credit) in the United States. As a reasonable estimate, we infer the average assets of nontaxable deaths from other sources.

Third, double counting is possible in taxable deaths. When a wealthy husband dies first, he bequeaths a portion to children and a portion to his widow. This shows up in the taxable death data. Some years later, the widow dies with a bequest to children that is still sufficiently large to be caught in bequest tax. Age and sex of decedents in the Japanese bequest taxation are not available, so that we may not know how extensive this problem is. We simply assume for the Japanese data that the double counting problem is minor and that taxable deaths are all male and 50 years or older. This is the only assumption that might bias our estimate of intergenerational transfers upward. The wealthiest persons certainly plan to avoid double taxation, in addition to natural depletion of assets by the widow. The widow typically receives only a portion of the husband's bequest, and she would have many years to spend this bequest and make inter vivos transfers to children. By the time of her death, we assume that the wealthiest widows' assets are substantially reduced so that they would not be taxable. This leads to another stage of assumption, about how much of the bequest, taxable and nontaxable, to a spouse ultimately is handed down to children.

Fourth, we will reduce the amount of bequest in the calculation of intergenerational transfers, as an allowance for the widow who consumes the bequeathed assets. In Japan, the amount bequeathed to the widow is inferred from the amount of tax credit for a spouse. Then we calculate the upper and lower bounds for intergenerational transfers. At the lower bound, the wife is assumed to consume all assets bequeathed to her. (In this case, the double counting problem above disappears automatically.) At the upper bound, the widow is assumed to live off her own assets and returns from her husband's bequest and to bequeath eventually the principal components of her husband's bequeathed assets to children. (Under this assumption, the double counting problem above would additionally bias the estimate upward.)

In order to correct for taxable versus nontaxable deaths, we examine the proportion of taxable deaths in table 10.9. Among all deaths, taxable deaths were only 2 percent in 1975 but rose to about 8 percent in 1987. During those thirteen years, inflation and wealth accumulation over a half generation increased the nominal value of bequeathed property, while virtually all tax deductions, credits, and brackets were kept unchanged.[2]

---

2. The reduction from 1987 to 1988 is due to the tax reform of 1988. The 1988 tax reform was advertised as a revenue-neutral package consisting of an introduction of a consumption tax and a reduction in income, excise, and inheritance taxes. However, a reduction in taxable deaths pushed back the clock by only two years, out of twelve years of bracket creep.

Table 10.9   Death, Taxable Death, and Land and Total Bequest per Taxable Decedent, Japan

	Deaths				Per Taxable Death	
	All Ages, Both Sexes (1)	50+ Years, Males (2)	Taxable (3)	TAXDTHR (%) (3/1)	TAXD50MR (%) (3/2)	Land (billions of yen) (Land/3)	Total (billions of yen) (Total/3)
1973	709,416	300,655	29,231	4.12	9.72	0.0417536	0.058852
1974	710,510	302,497	32,896	4.63	10.87	0.0437074	0.061102
				Tax Reform			
1975	702,275	301,456	14,587	2.08	4.84	0.0768492	0.109193
1976	703,270	305,528	15,932	2.26	5.21	0.0756716	0.103854
1977	690,074	301,741	17,853	2.58	5.91	0.0755671	0.104403
1978	695,821	307,504	20,208	2.90	6.57	0.0761481	0.106146
1979	689,664	307,715	22,658	3.28	7.36	0.0762998	0.106726
1980	722,801	326,795	26,789	3.70	8.19	0.0800328	0.111617
1981	720,262	327,472	31,569	4.38	9.64	0.0878552	0.120083
1982	711,883	326,199	35,944	5.04	11.0	0.0926719	0.123395
1983	740,038	341,630	39,523	5.34	11.5	0.0925031	0.125454
1984	740,247	344,846	43,025	5.81	12.4	0.0910819	0.124872
1985	752,283	352,822	48,114	6.39	13.6	0.0922268	0.128536
1986	750,620	353,563	51,822	6.90	14.6	0.0903593	0.129256
1987	751,172	357,195	59,007	7.85	16.5	0.0974003	0.138677
				Tax Reform			
1988	793,014	377,996	50,625	6.38	13.3	0.1464000	0.194177

Note: Bequest tax statistics do not contain information on the age and sex of decedent. TAXDTHR = ratio of taxable deaths to all deaths; TAXD50MR = ratio of taxable deaths to deaths of males age fifty and over.

Sources: Ministry of Health and Welfare, *Vital Statistics Japan* (various issues); Ministry of Finance, Tax Bureau, *Tax Bureau Statistics* (various issues).

As a proxy for a death of a representative member of a "generation," the number of deaths among the male cohort of 50 years or older is shown in table 10.9 (second column). The ratio of taxable deaths to deaths in this cohort of older males was 5 percent in 1975 and 16.5 percent in 1987, assuming that all taxable deaths are part of generational deaths.

The last two columns of table 10.9 show land and total wealth per taxable death (in billions of yen). The jump in these two values from 1988 to 1989 reflects both the truncation of the sample due to the tax reform and high land price inflation.

Since nontaxable deaths did not get taxed, their bequeathed property value was less than the amount of the basic deduction plus other deductions and values toward other credits, barring illegal transfers. Here we assume that a nontaxable decedent bequeaths property that equals ratio K of the basic deduction for three heirs (wife and two children).[3] In the simulation, we allow K to

3. With three heirs, the basic exemption of ¥(20 + 4 × 3) million from 1975 to 1987 and the current exemption of ¥(40 + 8 × 3) million are completely tax free. In a sense, we assume

vary from 0 to 1. Approximately half of the asset value of bequeathed property was held in the form of land. In section 10.5.2 we discuss how to guess a reasonable value for K.

We require a series of assumptions to undertake our simulations. First, liabilities, funeral expenses, and bequest taxes (after tax credit) are deducted in the calculation of intergenerational transfers of taxable decedents. The ratio of these liabilities, etc., to the bequeathed gross amount is assumed to be the same for nontaxable deaths, too.

Second, an assumption is made with regard to how the transfers to the widow(er) will be dissaved before the widow(er)'s death. Recall that bequests to a spouse receive a special tax credit in Japan (unlike in the United States where unlimited deduction is possible). Thus, "intra"-generational transfers are estimated from the ratio of claimed spouse tax credit to the total bequest tax (before tax credit). Then, it is assumed that a constant fraction, MM, (benchmark is $MM = 0.5$) of the transfers to the spouse is later bequeathed to children, upon the widow(er)'s death. The transfer is assumed to be free from the inheritance tax, because only a portion of the original property was given to the spouse, and then a portion is dissaved by the spouse. As variations, we prepare two tables with $MM = 0.0$ and 1.0 The former implies that a wife consumes all of the assets she received upon her husband's death so that she would bequeath no assets to her children, and the latter that a wife consumes none of the assets, presumably living off her own life-cycle savings (including any inter vivos transfers from her husband).

Third, suppose that one generation consists of twenty-five years. Hence, we take the average of the bequest transfers over twelve years and blow it up by 25. In the steady state, this procedure amounts to the following assumption. At one point in time, we would classify wealth in two categories, bequest wealth that is transferred from the ancestor and will be handed down to heirs, and life-cycle wealth that is saved when young but will be dissaved when old. We consider that the steady state is defined by a constant ratio of bequest wealth to total wealth. Conceptually, the returns of the bequest wealth, with the return being the same as on other types of assets, are assumed to be compounding and included in bequest wealth. Otherwise the conditions of the steady state would be violated.

Fourth, the assessment of land has to be adjusted. In Japan, land for bequest is underassessed, as argued in section 10.4.2. Accordingly, the value of land has to be inflated from that reported in the taxation data. The ratio of Rosen Ka (assessment for bequest tax) to Koji Kakaku (the monitoring price that is believed to be used in National Accounts, Stock Division survey) is defined as U. The lower bounds estimate for intergenerational transfer is obtained when $U = 1$. However, a more realistic number is 0.56 (recall discussion of

---

two parents are on average survived by two children, but at the time of the husband's death, the wife is still alive. Therefore, a male decedent of 50 years or older is assumed to be survived by two children and and wife in the taxation statistics.

the estimates by Homma and Atoda 1989 in section 10.4.2). If the typical residential real estate is less than 200 square meters, however, an assessment will further be reduced by 50 percent (so that $U = 0.28$). Of course, some families own a second house or manage rental housing. The correction should not be 50 percent from 0.56. On the other hand, agricultural land has much more favorable treatment. Allowing for some large properties, it may be plausible to consider U somewhere between 0.26 and 0.56. Hence, for the simulation, we select $U = 0.34$, 0.56, 0.78, and 1.0. We believe the truth is a value of U somewhere between 0.34 and 0.56.

The last and most difficult stumbling block is to guess how much an average nontaxable decedent bequeaths to heirs, and how the assets are divided among land and other assets. We will make our best effort on this front in the section 10.5.2.

10.5.2 Estimation of Transfers from Nontaxable Decedents

The next important step is to guess the amount of transfers by the nontaxable decedents, and narrow the upper and lower bounds on parameter K. The following calculation is done for calendar year 1988.

For the average assets of households, we use a table from the Family Saving Survey, which lists the average "savings" (financial assets only) and liabilities of households classified by age brackets (see columns 5 and 6 of table 10.10). However, we have to make several adjustments. First, the statistics show only those elderly who remain as household heads. The elderly person who lives with his or her children (that is, forming a "merged" family) is typically a dependent instead of a household head. (Usually, the household head is defined in various statistics as the person who earns the most in the family located at the same address.) If the household heads and the merged have different asset characteristics, we have to adjust for the difference. Second, the survey does not have information on the sex of household heads. Third, the survey has only financial saving.[4] However, the survey does contain a "home ownership ratio," that is the ratio of "owner-occupied" household heads to all household heads.

In order to correct for the first point, from the Basic Life Survey (Kokumin Seikatsu Kiso Chosa), statistics on the household status of the elderly (sixty years and over) can be estimated. This survey classifies the elderly into eight different categories with respect to their relationship to household heads.[5]

---

4. Takayama (1991) estimated the value of landholdings by age of household heads from individual responses to the National Survey of Family Income and Expenditure. In 1987 the *median* of land values held by those aged 60–64, 65–69, 70–74, and 75 and over is ¥22, ¥24, ¥22, and ¥24 million, respectively. The *mean* of land values for the same age groups is ¥44, ¥44, ¥38, and ¥44 million. Dekle (1990) used a different survey and estimated landholdings of the typical household head of age 60–64, 65–69, and 70–74 to be ¥27, ¥30, and ¥34 million.

5. The eight categories are as follows: (1) single household (the elderly becomes household head); (2) household with the elderly couple only (the elderly becomes household head); (3) living with children but maintaining a household head status; (4) living with children, and the elderly is

Table 10.10 **Average Net Assets of Japanese Households, 1988**

| Age | Households (in thousands) | | | Non-household-head Males (in thousands) | | Weights | Financial Assets (thousands of yen) | Financial Liability (thousands of yen) | Net Assets Male Household Head | Net Assets of Males | Male Deaths |
	Male (1)	Female (2)	Both Sexes (3 = 1 + 2)	(N1)	(hp = 1/(1 + N1))	(4)	(5)	(6)	(7)	(8 = 7 × hp)	(9)
50–54	4,200	250	4,450	0	1.00	0.1248	13,108	3,808	9,568	9,568	22,209
55–59	3,600	200	3,800	0	1.00	0.1029	15,749	3,204	12,884	12,884	32,928
60–64	2,458	354	2,812	470	0.839	0.0893	19,333	1,625	18,897	15,854	38,238
65–up	4,285	1,220	5,505	1,253	0.773	0.1139	17,412	1,307	18,111	14,000	285,044
Average of (8) weighted by (9) 13,826											

Notes: Column 1: For age group 60–64 and 65–up, one-man households, male-headed households of couples, plus (0.8 times those who are classified as household heads of the elderly who live with child[ren]). The last term does not have a breakdown to male and female, so that it was multiplied by 0.8 to allow for female household heads living with child(ren). The multiplier 0.8 is a guess (Basic Life Survey 1988). For age groups 50–54, and 55–59, inferred from column 4. This is a guess.

Column 2: For age groups 60–64 and 65–up, one-woman households. For age groups 50–54 and 55–59, inferred from 4. This is a guess.

Column N1: Male population for that age bracket minus column 1.

Column hp: ratio of male household heads to total males.

Column 4: Estimated weights of household number for that age bracket used in the Family Savings Survey (1988).

Columns 5 and 6: Family Savings Survey (1988).

Column 7: First, subtract liabilities form assets. Then assume that a household headed by female has a net asset equal to half of a male-headed household. (7) = ((5 − (6)) × (3)/((1) + (2)/2).

Column 8: Correct for those who are not household heads. Assume those who are not a household head own 0 assets. These are typically merged in children's household.

Column 9: Ministry of Health and Welfare, *Vital Statistics Japan*.

Average net financial assets   A = ¥13,826,000
Taxable decedent's average net financial assets   B = ¥41,760,000
(securities + cash + miscellaneous − liabilities, tables 10.4 and 10.5)/50,625
Weight (TAXD50MR in table 10.9)   w = 0.133
Nontaxable decedent's average financial assets   N
Weight (1 − TAXD50MR)   0.867
N = (A) − (B × w)/(1 − w) =   ¥9,541,000
Nontaxable decedent's average financial assets plus land (assessed at Rosen Ka)   N/M
K = (N/M)/64,000,000 =   0.426

From the survey, we may infer the numbers of the male household heads and male non–household heads. The non-household-head elderly are assumed to hold zero assets (an underestimate bias); and the female household heads are assumed to hold half the assets of the male. With these assumptions, the average household head assets and liabilities statistics in the Family Saving Survey are corrected to become the average male elderly assets and liabilities, regardless of household head status. This is shown in column 8 of table 10.10. In order to be consistent with the bequest tax statistics, where no age information is available, column 8 is aggregated over age brackets with weights taken from the frequency of death by age bracket. Finally, we obtain the inferred average net asset for an average dying male person, ¥13,826,000.

Suppose that the Family Saving Survey samples both the wealthy and the poor correctly. (It may be that the highest income bracket is undersampled. This would make our estimate for nontaxable decedents' assets biased downward.) We then calculate the average financial holdings of taxable decedents from table 10.5 to be ¥41,760,000.

Recall that the fraction of taxable deaths per generation was 0.133 (table 10.9). In order to arrive at ¥13,826,000 as an average of taxable and nontaxable deaths, the nontaxable death average financial asset is inferred to be ¥9,541,000.

The last adjustment we have to make is to estimate the landholding of nontaxable decedents. The financial share in a nontaxable decedent's portfolio is denoted by M. Here, we assume a ratio similar to the taxable decedent, $M = 0.35$. (The case for $M = 0.5$ is shown in table 10.12.) Since the home owner ratio does not seem to decline with age according to the Family Saving Survey, the assumption is not unreasonable. Then K, the average net asset holding of nontaxable decedents, is calculated as 0.426.

10.5.3 Simulation

Since the parameter of land underassessment and that of nontaxable death may not be absolutely reliable, we conducted simulations to ascertain the robustness of the results.

Results of simulation are shown in tables 10.11 and 10.12. In the benchmark case, table 10.11, the widow(er) is assumed to dissave 50 percent of the

---

a spouse of the household head (typically, the female elderly, where the male elderly is a household head); (5) living with children, and a child is a household head; (6) living with children, and the elderly is a parent of the spouse of the household head; (7) living with children with other kinds of relationships; and (8) other living arrangements. For categories 1, 2, and 8, male and female statistics are shown separately. Only the sum of 3 through 7 can be decomposed into males and females. The male household heads are calculated as the sum of 1, 2, and 80 percent of 3. The 80 percent multiplier in the last term is necessary because for 3, male and female decomposition is not available, and some household heads living with children are females. If taken as 100 percent of 3, the highest age bracket would have a higher household head ratio than the second highest age bracket. Consequently, we made the 80 percent adjustment.

Table 10.11   **Simulation of the Ratio of Bequest Wealth to Total Wealth, Japan**

	$u = 0.34$		$u = 0.56$		$u = 0.78$		$u = 1.0$	
K	Land	Asset	Land	Asset	Land	Asset	Land	Asset
0.0	29.8	17.9	18.1	11.5	13.0	8.7	10.1	7.1
0.1	38.8	23.6	23.6	15.3	16.9	11.7	13.2	9.7
0.2	47.9	29.4	29.0	19.1	20.8	14.7	16.2	12.2
0.3	56.9	35.1	34.5	23.0	24.8	17.7	19.3	14.7
0.4	65.9	40.9	40.0	26.8	28.7	20.7	22.4	17.3
0.426	68.3	42.3	41.4	27.8	29.7	21.5	23.2	17.9
0.5	74.9	46.6	45.5	30.7	32.6	23.7	25.4	19.8
0.6	84.0	52.4	51.0	34.5	36.6	26.7	28.5	22.4
0.7	93.0	58.1	56.5	38.3	40.5	29.7	31.6	24.9
0.8	102.0	63.9	61.9	42.2	44.5	32.7	34.7	27.4
0.9	111.1	69.6	67.4	46.0	48.4	35.7	37.7	30.0
1.0	120.1	75.3	72.9	49.9	52.3	38.7	40.8	32.5

Notes: This simulation assumes $M = 0.35$, $MM = 0.5$, and $K = 0.426 = (9,541/M)/64,000$.

$M =$ (portfolio parameter of nontaxable decedent) the ratio of financial assets to total net assets among the nontaxable decedent's portfolio.

$MM =$ (dissaving of widow parameter) the ratio of the widow's bequest to children to husband's bequest to the wife.

$K =$ (nontaxable death wealth parameter) the ratio of assets (financial and land) to the basic deduction amount for nontaxable death. If an estimate of average net "financial" asset for nontaxable death of ¥ 9,541 million in 1988 is adopted, and if $M = 0.35$, then K is equal to 0.426.

$U =$ (underassessment of land) the ratio of land value for bequest to land value of National Accounts.

property inherited from the spouse. The widow(er) is assumed to dissave 0 percent in table 10.12A and 100 percent in table 10.12B.

In the benchmark case, suppose that the land underassessment ratio is 0.56 and that nontaxable deaths on average leave 0.426 of the basic deduction. Then 41 percent of land and 28 percent of net household assets are obtained by bequest. If the land underassessment ratio is 0.34, then 68 percent of land and 42 percent of net household assets are obtained by bequest.

10.6   Estimating Bequeathed Assets in Outstanding Assets in the United States

In this section, we attempt to make an estimate, comparable to those estimates for Japan, of the proportion of national wealth transferred from one generation to the next in the United States. Table 10.13 presents data for the United States which are roughly comparable to the data of table 10.10 for Japan. Unfortunately, the Federal Reserve's definition of household includes the assets and liabilities of personal trusts and nonprofit organizations. While it is certainly appropriate to include personal trusts in an analysis of bequest and gift behavior, the inclusion of nonprofit organizations may or may not be

Table 10.12   **Simulations, Japan**

K	$u = 0.34$ Land	Asset	$u = 0.56$ Land	Asset	$u = 0.78$ Land	Asset	$u = 1.00$ Land	Asset
	A. $M = 0.35$, $MM = 0.00$, $K = 0.426 = (9{,}541/M)/64{,}000$							
0.3	45.8	29.2	27.8	19.4	20.0	15.2	15.6	12.8
0.4	53.7	34.2	32.6	22.8	23.4	17.8	18.2	15.0
0.426	55.8	35.5	33.9	23.6	24.3	18.5	18.9	15.6
0.5	61.6	39.2	37.4	26.1	26.8	20.4	20.9	17.2
0.6	69.6	44.2	42.2	29.5	30.3	23.0	23.6	19.4
	B. $M = 0.35$, $MM = 1.0$, $K = 0.426 = (9{,}541/M)/64{,}000$							
0.3	69.1	41.5	41.9	26.7	30.1	20.3	23.5	16.7
0.4	79.3	47.9	48.1	31.0	34.5	23.7	26.9	19.6
0.426	81.9	49.6	49.7	32.2	35.7	24.6	27.8	20.3
0.5	89.4	54.4	54.3	35.4	39.0	27.1	30.4	22.4
0.6	99.6	60.9	60.5	39.7	43.4	30.4	33.8	25.3
	C. $M = 0.5$, $MM = 0.5$, $K = 0.298 = (9{,}541/M)/64{,}000$							
0.298	50.5	32.8	30.6	22.0	22.0	17.3	17.1	14.7
0.3	50.6	32.9	30.7	22.1	22.0	17.4	17.2	14.7
0.4	57.6	37.9	34.9	25.6	25.1	20.3	19.5	17.3
0.5	64.5	42.9	39.2	29.2	28.1	23.2	21.9	19.8
0.6	71.5	47.9	43.4	32.7	31.1	26.1	24.3	22.4

Table 10.13   **Household Assets and Liabilities at Year End 1976–89, United States** (in billions of dollars)

Year	Assets	Liabilities	Net
1976	6,052.6	869.2	5,183.4
1977	6,730.9	1,006.2	5,724.7
1978	7,695.8	1,172.2	6,523.6
1979	8,866.1	1,344.6	7,521.5
1980	10,129.7	1,472.0	8,657.7
1981	10,971.9	1,589.7	9,382.2
1982	11,508.6	1,664.0	9,844.6
1983	12,587.8	1,832.1	10,725.7
1984	13,376.5	2,050.4	11,326.1
1985	14,716.2	2,319.6	12,396.6
1986	16,066.5	2,627.9	12,438.6
1987	17,151.8	2,891.4	14.260.4
1988	18,464.3	3,185.4	15,278.9
1989	20,278.4	3,468.1	16,810.3

Source: U.S. Board of Governors of the Federal Reserve System, Flow of Funds Accounts (1990).

Note: Includes holdings and liabilities of households, personal trusts, and nonprofit organizations. However, the holdings of land, residential structures, and plant and equipment by tax-exempt organizations are deleted from the compilation of assets, while liabilities of tax-exempt debt are deleted from the compilation of liabilities.

Table 10.14   **Composition of Bequeathed Assets, United States** (in millions of dollars)

Year	Real Estate	Financial Assets[a]	Other Assets[b]	Funeral and Administrative Expense	Liabilities	State Taxes[c]	Federal Taxes	Net Bequest[d]
1976	12,920.9	30,508.1	4,772.6	2,022.1	2,649.0	552.3	4,979.1	37,999.1
1981	10,974.3	26.722.1	7,263.5	1,654.0	2,600.7	919.7	6,226.0	33,559.1
1984	13,948.4	35,823.1	9,796.3	1,885.4	3,608.4	1,077.6	5,035.4	47,961.0
1987	13,564.8	43,401.1	13,659.5	1,898.1	3,238.2	1,567.5	6,299.2	57,662.4

Source: Internal Revenue Service, Statistics of Income Division.

[a]Includes value of noncorporate businesses.

[b]Sum of household goods and lifetime transfers.

[c]Value of state death tax credit, hence an underestimate of all state taxes.

[d]Calculation nets all expenses, liabilities, and taxes against total assets.

appropriate. To the extent the holdings of nonprofit organizations represent pension fund assets that are held on behalf of individuals, the net holdings should be included. To the extent the holdings of nonprofit organizations are endowments of universities or other charitable organizations, the net holdings should be excluded.

The inclusion of trusts and nonprofit organizations has a large effect. For example, in 1984 the Federal Reserve calculated the holdings of financial assets of households at $8.8 trillion and the holdings of financial assets of individuals at $6.9 trillion. The liabilities of households were $2.1 trillion and the liabilities of individuals were $3.2 trillion.[6] Consequently, the net financial assets of households were $6.7 trillion and the net financial assets of individuals were $3.7 trillion. To partially correct for this we have netted from the asset data the value of residential structures, plant and equipment, and land held by tax-exempt organizations. We also have netted from the liability data the value of tax-exempt debt, which presumably can only be issued by tax-exempt organizations. However, we are unable to make any consistent corrections for holdings of financial assets by tax-exempt organizations. We observe that the estimated net worth of households reported in table 10.13 exceeds the estimates of the PSID and SIPP studies for 1984 cited in section 10.3.

Table 10.14 provides a composition of bequeathed assets for the years 1976, 1981, 1984, and 1987 for taxpayers who filed estate tax returns in 1977, 1982, 1985, and 1988. The data do not precisely correspond to bequests for each year because some estate tax returns filed in any particular year are not returns for a death in the year immediately preceding filing. We calculated the net bequest (last column on the right) by subtracting all liabilities, expenses,

6. Federal Reserve Boards of Governors, "Financial Assets and Liabilities Year-End, 1964–87," September 1988. In addition to the exclusion of trusts and nonprofit organizations, the data for individuals include the assets and liabilities of nonfarm noncorporate businesses and corporate farms. The Federal Reserve does not separately report the assets and liabilities of nonprofit organizations.

and taxes against the value of financial assets in the estate. As such it is comparable to table 10.13. Unlike the comparable data in table 10.10 for Japan, these data are defined by those estates that filed returns, regardless of whether there ultimately was a tax liability.

Table 10.15 reports taxable estate tax returns as a percentage of annual deaths. Generally, for each taxable return filed, a nontaxable return is filed. Table 10.15 shows that the percentage of taxable deaths rose from 1935 to 1977, since which time it has declined. As discussed above, in the absence of changes in the estate tax, inflation and the growth in per capita wealth causes more decedents' estates to incur an estate tax liability. This was the case until 1977. The Tax Reform Act of 1976 increased the estate tax exclusion from $30,000 to $60,000. The Economic Recovery Tax Act of 1981 further increased the annual exclusion to $600,000.[7] In addition, as discussed in appendix B, the 1981 act created an unlimited marital reduction, which further reduces the number of estates subject to tax. The increase in the estate tax exclusion and the marital deduction removed a substantial number of estates from federal estate taxation, as table 10.15 documents. Even when the marital deduction results in no tax liability, however, a return must be filed. To arrive at a comparable figure for the United States for intergenerational deaths, we use the 1986 ratio of deaths of males aged 55 or older to total deaths, 42 percent.

In table 10.16 we make a lower bound estimate of the ratio of transferred assets to outstanding assets. As discussed in section 10.2, U.S. law and practice generally value all assets at market value. In addition, unlike Japan, the U.S. data reveal no preference for real estate or other specific assets as a tax planning device.[8] To arrive at an estimate of generational bequests we divide

7. The 1976 increase in the exclusion was phased in over 1977 to 1980, and the 1981 increase was phased in annually from 1982 through 1987.

8. Patric Hendershott has raised to us the question of whether "flower bonds" constitute a significant preference that might alter the composition of the portfolios of American decedents. Prior to March 3, 1971, the Treasury could issue bonds that could be redeemed at par in payment of an estate or gift tax liability, if the taxpayer had purchased such bonds prior to his or her death. The Treasury issued limited series of such bonds, which became known as flower bonds. When issued in the 1950s and early 1960s, flower bonds carried competitive coupon rates. Subsequent increases in the rate of inflation and interest rates have caused the outstanding bonds to trade at substantial discounts to par. Consequently, purchase of the bonds at discount for redemption at par to pay estate taxes may be quite profitable, even though the value of the bonds must be carried at par for purposes of determining the gross estate.

Since 1980 only nine series of these bonds have been outstanding (all issued prior to 1964). At present, only five series of flower bonds have yet to reach maturity. In 1988, approximately 1,000 estates redeemed approximately $200 million worth of flower bonds at par to pay the estate tax. More than 18,000 taxable estates were taxable that year. Moreover, the value of bonds redeemed at par represented approximately 3 percent of total estate tax liability, only 11 percent of the value of all federal bonds in filers' estates, less than 3 percent of the value of all bonds in filers' estates, and approximately 0.5 percent of the value of the gross estate of those filers who incurred a tax liability. In earlier years flower bonds were more prominent. In 1982 approximately 10 percent of taxable returns redeemed flower bonds worth approximately 10 percent of their tax estate of their tax liability, but less than 2 percent of value of the gross estate of those filers who incurred a tax liability. However, the composition of estates looks quite similar in 1982 and 1988 (see appendix

Table 10.15   **Number of Taxable Estate Tax Returns Filed as a Percentage of Adult Deaths, Selected Years 1935–88, United States**

Year	Deaths	Taxable Estate Tax Return Filed[a]	
		Number	Percentage of Deaths
1935	1,172,245	8,655	0.74
1940	1,237,186	12,907	1.04
1945	1,239,713	13,869	1.12
1950	1,304,343	17,411	1.33
1955	1,379,826	25,143	1.82
1961	1,548,665	45,439	2.93
1966	1,727,240	67,404[b]	3.90
1970	1,796,940	93,424[b]	5.20
1973	1,867,689	120,761[b]	6.47
1977	1,819,107	139,115[b]	7.65
1982	1,897,820	41,620[b,c]	2.19
1983	1,945,913	35,148[b,c]	1.81
1984	1,968,128	31,507[b,c]	1.60
1985	2,086,440	30,518[b,c]	1.46
1986	2,105,361	23,731[b,c]	1.13
1987	2,123,323	21,335[b,c]	1.00
1988	2,167,999	18,948[b,c]	0.87

Sources: Pechman (1987); Internal Revenue Service, Statistics of Income Division; U.S. National Center for Health Statistics.

[a]Estate returns need not be filed in the year of the decedent's death.

[b]Not strictly comparable with pre-1966 data. For 1966 and later years, the estate tax after credits was the basis for determining taxable returns. For prior years, the basis was the estate tax before credits.

[c]Although the filing requirement was for gross estates in excess of $225,000 for 1982 deaths, $275,000 for 1983 deaths, and $325,000 for 1984 deaths, the data are limited to gross estates of $300,000 or more. The filing requirement increased to $400,000 for 1985 deaths, $500,000 for 1986 deaths, and $600,000 for deaths in 1987 and thereafter.

Table 10.16   **Bequeathed Assets as a Percentage of Net Household Assets, United States**

Year	Net Bequests (millions of $)	Net Total Assets (billions of $)	Bequest Ratio (%)	Generational Bequest Ratio		
				$MM = 1$	$MM = 0.5$	$MM = 0$
1976	37,999.1	5,183.4	0.733	18.33	14.66	11.00
1981	33,559.5	9,382.2	0.358	8.94	7.15	5.36
1984	47,961.0	11,326.1	0.423	10.58	8.46	6.35
1987	57,622.4	14,260.4	0.404	10.10	8.08	6.06

B). Consequently, we do not believe that the existence of flower bonds has significantly altered the composition of the portfolios of American decedents.

the net bequest (as defined in table 10.14) by the household sector's net worth (as reported in table 10.13). This produces the bequest ratio in table 10.16. As above, we multiply the bequest ration by 25 to convert the bequeathed stock of assets into a flow.

Lastly we make an adjustment to the generational bequest ratio to account for the marital deduction permitted under the U.S. transfer taxes. The U.S. bequest data are for those who file, not for taxable returns. A husband could die and his estate would file a return, even if under the marital deduction all his wealth was bequeathed to his wife. If the wife died the next year, her estate would file a return, which could contain nearly the identical assets. When this occurs, assets bequeathed to the surviving spouse would be counted twice in our analysis. Consequently, we compute an "adjusted generational bequest ratio."

In practice, the data reveal that decedents do not leave their entire estate to their surviving spouse. The 1977 estate tax data report approximately 20 percent of the gross estate claimed the marital deduction. However, prior to 1982 not all assets bequeathed to a surviving spouse qualified for the marital deduction. The experience from 1985 and 1988 when an unlimited marital deduction was in effect reveals that approximately one-third of the gross estate is bequeathed to the surviving spouse. For 1988 returns, this represents approximately 40 percent of the net after-tax bequest. To be conservative, we assume each estate has a surviving spouse to which 40 percent of the net bequest is made. We present three possible scenarios: (1) the surviving spouse consumes none of the bequeathed assets and bequeaths the assets to the next generation upon death ($MM = 0$); (2) the surviving spouse consumes one-half of bequeathed assets and bequeaths the remaining assets upon death ($MM = 0.5$); and (3) the surviving spouse consumes all of the assets, passing on none to the next generation ($M = 1.0$).

This computation suggests that, at a minimum, 5.4 percent of U.S. household wealth in the 1980s is intergenerational bequeathed wealth. The result for 1976 substantially exceeds that of the other years because in 1976 more than 7 percent of decedents had to file federal estate tax returns, whereas since 1982 fewer than 2 percent have had to file. These data may suggest that the next five percentiles of decedents bequeath 75 percent as much wealth as the wealthiest 2 percent of decedents. These figures are comparable to those for Japan when one recognizes that table 10.10 generally represents the wealthiest 6 percent of Japanese decedents and the figures for the United States from the 1980s represent the wealthiest 1 to 2 percent.

This estimate for the United States likely substantially understates reality. As noted above, we have used for our measure of household wealth an adjusted version of the Federal Reserve's accounting of household wealth, which includes the financial holdings of tax-exempt organizations. For example, for 1984 the generational bequest ratio would be even greater if the

PSID or SIPP wealth data, which do not include tax exempt organizations, were used. In addition, many observers believe that the U.S. estate tax is ineffectual in taxing intergenerational wealth transfers. See, for example, Cooper (1979), Bernheim (1987), and Munnell (1988). They argue that substantial opportunities exist for legal tax avoidance.

We attempt to estimate adjusted generational bequest ratios for net wealth while recognizing that many nonfiling decedents make bequests by the following procedure. We use 1987 deaths (1988 filing) as our base year. From the almost 2.2 million deaths in the United States that year, some 43,000 estate tax returns were filed. We assume that 42 percent of the remaining 2.1 million decedents were males aged 55 or older. We let K represent the fraction of the $600,000 exemption level that the average nonfiling decedent bequeathed. (A value of $K = 1$ corresponds to an average bequest of $600,000.) The value of such bequests is then divided by the 1987 value of net household assets and multiplied by 25. If we assume that all such bequests either go directly to the next generation or that any bequest received by a surviving spouse is not consumed and ultimately bequeathed intact, further adjustment is not necessary. This is equivalent to the case of $MM = 1$ in table 10.16. In addition, we assume that each male decedent bequeaths 40 percent of his estate to a surviving spouse and the surviving spouse consumes half ($MM = 0.5$) or all ($MM = 0$) of the bequest. To these results, we add the corresponding 1987 adjusted generational bequest ratios of the estate tax filers. Table 10.17 reports the results.

Obviously, a value of $K = 1$ is unlikely to represent the average bequest of nonfilers. However, we observe that the SIPP data report that for 1984 the median net worth of householders aged 55 to 64 was $130,498 and for householders age 65 and older, $104,851. With growth in net worth, this would imply a value of K of at least 0.2. We would hazard the guess that in the United States at least one-quarter of national wealth is transferred from one generation to the next.

To add some perspective, recall that for $MM = 1$, for 1976, the generational bequest ratio was 18.33. If all nonfiling decedents made an average bequest of $6,000 ($K = 0.2$), the generational bequest ratio equals 20.27. This is only modestly lower than the similar calculation for 1987 decedents in table 10.17.

10.7   Summary and Concluding Remarks

We have compared the transfer taxation systems in Japan and the United States, and we have estimated the amount of transfers through bequests. We also have estimated the share of bequeathed assets in total household assets in the two countries.

Table 10.17   **Estimates of Bequeathed Household Assets in Proportion to Outstanding Assets, United States (%)**

	Adjusted Generational Bequest Ratio		
K	$MM = 1$	$MM = 0.5$	$MM = 0$
0.0	10.10	8.08	6.06
0.1	19.50	15.60	11.70
0.2	28.89	23.11	17.34
0.3	38.29	30.63	22.97
0.4	47.69	38.15	28.61
0.5	57.08	45.67	34.25
0.6	66.48	53.18	39.89
0.7	75.88	60.70	45.53
0.8	85.27	68.22	51.16
0.9	94.67	75.73	56.80
1.0	104.07	83.25	62.44

In both countries, all bequeathed property of the decedent becomes subject to bequest or estate tax. However, the estate tax in the United States is imposed on the bequeathed estate (the donor side), while the bequest tax of Japan is imposed on beneficiaries of the bequest (the donee side). In Japan, there are presumed heirs, called statutory heirs. As the number of statutory heirs becomes large, so that the per person bequest becomes small, the tax burden is reduced. There is no such system in the United States, that is, the size of the estate determines the basic tax liability. In Japan, at least up to a half of bequeathed property may be given to a spouse tax free, while in the United States any bequest to a spouse is tax free.

Land and real estate are assessed for bequest tax purposes at a value substantially lower than the market value in Japan. There is no such favorable treatment in the United States. This incentive induces the Japanese elderly who intend to bequeath to invest heavily in real estate. At least three-quarters of the Japanese taxable bequest is in real estate. Only one-quarter of the U.S. taxable bequest is in real estate.

This paper does not distinguish between intended and unintended bequests. If unintended capital gains occurred, in particular in the value of land and housing, in favor of the elderly, then it may be difficult for the elderly to realize the gain in the form of an additional annuity in a world of imperfect markets. Land inflation in Japan would tend to increase the amount of unintended bequests. However, the relatively stable ratio, through time, of land in bequeathed property value implies that a significant portion of bequest was planned.

In the United States, the ratio of taxable deaths to total deaths is much lower than in Japan, so that our simulations are very sensitive to the parameter K. Suppose that on average $120,000 (that is, 20 percent of the maximum basic deduction) is bequeathed by the nontaxable decedents in the United States. Then at least one-quarter of household assets in the United States are obtained by intergenerational transfers, as opposed to live-cycle hump saving.

From the Japanese Family Saving Survey and Basic Life Survey, we consider that on average ¥24 million, that is, 40 percent of the maximum basic deduction, is bequeathed by an average nontaxable (male) decedent (of age 50 or more). Then, at least 30 to 40 percent of the household wealth and 40 to 60 percent of land were formed by intergenerational transfer.

Our results from our most preferred case for Japan ($K = 0.426$ with $U = 0.56$) and the United States (K between 0.2 and 0.3) show that the ratio of transferred saving as opposed to life-cycle saving is somewhat greater in Japan than in the United States. Hayashi, Ando, and Ferris (1988) have conjectured that the higher Japanese saving rate is due to nondissaving of the elderly. Their conjecture would be consistent with the results derived here.

However, for some simulations the United States ratio is higher than the Japanese. Given the high Japanese personal saving rate, this may be counterintuitive. We offer two factors that raise the U.S. ratio of transferred assets compared to the Japanese ratio. First, social security and corporate pensions, which essentially constitute a form of life-cycle saving, do not show up as household assets while accumulating prior to retirement. This lowers the denominator of the transferred assets to total asset ratio. To the extent that the United States has more social security and corporate pension plans than does Japan, the ratio is biased comparatively upward in the United States. (If pensions, or retirement severance payments, are unfunded, and the liabilities are reflected in the value of corporate stock, which is ultimately owned by the household sector, then the bias would disappear.)

Second, corporate pensions in the United States are predominantly distributed as an annuity, while the Japanese corporate pensions are traditionally paid as a lump-sum severance payment upon retirement. With lump-sum distribution, household assets in Japan typically increase upon retirement, that is, at age 55 to 60. This would increase the denominator of the ratio. Moreover, a lump-sum payment as opposed to an annuity payment leaves a larger possibility of intended and unintended bequests.

Our results suggest that in both Japan and the United States a substantial portion of the national capital stock is the result of intended and unintended intergenerational transfers. Kotlikoff and Summers (1981) suggested that between 15 and 70 percent of the American capital stock resulted from such transfers and argued that, in fact, the intergenerational transfers were primarily responsible for the existing capital stock. Utilizing a different methodology, our preferred cases suggest that for the United States and Japan between 25 and 40 percent of the capital stock results from intergenerational transfers, which is roughly the middle of the Kotlikoff and Summers range. Whether our calculations or those of Kotlikoff and Summers are closer to the truth requires further research.

Appendix A
Transfer Taxation in Japan

Historical Background[9]

Japan established its first transfer tax in 1905. Until 1949, it was an estate tax, in that the tax base was the value of properties of the decedent. In 1950, in accordance with the tax mission of Carl Shoup, it became an accession tax, in that the tax was imposed on the recipient of inherited properties, gifts, or bequests, and the value of properties used as the tax base was computed cumulatively over the recipient's lifetime. The 1953 revision divided the accession tax into an inheritance tax and a gift tax, and the method of cumulative taxation was repealed.

The gift tax was introduced as a complement to the inheritance tax. Without the gift tax, one could distribute one's wealth to one's heirs prior to death in order to avoid or reduce the inheritance tax burden. Each heir (or donee in the case of the gift tax) was separately liable for the tax on the property received. Hence, how wealth was distributed among heirs (or donees) could make a great difference in the total tax burden. In some cases, distribution was distorted in order to reduce the tax burden.

In 1958, the system was revised, so that the inheritance tax is calculated on the basis of the total property bequeathed and the number of statutory heirs (and not distribution among them or nonstatutory heirs). The 1988 tax reform included revision of inheritance and gift tax schedules and some revisions closing loopholes. The method of calculating the bequest tax will be explained in detail below.

Taxpayers

Residency status and location of the transferred property determine potential tax liability. An individual who acquires property by inheritance, bequest, or gift and who has a domicile in Japan at the time of acquisition of such property is an "unlimited taxpayer." An individual who acquires any property located in Japan by inheritance, bequest, or gift and who has no domicile in Japan at the time of acquisition of the property is a "limited taxpayer" (Ministry of Finance 1990).

An unlimited taxpayer is responsible for all bequeathed assets, located either in Japan or in foreign countries. A limited taxpayer is responsible for bequeathed assets located only in Japan, but not those in foreign countries. A Japanese national employed in Japan is an unlimited taxpayer even if he or she is temporarily traveling or residing in a foreign country (Ministry of Finance 1990).

Note that the inheritance tax in Japan is paid by those who receive proper-

---

9. This section is based on Ministry of Finance (1990, section IV).

ties as opposed to the estate of the decedent in the United States. Beneficiaries, however, have to mutually agree on how to divide the properties. The inheritance tax form signed by beneficiaries is usually filed at the Tax Bureau's branch that covers the residence of the decedent. Inheritance and gift taxes in Japan are a national tax. The same rate schedule, exemptions, and tax credit applies to all properties in Japan. No local government may impose additional bequest or gift tax.

Statutory Heirs and Statutory Shares

The Japanese civil law concept of "statutory heir" is critical to an understanding of the inheritance tax. There are three mutually exclusive ways to calculate the number of statutory heirs. (1) Lineal descendants. When there are surviving children, the spouse and children become statutory heirs. If there are no surviving children, but grandchildren are alive, the grandchildren substitute for the children. (2) Lineal ascendants. When there are no children (or grandchildren), the spouse and the parents of the deceased constitute statutory heirs. (3) Lateral. When there are no children and parents, statutory heirs consist of the spouse and brothers and sisters of the decedent.

The total number of statutory heirs determines the size of the basic exemption (explained below). The concept of statutory heirs also determines an estate's "statutory shares" (Civil Law, article 900). In case 1, the spouse is entitled to half the estate and each child is entitled to the other half divided by the number of children.[10] In case 2, the spouse is entitled to two-thirds and parents receive one-third (or each parent receives a half of one-third). In case 3, the spouse is entitled to three-quarters, and surviving siblings receive one-quarter (or each brother and sister receives one-quarter divided by the total number of surviving siblings).

When no will exists, heirs may mutually decide how to divide the property (Civil Law, article 902). However, when heirs cannot reach a mutually acceptable agreement on the division of property the statutory shares actually determine the division of property (Civil Law, articles 900, 901). Moreover, even if the decedent leaves a will specifying transfer of the entire estate to a sole recipient, statutory heirs may sue for the automatic entitlement of bequest, that is, a half of statutory share.[11] More important, regardless of the actual

10. A child born out of wedlock, or born to a different spouse, is entitled to only a half of a share of child.

11. A dying person cannot control the distribution of bequeathed property. One-half of the statutory share is reserved for each statutory heir, no matter how the dying person wishes to distribute his or her property postmortem (Civil Law, article 1028). (In the case where there is no child, grandchild, or spouse, the guaranteed share of the parents of the decedent is one-third.) This guaranteed minimum share is called *iryubun*. (*Pflichtteil* in German, and *réserve* in French. There is no word in Anglo-Saxon law.) From the perspective of a strategic bequest motive (Bernheim, Shleifer, and Summers 1985), *iryubun* creates a very weak threat point for the parents. Unless parents have illiquid assets, such as land and structures, heirs are assured of wealth transfer with an uncertain timing in the future. This would reduce the amount of children's care of parents

distribution of property, the statutory shares determine the total inheritance tax liability.

Taxable Property, Exemptions, and Tax Base

The inheritance tax base is equal to the value of all the property owned by the decedent at the time of his or her death, including any life insurance and severance payments paid upon death. Benefits of life insurance or accidental death insurance are included, provided that the decedent had paid insurance premiums. In addition, all gifts made during the last three years of life are added to the total.[12] From this total, the funeral expenses, liabilities of the decedent, and exemptions for charity, life insurance, and retirement severance are subtracted. Lastly, the basic exemption is subtracted from this amount to determine total taxable property.

The bequeathed properties, securities, and real estate are in principle valued at the fair market price. However, there are two well-known deviations from the principle. Real estate, such as residential land and land and structures for self-employed business, is in practice assessed less than the market price, partly because there is a special provision for small property and partly because, in practice, assessments for inheritance purposes are underestimated.

The former aspect is a provision for the small sites for residence or for business, such as rental housing. The assessment for the portion of 200 square meters of such property is reduced by 50 percent, and by 60 percent for business sites. If the property was partly residential and partly for business, the business portion is reduced by 60 percent and the residential portion is reduced by 40 percent, provided that the average rate is above 50 percent.

The second source of undervaluation is entirely due to ministerial practice. Land, which is a major portion of real properties in Japan, for bequest purposes is assessed by a valuation map (known as Rosen Ka) in the Tax Bureau's office. This is different from the land price survey (known as Koji Kakaku) done by the Land Agency of the Japanese government, or the land valuation for real estate (property) tax (imposed by municipal government). This problem will be discussed later.

Another provision effectively underassesses the value of agricultural land. This is accomplished by a special deferment and eventual exemption of inheritance tax if a beneficiary continues agriculture on that piece of property. This will be explained later.

There are four major categories for special exemptions from the inheritance tax. Property acquired through inheritance by a person or an organization engaged in religious, charitable, scientific, or other activities for public welfare

---

in equilibrium. In contrast, if the parent-heir relationship is essentially a cooperative game involving an exchange of terminal care and bequest, then the *iryubun* works as a precommitment that would increase the utility of both the elderly and the heirs-to-be. However, an economic analysis of *iryubun* is beyond the scope of this paper.

and to be used for public purposes is exempt from taxation. Payment from the mutual aid systems for handicapped persons carried out by local public entities according to their regulations is exempt from taxation.

Although life insurance payments and severance payments are included in property value, there are deductions for those payments. (Corporate severance payments are prevalent in Japan. The onetime, lump-sum payments upon retirement usually amount to three times annual salary. They play the role of annuity and pensions for U.S. workers.) A tax credit to each of these payments is equal to ¥5 million times the number of statutory heirs.[13]

In addition to special exemptions, all bequests benefit from a basic exemption. The basic exemption under current law is ¥40 million + (¥8 million × the number of statutory heirs).[14]

Tax Base, Tax Table, and Calculation of Tax

The total amount of inheritance tax owed by all heirs is determined as follows. First, assign the total tax base (property values after all exemptions) to each statutory heir by the statutory share (defined above). Then apply the tax schedule shown above in table 10.1 to the assigned amount for each heir (that is, the total tax base times statutory share) to calculate a tax amount for each heir. Deduct any tax credit (to be explained shortly) from this individual tax amount. Then sum up the individual tax amounts to the total inheritance tax liability. Below we provide an example of how to calculate and distribute inheritance tax liability to clarify any questions arising from this description.

Tax Credit and Surcharge

Spouse Provision

A surviving spouse receives a special property value deductible that works like a tax credit. If a surviving spouse inherits property, she or he may deduct

---

12. If a beneficiary of inheritance received properties by gift from the deceased within three years before his or her death, the value of such properties are included in the value of total properties bequeathed. The gift tax with respect to such properties is credited against the inheritance tax due to the beneficiary. This eliminates the potential double taxation of the gift. Although the marginal tax rate for gifts is higher than that of the inheritance tax if the same amount is given, it is possible to lower the total tax burden if only a portion of the intended bequest is given as an inter vivos transfer near death. This provision is intended to deter a near-death rush to divide up properties.

13. There were changes in the amounts of these types of exemptions in the 1988 reform. The old exemption (1975–87) for severance pay due at death was ¥2 million × number of statutory heirs; the new exemption (1988–present) is ¥5 million × number of statutory heirs. The old exemption for life insurance payments was ¥2.5 million × number of statutory heirs; the new exemption is ¥5 million × number of statutory heirs.

14. History of basic deduction: (in million yen) 1958–61, 1.5 + (0.3 × number of statutory heirs); 1962–65, 2.5 + (0.5 × number of statutory heirs); 1966–70, 4.0 + (0.8 × number of statutory heirs) + (4.0 maximum spouse allowance); 1971–72, 6.0 + (0.8 × number of statutory heirs) + (4.0 maximum spouse allowance); 1973–74, 6.0 + (1.2 × number of statutory heirs) + (6.0 maximum spouse allowance); 1975–87, 20.0 + (4.0 × number of statutory heirs); 1988–present, 40.0 + (8.0 × number of statutory heirs).

from her or his inheritance taxable property value the following amount (but not exceeding the inheritance tax less any applicable gift tax credit):

$$\begin{matrix} \text{Tax credit} \\ \text{for spouse} \end{matrix} = \begin{matrix} \text{Total} \\ \text{inheritance} \\ \text{tax} \end{matrix} \times \frac{\begin{matrix} \text{Min (Max [¥80 million, spouse's} \\ \text{statutory share times taxable} \\ \text{property value], value of property} \\ \text{actually given to spouse)} \end{matrix}}{\text{Total taxable property value}}$$

In order to understand the above formula with respect to the spouse's tax liability, it is instructive to consider several scenarios. First, if the spouse actually inherits only up to the portion of statutory share, the inherited amount is free from inheritance tax, however large the property is. This is a revised clause from the 1988 tax reform. In the old formula, this part read "a half of taxable property value." The consequences of the new and old clause differ when there are no children as statutory heirs, since the statutory share of the spouse becomes greater than one-half in such a case. Second, even if the spouse actually inherits more than a statutory share, a bequest to the spouse of less than ¥80 million is again free from inheritance tax. The amount was raised from ¥40 million in the 1988 tax reform. (This revision was commensurate with other revisions of other deductible amounts in the inheritance tax.)

Tax Credit to Certain Heirs and Certain Kinds of Property

After the bequest tax is calculated, there are several provisions for tax credit (table 10A.1). First, if the beneficiary is a child of the decedent and a minor (under age twenty), the tax liability is reduced by ¥60,000 for each year the child is short of his or her twentieth birthday. Second, if a beneficiary is a handicapped child of the decedent, a further tax reduction is provided. The credit equals ¥60,000 times the number of years until the handicapped child attains age seventy. The amount doubles for the severely handicapped.

Other Tax Credits

Recall that any gifts that were made within three years prior to the death are counted toward an inheritance property value. In order to avoid double taxation, the gift tax paid for such gifts is applied as tax credit for inheritance tax.

If the decedent had received property by inheritance within ten years of his or her death, a certain percentage of inheritance tax is reduced for the new

Table 10A.1   **Tax Credit Summary** (in yen)

	Old (1975–87)	New (1988–present)
Handicapped	$(70 - \text{age}) \times 30,000$	$(70 - \text{age}) \times 60,000$
Severely handicapped	$(70 - \text{age}) \times 60,000$	$(70 - \text{age}) \times 120,000$
Minor	$(20 - \text{age}) \times 30,000$	$(20 - \text{age}) \times 60,000$

beneficiary. This alleviates an excess burden imposed by the succession of inheritance from one generation to the grandchildren's generation. The formula is complicated; an interested reader should consult a detailed tax book (Ministry of Finance 1989).

Surcharge

If a beneficiary is not a child (or a grandchild if there are no children), a parent, or a spouse of a child (or a grandchild if there are no children), then there is a 20 percent surcharge on the amount of tax calculated above. This provision works against a generation-skipping inheritance as well as lucky strangers.

Example

Suppose that a property valued at ¥200 million is bequeathed to a spouse and four children. (This example is taken from Ministry of Finance [1990, 129], but case C is added to take into account a second bequest from a spouse to children.) The amount of basic exemption is ¥40 million (a constant) plus ¥8 million times 5 (a spouse and four children), for a total of ¥80 million. Assuming no other exemptions, the tax base is ¥120 million (200 − 80). Next, the statutory share assigns the following distribution of tax base: for the spouse, ¥60 million (120 × ½); for each child, ¥15 million (120 × ⅛). Applying the tax table, individual tax amounts are ¥17.3 million for the spouse and ¥2.45 million for each child. The total tax liability, before tax credit, is thus, ¥27.1 million (17.3 + 2.45 × 4).

Case A. Suppose that heirs decide to actually distribute the property of ¥200 million according to the statutory share. Each child receives ¥25 million (100/4). The spouse tax credit applies in full, so there is zero tax liability for the spouse. Assuming no other tax credits, each child's tax liability is ¥27.1 million multiplied by (25/200), or ¥3.3875 million. The total tax liability is ¥13.55 million.

Case B. A confusing case arises when the actual distribution of the property deviates from the statutory share. The key in such a case is that the total tax liability, ¥27.1 million, does not change. Suppose that the actual distribution of the property is such that the spouse receives a half (that is, ¥100 million) as in case A, but four children, say C_1, C_2, C_3, and C_4, receive ¥40, ¥30, ¥20, and ¥10 million, respectively. Then the actual tax liability becomes, for C_1, 27.1 × (40/200) = ¥5.42 million; for C_2, 27.1 × (30/200) = ¥4.065 million; for C_3, 27.1 × (20/200) = ¥2.71 million; and for C_4, 27.1 × 10/200) = ¥1.355 million. The total tax liability remains ¥13.55 million.

Case C. Note that Cases A and B consider only one aspect of intergenerational transfers. Suppose case A, and assume that the surviving spouse dies some years later without spending the ¥100 million. Then that amount is bequeathed to the four children. The basic deduction this time is ¥72 million (40 + (8 × 4)). Hence the total tax base is ¥28 million (100 − 72), implying that each statutory heir is responsible for ¥7 million (28/4). From the tax table, that would trigger a tax liability of ¥0.85 million per person, for a total inheritance tax of ¥3.4 million. Hence, the total inheritance tax on the intergenerational transfer (in two transactions) is ¥13.55 plus ¥3.4 million for a total of ¥16.95 million on a ¥200 million estate.

Special Treatment and Agricultural Land

When a farmer bequeaths farmland to an heir and the heir continues to use the land in an agricultural (family) business, the inheritance tax on the difference between the value as an agricultural land and the value otherwise may be deferred, and will be exempted if (1) the beneficiary continues agricultural use for twenty years after the inheritance, (2) the beneficiary dies, or (3) the beneficiary makes a gift to a person who continues farming.

Suppose that there is a parcel of land in a residential area. It is not productive as an agricultural business, so that its value as agricultural land would be relatively low. (In practice, the value is calculated as a present discounted value of agricultural income from the land.) However, if it is converted to residential use, the market value would be ten times its agricultural value. An heir generally would be better off to continue farming for twenty years to gain an exemption from the inheritance tax for most of the land value. After twenty years, the heir may sell at the higher market price. If the heir quits farming before ten years, a recapture provision for higher tax applies.

Filing Requirement

After these calculations, those who do not owe any inheritance tax are not required to report to the Tax Bureau's office, except for a spouse who benefits from the special spouse tax credit to become nontaxable. The filing has to be completed within six months of death. If mistakes in filing are found later, corrections may be submitted.

Inheritance Tax Distortion

Token Adoption

It is apparent from the calculation of the inheritance tax that the number of statutory heirs plays an important role. The number of statutory heirs need not equal the true number of heirs. More statutory heirs reduces total inheritance taxes imposed upon actual heirs. This is independent of how a decedent actually divides his or her properties. Three features of the inheritance tax produce this result. First, the basic exemption depends on the number of statutory heirs. Second, the total property value after exemptions is divided by the number of statutory heirs before a progressive tax schedule is applied. Third, the tax credit for life insurance payment and severance payment depends on the number of statutory heirs.

Hence, a family may reduce inheritance tax payments by adopting children to increase the number of statutory heirs, with an understanding that the adopted children receive only a nominal compensation for this service. This loophole was widely recognized and exploited by wealthy families. Table 10.8 reveals a strong correlation between the size of the estate and the number of statutory heirs.

To close this loophole, the 1988 revision included a cap on the number of adopted children counted toward statutory heirs. Under the new rule, an adopted heir may be counted as a statutory heir only if the adopted heir is (1) a biological child of the spouse of the decedent; (2) a grandchild (if there is no child); or (3) an adopted child under the special adoption clause (Civil Law, article 817, 2–11);[15] *and* (4) the only adopted heir or one of only two adopted heirs, if there is no adopted heir in (1)–(3), a natural child, or a grandchild.

However, the effective date for this change was not until December 31, 1988, unlike most other changes, which became effective on January 1, 1988. Hence, we have to wait one more year to see what difference this tax reform has made.

Use of Real Estate

As explained in the text, real estate is a good vehicle for integenerational transfers. The value of real estate is in practice assessed at about half to two-thirds of the market value. In addition, assessments on up to 200 square meters of bequeathed residential property are further reduced by 50 percent (60 percent for business).

Bequests carried in the form of real estate are subject to less inheritance tax than those carried in the form of securities. Moreover, since the amount of debt is deductible in full, an effective way to reduce inheritance tax is to borrow a large sum of money to purchase real property, preferably shortly before death, so that the property is still highly leveraged at the time of intergenerational transfer.

To curtail such tax planning, the 1988 tax reform mandated that any real estate (land and structures, excluding the decedent's personal residence) purchased within three years of the date of death is assessed at its purchase price. (This is evidence that the tax authorities admit that assessed value is in practice less than the market value.) This rule still permits a tax advantage in a period of high land inflation. This change is also effective as of December 31, 1988.

We expect that this kind of tax incentive will manifest itself in land's repre-

15. The special adoption clause was introduced in 1987 to make children adopted at an early age (younger than six years) have rights and obligations in the family relationship similar to biological children. Unlike traditional adoption, special adoption severs the child's ties with his or her biological parents.

senting a larger fraction of bequests than otherwise. First, the share of land in tax-filing bequeathed property value is higher than the share of land in outstanding property value of a household. In 1988, the former was 69 percent, while the latter was 53 percent. Second, the share of land in the value of bequeathed property is higher in Japan than in the United States.

Gift Tax

A person may receive a gift of up to ¥600,000 a year free of gift tax. In addition, without gift tax, a spouse who has been married for more than twenty years may receive a gift of residential property of up to ¥20 million for personal use or a financial gift up to ¥20 million toward a purchase of residential property for personal use. This clause was created in 1966 with a twenty-five-year marriage requirement and with a ¥1.6 million deductible. The requirement had been twenty years since 1971, and the deductible amount was ¥10 million from 1975 to 1988.

A gift beyond these exemptions is subject to gift tax according to the tax schedule in table 10A.2. Table 10A.3 shows the gift tax filings for recent years.

Table 10A.2   **Gift Tax Table** (in millions of yen, beyond exemptions)

Old Taxable Transfer (1975–87)			New Taxable Transfer (1988–present)		
More Than	But Less Than	MTR (%)	More Than	But Less Than	MTR (%)
0.0	0.5	10	0.0	1.0	10
0.5	0.7	15	1.0	1.5	15
0.7	1.0	20	1.5	2.0	25
1.0	1.4	25	2.0	3.0	30
1.4	2.0	30	3.0	4.0	35
2.0	2.8	35	4.0	6.0	40
2.8	4.0	40	6.0	8.0	45
4.0	5.5	45	8.0	12.0	50
5.5	8.0	50	12.0	20.0	55
8.0	13.0	55	20.0	30.0	60
13.0	20.0	60	30.0	70.0	65
20.0	35.0	65	70.0	—	70
35.0	70.0	70			
70.0	—	75			

Source: Ministry of Finance, Tax Bureau, *An Outline of Japanese Taxes* (various issues).

Table 10A.3   **Gift Tax Filing Record** (in billions of yen)

	1986	1987	1988
Gift property value	960.600	1,418.543	1,109.786
Spouse exemption	165.018	357.432	179.096
Basic exemption	252.259	303.400	275.873
Tax base	543.213	772.927	653.528
Gift tax	151.858	225.454	168.670

Note: There was a tax reform (reduction) in 1988.
Source: Ministry of Finance, Tax Bureau, *Tax Bureau Statistics Annual* (various years).

Appendix B
Transfer Taxation in the United States

Overview

United States law formally structures the gift and estate taxes as excise taxes on the transfer of wealth.[16] A gift tax is imposed on transfers by gift during life, and an estate tax is imposed on transfers at death. The gift and estate taxes are a unified transfer tax system in that one progressive tax is imposed on the cumulative transfers during the lifetime and at death.

In theory, the tax applies to a family's wealth once per generation. In its present configuration, U.S. transfer taxes treat husband and wife as a family unit for purposes of transfers. Transfers between spouses are free of tax. However, the husband and wife independently use the basic exemption and tax rate schedule.

Taxable Estate and Taxable Gift

A decedent's gross estate is the market value of all the decedent's assets.[17] The law permits an unlimitied deduction for transfers between spouses. In addition, transfers and bequests to charities are deductible.[18] Funeral and burial expenses and expenses of administration of the estate are also deductible. Consequently, in its simplest terms, the taxable estate is the market value of all assets less the estate's expenses, charitable bequests, and transfers to the surviving spouse.

An individual may make annual gifts of $10,000 to any other individual

16. This is a consequence of an 1895 Supreme Court decision that invalidated the existing income tax, which treated gifts and inheritances as income and taxable as such. Congress enacted the current form of the estate tax in 1916. To eliminate avoidance through inter vivos transfers, Congress enacted the gift tax in 1932.
17. Special-use valuation of farm and other property is discussed in the main text and below.
18. Transfers are charitable only if they go to qualifying organizations. The Internal Revenue Service certifies qualifying charitable organizations.

without being subject to tax.[19] A husband and wife may jointly make $20,000 of tax-free gifts to each recipient. For example, a husband and wife with three children may annually transfer $20,000 to each child free of any gift tax, for a total of $60,000 in tax-free transfers. Moreover, a husband and wife may transfer $20,000 annually to each child for as long as they live. Such transfers are free from transfer taxes, and they do not constitute taxable income to the children. A program of annual giving permits the transfer of considerable wealth free of tax. Our hypothetical husband and wife could transfer $1.2 million tax free to their three children over a twenty-year period.

Prior to the Economic Recovery Tax Act of 1981 the treatment of interspousal transfers and other gifts was not quite as liberal. At that time the annual gift tax exclusion was $3,000 ($6,000 for joint gifts). The entire value of the first $100,000 of lifetime transfers between spouses was exempt from tax. Thereafter, a deduction was allowed for 50 percent of interspousal lifetime transfers in excess of $200,000. The estate tax marital deduction generally was equal to the greater of $250,000 or one-half of the decedent's adjusted gross estate.

Rates and Unified Credit

Under present law, the gift and estate tax rates begin at 18 percent on the first $10,000 of taxable transfers and reach 55 percent on transfers over $3 million.[20] In addition, for transfers between $10 million and $21,040,000,[21] the benefits of the lower rates and the unified schedule are phased out at a rate of 5 percent, making the effective marginal tax rate 60 percent. After this phase-out range, the marginal and average tax rate equals 55 percent.

The cumulative amount of any gift or estate tax is reduced by a unified credit. The gift or estate tax is first computed without any exemption, and then the unified credit is subtracted to determine the amount of gift or estate tax payable before the allowance of other credits. The Tax Reform Act of 1976 created a unified credit of $47,000, which had the effect of exempting transfers of up to $175,625 from tax. The Economic Recovery Tax Act of 1981 increased the credit in six annual steps to $192,800, which has the effect of exempting transfers of up to $600,000 from tax.[22] As a consequence, the first dollar of a taxable estate faces a 37 percent marginal tax rate.[23] The unified

19. Payment of qualifying educational expenses, such as the tuition and fees charged by a university, and medical expenses do not count toward the annual limit.

20. In 1993 the top rate is scheduled to be reduced to 50 percent. Prior to 1981, the top rate was 70 percent for transfers in excess of $5 million. Brackets at 60 and 65 percent also existed. The reduction from a top rate of 70 percent to the current rate structure was phased in.

21. $18,340,000 after 1992.

22. The unified credit was $62,800 for 1982, $79,300 for 1983, $96,300 for 1984, $121,800 for 1985, and $155,800 for 1986.

23. The rate structure for transfers of less than $600,000, reported above, has been retained over the past fifteen years. Lower-end relief has been provided by increases in the unified credit. As noted above, the top bracket rates have been reduced.

credit is not indexed for inflation. Tax liability accounts for any prior gift taxes paid or unified credit claimed.

While the gift and estate taxes are unified and unlimited tax-free transfers are permitted between spouses, the husband and wife do not jointly face one tax rate schedule for transfers of household wealth. This implies that simple tax planning can reduce significantly taxes on transfers. Suppose a husband and wife receive an annuity that provides for their living expenses and the husband owns $1.2 million of assets. The husband could bequeath all assets to his wife, and his estate would pay no tax. Upon the wife's subsequent death, however, $1.2 million would be in her estate. After using the unified credit, the estate would owe $235,000 in tax, and $965,000 would be bequeathed to their children. The superior strategy is for the husband to bequeath $600,000 to his wife, which is untaxed under the marital deduction, and to bequeath $600,000 to their children, which is untaxed by his estate's use of the unified credit. Upon the wife's subsequent death, her estate could transfer the remaining $600,000 to their children free of tax as her estate uses the unified credit. With an increasing marginal tax rate schedule, equal bequests from each spouse minimize the total tax burden.

A limited credit is available for any state death or inheritance taxes paid.[24] The state credit works as revenue sharing with the states, encouraging them to establish a death tax at least to soak up the benefit of the dollars that the federal government would otherwise tax. Twenty-six states impose only a so-called soak-up or pick-up tax. For example, Florida has such a tax. Nine states, for example, New York, impose estate taxes in excess of what is creditable against the federal estate tax, thereby increasing the total tax burden. Another eighteen states, for example, Pennsylvania, impose a bequest tax in addition to an estate soak-up tax.[25] Such taxes also increase the total tax burden.

Tax-Inclusive versus Tax-Exclusive Rate Structures

While the credit is unified, the rate structure is not. The estate tax is calculated on a tax-inclusive basis while the gift tax is calculated on a tax-exclusive basis. What this means is that, for transfers from an estate, bequests are paid from the after-tax estate. The tax is "included" in the estate. For gifts, the amount transferred defines the tax base. The tax is "excluded" from the gift received by the beneficiary. Hence, to think of the gross of tax transfer, one must gross up the gift by the tax subsequently paid.

Assume Smith has $1.5 million in wealth and that the transfer tax rate is 50

---

24. The current state death tax credit provides a credit for state death taxes up to 80 percent of the tax imposed by the 1926 federal tax rate schedule. It is somewhat of a historical anomaly, but its more than sixty-year existence and the off-budget revenue sharing it provides make it unlikely that it will be modified in the future, although an attempt was made to convert it to a deduction in 1987.

25. The U.S. Advisory Commission on Intergovernmental Relations (1991) describes the estate or bequest tax rate structure of each state.

percent. Assume Smith wants to transfer wealth to Jones. If Smith accomplishes the transfer by bequest, Smith's estate applies the 50 percent tax rate (inclusive) and pays $750,000 to the government. Jones receives $750,000. However, if Smith made a gift to Jones of $1 million, a 50 percent tax is assessed (exclusive) on the gift, and Smith must pay $500,000 to the government. Smith faced an effective tax rate of 50 percent on his wealth when transferred through his estate and an effective tax rate of 33 percent on his wealth when transferred by gift.

Taxation of Life Insurance

In the main text we explained that the gross estate does not include the proceeds of a life insurance policy if the decedent, at least three years prior to death, irrevocably designates beneficiaries of the policy and transfers all other incidents of ownership to another person. Such a strategy effectively avoids all estate taxes but not necessarily gift taxes, as payments of the insurance premium may be a taxable gift. For example, if a father pays a $12,000 insurance premium on a policy that is owned by his son, the father has made a taxable gift of $2,000 ($12,000 less the $10,000 annual exclusion).

Taxation of Farm Property and Closely Held Businesses

As explained in the text, an executor may elect to have certain real property used in farming and other closely held businesses valued at its current use, rather than at fair market value, for estate tax purposes. The election effectively lowers the estate tax burden on family farms and other family-owned businesses. In addition, where the estate is illiquid, the tax may be paid, with interest, over a fifteen-year period. To the extent that the interest rate charged is less than the heirs' opportunity cost, this can present a substantial deferral advantage.

Generation-Skipping Transfers

In 1976 Congress created a generation-skipping transfer tax to apply to transfers that deviate from the normal succession of bequests by skipping one or more generations. Prior to 1977, trusts were used frequently to effect generation skips, because the death of a life beneficiary in the trust did not necessarily create a taxable transfer to the trust's remainderman. Pechman (1987) presents evidence that in the 1940s and 1950s more than 60 percent of millionaires in the United States transferred at least some of their property in trusts and trusts accounted for more than one-third of the value of noncharitable transfers by millionaires. The 1976 legislation effectively taxed the assets in a generation-skipping trust at the marginal estate tax rate of the life beneficiary. The Tax Reform Act of 1986 simplified this tax by imposing the tax at a flat rate, independent of the tax status of the life beneficiary. The 1986 legislation also extended this tax to apply to direct generation skips (outright gifts that skip a generation).

This tax subjects generation-skipping transfers to a flat rate of tax equal to the highest rate of the estate tax (currently 55 percent) after allowing a $1 million exemption per taxpayer. A gift from grandparent to grandchild is potentially subject to both the gift tax and the generation-skipping transfer tax. If the grandchild's parents have predeceased his or her grandparent, the generation-skipping tax does not apply. The generation-skipping transfer tax is imposed only once per transfer. The tax liability created by a gift from parent to great-grandchild is no different than the tax liability created by a gift from parent to grandchild.

Composition of Wealth of Decedents in the United States

In the main text we presented data on the composition of wealth of decedents from estate tax returns filed in 1985. Tables 10B.1 through 10B.7 present comparable data from estate tax returns filed in 1977, 1982, 1983, 1984, 1986, 1987, and 1988. It is important to note that in 1981, as discussed above, substantial changes were made to the estate tax, some of which were not fully phased in until 1987.

Table 10B.1   **Estate Tax Returns Filed in 1977**

	Returns		Value	
	Number	%	Millions of $	%
Gross estate	200,747	100.0	48,201.7	100.0
Real estate	159,032	72.9	12,920.9	26.8
Bonds (total)	90,093	44.9	3,897.8	8.1
Federal savings	51,922	25.9	730.9	1.5
Federal other	18,438	9.2	1,260.3	2.6
State and local	13,184	6.6	1,192.5	2.5
Corporate and foreign	38,519	19.2	714.1	1.5
Corporate stock	128,817	64.2	12,483.6	25.9
Noncorporate business	25,871	12.9	1,010.3	2.1
Cash	195,016	97.1	8,444.3	17.5
Notes and mortgages	50,426	25.1	1,736.0	3.8
Life insurance	124,231	61.9	2,683.0	5.6
Annuities	17,478	8.7	253.1	0.5
Household goods	172,757	86.1	1,538.7	3.2
Lifetime transfers	25,329	12.6	3,233.9	6.7
Deductions (total)	200,747	100.0	28,065.4	58.2
Funeral and administrative				
expenses	197,159	98.2	2,022.1	4.2
Debts and mortgages	162,562	81.0	2,649.0	6.2
Charity	24,401	12.2	2,993.9	6.2
Marital	94,578	47.1	9,952.4	20.7
Exemption	174,139	86.7	10,445.9	21.7
Orphans	72	0.0	1.9	0.0
Taxable estate	148,194	73.8	20,904.2	43.4
Estate tax before credits	148,194	73.8	6,172.0	12.8
Credits (total)	91,272	45.5	1,192.9	2.5
State death taxes	81,292	40.5	552.3	1.1
Federal gift taxes	1,450	0.7	28.1	0.1
Unified credit in lieu of				
exemption	21,633	10.8	523.6	1.1
Other	8,489	4.2	88.9	0.2
Estate tax	139,115	69.3	4,979.1	10.3

Source: Internal Revenue Service, Statistics of Income Division.

Table 10B.2   **Estate Tax Returns Filed in 1982**

	Returns		Value	
	Number	%	Millions of $	%
Gross estate	59,597	100.0	45,412.0	100.0
Real estate	48,166	80.8	10,974.3	24.2
Corporate stock	47,978	80.5	11,889.4	26.2
Bonds (total)	29,795	50.0	3,538.6	7.8
Federal savings	10,151	17.0	245.3	0.5
Federal other	11,446	19.2	1,370.7	3.0
State and local	12,976	21.8	1,452.1	3.2
Corporate and foreign	14,918	25.0	470.4	1.0
Cash	56,851	95.4	5,993.7	13.2
Notes and mortgages	21,994	36.9	1,466.3	3.2
Life insurance	35,902	60.2	1,854.4	4.1
Annuities	8,205	13.8	441.8	1.0
Noncorporate business	16,323	27.4	1,537.8	3.4
Household assets	52,204	87.6	1,807.7	4.0
Lifetime transfers	12,678	21.3	5,455.8	12.0
Deductions (total)	—	—	17,897.5	39.4
Funeral expenses	56,781	95.3	214.2	0.5
Administrative expense (total)	50,945	85.5	1,439.8	3.2
Executors	22,337	37.5	430.3	0.9
Attorneys	42,882	72.0	626.8	1.4
Other	49,698	83.4	382.7	0.8
Debts and mortgages	51,560	86.5	2,600.7	5.7
Charity	8,728	14.6	2,250.2	5.0
Marital	31,753	53.3	11,385.7	25.1
Orphans	236	0.4	6.8	0.0
Taxable estate	57,928	97.2	27,567.9	60.7
Adjusted taxable gifts	917	1.5	31.0	0.1
Adjusted taxable estate	57,928	97.2	27.598.8	60.8
Estate tax before credits	57,927	97.2	9,775.3	21.5
Credits (total)	57,914	97.2	3,549.3	7.8
Unified	57,914	97.2	2,520.1	5.5
State death taxes	41,716	70.0	919.7	2.0
Other	—	—	109.6	0.2
Estate tax	41,620	69.8	6,226.0	13.7

Source: Internal Revenue Service, Statistics of Income Division.

Table 10B.3   Estate Tax Returns Filed in 1983

	Returns		Value	
	Number	%	Millions of $	%
Gross estate	63,251	100.0	50,390.4	100.0
Real estate	43,302	68.5	12,009.1	23.8
Corporate stock	40,263	63.6	11,509.8	22.8
Bonds (total)	26,946	42.7	4,049.9	8.0
Federal savings	8,089	12.8	313.9	0.6
Federal other	9,229	14.6	1,358.9	2.7
State and local	13,636	21.6	1,978.0	3.9
Corporate and foreign	11,779	18.6	399.1	0.8
Cash	51,126	80.8	5,878.5	11.7
Notes and mortgages	19,957	31.6	1,904.0	3.8
Life insurance	36,975	58.5	1,952.0	3.9
Annuities	7,576	12.0	403.5	0.8
Noncorporate business	14,828	23.4	2,060.1	4.1
Household assets	47,866	75.7	2,079.2	4.1
Lifetime transfers	8,671	13.7	4,729.3	9.4
Deductions (total)	—	—	24,321.9	48.3
Funeral expenses	59,187	93.6	345.1	0.7
Administrative expense				
(total)	42,120	66.6	1,256.0	2.5
Executors	18,497	29.2	400.8	0.8
Attorneys	34,383	54.4	543.5	1.1
Other	40,529	64.1	311.8	0.6
Debts and mortgages	53,979	85.3	3,209.5	6.4
Charity	9,949	15.7	2,545.4	5.1
Marital	32,247	51.0	16,964.9	33.7
Orphans[a]	—	—	—	—
Taxable estate	55,588	87.9	26,235.4	52.1
Adjusted taxable gifts	2,905	4.6	247.8	0.5
Adjusted taxable estate	55,601	87.9	26,483.3	52.6
Estate tax before credits	55,585	87.9	9,264.8	18.4
Credits (total)	55,585	87.9	4,094.8	8.1
Unified	55,585	87.9	3,155.0	6.3
State death taxes	36,971	58.5	848.0	1.7
Other[a]	—	—	—	—
Estate tax	35,148	55.6	5,170.0	10.3

Source: Internal Revenue Service, Statistics of Income Division.

[a]Information not disclosed.

Table 10B.4   **Estate Tax Returns Filed in 1984**

	Returns		Value	
	Number	%	Millions of $	%
Gross estate	60,316	100.0	49,953.6	100.0
Real estate	41,915	69.5	10,316.9	20.7
Corporate stock	40,363	66.9	13,267.7	26.6
Bonds (total)	26,346	43.7	3,423.4	6.9
Federal savings	7,749	12.8	169.3	0.3
Federal other	7,758	12.9	1,090.0	2.2
State and local	14,454	24.0	1,831.1	3.7
Corporate and foreign	11,415	18.9	338.1	0.7
Cash	48,742	80.8	5,547.6	11.1
Notes and mortgages	17,818	29.5	1,625.6	3.3
Life insurance	32,798	54.4	1,958.8	3.9
Annuities	12,247	20.3	950.8	1.9
Noncorporate business	14,251	23.6	1,746.1	3.5
Household assets	47,415	78.3	2,098.5	4.2
Lifetime transfers	7,823	13.0	5,606.2	11.2
Deductions (total)	—	—	25,553.3	51.2
Funeral expenses	55,639	92.2	307.0	0.6
Administrative expense				
(total)	39,640	67.7	1,090.9	2.2
Executors	15,849	26.3	357.2	0.7
Attorneys	31,505	52.2	479.2	1.0
Other	37,304	61.8	254.5	0.5
Debts and mortgages	49,394	81.9	2,722.0	5.4
Charity	9,151	15.2	3,091.3	6.2
Marital	29,691	49.2	18,341.7	36.7
Orphans[a]	—	—	—	—
Taxable estate	54,472	90.3	26,420.7	52.9
Adjusted taxable gifts	3,745	6.2	279.5	0.6
Adjusted taxable estate	54,473	90.3	26,700.2	53.5
Estate tax before credits	54,473	90.3	9,378.6	18.8
Credits (total)	54,473	90.3	4,711.9	9.4
Unified	54,473	90.3	3,760.7	7.5
State death taxes	32,851	54.5	867.1	1.7
Other[a]	—	—	—	—
Estate tax	31,507	52.2	4,666.7	9.3

Source: Internal Revenue Service, Statistics of Income Division.

[a]Information not disclosed.

Table 10B.5   **Estate Tax Returns Filed in 1986**

	Returns		Value	
	Number	%	Millions of $	%
Gross estate	42,125	100.0	59,805.0	100.0
Real estate	32,806	77.8	12,361.6	20.7
Corporate stock	33,747	80.1	17,029.1	28.5
Bonds (total)	—	—	6,315.2	10.6
Federal savings	6,308	15.0	321.6	0.5
Federal other	10,365	24.6	1,656.9	2.8
State and local	16,806	39.9	3,927.9	6.6
Corporate and foreign	10,350	24.6	408.8	0.7
Cash	40,957	97.2	6,853.3	11.5
Notes and mortgages	14,663	34.8	1,917.1	3.2
Life insurance	23,741	56.4	1,866.2	3.1
Annuities	11,244	26.7	1,349.8	2.3
Noncorporate business	11,202	26.6	2,069.9	3.5
Household assets	38,017	90.2	2,346.2	3.9
Lifetime transfers	8,581	20.4	7,696.7	12.9
Deductions (total)	42,124	100.0	28,312.9	47.3
Funeral expenses	39,318	93.3	177.4	0.3
Administrative expense (total)	—	—	1,494.9	2.5
Executors	15,615	37.1	533.6	0.9
Attorneys	27,200	64.6	591.2	1.0
Other	31,337	74.4	370.1	0.6
Debts and mortgages	35,890	85.2	2,941.7	4.9
Charity	7,835	18.6	3,573.3	6.0
Marital	20,010	47.5	20,125.7	33.7
Taxable estate	38,054	90.3	31,634.7	52.9
Adjusted taxable gifts	3,650	8.7	438.4	0.7
Adjusted taxable estate	38,124	90.5	32,073.2	53.6
Estate tax before credits	38,134	90.5	12,074.4	20.2
Credits (total)	—	—	5,691.3	9.5
Unified	38,033	90.3	4,243.1	7.1
Other	25,166	59.7	1,448.2	2.4
Estate tax	23,731	56.3	6,383.1	10.7

Source: Internal Revenue Service, Statistics of Income Division.

Table 10B.6   **Estate Tax Returns Filed in 1987**

	Returns		Value	
	Number	%	Millions of $	%
Gross estate	45,113	100.0	66,564.1	100.0
Real estate	35,519	78.7	12,826.6	19.3
Corporate stock	34,987	77.6	18,667.8	28.0
Bonds (total)	—	—	7,544.7	11.3
Federal savings	6,552	14.5	289.7	0.4
Federal other	9,990	22.1	1,659.0	2.5
State and local	18,361	40.7	5,028.6	7.6
Corporate and foreign	10,679	23.7	567.4	0.9
Cash	43,726	96.9	7,212.2	10.8
Notes and mortgages	13,290	29.5	1,823.7	2.7
Life insurance	24,489	54.3	1,990.0	3.0
Annuities	11,981	26.6	1,494.1	2.2
Noncorporate business	11,354	25.2	2,736.9	4.1
Household assets	40,947	90.8	2,516.0	3.8
Lifetime transfers	8,889	19.7	9,752.3	14.7
Deductions (total)	45,084	99.9	30,873.4	46.4
Funeral expenses	42,246	93.6	199.7	0.3
Administrative expense (total)	—	—	1,678.4	2.5
Executors	16,128	35.8	612.7	0.9
Attorneys	27,634	61.3	622.5	0.9
Other	32,874	72.9	443.2	0.7
Debts and mortgages	38,067	84.4	3,566.6	5.4
Charity	8,987	19.9	3,978.0	6.0
Marital	20,191	44.8	21,540.9	32.4
Taxable estate	40,874	90.6	35,913.7	54.0
Adjusted taxable gifts	3,648	8.1	541.4	0.8
Adjusted taxable estate	40,935	90.7	36,455.0	54.8
Estate tax before credits	40,908	90.7	13,767.3	20.7
Credits (total)	—	—	7,409.3	11.1
Unified	40,907	90.7	5,803.4	8.7
Other	25,128	55.7	1,605.9	2.4
Estate tax	21,335	47.3	6,358.0	9.6

Source: Internal Revenue Service, Statistics of Income Division.

Table 10B.7   **Estate Tax Returns Filed in 1988**

	Returns		Value	
	Number	%	Millions of $	%
Gross estate	43,683	100.0	70,625.4	100.0
Real estate	35,077	80.3	13,564.8	19.2
Corporate stock	34,333	78.6	19,638.8	27.8
Bonds (total)	26,803	61.4	8,077.5	11.4
Federal savings	6,225	14.3	243.3	0.3
Federal other	9,239	21.2	1,539.2	2.2
State and local	19,521	44.7	5,823.1	8.2
Corporate and foreign	9,391	21.5	471.9	0.7
Cash	42,345	96.9	7,614.4	10.8
Notes and mortgages	12,568	28.8	1,708.7	2.4
Life insurance	23,741	54.3	2,150.0	3.0
Annuities	11,985	27.4	1,692.3	2.4
Noncorporate business	10,916	25.0	2,519.4	3.6
Household assets	39,374	90.1	2,547.4	3.6
Lifetime transfers	9,382	21.5	11,112.1	15.7
Deductions (total)	43,596	99.9	33,523.9	47.5
Funeral expenses	40,274	92.2	197.5	0.3
Administrative expense (total)	31,846	72.9	1,700.6	2.4
Executors	15,408	35.3	632.6	0.9
Attorneys	25,702	58.8	604.9	0.9
Other	30,762	70.4	463.1	0.7
Debts and mortgages	35,514	81.3	3,238.2	4.6
Charity	8,376	19.2	4,822.1	6.8
Marital	20,593	47.1	23,539.6	33.3
ESOP[a]	—	—	—	—
Taxable estate	39,480	90.4	37,250.2	52.7
Adjusted taxable gifts	4,582	10.5	918.2	1.3
Adjusted taxable estate	39,551	90.5	38,168.4	54.0
Estate tax before credits	39,551	90.5	14,588.7	20.7
Credits (total)	39,550	90.5	8,187.3	11.6
Unified	39,550	90.5	6,559.5	9.3
State death taxes	21,900	50.1	1,567.5	2.2
Other	919	2.1	60.3	0.1
Estate tax	18,948	43.4	6,299.2	8.9

Source: Internal Revenue Service, Statistics of Income Division.

[a]Employee Stock Ownership Plan; information not disclosed.

References

Bernheim, B. Douglas. 1987. Does the Estate Tax Raise Revenue? In *Tax Policy and the Economy*, ed. Lawrence H. Summers, vol. 1. Cambridge, Mass.: MIT Press.

Bernheim, B. Douglas, Andrei Shleifer, and Lawrence H. Summers. 1985. The Strategic Bequest Motive. *Journal of Political Economy* 93 (6): 1045–76.

Cooper, George. 1979. *A Voluntary Tax? New Perspectives on Sophisticated Tax Avoidance*. Washington, D.C.: Brookings Institution.

Cox, Donald. 1990. Intergenerational Transfers and Liquidity Constraints. *Quarterly Journal of Economics* 105 (February): 187–217.

David, Martin, and Paul L. Menchik. 1979. The Effect of Social Security on Lifetime Wealth Accumulation and Bequest. *Economica* 52: 421–34.

Dekle, Robert. 1989a. A Simulation Model of Saving, Residential Choice, and Bequests of the Japanese Elderly. *Economics Letters* 29: 129–33.

———. 1989b. The Unimportance of Intergenerational Transfers in Japan. *Japan and the World Economy* 1: 403–13.

———. 1990. Do the Japanese Elderly Reduce Their Total Wealth? A New Look with Different Data. *Journal of the Japanese and International Economies* 4: 309–17.

Economic Planning Agency. 1985–90. *Annual Report on National Accounts*. Tokyo: Printing Bureau, Ministry of Finance.

Hayashi, Fumio. 1986. Why Is Japan's Saving Rate So Apparently High? *NBER Macroeconomics Annual* 1: 147–210. Cambridge Mass.: MIT Press.

Hayashi, Fumio, Albert Ando, and Richard Ferris. 1988. Life Cycle and Bequest Savings: A Study of Japanese and U.S. Households Based on Data from the 1984 NSFIE and the 1983 Survey of Consumer Finances. *Journal of the Japanese and International Economies* 2: 417–49.

Hayashi, Fumio, Takatoshi Ito, and Joel Slemrod. 1988. Housing Finance Imperfections, Taxation, and Private Saving: A Comparative Simulation Analysis of the United States and Japan. *Journal of the Japanese and International Economies* 2: 215–38.

Homma, Masaaki, and Masumi Atoda. 1989. *Empirical Analysis of Tax Reform* (In Japanese). Tokyo: Toyo Keizai Shinposha.

Hurd, Michael D. 1987. Savings of the Elderly and Desired Bequests. *American Economic Review* 77 (3): 298–312.

Internal Revenue Service. Various years. *Statistics of Income*. Estate Tax Returns. Washington, D.C.

Ishi, Hiromitsu. 1989. *The Japanese Tax System*. Oxford: Clarendon Press.

Ishikawa, Tsuneo. 1988. Saving and Labor Supply Behavior of Aged Households in Japan. *Journal of the Japanese and International Economies* 2: 414–49.

Kotlikoff, Laurence J. 1988. Intergenerational Transfers and Savings. *Journal of Economic Perspectives* 2 (2): 41–58.

Kotlikoff, Laurence J., and Lawrence H. Summers. 1981. The Role of Intergenerational Transfers in Aggregate Capital Accumulation. *Journal of Political Economy* 89 (4): 706–32.

Menchik, Paul L., and Martin David. 1983. Income Distribution, Lifetime Savings, and Bequests. *American Economic Review* 73 (4): 627–90.

Ministry of Finance, Tax Bureau. 1977–90. *Tax Bureau Statistics Annual*. Tokyo: Ministry of Finance.

———. 1990. *An Outline of Japanese Taxes, 1989*. Tokyo: Printing Bureau, Ministry of Finance.

———, ed. 1989. *Easy Inheritance Tax*. Tokyo: Okkura Zaimu Kyokai.

Ministry of Health and Welfare. 1977–90. *Vital Statistics Japan*. Tokyo: Printing Bureau, Ministry of Finance.

———. 1988. *Basic Life Survey*. Tokyo: Printing Bureau, Ministry of Finance.

Modigliani, Franco. 1988. The Role of Intergenerational Transfers and Life Cycle Saving in the Accumulation of Wealth. *Journal of Economic Perspectives* 2 (2): 15–40.

Munnell, Alicia H., with Nicole Ernsberger. 1988. Wealth Transfer Taxation: The Relative Role for Estate and Income Taxes. *New England Economic Review* (November/December): 3–28.

Noguchi, Yukio, Kyoko Uemura, and Yumiko Kitoh. 1989. Structure of Intergenerational Transfers of Wealth by Bequest. *Shakai Hosho Kenkyu* (2): 136–44.

Pechman, Joseph A. 1987. *Federal Tax Policy*. Washington, D.C.: Brookings Institution.

Takayama, Noriyuki. 1991. *Greying Japan: An Economic Perspective on Public Pensions*. Tokyo: Kinokuniya; and Oxford: Oxford University Press.

U.S. Advisory Commission on Intergovernmental Relations. 1991. Significant Features of Fiscal Federalism, Volume 1, Budget Process and Tax Systems. Washington, D.C.: February.

U.S. Board of Governors of the Federal Reserve System, Flow of Funds Accounts. 1988. Financial Assets and Liabilities Year-End, 1964–87. Washington, D.C.: September.

———. 1990. Balance Sheets for the U.S. Economy 1945–89. Washington, D.C.: April.

Comment   Ching-huei Chang

I offer the following comments on Thomas Barthold's and Takatoshi Ito's paper. In terms of the first objective of this paper, they did a very good job in detailing the bequest (inheritance) and gift tax systems in Japan and the United States. But it seems to me this paper would be more helpful if the authors made a comparison between the two tax systems, rather than concentrating on the institutional elements. Some important questions could have been addressed. For example, what are the two systems' similarities and differences? What accounts for these differences? Do these differences have implications for variations in households' bequest, saving, and other economic behaviors?

My second comment is more on the U.S. tax system than on the paper itself. It seems to me that there is a fundamental difference between the two systems. Japan treats inheritance and gift taxes as supplements to income taxes. The theoretical basis of these taxes is the concept of ability to pay. Therefore, corresponding to the individual income tax, there are exemptions, a tax base, credits, and a progressive rate structure in the Japanese transfer tax system. On the other hand, as Appendix 2 indicates, the United States treats these taxes as excise taxes on the transfer of wealth. If it is so, why does the United States use a progressive rate structure? As I understand it, progressive rates are usually related to the ability-to-pay principle. In the case of an excise

Ching-huei Chang is a research fellow of Sun Yat-sen Institute for Social Sciences and Philosophy, Academia Sinica, Taiwan.

tax, there may be different rates for different commodities or services, depending on price elasticities in demand. I do not see any justification for using a progressive rate system in estate and gift taxes.

Third, Ito and Barthold point out in section 10.4.1 the loopholes in Japan's transfer tax system, loopholes created by relying on the number of statutory heirs, rather than true heirs, in calculating liability for inheritance tax. They also provide a set of statistical data that reveal a positive correlation between the size of an estate and the number of statutory heirs. An estimate of the size of the distortion, however rough it is, would make a great contribution to our understanding of how serious the problem is. An estimate of the size of the distortion caused by the use of real estate would also be useful.

Finally, if I understand the paper correctly, Ito and Barthold seem to imply that the fact that at least one-third of household assets in Japan and the United States are obtained by intergenerational transfers is against the life-cycle model of saving. But suppose that a person saves in the way the life-cycle model predicts; that is, he accumulates wealth during his working period and plans to consume the total amount of wealth after he retires. Due to an unexpected accident, however, he dies earlier than he expected. Thus he leaves an estate to his daughter. Statistical data show us an intergenerational transfer of wealth, which is evidence against the life-cycle saving behavior, but, in fact, the person followed the life-cycle model. Of course, this is only a hypothetical example, but it may have some relevance to any policy implications drawn from statistical evidence.

Comment   Hiromitsu Ishi

This ambitious paper addresses a difficult issue that many economists have attacked. Although the arguments need strong reservations to be accepted by other economists, this seems to be a pioneering paper.

Statistics of inheritance tax are only one available data source to estimate bequest assets transferred from one generation to another. However, coverage of the inheritance tax data is so limited that anyone would hesitate to attempt such an empirical study. In fact, the ratio of decedents shows only 5 or 6% are taxable in Japan, and consequently some technique is required to expand the sample data to full, nationwide coverage of bequest transfers.

Thomas Barthold and Takatoshi Ito begin with a detailed explanation of inheritance and gift tax structure. In addition, they explain a little bit about the current situation of land issues in Japan in connection with the inheritance tax.

In this paper, the most crucial point is how to handle bequests from nontax-

Hiromitsu Ishi is professor of economics at Hitotsubashi University.

able decedents, because the tax data never cover this type of bequest and this amount must be substantial. Barthold and Ito use a "k ratio" hypothesis by which the maximum basic exemption is multiplied. If k is 50%, it means that half the basic exemption was left by a nontaxable decedent for his or her heirs.

Since it is impossible to get directly an accurate value of k, Barthold and Ito give various values between 1.0 and 0 on an ad hoc or arbitrary basis. As a preliminary approach this rough procedure might be permitted, but they might make more effort to determine the k value within a certain significant range, not relying on guesswork.

May I propose a couple of enhancements to the reliability of the k value?

First, the authors haven't already done so, they should interview tax collectors or tax assessors in the division of inheritance tax at the National Tax Administration. I think one could obtain some useful information about the bequest of a nontaxable decedent. This is merely an indirect approach.

Second, they might address the time period of institutional change. For instance, in 1974 and 1988, basic exemption levels were greatly raised, from one threshold to another. If one compares the number of taxpayers and other related data in two successive years before and after tax changes, one might gather some information about untaxable bequests, which are dropped from the new tax code. This is imperfect information but useful.

Third, I think the k value must change depending on business conditions, in particular on land price variations. During periods of higher land prices, k may be reduced. Therefore, the estimation period might be divided into two or three variations of land price, instead of using one period of 1976–88.

I would like to add one more point, apart from the k ratio issues. In conclusion Barthold and Ito stress that *at least one third* of household assets in Japan and the United States are obtained by intergenerational transfers, as opposed to life-cycle lump-sum saving. In spite of their painstaking estimates, they might need to explain further, to strengthen their position. In order to reject life-cycle saving behavior, is the value of one-third enough? Is there a critical percentage that would be more convincing, say 40 or 50%? What kind of theoretical implications can Barthold and Ito derive from their estimated results? How do they explain the same ratio of bequests in the United States and Japan, given different levels of household savings?

11 Taxation of Income from Foreign Capital in Korea

Kun-Young Yun

11.1 Introduction

11.1.1 Foreign Capital and the Economic Growth of Korea

During the past three decades, foreign capital played an important role in the economic development of Korea. In particular, in the 1970s, when the government placed a high priority on the development of heavy and chemical industries, foreign capital was essential in financing major investment projects. Table 11.1 shows that, in 1975, foreign savings financed as much as 22.0% of total national investment. However, with economic growth the national savings rate increased and the gap between national savings and investment began to close. By 1986, national savings were more than sufficient to finance national investment. As a result, the importance of foreign savings in financing national investment diminished. In 1989, foreign savings supported less than 3% of national investment.

Even though the inflow of foreign capital was essential for the rapid growth of the Korean economy, the government was careful not to attract too much foreign capital in the form of equity. Most of the foreign capital was either government borrowings or government-guaranteed commercial loans. Foreigners were not allowed to participate directly in the capital market, and foreign direct investment accounted for a very small fraction of total foreign capital in Korea.

With the decline in the importance of foreign capital as a source of national investment financing, the composition of foreign capital inflow changed substantially. In the late 1970s, when the government was emphasizing invest-

Kun-Young Yun is an associate professor of economics at Yonsei University, Seoul.

The author has benefited from comments by Toshihiro Ihori, Takatoshi Ito, Charles McLure, Assaf Razin, Toshiaki Tachibanaki, John Whalley, and other conference participants. He is also grateful to an anonymous referee for helpful comments.

Table 11.1 **Foreign Capital and Economic Growth** (in millions of U.S. dollars, %)

				Foreign Savings							
Year	GNP (A)	National Investment (B)	National Savings (C)	Government Borrowings (D)	Commercial Loans (E)	FDI (F)	D+E+F (G)	B/A	C/A	G/A	G/B
1972	10,890	2,337	1,903	—	—	—	—	21.4	17.5	—	—
1973	13,501	3,460	3,097	—	—	—	—	25.6	22.9	—	—
1974	17,237	5,579	3,552	317	616	124	1,057	32.2	20.6	6.1	18.9
1975	20,941	6,122	3,854	482	805	62	1,349	29.1	18.4	6.4	22.0
1976	28,745	7,802	7,130	711	843	86	1,640	27.1	24.8	5.7	21.0
1977	36,790	10,677	10,365	638	1,241	102	1,981	28.9	28.2	5.4	18.6
1978	49,590	16,656	15,146	817	1,913	100	2,830	33.5	30.5	5.7	17.0
1979	63,640	23,323	18,447	1,089	1,578	126	2,793	36.6	29.0	4.4	12.0
1980	59,278	19,492	14,037	1,516	1,402	96	3,014	32.8	23.7	5.1	15.5
1981	66,933	20,612	15,690	1,689	1,247	105	3,041	30.7	24.4	4.5	14.8
1982	72,010	21,605	18,025	1,868	913	128	2,909	29.8	25.0	4.0	13.5
1983	80,096	23,939	22,506	1,493	973	122	2,588	29.7	28.1	3.2	10.8
1984	86,544	26,811	25,927	1,424	858	193	2,475	30.9	30.0	2.9	9.2
1985	91,113	27,738	26,880	1,024	964	236	2,224	30.3	29.5	2.4	8.0
1986	103,760	30,504	34,462	880	1,620	976	3,476	29.2	33.2	3.4	11.4
1987	128,748	39,187	47,413	1,109	1,558	625	3,292	30.1	36.8	2.6	8.4
1988	171,684	53,531	66,199	891	988	894	2,773	31.0	38.6	1.6	5.2
1989	210,107	73,653	76,496	475	859	812	2,146	34.8	36.4	1.0	2.9

Sources: Bank of Korea. *Economic Statistics Yearbook* (various issues), and *National Accounts* (1989); Ministry of Finance, *Fiscal and Financial Statistics* (various issues).
Note: FDI = foreign direct investment in Korea.

ment in heavy and chemical industries, foreign borrowings accounted for most of the capital inflow. During the 1980s, however, the share of foreign borrowings in total capital inflow declined, while that of foreign direct investment increased.

11.1.2 Internationalization of the Capital Market

Since 1981, Korea has been pursuing internationalization of its capital market, although the process has been slow. As of 1990, foreigners are not allowed to participate in the Korean capital market directly. Foreign portfolio investors can participate only through indirect channels such as investment funds for foreigners[1] and convertible bonds issued overseas. However, most of the restrictions on foreigners' participation in the capital market will be removed in the next few years.

In December 1988, the government put forward a long-term plan for the internationalization of the capital market. According to this plan, foreign securities companies will be allowed to open branch offices in Korea by 1991. They will also be allowed to join Korean companies in establishing new se-

1. Investment funds for foreigners include investment trusts (beneficiaries certificates since 1981), Korea Fund (1984), and Korea Europe Fund (1987).

curities companies. By 1992, foreigners will be able to participate directly in the Korean stock market.

While working on the internationalization of the domestic capital market, the government has allowed Korean financial investors to participate in the world capital market. Since 1988, Korean financial investors such as securities companies, insurance companies, investment trusts, etc., were allowed to invest in foreign securities. Beginning in 1991, Korean securities companies will also be allowed to open branch offices and establish subsidiaries abroad.

As the Korean capital market matures and its participants become more experienced, the government will be able to pursue more aggressive policies for the internationalization of the capital market. At the same time, it will also encourage Korean investors, securities companies, and other financial institutions to participate actively in the world capital market.

Opening the capital market directly to foreign portfolio investors will affect the composition as well as the level of foreign capital inflow. It will also affect investment financing of the firms by allowing them to choose from a richer menu of financial instruments in a larger capital market. Perhaps even more important is that internationalization of the capital market will change the way savings and investment respond to tax policies, and other economic policies. For example, it may affect the optimal size of the tax burden on capital. Furthermore, the relative tax burden on corporate and individual capital income may affect national savings and investment.

In light of these tax-policy implications, opening of the capital market requires a careful reexamination of the tax treatment of capital income. In order to derive practical tax-policy implications of the opening of the capital market, we need a comprehensive model of the tax system as well as information on the behavioral response of the savers and investors to tax policy. The purpose of this paper, however, is a modest one. I focus on the narrow issue of the taxation of income from foreign capital in Korea. In particular, I describe Korean tax policies pertaining to income from foreign capital in Korea and estimate the effective tax rate of investment financed with foreign capital.

In section 11.2, I describe the tax treatment of income from foreign capital in Korea, in particular, the provisions of the tax laws, tax treaties, and the Foreign Capital Inducement Law. In section 11.3, I first estimate the effective rate of the corporate income tax for investments financed with foreign capital. I then consider the comprehensive effective tax rate, taking account of both the corporate and the nonresident withholding taxes on interest and dividends. In section 11.4, I consider some implications of my findings for tax policy.

11.2 Tax Treatment of Income from Foreign Capital

11.2.1 The Individual and the Corporate Income Tax Laws

The Individual Income Tax Law and the Corporate Income Tax Law provide the basic framework of tax policy pertaining to income from foreign capital in Korea. According to these laws, income from foreign capital is either taxed on a global basis or taxed separately by income category, depending on the tax status of the taxpayer.

Nonresident Taxpayer

If a taxpayer has permanent establishments[2] or draws income from real estate in Korea,[3] all of the taxpayer's income originating within Korea, with the exception of capital gains on land and buildings, pension and retirement income, and timber income, are lumped together in a single category of global income. Global income so defined is then taxed in accordance with a progressive rate schedule. For taxpayers without a permanent establishment or real estate income, each category of income is taxed separately. Capital gains on land and buildings, pension and retirement income, and timber income are taxed separately for all taxpayers regardless of the existence of permanent establishments or real estate income.

The marginal tax rate for global income is graduated from 5 to 50%. For retirement income and timber income, the rate schedule is the same as that which applies to global income. The tax rate for capital gains on land and buildings is also graduated, but the marginal tax rates are much higher, ranging from 40 to 60%. The taxation of nonresidents without a permanent establishment or real estate income distinguishes three categories of capital income with the following withholding tax rates:

1. Business income and rental income from vessels, airplanes, motor vehicles, heavy machinery, and equipment: 2%.
2. Interest, dividends, and royalties: 25%.
3. Capital gains on securities: 10% on transaction or 25% on capital gains, whichever is smaller.

Corporations

If a foreign corporation has either a permanent establishment, real estate income (including capital gains on land and buildings), or timber income, it is taxed like a resident corporation. The tax rate for corporate income is 20%, for the first 80 million won of the adjusted taxable income and 30% for the remainder. For other foreign corporations, income taxes are withheld at the source, with the tax rates the same as those for nonresident individuals.

11.2.2   Defense Tax and Inhabitant Tax

In addition to the income tax, the defense and inhabitant taxes are levied on individuals and corporations. The tax base of the defense and inhabitant taxes

2. "Permanent establishment" includes branch offices, business offices, stores and other fixed sales places, factories, warehouses, construction sites, places for installation or assembly work, places for direction or supervision, places for provision of technological services, mines, quarries, and places for exploration or gathering of natural resources.

3. "Real estate income" includes rental income, income from operation of real properties, capital gains on real estate other than land and buildings, and capital gains on property rights such as the right for mining, oil exploration, and quarrying.

is the income tax liability of individuals and corporations. The defense tax is levied on individuals and corporations with real estate income other than capital gains on land and buildings or with permanent establishments. For individuals, the tax rate is 10% if the total adjusted taxable income is not more than 8.4 million won per year, and 20% otherwise. For corporations, the tax rate is 20% if the adjusted taxable income is not more than 500 million won per year, and 25% otherwise. The inhabitant tax rate is 7.5% for both individuals and corporations.

11.2.3   Foreign Capital Inducement Law

As amended extensively in 1983, the principal objective of the Foreign Capital Inducement Law is to protect and provide incentives for foreign capital inflow. The law places special emphasis on those foreign direct investments that contribute to the development of the Korean economy and help improve the balance of payments. Specifically, the law provides generous tax incentives for foreign direct investments in the following areas:

1. Investments with substantial contributions to the improvement of balance of payments.
2. Investment projects that employ advanced technologies or require a large amount of capital.
3. Investments by overseas Korean residents.
4. Investments by firms in the export free zones.
5. Other foreign direct investments that require tax incentives.

Tax incentives for foreign direct investment include a five-year tax holiday for individual business income, corporate income, and royalties; accelerated depreciation; exemption from the acquisition tax, property tax, and global land tax; reduction of import duties, special excise tax, and value-added tax (VAT).

Specifically, eligible foreign direct investors can take either the 100% special depreciation, which doubles the speed of tax depreciation, or the tax holiday for corporate income and dividends for any five consecutive years within the first ten taxable years after the registration of the business. Since the taxpayer decides when to take the five-year tax holiday within the first ten taxable years, with appropriate tax planning the taxpayer may be able to reduce his or her tax burden substantially for the first ten taxable years.

The acquisition tax, property tax, and global land tax are exempt for the first five years after the registration of the business. Similarly, royalties based on the agreement for technology transfer, as reported to the minister of finance, are tax exempt for the first five years after the agreement is reported. Finally, import duties, special excise tax, and VAT are reduced by 70% for capital goods that are imported as an equity investment of the foreign investor. The same tax preferences are extended to the import of capital goods if they are paid for with dividends received by the foreign investor or with foreign currency paid in by the foreign investor.

In addition to the tax preferences for foreign direct investment in Korea, the

Foreign Capital Inducement Law provides tax exemptions for interest on government borrowing and commercial loans. The law provides a variety of tax incentives for foreign direct investment, but tax exemption of interest income is the only incentive for foreign borrowing. Since the value of outstanding foreign borrowing is much larger than that of foreign direct investment, however, tax exemption of interest income has been a crucial element of tax policy for income from foreign capital.

11.2.4   Tax Treaties

As of January 1, 1990, Korea has concluded tax treaties with twenty-eight countries, including Japan, the United States, the United Kingdom, Germany, Canada, France, Australia, Sweden, Norway, Thailand, and Indonesia. In all of the tax treaties, the maximum withholding tax rates for interest, dividends, and royalties are in the 10–15% range, which is substantially lower than the corresponding tax rates for domestically owned capital income. It is also true that the withholding tax rates are lower than the regular income tax rates in the home country of the capital. This feature of the tax treaties reflects a compromise between the host and the home countries that collect taxes from the same source.

The Individual Income Tax Law and the Corporate Income Tax Law also define the nonresident withholding tax rates. For dividends, interest, and royalties, the withholding tax rate as defined by the domestic laws is 25%, which is higher than the maximum withholding rates allowed under the tax treaties. Since virtually all of the foreign capital in Korea is covered by the tax treaties, the nonresident withholding tax rates for dividends, interest, and royalties are determined by the tax treaties, and the provisions of the domestic tax laws that define the withholding tax rates for these categories of income are practically meaningless.

11.2.5   Tax Revenues

Table 11.2 presents statistics on tax collections from foreign corporations with permanent establishments in Korea. It is evident from the table that the

Table 11.2   Taxation of Foreign Corporations with Permanent Establishment or Real Estate Income

Year	Number of Corporations	Total Income (billion won)	Tax Revenue (billion won)	Average Tax Rate (%)
1985	353	204.5	52.5	25.6
1986	408	163.6	44.7	27.3
1987	457	207.4	57.3	27.6
1988	609	244.9	69.1	28.2

Source: Ministry of Finance.

number of foreign corporations investing in Korea has been steadily increasing in recent years along with the total income generated by them and the total amount of tax paid. Note that the average tax rate faced by the foreign corporations shows a slightly rising trend, which may be attributed to the graduation of the tax rate and the lack of indexation of the tax brackets.

Table 11.3 presents similar information on tax collections from the taxpayers without permanent establishments. Of total income, royalties account for the largest share and the remainder is accounted for by business and real estate income, dividends, and interest income.[4] Table 11.3 also shows that business and real estate incomes are the most favored by the tax policy. The average tax rate for business and real estate incomes has been only 2.0% as opposed to 7.6–25.0% for other categories of income. Until 1987, royalties and interest were taxed more heavily than dividends, but in 1988 the differences among the average tax rates of royalties, dividends, and interest narrowed substantially.

11.3   Effective Tax Rate of Foreign Investment

11.3.1   Effective Tax Rate and the Cost of Capital

The taxation of corporate income or personal business income is complicated due to the difficulties of measuring taxable income, differential tax treatment of debt and equity, and the various provisions for tax incentives. Because of the complexity of the capital income tax system, it is practically impossible to figure out from the tax laws the tax burden imposed on investment.

If the taxation of income from domestically owned and operated capital is complicated, even more complicated is the taxation of income from foreign capital. For foreign capital, the home country also levies taxes on foreign investment income after the host country has taken its share. For example, in the case of foreign corporate investment, the host country levies corporate income taxes and nonresident withholding taxes on dividends, interest, royalties, etc. The home country then levies its own corporate and individual income taxes.

For a reliable analysis of the effect of taxation on foreign investment, it is convenient to have a summary measure of the overall tax burden on investment. One such measure is the effective tax rate on investment. The effective tax rate condenses the effects of various provisions of the tax laws and the behavior of the taxpayers into a single number that represents the total tax burden on investment. In this section, I discuss the effective tax rate of corporate investment that is financed with foreign capital.

---

4. The fact that royalties account for the largest share of capital income may be related to the fact that, like interest payments, royalties are deductible for corporate income tax purposes and that royalties are eligible for tax preferences that are similar to those applicable to dividends.

Table 11.3   **Taxation of Foreign Taxpayers without Permanent Establishment: Individuals and Corporations** (billion won)

Type of Income	1984	1985	1986	1987	1988
Business and real estate					
Income	17.84	17.72	15.43	40.46	82.08
Tax revenue	0.36	0.36	0.31	0.81	1.63
ATR (%)	2.00	2.02	2.00	2.00	1.98
Interest					
Income	8.60	3.03	3.98	3.07	7.21
Tax revenue	2.15	0.42	0.49	0.48	0.95
ATR (%)	25.00	13.88	12.22	15.71	13.11
Dividends					
Income	9.41	29.79	51.68	39.85	40.75
Tax revenue	1.38	3.41	3.90	3.91	5.64
ATR (%)	14.70	11.45	7.55	9.82	13.85
Royalties					
Income	20.36	48.38	58.30	95.34	109.81
Tax revenue	3.60	6.30	7.84	11.57	17.37
ATR (%)	17.69	13.02	13.45	12.13	15.82
Human services					
Income	13.02	10.59	11.05	13.69	20.42
Tax revenue	2.60	2.10	2.16	1.97	3.88
ATR (%)	19.96	17.79	19.58	14.42	19.01
Other					
Income	8.07	2.84	4.32	3.21	17.41
Tax revenue	1.68	0.71	1.08	0.56	2.04
ATR (%)	20.78	25.00	24.95	17.37	11.72
Total					
Income	77.29	112.36	144.76	195.61	277.67
Tax revenue	11.77	13.30	15.78	19.30	31.51
ATR (%)	15.22	11.83	10.90	9.87	11.34

Source: Ministry of Finance.
Note: ATR = average tax rate.

We start with the effective corporate tax rate on investment, which is defined by

(1) $$(1 - E_c) F_k = r_c$$

where E_c is the effective corporate income tax rate, F_k is the marginal productivity of capital net of depreciation, and r_c is the corporate after-tax rate of return on investment. Eq. (1) may be rewritten as

(2) $$E_c F_k = F_k - r_c.$$

Eq. (2) implies that the effective burden of income tax on one unit of investment is equal to $E_c F_k$, which is the difference between the marginal productivity of capital (or the social rate of return) and the after-tax rate of return.

Eq. (1) or (2) can be modified to define other effective tax rates on investment. In particular, we can define a comprehensive effective tax rate that encompasses both the corporate and the withholding taxes by

$$(1') \qquad\qquad\qquad (1 - E_a) F_k = r_{p'}$$

where E_a is the comprehensive effective tax rate and r_p is the rate of return on investment after the corporate and withholding taxes.

In order to measure the effective tax rate, we need to know the marginal productivity of capital and the after-tax rate of return on investment. Measuring the latter is relatively straightforward. However, it is difficult, if not impossible, to obtain a direct measure of the marginal productivity of capital. Thus we assume that the producer is in equilibrium in the sense that the cost of capital is equalized to the marginal productivity of capital.

11.3.2   Financial Behavior of the Firm

In measuring the effective tax rate on investment, we need to be specific about the assumptions concerning dividend behavior and capital structure of the firm. There are two competing views on the dividend behavior of a firm. One is the so-called traditional view that implies that firms pay out a fixed fraction of the after-tax profits. Under this view, the marginal source of equity finance is new share issues. The alternative view, which is known as the new view or the trapped equity view, implies that the firm adjusts dividend payments according to the need for investment funds. Under this view, the marginal source of equity finance is retention of profits. It may be noted that the traditional view does not rule out retention; neither does the new view preclude new share issues altogether. The two competing views differ in the way in which marginal equity funds are raised.

In reality, the marginal source of equity finance can be either new share issues or retention, depending on the firm's financial condition. For a new or a fast-growing firm, the marginal source of equity finance is likely to be new share issues. In contrast, a mature firm with stable cash flow may choose retention, which is the cheaper method of equity finance. It is difficult to identify the pattern of financial behavior of individual firms however, or even to determine the proportion of the firms that can be classified under either view of dividend behavior.

Under the traditional view, the marginal withholding tax rate on equity income is a weighted average of the withholding tax rates for dividend and capital gains. Under the new view, the marginal withholding tax rate is the withholding tax rate on capital gains. In this paper, I take the traditional view. Since the withholding tax rates for dividend and capital gains are similar, however, the results are not sensitive to the assumption on dividend behavior (see section 11.3.4).

Regarding the capital structure of the firm, we assume that the firm has a maximum debt capacity and takes advantage of the tax deduction of interest payment by maintaining the debt/capital ratio at the maximum level, where "capital" refers to the total value of debt and equity claims on the firm. It follows that the firm borrows a fixed fraction of the investment funds and raises the remainder by issuing new shares and/or retaining profits.

11.3.3   Effective Corporate Tax Rates

Under the above assumptions about the firm's financial behavior, maximization of the shareholder's wealth yields the following expression for the cost of capital:[5]

$$(3) \qquad F_k + \delta = \frac{1 - k - t_c(z + y)}{1 - t_c}[R + \delta] + t_p,$$

where

$$(4) \qquad R = (1 - \beta)r_e + \beta[(1 - t_c)i - \pi].$$

The notations in (3) and (4) are δ = rate of economic depreciation; k = rate of investment tax credit; z = present value of tax depreciation; y = present value of tax deduction due to the tax deferral of investment reserve; β = debt/capital ratio, or debt/(debt + equity) ratio; t_c = corporate income tax rate; t_p = property tax rate; r_e = corporate after-tax rate of return on equity; i = nominal interest rate; and π = rate of inflation.

In order to determine the cost of capital for corporate investment, we allocate the after-tax rate of return on corporate capital, as reported in the corporate income statement, between the returns to debt and equity. Within the accounting framework of corporate income statement, the real return to debt is $\gamma i - \beta \pi$, where γ is the ratio of interest-bearing debt/capital ratio. The remainder of the after-tax rate of return is allocated to equity according to

$$(5) \qquad r_{np} = (1 - \beta)r_e + \gamma i - \beta \pi,$$

where r_{np} is the after-tax rate of return reported in the income statement.

It is clear from (5) that r_{np} is smaller than the real after-tax rate of return on corporate capital by the amount of implicit interest on the non-interest-bearing debts. We assume that the implicit interest on non-interest-bearing debts is the same as that on interest-bearing debt, and add the implicit interest on both sides of (5). The result is

$$(5') \qquad r_{np} + (\beta - \gamma)i = (1 - \beta)r_e + \beta(i - \pi).$$

We refer to the right-hand side of (5') as the real after-tax rate of return on corporate capital and denote it by r_c. Thus

$$(6) \qquad r_c = (1 - \beta)r_e + \beta(i - \pi).$$

---

5. See Jorgenson and Yun (1991) for derivation.

In the calculation of the cost of capital, we set the debt/capital ratio and the nominal interest rate of corporate debt at their 1977–86 averages in the manufacturing sector, i.e., $\beta = 0.79$ and $i = 14.7\%$, respectively. In order to establish a point of reference for the calculation of the various rates of return and the effective tax rates, we hold the real after-tax rate of return on corporate capital, before adjustment for the implicit interest on non-interest-bearing debts, at its 1977–86 average, that is, $r_{np} = 8.4\%$.

Eqs. (5) and (6) are used to calculate the real after-tax rate of return on equity, r_e, and the after-tax rate of return on corporate capital (debt + equity), r_c. The nominal interest rate on corporate debt is held constant to reflect the insensitivity of nominal interest rate with respect to the rate of inflation.[6]

The corporate tax rate, t_c, is calibrated to reflect the effects of the defense tax and the inhabitant tax as well as corporate income tax. Specifically, t_c is set equal to the statutory tax rate for corporate income multiplied by 1.325, reflecting that the defense and inhabitant taxes are 25% and 7.5%, respectively, of the corporate income tax. Using the statutory corporate tax rate of 30%, we set t_c at 39.75%.

We do not have any estimates of the economic depreciation rates of capital assets employed in Korea. We take the economic depreciation rates of the various categories of assets estimated by Hulten and Wykoff (1981) for the United States, then calculate the weighted averages for machinery and equipment and for buildings and structures. The shares of each category of assets in the net national capital stock from the National Wealth Survey of Korea (Economic Planning Board 1977) are used as the weights. We obtain $\delta = 13.07\%$ for machinery and equipment, and $\delta = 3.3\%$ for buildings and structures.

For tax depreciation, the taxpayer can choose either the straightline method or the declining balance method. Under the current law, the depreciation rate for the declining balance method is calibrated so that 10% of the capital cost remains undepreciated after the tax life of an asset. Since the declining balance method results in a larger present value for the tax deduction, we assume that the taxpayer chooses the declining balance method. Using the same weights used in the economic depreciation calculation, we estimate the depreciation rate for tax purposes to be 21.69% for machinery and equipment and 5.9% for buildings and structures.

Once the cost of capital, which is equated to the marginal productivity of capital, and the after-tax rate of return are calculated, the effective corporate tax rate can be estimated according to

---

6. With the nominal interest rate constant, holding r_{np} constant is equivalent to holding r_c constant. To see this, subtract (5) from (6) and rearrange the terms to obtain

$$r_c = r_{np} + (\beta - \gamma)i.$$

$$(7) \qquad\qquad E_c = \frac{F_k - r_c}{F_k}.$$

I considered eight tax incentives and calculated the effective corporate tax rates under each of them. To provide a reference of comparison, I also calculated the effective tax without any tax preference. In order to test for sensitivity, I repeated the calculations for three different rates of inflation. Table 11.4 presents the estimated effective corporate tax rates for machinery and equipment (see the three rows with E_c). Similarly, table 11.5 presents the effective tax rates for buildings and structures.

The effective corporate tax rates are negative in all the cases considered both for machinery and equipment and for buildings and structures. In particular, the effective tax rates have large absolute values when a generous tax preference, such as 100% special depreciation, 50% expensing, 10% investment tax credit, or 15% investment reserve, is available. It follows that the corporate income tax in Korea effectively serves as an incentive system for investment.

It should be emphasized that the effective tax rates in table 11.4 and 11.5 are estimated under the assumption that the firm is eligible for at most one category of incentives for a given investment. The tax laws indeed have provisions that prohibit taxpayers from taking more than one tax preference for the same activity. In practice, however, there are cases in which firms are eligible for more than one tax preference. For example, a firm that finances an investment project with the funds from investment reserve may be eligible for investment tax credit, expensing, or special depreciation for the same project. In such a case, the effective tax rate must be lower than tables 11.4 and 11.5 indicate.

Since nominal interest payments are deductible, the effective corporate tax rate decreases with the rate of inflation. The real after-tax rate of return on equity, r_e, is very sensitive to the rate of inflation. In particular, r_e is as high as 44.7% when the rate of inflation is 10% per year. Underlying these phenomena are the high debt/capital ratio in the firms' capital structure and the insensitivity of nominal interest to inflation.

In interpreting the estimated effective tax rates, two caveats are in order. First, my estimate of the debt/capital ratio is likely to be an overestimate of the true value because my figures are based on book values, rather than the replacement cost, of the corporate assets. Since interest payments are tax deductible while dividend payments are not, to the extent the debt/capital ratio is overestimated, the effective tax rate is underestimated. Second, my estimates of the economic depreciation rates are also problematic. One may easily argue that the economic depreciation rates of the assets in Korea are higher than those in the United States. Unfortunately I do not have any solid evidence as to the direction and magnitude of the biases in my calculation.

Table 11.4   **Effective Tax Rate: Machinery and Equipment (%)**

π	No Incentives	Special Depreciation			Expensing		Investment Tax Credit		Investment Reserve
		30	50	100	30	50	3.0	10.0	15.0
0.0									
F_k	12.1	11.5	11.2	10.7	11.0	10.2	11.1	8.7	9.5
E_c	−8.0	−13.9	−17.0	−22.6	−19.2	−28.3	−17.0	−49.9	−37.3
E_a	5.2	0.3	−2.4	−7.2	−4.2	−12.4	−3.3	−31.8	−20.7
	$r_e = 7.1$				$r_p = 11.5$		$r_c = 13.1$		
6.0									
F_k	11.9	11.3	11.0	10.4	10.8	10.0	10.9	8.5	9.3
E_c	−10.4	−16.5	−19.6	−25.4	−21.9	−31.4	−20.6	−53.8	−40.8
E_a	9.9	5.1	2.5	−3.1	0.7	−7.2	1.6	−26.1	−15.3
	$r_e = 29.7$				$r_p = 10.7$		$r_c = 13.1$		
10.0									
F_k	11.7	11.1	10.8	10.3	10.6	9.8	10.7	8.4	9.2
E_c	−12.0	−18.2	−21.5	−27.4	−23.8	−33.5	−22.5	−56.6	−43.1
E_a	12.7	8.0	5.4	0.8	3.7	−4.2	4.6	−21.6	−11.0
	$r_e = 44.7$				$r_p = 10.2$		$r_c = 13.1$		

Parameters: $\delta = 13.07$, $d = 21.69$, $\alpha = 34.0$, $\beta = 79.0$, $\gamma = 47.0$, $i = 14.7$, $i^e = 18.0$, $r_{np} = 8.4$, $t_c = 39.75$, $t_d = t_g = t_i = 12.5$, $t_p = 0.0$

Notes: π = rate of inflation; F_k = marginal productivity of capital, net of depreciation; E_c = effective corporate tax rate; E_a = comprehensive effective tax rate, corporate and withholding taxes; r_c = real rate of return on capital (equity + debt), after corporate tax; r_e = real rate of return on equity, after corporate tax; r_p = real rate of return on capital (equity + debt), after corporate and withholding taxes. δ = rate of economic depreciation; d = rate of tax depreciation; α = dividence payout ratio; β = debt/capital ratio, where capital = debt + equity; γ = interest bearing debt/capital ratio; i = nominal interest rate on corporate debt; i^e = present value of income deduction for new share issue; r_{np} = after-tax rate of return on corporate capital as reported in income statement; t_c = corporate income tax rate; t_d = withholding tax rate on dividend; t_g withholding tax rate on capital gains, accrual based; t_i = withholding tax rate on interest income; t_p = property tax rate.

11.3.4   Comprehensive Effective Tax Rate

I have estimated the effective corporate tax rate of investment. From a foreign investor's point of view, however, a more comprehensive measure of effective tax burden would be desirable, possibly encompassing all the taxes levied by the host and the home countries. Incorporating the home country taxes in my measure of effective tax rate is beyond the scope of this paper. Instead I estimate the effective burden of all the income taxes imposed in Korea.

The real rate of return on corporate capital after withholding taxes is a weighted average of the returns to equity and debt, both after withholding taxes, i.e.,

Table 11.5   **Effective Tax Rate: Buildings and Structures (%)**

π	No Incentives	Special Depreciation			Expensing		Investment Tax Credit		Investment Reserve
		30	50	100	30	50	3.0	10.0	15.0
0.0									
F_k	12.8	12.3	12.0	11.4	11.5	10.6	12.2	10.9	9.9
E_c	−2.6	−6.9	−9.4	−14.7	−14.3	−23.8	−7.2	−19.9	−33.0
E_a	10.4	6.8	4.4	−0.6	0.3	−8.2	6.0	−5.2	−15.8
	$r_e = 7.1$				$r_p = 11.5$		$r_c = 13.1$		
6.0									
F_k	12.5	12.0	11.7	11.2	11.2	10.3	11.9	10.7	9.6
E_c	−5.0	−9.5	−12.1	−17.5	−17.1	−27.0	−9.8	−22.9	−36.4
E_a	14.2	10.7	8.4	4.3	4.3	−4.1	9.9	−0.2	−11.7
	$r_e = 29.7$				$r_p = 10.7$		$r_c = 13.1$		
10.0									
F_k	12.3	11.8	11.5	11.0	11.0	10.2	11.7	10.5	9.4
E_c	−6.8	−11.3	−14.0	−19.5	−19.1	−29.1	−11.6	−24.9	−38.8
F_a	17.0	13.5	11.2	7.2	7.2	−0.1	12.7	2.7	−8.6
	$r_e = 44.7$				$r_p = 10.2$		$r_c = 13.1$		

Notes: Parameters: $\delta = 3.3$, $d = 5.9$. For other parameters and notes, see table 11.4.

$$(8) \qquad r_p = (1 - \beta)(r - \pi) + \beta[(1 - t_i)i - \pi],$$

where r_p is the real rate of return to corporate capital after the withholding taxes, r is the nominal rate of return on equity after withholding tax, and t_i is the marginal withholding tax rate on interest income. Notice that the expression in the brackets represents the real rate of return to debt, after withholding tax.

In order to measure the comprehensive effective tax rate we need to calculate r_p. For this purpose we need to distinguish the sources of equity finance. Under the traditional view, the marginal source of equity finance is new share issues and the relevant marginal withholding tax rate for equity income is a weighted average of the withholding tax rates on dividends and capital gains. Under the new view, the marginal source is retention and the corresponding marginal tax rate is the withholding tax rate on capital gains.

Specifically, under the traditional view

$$(9) \qquad r_e = \frac{r - \pi(1 - t_g)}{1 - (\alpha t_d + (1 - \alpha)t_g)},$$

where t_d and t_g are the marginal withholding tax rates on dividend and capital gains, respectively. Under the new view,

$$(9') \qquad\qquad r_e = \frac{r - \pi(1 - t_g)}{1 - t_g}.$$

Making use of $(1')$, (8), and (9) or $(9')$, we can calculate the comprehensive effective tax rate on corporate investment, encompassing both the corporate and withholding taxes.

In the above discussion, the tax rate for capital gains is accrual based. In practice, however, capital gains are taxed on a realization basis, and the statutory tax rate on capital gains is defined accordingly. Thus we need to convert the realization-based tax rate into an accrual-based one. A rule of thumb for the conversion is to cut the realization-based tax rate by one-half to obtain an accrual-based tax rate. This is roughly equivalent to assuming that the holding period of equity is ten years and the appropriate discount rate is 7% per year.

Since the statutory withholding tax rate is 25% on realized capital gains, it is reasonable to assume that the accrual-based withholding tax rate is in the range of 10–15%, which is the same as the range of withholding tax rates on dividend and interest incomes. In estimating the comprehensive effective tax rate, we set the withholding tax rates on dividends, interest, and accrued capital gains at 12.5%, i.e., $t_d = t_g = t_i = 12.5\%$. With the withholding tax rates the same for dividends and capital gains, the comprehensive effective tax rates are the same under either view of dividend behavior.

The estimated effective tax rates are reported in tables 11.4 and 11.5. Since all the withholding tax rates are set at 12.5%, the comprehensive effective tax rates are substantially higher than the corresponding effective corporate tax rates. In particular, the comprehensive effective tax rates are substantially closer to zero than the effective corporate tax rates. In the central case of 6% inflation, the comprehensive effective tax rates are between -26.1 and 9.9% for machinery and equipment and between -11.7 and 14.2% for buildings and structures.

Since nominal interest and nominal capital gains are taxed at the withholding level, the differences between the effective corporate tax rates and the corresponding comprehensive effective tax rates increase with inflation. The value of interest deduction at the corporate level increases with inflation, while the tax burden increases with inflation at the withholding level. The comprehensive effective tax rates in tables 11.4 and 11.5 suggest that, on balance, tax burden increases with inflation.

In the calculation of the comprehensive effective tax rates, we assumed that the government collects 12.5% of withholding tax on foreign capital income. Although this assumption provides a useful benchmark, it is not realistic. As I discussed in section 11.2, in accordance with the Foreign Capital Inducement Law, the government exempts most dividends and interest income from taxation. Since government borrowing and commercial loans are the principal forms of foreign capital in Korea, tax exemption of interest on foreign debt is particularly important. For foreign direct investment, the firm can choose either the 100% special depreciation or the five-year tax holiday for corporate income and dividends. If these tax preferences are taken into account, the actual comprehensive effective tax rates must be similar to the effective corporate tax rates in tables 11.4 and 11.5.

11.4   Policy Issues

11.4.1   Are the Current Tax Preferences Excessive?

A natural question at this point is whether Korea's current tax treatment of income from foreign capital is appropriate. This question cannot be answered definitively without knowing the optimal effective tax rate. However, my analysis suggests strongly that Korea's tax policy is too generous for the income from foreign capital. In order to justify the current tax policy, we need a convincing argument such as that foreign capital generates large positive external effects.

Many of Korea's tax treaties with its trading partners include tax-sparing provisions for capital income. One implicit assumption underlying the tax-sparing provisions is that lowering the overall tax burden, including the tax burden of the home country, on foreign capital attracts more foreign capital into Korea. It may be true that the supply of foreign capital is indeed responsive to the after-tax rate of return. However, the fact that a tax-sparing provision prevents the tax preference provided by the host country from being offset by home country taxes is not sufficient to justify the substantially negative effective tax rates. With the national savings rate well above 30% and higher than the national investment rate, it would be difficult to find convincing evidence in support of the current negative effective tax rates.

If the current tax policy is excessively generous to foreign capital, what are the necessary policy changes? The most obvious approach is to eliminate the tax preferences for foreign capital. It is especially worth considering the abolition of the tax preferences provided by the Foreign Capital Inducement Law, such as the five-year tax holidays, 100% special depreciation, tax exemption of interest, reduction of special excise tax, exemption from property tax, etc.

One of the main reasons the effective corporate tax rates are negative is that interest payments are deductible at the firm level while investments financed by debt are eligible for all the tax preferences that apply to equity-financed investment. Given the tax treatment of debt-financed investment at the firm level, the exemption of interest income from withholding tax guarantees a negative comprehensive effective tax rate for debt-financed investment. In this situation, the abolition of tax exemption for interest on foreign loans would be of particular importance.

One might consider increasing the tax burden on foreign capital at the firm level. However, this approach is less attractive than eliminating the tax preferences specific to foreign capital. Because of the nondiscrimination clauses of the tax treaties, increasing the tax burden on foreign capital at the firm level will increase the tax burden of domestically owned capital as well. If the overall tax treatment of domestically owned capital is excessively generous, there are no difficulties. Otherwise, my analysis cannot be relied upon to justify such a policy.

11.4.2   Internationalization of the Capital Market

Foreign portfolio investors are not eligible for the tax preferences provided by the Foreign Capital Inducement Law. As a result, it seems reasonable to assume that the comprehensive effective tax rates on foreign portfolio investments are close to those presented in tables 11.4 and 11.5. If 6% inflation is assumed, all of the comprehensive effective tax rates I consider for buildings and structures are not far from zero. A similar pattern is observed for machinery and equipment, with the exception of the cases with the 10% investment tax credit and 15% investment reserve.

The above analysis suggests that the current framework of Korean tax policy need not be modified in any fundamental way to accommodate internationalization of the capital market. The main tax policy issue appears to be in tax administration. For example, since the capital gains on financial assets owned by resident individuals are exempt from taxation, it might be difficult to tax effectively the capital gains on financial assets owned by foreign investors. The issue of tax administration becomes particularly serious because financial assets can be traded among residents under pseudonyms.

The issue of taxing capital gains on financial assets has long been debated in Korea. Similarly, the abolition of financial transactions under pseudonyms has been on the government agenda for about a decade. At present, the consensus is that the capital gains should be taxed and financial transactions under pseudonyms should be abolished. With internationalization of the capital market, the issues of taxing capital gains on financial assets owned by nonresident individuals will become more important. Internationalization of the capital market adds new reasons for going forward with the reforms in tax policy on capital gains and the practice of financial transactions under pseudonyms.

11.5   Conclusion

I have described the tax treatment of income from foreign capital in Korea and estimated the effective tax rate of corporate investment financed with foreign capital. The analysis of section 11.3 shows that the effective rates of corporate income tax are negative under realistic assumptions and that the absolute values of the effective tax rate are large when generous tax preferences are available. Without further tax preferences, especially at the withholding level, the comprehensive effective tax rates are not far from zero. With the tax exemption of interest and the five-year tax holidays for corporate income and dividends, however, the comprehensive effective tax rates are negative and close to the effective corporate tax rates.

The overall tax preferences for foreign capital in Korea are excessive, and the tax preferences need to be curtailed. The obvious approach is to reduce or eliminate the most generous preferences, such as tax exemption of interest income, 100% special depreciation, and the five-year tax holidays for corporate income and dividends. In addition to these changes in the income tax policy, the exemption of the acquisition tax, property tax, and global land tax and the reduction of the special excise tax, VAT, import duties, etc., may also be reconsidered.

The basic framework of Korean tax policy need not be changed to accommodate the internationalization of capital market. However, unless the capital gains on domestically owned financial assets are taxed and the practice of financial transactions under pseudonyms is abolished, it would be difficult to tax effectively the capital gains on financial assets owned by nonresident individuals. In this sense, internationalization of the capital market has salutary effects on the development of the Korean economic system.

References

Auerbach, A. J. 1979. Wealth Maximization and the Cost of Capital. *Quarterly Journal of Economics* 93(3): 433–46.
———. 1983. Taxation, Corporate Financial Policy, and the Cost of Capital. *Journal of Economic Literature* 21(3): 905–40.
Ault, H. J., and D. F. Bradford. 1990. Taxing International Income: An Analysis of the U.S. System and Its Economic Premises. In *Taxation in the Global Economy,* ed. A. Razin and J. Slemrod. Chicago: University of Chicago Press.
Caves, R. E. 1982. *Multinational Enterprise and Economic Analysis.* New York: Cambridge University Press.
Economic Planning Board. 1977. *National Wealth Survey of Korea.* Seoul.
Fama, E. F. 1974. The Empirical Relationships between Dividend and Investment Decisions of Firms. *American Economic Review* 64(3): 304–18.
Feldstein, M. S., and D. G. Hartman. 1979. The Optimal Taxation of Foreign Source Investment Income. *Quarterly Journal of Economics* 93(4): 613–29.
Feldstein, M. S., and C. Horioka. 1980. Domestic Saving and International Capital Flows. *Economic Journal* 90(June): 314–29.
Frisch, D. J. 1983. Issues in the Taxation of Foreign Source Income. In *Behavioral Simulation Methods in Tax Policy Analysis,* ed. M. S. Feldstein. Chicago: University of Chicago Press.
Goulder, L. H., and B. Eichengreen. 1989. Savings Promotion, Investment Promotion, and International Competitiveness. In *Trade Policies for International Competitiveness,* ed. R. C. Feenstra. Chicago: University of Chicago Press.
Harberger, A. C. 1980. Vignettes on the World Capital Market. *American Economic Review* 70(2): 331–37.
Hartman, D. G. 1985. Tax Policy and Foreign Direct Investment. *Journal of Public Economics* 26(1): 107–21.

Hines, J. R., and R. G. Hubbard. 1990. Coming Home to America: Dividend Repatriations by U.S. Multinationals. In *Taxation in the Global Economy,* ed. A. Razin and J. Slemrod. Chicago: University of Chicago Press.

Horst, T. 1977. Americal Taxation of Multinational Firms. *American Economic Review* 67(3): 376–89.

———. 1980. A Note on the Optimal Taxation of International Investment Income. *Quarterly Journal of Economics* 94(4): 793–98.

Horst, T., and G. Hufbauer. 1984. International Tax Issues: An Aspect of Basic Income Tax Reform. In *New Directions in Federal Tax Policy for the 1980s,* ed. C. E. Walter and M. A. Bloomfield. Cambridge, Mass.: Ballinger for American Council for Capital Formation.

Hulten, C. R., and F. C. Wykoff. 1981. The Measurement of Economic Depreciation. In *Depreciation, Inflation, and the Taxation of Income from Capital,* ed. C. R. Hulten. Washington, D.C.: Urban Institute.

Jorgenson, D. W., and K.-Y. Yun. 1986. Tax Policy and Capital Allocation. *Scandinavian Journal of Economics* 88(2): 355–77.

———. 1990. Tax Reform and U.S. Economic Growth. *Journal of Political Economy* 98(5), part 2: S151–93.

———. 1991. *Tax Reform and the Cost of Capital.* New York: Oxford University Press.

Lintner, J. V. 1956. Distribution of Incomes of Corporations among Dividends, Retained Earnings, and Taxes. *American Economic Review* 46(2): 97–113.

Pechman, J. A., ed. 1988. *World Tax Reform: A Progress Report.* Washington, D.C.: Brookings Institution.

Summers, L. H. 1981. Taxation and Corporate Investment: A q-Theory Approach. *Brookings Papers on Economic Activity* 1: 67–127.

Yun, K.-Y. Taxation of Capital Income and the Allocation of Capital in Korea (in Korean) *Journal of Korean Tax Association* 4: 122–58.

Comment   Toshihiro Ihori

Kun-Young Yun's paper provides a framework for the analysis of the impact of taxation of income from foreign capital on a small capital-importing country, Korea. In contrast with much of the earlier work in this area, an attempt is made to ground some of the equations on standard microtheory. I think the paper is useful in that it attempts to explain the Korean tax policy from the optimal taxation perspective. I have a few comments and questions for the author.

This paper estimates the effective tax rate of corporate investment financed with foreign income. It would be useful to estimate the effective tax rate of corporate investment financed with domestic income as well. If the former tax rate is less than the latter, it would mean that the tax preferences for foreign capital in Korea are excessive. If both rates were almost the same, it would imply that Korea's tax policy is not necessarily generous for the income from foreign capital.

Toshihiro Ihori is associate professor of economics at Osaka University.

It would be useful to discuss the normative aspects of tax policy on the whole capital income, domestic or foreign, in Korea. In order to stimulate economic growth, it might be necessary to reduce capital income taxes.[1] If so, the generous treatment of foreign capital in Korea may be justified.

Equation (3) assumes that foreign capital can move freely into Korea, so that the optimal marginal condition is satisfied. Is such an assumption realistic in Korea? Were there any restrictions on importing capital in the 1970s?

International capital movements are crucially dependent on the tax system. In a territorial system capital income tax burdens depend on where the income is earned, but not on the consumer's country of residence. Conversely, under a residence system, tax burdens depend on the country of residence, not on where income is earned. Hence, if the residence system is realistic, the generous tax treatment of foreign capital in Korea may be offset by the tax treatment in the rest of the world, so that the supply of foreign capital may not be responsive to the after-tax rate of return.

Overall, this is a very useful paper investigating taxation of income from foreign capital. I hope that the normative aspects of tax policy in Korea will be explored more fully in future research.

Comment   Toshiaki Tachibanaki

The paper by Kun-Young Yun investigates the tax treatment of income from foreign capital in Korea and examines the effect of tax policy on capital inflow. The paper is a useful application of neoclassical economic theory, providing us with an interesting policy implication for Korea. My comments are concerned with an overview of foreign capital in Korea and the empirical results obtained in this paper.

First, section 11.2 gives an overview of foreign capital in Korea. The paper does not show in detail what percentage of all capital is foreign. Moreover, it would be useful to describe from what countries capital is imported and in what form, say direct investment or financial investment. That information would be helpful to understand and judge the usefulness of the theoretical and empirical parts of the paper.

Second, related to the first point, the utility of the maximization of the tax revenue from foreign capital is doubtful. If the share of the tax revenue from foreign capital in Korea were negligible, it would not be effective for the government in Korea to use the maximization principle; other behavioral principles would be more useful.

---

1. See, for example, R. J. Barro, "Government Spending in a Simple Model of Endogenous Growth," *Journal of Political Economy* 98: S103–25.

Toshiaki Tachibanaki is professor of economics at Kyoto University.

Third, the theory part neatly develops the neoclassical growth and tax model. Although several stringent assumptions are imposed, it would be unfair to fault Yun for that. I am impressed with the Jorgensonian neoclassical approach throughout the paper.

Fourth, it is quite impressive to see the negative effective tax rates for investment in the empirical part. This implies a subsidy. The paper does not present in detail the reasons for the negative rates; it would be useful to have a decomposition analysis to draw some conjectures for rates, or a sensitivity analysis to confirm that the negative values are right. I would guess that the reasons are a very high debt/equity ratio in Korea or generous depreciation allowances. These were quite effective for promoting high investment activity in postwar Japan and are supposed to be very effective in the process of industrialization. It is impressive to see that two countries, namely Korea and Japan, had the common policy tools for strong industrialization.

Comment   Twatchai Yongkittikul

Kun-Young Yun's extremely well-organized paper formulates a very elaborate theoretical framework for an evaluation of the tax policy, and then painstakingly measures the effective tax rate in Korea. The empirical results are compared with the theoretical conclusions to draw the policy implications. I have just a few general comments.

First, since the theoretical framework is quite elaborate, Yun inevitably discovered a considerable gap between the theoretical and the empirical data. He therefore found it necessary to make a number of assumptions in order to bridge this gap. He thus noted that his estimate of the effective tax rate was only as good as the assumptions made in the calculation. Since the policy implications were drawn from these empirical results, one could not help but wonder how sensitive these results were regarding the assumptions made. The readers might feel a bit more comfortable if some of these assumptions were varied to ascertain the sensitivity of the results.

Second, Yun found that, although the overall tax burden levied by the Korean government on foreign capital is reasonable, the extremely generous tax treatments provided by the Foreign Capital Inducement Law for foreign direct investment in Korea are not justified. In the presence of the foreign tax credit system in the home country, the tax exemption provided by the law merely benefits the treasury of the home country without affecting the effective tax burden of the investor. This conclusion is quite relevant for the small developing countries that are competing with each other to attract foreign capital

Twatchai Yongkittikul is director of planning and development at the Thailand Development Research Institute Foundation.

by providing excessively generous incentives. A better-coordinated tax policy among the developing countries in this regard would clearly increase their benefits from foreign investment.

Third, this paper focused on taxes as the only policy instrument affecting capital flows. I believe that there are a number of factors that would encourage or discourage foreign capital, the major ones being interest rates and foreign exchange rates. These have been used extensively in many countries as policy instruments, and they have played an important role in attracting foreign capital. In Korea's case, the won was kept undervalued up to the first half of the 1980s, and the exchange rate policy clearly played as important a role as taxes in promoting export as well as capital inflow.

Finally, Yun stated in the first part of his paper that Korea has pursued internationalization of its capital market since 1981. He did not mention the reasons why this policy was being pursued. Foreign investment has always been looked at with wariness in Korea, and this attitude has changed very slowly. Why is Korea so interested in liberalizing its capital market now? What is the impetus for this recent change? Is it driven by internal forces— such as the prevalence of excess liquidity—or is Korea yielding to external pressure to open its capital market? Are there any preconditions that must be achieved before a country can internationalize its capital market? The answer to this last question would be useful for other developing countries in deciding when they would be in a position to open up their capital market.

12 Tax Policy and Foreign Direct Investment in Taiwan

Ching-huei Chang and Peter W. H. Cheng

12.1 Introduction

Over the past three decades, Taiwan has experienced one of the world's highest sustained economic growth rates. From 1953 to 1988, real gross national product (GNP) grew at an average annual rate of 8.82 percent. Foreign trade has grown at an even faster pace. Over the same thirty-five-year period, for example, exports and imports increased at average annual rates of 21.87 percent and 19.25 percent, respectively. Consequently, the foreign sector has become the most important sector of Taiwan's economy. Exports of goods and services have accounted for more than 50 percent of GNP since 1978. Taiwan's persistent trade surplus, which occurred during most years in the 1970s and 1980s, has resulted in huge international currency reserves and has become a major source of economic instability in recent years.[1]

A number of previous studies have argued that foreign direct investment (FDI) contributed to the growth process in Taiwan by providing funds for capital formation and facilitating technology transfers.[2] Furthermore, FDI with a high export orientation also contributed significantly to Taiwan's trade

Ching-huei Chang is a research fellow at Sun Yat-sen Institute for Social Sciences and Philosophy, Academia Sinica, Taiwan. Peter W. H. Cheng is an associate professor at the Department of Public Finance and Taxation, National Chengchi University, Taiwan.

The authors are indebted to Professors Ihori, Choi, and other participants of the conference for their valuable comments on and suggestions for the earlier draft of this paper.

1. Taiwan's international reserves have been at around U.S. $65 billion since 1987, ranking third in the world behind Japan and West Germany. Not surprisingly, Taiwan's currency appreciated from New Taiwan (N.T.) $39.85 per U.S. dollar at the end of 1985 to N.T. $25.90 per U.S. dollar in June of 1989. The external imbalance not only created tensions and disputes with major trading partners but also generated excess liquidity and raised strong inflationary pressures in the domestic economy.

2. These conclusions have been reached mostly by qualitative analysis. For a brief review, see Lee and Hu (1989) and Tsai (1991).

surplus, which helped alleviate the foreign exchange shortages prevalent in previous decades.[3]

In fact, more than 40 percent of Taiwan's gross domestic capital formation (GDCF) in 1952–60 was financed by foreign capital, predominantly U.S. aid. However, the importance of foreign capital has declined significantly since the termination of U.S. aid in 1965. Although private FDI has risen steadily in nominal terms since then, FDI as a percentage of GDCF has dropped from 8.03 percent in 1966–70 to 2.94 percent in 1976–80 before swinging back to 4.39 percent in 1981–86 (R. Wu 1989). In addition, FDI in Taiwan as a percentage of global FDI has remained quite stable between 0.2 and 0.5 percent during 1965–84 (Tsai 1991).

In general, government policies have been very favorable toward FDI in Taiwan, though there were various forms of government manipulation that affected the amount and direction of FDI.[4] The treatment afforded foreign enterprises in Taiwan has been essentially the same as that given to the corresponding types of local enterprises. Since before 1980 Taiwan followed the dual development strategies of import substitution and export promotion, foreign investors could enjoy all kinds of tariff and nontariff protection if they produced for the domestic market.[5] They could also take advantage of various assistance measures such as export processing zones, tax rebates, and export loans if they produced for international markets.

Furthermore, since the major concern of national tax policy has been stimulation of investment, in addition to low corporate income tax rates very generous tax incentives have been provided. The highest marginal tax rate on corporate income remained 25 percent for most of the years after 1956, with the exception of 1974–85.[6] Major tax incentive measures, such as tax holidays and a tax ceiling, were first introduced in 1960, and accelerated depreciation and investment tax credit were added in the 1970s and 1980s. Nowadays Taiwan has one of the most complex tax incentive systems in the world.[7]

Taiwan's major economic objective in recent years, however, has been the establishment of an international and more liberalized economy. Strategies adopted include loosening restraints on foreign exchange control, reducing tariff and nontariff barriers, and opening domestic markets.[8] Foreign invest-

3. Though the export ratio of foreign firms in Taiwan has declined gradually in recent years, it was over 50 percent before 1985. The exports of foreign firms in 1980–84 accounted for about 20 percent of Taiwan's total exports and caused more than 30 percent of the trade surplus in Taiwan (cf. R. Wu 1989, table 13).

4. Like most developing countries, Taiwan applies restrictions on the ownership, size, foreign exchange transactions, scope of operation, etc. Cf. Peat, Marwick, Mitchell and Co. (1987).

5. For an analysis of industrial and trade policies in Taiwan, see R. Wu (1989).

6. The highest marginal tax rate on corporate income has been adjusted many times over the past three decades. It was 18 percent in 1961–66; 25 percent in 1956–60, 1967–73, and 1986–90; 30 percent in 1985; and 35 percent in 1974–84.

7. A brief review of the major tax incentives in Taiwan and a comparison with selected other countries is presented in tables 12.1 and 12.2.

8. As regards foreign exchange transactions involving international commodities, the tariff rate dropped from 20.1 percent in 1987 to 12.8 percent in 1988. Moreover, a constantly increasing

ment is now permitted in almost all industries. Domestic shareholding and business operations requirements and restrictions on the repatriation of profits and capital have also been greatly reduced. Conspicuously, Taiwan has attracted more FDI in recent years, both in absolute and in relative terms.[9]

Against this background, the current tax policy toward FDI has been under critical review. The effectiveness of tax incentives in attracting FDI has been an area of controversy (Riedel 1975; Wu et al. 1980). A recent study (Tsai 1991) found that FDI in Taiwan was likely to be determined by supply-side factors, rather than by government policy. The side effects of FDI's contribution to Taiwan's trade surplus have also called for reconsideration of existing policies that were designed largely to cope with the earlier problem of a serious exchange shortage (R. Wu 1989). Furthermore, the cost of tax incentives in terms of losses in equity and efficiency has brought about a comprehensive review of national income taxation (Chen and Cheng 1990).

The ROC Tax Reform Commission (1987–89) has proposed a comprehensive package of income tax reforms that includes the integration of individual and business income taxes and the abolishment of most current tax incentives.[10] How FDI in Taiwan will be affected by the proposed tax policy change and how important this effect will be should be a subject for serious scrutiny. Current empirical results from cross-national studies can make little contribution to an evaluation of the suggested policy change (Agarwal 1980).

This paper provides some observations based on empirical studies of the effects of tax policy on FDI in Taiwan. For that purpose, firm-specific FDI data for 1984–86 and also aggregate time-series FDI data for 1972–87 are analyzed. While the data are severely limited, some basic policy implications may still be explored. Further investigations should be made to evaluate the impact of abolishing tax incentives in those industries where international competition to attract investment is severe.

This paper is organized as follows. Section 12.2 reviews some studies of the effects of tax policy on capital inflows in developing countries. Section 12.3 discusses tax preferences in Taiwan. Section 12.4 analyzes FDI in Taiwan by industry, sources of origin, and export orientation in order to display its changing characteristics. Section 12.5 presents the regression results ob-

---

number of imported goods are exempted from Taiwan's prior-permit requirements, and the range of allowable foreign investment, for which favorable status is granted, has been significantly extended from the manufacturing to the service industries.

9. Approved FDI has increased from U.S. $395 million (1981) to $2,418 million (1989), and its share as a percentage of domestic nonresidential investment increased from 3.56 percent (1981) to 8.56 percent (1989); see table 12.3. That table also shows that actual FDI as a percentage of FDI in nonoil developing countries increased from 1.03 percent (1981) to 6.03 percent (1987).

10. Since the government of Taiwan has taken a piecemeal, approach to tax reform, the extent to which reform proposals will be put into effect remains to be seen. According to the draft of a new act currently under consideration by the Legislative Yuan, however, only tax holidays will be eliminated entirely, while accelerated depreciation, tax credits, and other incentives will remain. For a brief summary of the proposed changes in Taiwan's income taxation made by the Tax Reform Commission, see Chen and Cheng (1990).

tained from firm-specific and time-series data to ascertain the relationship between FDI and tax policy. Section 12.6 summarizes some important results found in this study and discusses their policy implications.

12.2   Review of Literature

In theory the tax policy of both host country and home country should have a significant impact on international capital flow. Consider this simple example. A dollar investment in the home country yields the risk-adjusted, net rate of return $(1 - t)r$ each year, where t and r are the income tax rate and the before-tax rate of return, respectively. On the other hand, the investment earns $(1 - t_h)r_h$ in the host country, where subscript h represents the host country. If the subsidiary firm repatriates its earnings immediately, how much will the parent firm have at its disposal? Apparently, the answer depends on the tax policy on foreign source income that the home country adopts.[11]

Since the major sources of FDI in Taiwan are the United States and Japan, we will take the "residence approach" in our analysis where foreign tax credits are allowed.[12] We will also explicitly assume $t_h < t$.[13] In this case, the tax liability to the home country is $(t - t_h)$ for each dollar that the parent company receives, and total tax payments are $(t - t_h) + t_h = t$. Thus, the net rate of return on foreign investment is $(1 - t)r_h$, and the firm benefits by investing abroad if $r_h > r$. Neither the home country tax nor the host country tax affects the firm's international investment decision. This conclusion is consistent with the previous research in this area, which argued that taxing foreign income at the domestic rate with a credit provides for "capital export neutrality." It follows that any tax concessions offered by the host country will result in a transfer of tax revenue to the home country's government without affecting the firm's investment.

In the above discussion, we explicitly assume that the foreign subsidiary repatriates earnings immediately. The result may be different if this assumption is relaxed, since the tax the home country imposes on the firm's foreign investment is typically deferred until earnings are repatriated. In the most extreme case, the foreign subsidiary retains all of the earnings, and the effective tax rate on foreign income is equal to t_h, the host country's tax. This is the basis under which previous studies argued that, under the tax-sum-credit sys-

---

11. This assumes that the host country does not impose a withholding tax on repatriation.

12. In the United States and Japan, however, a deduction from taxable income may be taken in lieu of the tax credit. As such, the firm should invest in the foreign country if $(1 - t_h)r_h > r$. Then it is of interest to see that the home country tax applied to foreign source income, t, plays no role in the firm's marginal investment decision. Moreover, a tax reduction in the host country can potentially encourage capital flow.

13. The corporate income tax rates for the United States and Japan are currently 34 percent and 40 percent, respectively, compared with 25 percent in Taiwan. Cf. table 12.2.

tem, the ability to defer taxation on foreign source income confers a tax advantage on foreign investment.

The above view has recently been challenged by Hartman (1984, 1985). He correctly draws attention to the distinction between investment financed out of earnings abroad and investment financed by transfers from the home country. If the subsidiary is investing out of retained earnings, the home country tax on foreign source income does not affect the marginal investment decision. On the other hand, if the planned investment by the subsidiary is not sufficient to exhaust totally its retained earnings (i.e., if repatriation of earnings must take place), then the home country tax is unavoidable and its present value does not depend on the length of deferral. Thus the decision for investment out of retained earnings should depend only on net returns available in the home country or the host country.

Hartman's argument can easily be illustrated by using the simple example cited above. Suppose that the subsidiary has a dollar of after-tax earnings (previously taxed at the host country rate t_h), which can be either repatriated or reinvested. If the subsidiary firm repatriates the earnings immediately, after paying the home country tax the parent has at its disposal $(1 - t)/(1 - t_h)$ dollars. If the dollar is reinvested, the dollar plus the one-period earnings will be repatriated at the end of the period. Upon receipt of the dividend, the parent must pay the home country tax on the original dollar of earnings and the return earned during the period, but it can claim a credit for the taxes paid to the host country. So the parent receives $(1 - t) [1 + r_h (1 - t_h)]/(1 - t_h)$. The present value of this amount is equal to $(1 - t)/(1 - t_h)$, when discounted at the rate of return, net of the host country tax, $[1 + r_h (1 - t_h)]$.

Return to the case where the subsidiary repatriates its profits immediately; the dollar is in the form of a dividend to the parent company. After investing in the home country at a net rate of return, $(1 - t)r$, the parent has $(1 - t)$ $[1 + r (1 - t)]/(1 - t_h)$ at the end of the period. Comparing these two results, we see that the dollar should be reinvested in the host country rather than repatriated if $r_h (1 - t_h) > r(1 - t)$. Note that this is exactly the result obtained when the home country adopts the "territorial approach" to taxation of foreign source income. Hartman called this "capital import neutrality," that is, the same tax rates influence the decision of both domestic firms and foreign firms in the host country that finance investment through retained earnings.

The discussions above imply that fiscal incentives offered by developing host countries that lower the value of t_h will in most cases be effective in attracting FDI. How responsive FDI is to these tax concessions is of course an empirical question. There is no clear-cut conclusion about the effectiveness of these measures in attracting FDI. Most empirical evidence suggests that their overall impact on FDI is marginal at best (Root and Ahmed 1978, Shah and Toye 1978, Lim 1983, Goldsbrough 1985, Balasubramanyam 1986).

In his survey of the literature, Agarwal (1980) attributed the failure of these tax measures in attracting FDI to a host of disincentives that generally accompany the incentives provided by a host country. These include restrictions on ownership, size, location, dividends, royalties, fees, entry into certain industries and mandatory provisions for local purchases, as well as the requirement of being export-oriented. Moreover, the incentive policies of developing countries are generally quite restrictive in the sense that foreign investors must fulfill a number of conditions to be eligible for them. For example, in Taiwan the Investment Commission of the Ministry of Economic Affairs has been known to manipulate its power to regulate the inflow of capital (R. Wu 1989).

Many authors have also pointed out that tax incentives are so pervasive among developing nations that the benefits these measures confer on a country are very small (for example, Root and Ahmed 1978). However, Goldsbrough (1985) postulated that an individual country might lose much new investment were it to lower or abolish all its incentives unilaterally. This issue is particularly relevant for newly industrialized economies that wish to attract capital inflow on the one hand, while reducing unnecessary tax incentives on the other hand.

From the point of view of a host country, it is even more important to identify the demand-side determinants that it can control to some extent. For that purpose, case studies rather than cross-national analyses would be more relevant. In the case of Taiwan, Wu et al. (1980) found in their survey that most U.S. firms are concerned with tax concessions. Riedel (1975) concluded from his econometric results that the incentives in Taiwan have no impact on U.S. FDI, though they are effective in attracting capital inflow from Japan and Hong Kong. However, Tsai's recent study (1991) found that neither government incentive measures nor Taiwan's extraordinary economic performance were themselves significant factors in attracting FDI. Therefore, it is likely that FDI in Taiwan is determined by supply-side factors.

Since the variety and complexity of incentives make it difficult to evaluate their effectiveness, one would need more relevant data and a better methodology to ascertain clearly the relationship between FDI and tax policy. It is exactly in these areas that the present paper hopes to make a contribution to the existing literature.

12.3 Tax Preferences

There are two methods by which foreign investors may fulfill the requirements for capital investment in Taiwan. One requires approval by the ROC Investment Commission pursuant to the Statute for Investment by Foreign Nationals or the Statute for Investment by Overseas Chinese. The other is to set up branches or subsidiaries without foreign investment approval if the firm meets the requirements of minimal capital contribution, a resident manager, domiciled national stockholders and shareholdings, and a domiciled national chairman and supervisors. In either case, foreign firms and their local counterparts are treated equally.[14] In this section, we will discuss the tax prefer-ences that have been enjoyed both by FDI and domestic investment over the past three decades.

Almost all of Taiwan's major tax incentives are provided through the Statute for Encouragement of Investment, which was originally promulgated in Sep-tember 1960. This statute was initially supposed to be effective for only ten years; however, it has been extended and expanded for two decades. Current major tax incentives and their history are compiled and shown in table 12.1. Four types of businesses are identified, according to the tax preferences for which they qualify: general profit-seeking enterprises, general productive en-terprises, important productive enterprises, and firms eligible for tax holi-days.[15]

Four major measures were gradually introduced during the past three dec-ades: tax holidays and tax ceilings in the 1960s, accelerated depreciation in the late 1960s and 1970s, and more-specific depreciation measures and tax credits in the 1980s. With few exceptions, the provisions for tax preferences became more and more generous over time; the whole incentive system is now very complex. For example, an important productive enterprise may claim ten tax preferences that are listed in table 12.1. Some of them may be redundant (for example, tax ceilings), while some have multiple benefits (for example, tax credits and accelerated depreciation).

Table 12.2 compares tax and incentive systems among Taiwan, its major FDI sources, i.e., the United States and Japan, and its major FDI competitors, such as Korea, Singapore, and Thailand. Clearly, Taiwan currently has the lowest corporate income tax rate among these countries. Furthermore, Taiwan also provides the most generous incentives (except for tax holidays). Not only are tax credits and depreciation preferences provided for general capital in-vestment rather than for specific industries or purposes, but the degree to which both preference items are enjoyed by firms in Taiwan is quite large. It is clear that the incentive measures have actually reduced the tax burden of firms in Taiwan.

To give an idea of the extent of tax preferences for FDI, table 12.3 com-pares the average effective tax rates for foreign and domestic manufacturing firms in 1984–86. It should be noted that the highest marginal business in-come tax rate decreased annually during this period from 35 percent in 1984 to 30 percent in 1985 and 25 percent in 1986. The average rate on profit-seeking enterprises nationwide was 21.19 percent over the same period (Lee and Chu 1990). Table 12.3 indicates that foreign firms, as a whole, bore a

---

14. However, it should be noted that nontax favorable treatment is provided to foreign invest-ment with approval. For example, the restrictions on the percentages of foreign ownership and stockholders and on the chairman and supervisors may be waived. Moreover, there is a twenty-year guarantee against government expropriation or forced requisition. Cf. Peat, Marwick, Mitch-ell and Co. (1987).

15. For the definitions of the different types of firms, see the notes to table 12.1.

Table 12.1   **Major Tax Incentives for Firms in Taiwan**

Type of Firm	Tax Incentive	Beginning Year and Later Revisions
General profit-seeking enterprises[a]		
	2-year depreciation for pollution-control facilities	1981
	2-year depreciation for energy-saving facilities	1981
	30% tax credit for capital investment in major high-tech enterprises	1987
	20% tax credit for capital investment in venture capital projects	1987
General productive enterprises[b]		
	Tax ceiling	1960 (18%), 1971 (25%), 1987 (20% for large trade and venture capital)
	Accelerated depreciation for renovation of machinery and equipment	1965 (1/3), 1981 (1/2)
	Accelerated depreciation for R&D facilities	1977
	5–20% tax credit for machinery and equipment	1981
	20% tax credit for R&D expenses	1984
	All preferences enjoyed by profit-seeking enterprises	
Important productive enterprises[c]		
	Tax ceiling	1960 (18%), 1971 (22%), 1988 (20%)
	All preferences enjoyed by general productive enterprises	
Firms eligible for tax holidays[d]		
	5-year exemption for new firms	1960
	4-year exemption for expansion firms	1960 (5 yrs), 1971 (4 yrs)
	May elect to adopt accelerated depreciation	1971
	May elect to defer commencement of tax holiday	1977 (1–4 yrs), 1982 (2–4 yrs)

Source: Study on Tax Incentive Measures in the Statute for Encouragement of Investment (in Chinese), ROC Tax Reform Commission Technical Report no. 37 (Ministry of Finance, June 1989).

[a]Any public or private organization that engages in activities for profit-seeking purposes, organized in any form.

[b]A firm that is organized as a "company limited by shares" and operates in a set of specified industries including manufacturing, mining, agriculture, and most other industries except major service sectors.

[c]A firm in the metal, heavy machinery, or petrochemical industry that is capital-intensive and technology-intensive and "confirms the need for development of economic and national defense industries."

[d]A productive enterprise that conforms to regulated categories and criteria of encouragement and is newly established or effects an expanion of equipment through an increase of capital.

Table 12.2   **Comparison of Taxes and Incentives on Corporate Income, 1989**

Taxes and Incentives	Japan	Korea	Singapore	Taiwan	Thailand	United States
Highest marginal corporate tax rates	40%	27, 30, or 33%	Flat 32%	25%	Flat 30 or 35%	34%
Withholding tax rate on dividend income[a]	20%	25%	32% to be paid out of corporate tax	20%[b]	20%	30%
Tax holidays	Nil	Up to 5 years for FDI only	Up to 10 years	Up to 5 years	Up to 8 years	Nil
Other major incentives	Up to 7% tax credit or up to 30% special depreciation for energy savings. 20% tax credit for incremental R&D.	30% special depreciation for exports. Up to 10% tax credit or up to 50% special depreciation for energy savings, pollution control, R&D, etc.	Reduced rate, up to 5 years for international trade and services. Up to 50% investment allowances.	Up to 20% tax credit. Up to 2-year depreciation.	—	20% tax credit for incremental R&D

Sources: Corporate Taxes: A Worldwide Summary, 1988 (New York: Price Waterhouse); *1988 International Tax Summaries* (New York: Coopers and Lybrand); *Asian Pacific Taxation, 1989* (Tokyo: KPMG Peat Marwick).

[a]Rates may be reduced in accordance with the provisions in the double taxation agreements.

[b]Thirty-five percent is levied on nonapproved investment. However, these foreign investors may elect to file an income final return subject to progressive tax rates, in which case the effective tax rate may be lower than 20 percent.

Table 12.3   Comparison of Effective Tax Rates for Foreign and Domestic Manufacturing Firms in Taiwan, 1984–86 Average (%)

Industry	Foreign Firms with Tax Holiday					All Foreign Firms		All Domestic and Foreign Firms with Tax Holiday	
	Sample Size	Before Tax Concessions	Tax Holiday Benefit	Other Tax Benefit	After All Concessions	Number	Average Tax Rate	Sample Size	After All Concessions
Food and beverage	5	14.67	8.00	0	6.67	115	36.03[a]	7	11.20
Chemicals	32	17.00	9.00	3.00	5.00	342	16.03	80	10.60
Nonmetallic	3	24.00	1.67	09	22.33	87	17.19	11	21.80
Basic metals	9	19.00	6.67	0.33	12.00	296	18.13	21	19.30
Machinery	34	16.45	3.77	0.35	12.33	212	22.50	74	15.97
Electronics	109	17.73	4.50	0.90	12.33	604	17.22	212	11.31
Other manufacturing	8	17.67	1.33	1.00	15.33	419	20.64	25	21.72
Average[b]	200	17.46	5.11	1.09	11.26	2075	19.47	430	13.31

Sources: Effective tax rates for all domestic and foreign firms with tax holidays in Taiwan are calculated from the corporate income tax returns of the sampled data in Lee and Chu (1990). Effective tax rates and tax concessions for foreign firms with tax holidays are calculated from the subfile data used by Lee and Chu (1990). Effective tax rates for all foreign firms in Taiwan are calculated from the data in *An Analysis of Operations and Economic Effects of Foreign Enterprises* (in Chinese) (ROC, Investment Commission, Ministry of Economic Affairs, 1987).

[a]While the highest marginal tax rates were 35 percent (1984), 30 percent (1985), and 25 percent (1986), the exceptionally high average effective tax rate for food and beverage processing was due to the aggregation of positive profits of some firms with the large losses of other firms.

[b]Weighted average of the sample size or number of firms in each industry.

lower tax burden (19.47 percent) than the national average. It further shows that the effective tax rate for the foreign firms eligible for tax holidays and other incentives was 11.26 percent, only about one-half of the national average effective tax rate (21.29 percent), and about 2 percentage points lower than the average effective tax rate for all domestic and foreign firms eligible for tax holidays (13.31 percent).

However, to measure the extent of tax preferences more meaningfully, one should compare the after-tax concession rate (11.26 percent) with the before-tax concession rate (17.46 percent). This gives about a one-third, or 6.20 percent, tax savings to foreign firms eligible for tax holidays. This tax savings can be further decomposed into two parts: 5.11 percent for tax holidays, and 1.09 percent for other tax preferences, major tax credits, and tax ceilings.[16]

12.4   Changing Characteristics of FDI in Taiwan

12.4.1   FDI Trends

Summary data for the amount of approved and actual FDI in Taiwan are presented in table 12.4. Though approved investment figures vary annually, they were generally less than U.S. $1 billion before 1987, and clearly exhibited a pattern of gradual increase. In relative terms, however, approved FDI displayed a large swing during 1952–89. FDI was an important supplement to inadequate domestic savings in the 1960s and early 1970s. It accounted for 12.5 percent of nonresidential domestic investment in 1970. The importance of approved FDI has declined since then; however, it swung back to over 5 percent after 1984. Nevertheless, it should be noted that Taiwan has had a large amount of excess savings in recent years, totaling over 9 percent of GNP.[17] Table 12.4 also reveals that about one-third of annual approved FDI went into the expansion of old projects, while two-thirds went for new projects.

The annual data on the actual amount of FDI show the same increasing pattern as for approved FDI.[18] Before 1986, the ratio of actual to approved FDI remained relatively constant at about 40 percent. In the last two years, however, the realization ratio of approved FDI has been high: 81.07 percent in 1988 and 66.34 percent in 1989. The major reason for the large discrepancy between actual and approved FDI remains unknown, and future trends deserve

16. Since accelerated depreciation has been included as an expense in calculating before-tax profit, its degree of tax preference cannot be identified. In other words, the tax preferences enjoyed by foreign firms, such as tax holidays (as shown in table 12.3), are underestimated because of the exclusion of accelerated depreciation.

17. The percentages are 11.88 (1984), 14.83 (1985), 21.34 (1986), 18.39 (1987), 11.68 (1988), and 9.32 (1989). See *Quarterly National Economic Trends,* Directorate-General of Budget, Accounting Statistics, Executive Yuan, ROC, February 1990.

18. Both the approved and actual amounts of FDI in the Taiwanese data include equity investment and reinvested earnings, but the data do not include loans from parent firms to subsidiaries. Also, it should be noted that these two FDI statistics are obtained from different sources.

Table 12.4   Trends in Taiwan's Foreign Direct Investment

	Approved FDI			Actual FDI		
Year	Amount (millions of U.S. $)	Percentage of Expansion Projects	Percentage Nonresidential Investment[a]	Amount (millions of U.S. $)	Percentage of Approved FDI	Percentage of FDI in Nonoil LDCs
1952	1.067	—	2.43	—	—	—
1960	15.470	—	6.93	5.77	37.30	—
1970	138.900	44.05	12.50	61.93	44.59	4.80
1980	466.000	36.93	4.28	165.70	35.56	1.47
1981	395.800	42.50	3.56	150.90	38.13	1.03
1982	380.000	29.21	3.60	104.00	27.37	0.80
1983	404.500	38.51	3.98	149.00	36.84	1.48
1984	558.700	38.97	5.29	200.90	35.96	1.91
1985	702.500	30.72	7.32	340.20	48.43	3.06
1986	770.400	29.52	6.25	326.00	42.34	3.44
1987	1,419.000	35.30	7.75	715.00	˙50.39	6.03
1988	1,183.000	43.83	5.49	959.00	81.07	—
1989	2,418.000	32.87	8.51	1,604.00	66.34	—
Total/ average	10,950.000[b]	36.95[d]	5.99[c]	—	45.35[c]	2.67[c]

Sources: For approved FDI, Statistics on Overseas Chinese and Foreign Investment (Taipei: ROC Investment Commission, Ministry of Economic Affairs, various years). For actual FDI, Balance of Payments Statistics (Taiwan: Central Bank of China, 1989). For FDI in non-oil-exporting LDCs, Balance of Payments Statistics Yearbook (Washington, D.C.: International Monetary Fund, various years). For nonresidential domestic investment, Quarterly National Economic Trends Directorate-General of Budget, Accounting Statistics, Executive Yuan, ROC, Taipei February 1990.

[a]Gross fixed capital formation, excluding residential buildings.
[b]Total for the period from 1952 to 1989.
[c]Simple average for the selected years shown in the table.

to be followed closely.[19] The other important figure in table 12.4 is the share of Taiwan's FDI in total FDI of all non-oil-exporting LDCs. Tsai (1991) mentioned that the ratio remained quite stable during 1958–85. However, table 12.4 clearly shows that Taiwan has attracted an increasing share of the total FDI since 1982. Therefore, the demand-side determinants of FDI in Taiwan in recent years deserve further scrutiny.

12.4.2   Composition of FDI

Three aspects of the changing composition of FDI in Taiwan are presented in tables 12.5 and 12.6. From panel A of table 12.5, it can be seen that the dominant sector of FDI has been manufacturing. However, its share has dropped from 77.58 percent in the 1960s to 68.01 percent in 1985–89. The largest decline has been in the electronic and electrical appliance sector, which went from 36.61 percent of all FDI in the 1960s down to 21.21 percent in

19. Though the time lag for realizing investment may be part of the cause of the discrepancy, it cannot account for the size of the gap between approved and actual FDI. See Schive (1987).

Table 12.5   Composition of Foreign Direct Investment in Taiwan, 1960–89 (in millions of U.S. dollars)

	1960–69		1970–79		1980–84		1985–89	
	Amount	Percentage	Amount	Percentage	Amount	Percentage	Amount	Percentage
Total	400.16	100.00	1,895.00	100.00	2,205.00	100.00	6,492.00	100.00
			A. By industry					
Electronics	146.48	36.61	596.00	31.45	638.00	28.93	1,377.00	21.21
Chemicals	64.26	16.06	183.00	9.66	306.00	13.88	1,150.00	17.71
Machinery	12.51	3.13	137.00	7.23	267.00	12.11	513.00	7.90
Other manufacturing	87.18	21.79	457.00	24.12	563.00	25.53	1,440.00	22.18
Services	51.55	12.88	335.00	18.73	366.00	16.60	1,895.00	29.19
Others	38.18	9.45	187.00	9.87	65.00	2.95	117.00	1.80
			B. By area					
United States	169.78	42.43	624.00	32.93	829.00	37.60	1,476.00	22.74
Japan	66.03	16.50	342.00	18.05	621.00	28.16	1,947.00	29.99
Major European countries[a]	25.28	6.32	147.00	7.76	167.00	7.57	828.00	12.75
Other Asian countries[b]	113.88	28.46	556.00	29.34	434.00	19.68	968.00	14.91
Others	25.19	6.29	226.00	11.93	154.00	6.98	1,273.00	19.61[c]

Source: Statistics on Overseas Chinese and Foreign Investment (Taipei: ROC Investment Commission, Ministry of Economic Affairs, 1989).

[a]Including United Kingdom, West Germany, France, The Netherlands, and Switzerland.

[b]All Asian countries except Japan.

[c]The sharp increase is due to FDI from tax havens. It is calculated by the Investment Commission that FDI from tax havens in 1989 was U.S. 564% $ million, accounting for 23.33 percent of total FDI in that year.

Table 12.6　　　　　**Export Ratios of Foreign Firms in Taiwan, 1978–87 (%)**

	1978	1979	1980	1981	1982	1983	1984	1985	1986	1987
Total	60	54	53	54	55	51	52	49	46	47
Electronics	70	66	67	71	71	80	77	80	72	75
Chemicals	51	43	44	41	39	31	25	26	20	22
Machinery	31	25	28	34	48	20	30	18	33	19
Other manufacturing	59	57	52	52	50	52	48	51	38	47
Services	28	19	17	16	19	20	17	14	9	7
Others	76	78	69	67	80	79	77	71	74	80

Source: An Analysis of Operations and Economic Effects of Foreign Enterprises (in Chinese) (Taipei: ROC Investment Commission, Ministry of Economic Affairs, 1987).

1985–89. In contrast, there was a sharp rise in the share going to services, from 16.60 percent in 1980–84 to 29.19 percent in 1985–89. The change in the service industry is quite conspicuous, reflecting that Taiwan's domestic service markets have begun to open up to foreign competition.[20]

Panel B of table 12.5 also shows that the sources of FDI have substantially changed during the past three decades. The share of U.S. investment has declined from 42.43 percent in the 1960s to 22.74 percent in 1985–89. The United States' dominant role was taken over by Japanese investors whose share has increased from 16.50 percent to 29.99 percent in the same period. In the last five years, investment from the major European countries has also increased from 7.57 percent to 12.75 percent. However, the most conspicuous increase in recent years has been in investment from so-called tax haven countries or areas. It was estimated by the Investment Commission that as much as U.S. $564 million of FDI in 1989 came from such places, accounting for 23.33 percent of total FDI in that year. These investments are suspected to have been made by Taiwan residents so as to avoid Taiwan's highly progressive personal income tax rates.[21] This issue has prompted suggestions that the international and domestic aspects of income taxation should be regarded as an integrated rather than a separate system.

One of the major effects of FDI in Taiwan has been export expansion. Many believe that, in the past, foreign investors came mainly to take advantage of cheap labor in Taiwan and to produce for international markets where they had a comparative advantage. A survey by the Investment Commission revealed

20. It is also recognized that the openness of the service sector is one of the major topics that will be discussed during the upcoming Taiwan-U.S. trade negotiation sessions. Cf. *The Analysis of FDI in 1989,* prepared by the ROC Investment Commission, Ministry of Economic Affairs, 1990.

21. Tax havens are defined to include those countries without an income taxation system, those applying very low income tax rates, or those that exempt the foreign source income of their residents. Ironically, Taiwan still takes the territorial approach toward its residents' foreign source income and thus should be classified as a tax haven by the Investment Commission. For a review of the current international income taxation system in Taiwan, see Chen and Cheng (1990).

that direct and indirect exports made by foreign firms in Taiwan accounted for 29.06 percent of total national exports in 1978. This ratio declined to 17 percent in 1987.[22] Two factors contributed to the changes in the importance of FDI in national exports. One reflects the shift in the industrial structure of FDI. Specifically, electronics became the single most important export industry in Taiwan, with export values accounting for two-thirds to three-quarters of the total exports made by foreign firms in 1978–87. As shown in panel A of table 12.5, however, the electronics industry's share of total FDI has steadily declined over the last three decades. In contrast, other more domestic-oriented manufacturing industries such as chemicals and machinery have gained a greater share of total FDI. Needless to say, the increasing amount of FDI in the service sector is mainly geared toward the domestic market.

The second factor that may have contributed to the relative decline in the export share of foreign firms is the shift in the market orientation of each FDI industry. Table 12.6 exhibits the export ratio of foreign firms in Taiwan during 1978–87. Two different market tendencies can be observed. For export-oriented industries, mainly electronics and the "other" category, export ratios slightly increased over 1978–87. For domestic-oriented industries, such as chemicals, machinery, and services, a decline in export ratios during the decade is rather clear.

In summary, Taiwan's FDI has increased substantially in both absolute and relative terms during the 1980s, and structurally its focus has begun to turn more toward domestic markets. Since a foreign investor may have many locations to choose from in deciding where to produce for international markets, it makes sense to distinguish between export- and domestic-oriented FDI in order to evaluate the potential impact of tax incentives on the inducement of both kinds of FDI. It is also reasonable to conjecture that FDI in export-oriented industries, such as electronics, would be more likely to respond to tax incentives. In the following section we will present the regressional results of our analysis on total FDI in Taiwan, FDI in manufacturing, and FDI in the electronics industry.

12.5 Effects of Tax Incentives on FDI in Taiwan

Econometric attempts to ascertain the effects of tax policy on FDI have been unsuccessful for both theoretical and statistical reasons. Tax incentives in Taiwan, as shown in table 12.1, are so pervasive that they cannot be represented well by the dummy variable proxy commonly used in empirical studies. Our study tries to overcome this difficulty by measuring the extent of tax preferences that FDI has enjoyed. Two regressional analyses are made, one using time-series data and the other using firm-specific data.

---

22. *An Analysis of Operations and Economic Effects of Foreign Enterprises* (in Chinese) (Taipei: ROC Investment Commission, Ministry of Economic Affairs, 1987).

12.5.1   Time-Series Studies

According to Riedel (1975), Wu et al. (1980), and Tsai (1991), the potential demand-side determinants of FDI in Taiwan include the domestic market, incentive policies, and cheap cost. Since we are interested in explaining increasing FDI in Taiwan during the 1980s, we will use data from 1972–87.[23] However, the cost of labor in Taiwan during this period was not what could be called cheap. After having adjusted for the effects of foreign exchange rates, the increase in the unit labor cost in Taiwan reached 13 percent over 1970–82, which was higher than labor cost increases in the United States, Japan, Korea, and Singapore (Tsai 1991). Hence, in this study, we try to test for the adverse impact of rising labor costs on the inflow of FDI. Since strong export orientation is one characteristic of FDI in Taiwan, it is considered explicitly in the model.

The estimated regression equation is specified as follows:[24]

(1) $\text{FDI} = b_0 + b_1 \text{ GNP} + b_2 \text{ Export} + b_3 \text{ Wage} + b_4 \text{ Tax Pref,}$

where FDI = approved FDI in Taiwan in a given year, GNP = gross national product in a given year, Export = the ratio of foreign firms' exports to total national exports in a given year, Wage = wage index, and Tax Pref = tax preferences enjoyed by foreign firms in a given year, measured by the difference between the highest marginal corporate income tax rate and the average effective tax rate.

This equation is applied to the inflow of total FDI in Taiwan and disaggregate FDI, such as FDI from Japan and the United States, and FDI in the electronics industry. All coefficients except b_3 are expected to be positive. To eliminate supply-side effects, relative FDI, expressed as Taiwan's share of total FDI in non-oil-exporting LDCs, is also estimated using equation (1).

Table 12.7 gives the results of the estimation and provides comparisons with the results of a previous study (Tsai 1991). Three major findings can be summarized:

1. In terms of goodness-of-fit, as measured by the adjusted R^2, all equations, except FDI from the United States, perform very well.
2. In terms of testing hypotheses, the results consistently show that GDP has a positive effect, while rising labor costs have a negative effect; the other two variables, export orientation and tax preferences, have no significant effect.
3. Contrary to Tsai (1991), this study finds that Taiwan has attracted relatively more FDI than other non-oil-exporting LDCs. This may be due to the policy change that opened Taiwan's domestic markets, witnessed by

23. One of the other major reasons for using this time period is that more detailed data on tax preferences were made available beginning in 1972.
24. Other variables such as the growth rate of GDP, the political climate, and the status of the public infrastructure are also considered. However, no significant effects have been shown to be related to these variables.

Table 12.7   Comparison of Time-Series Regression Results for Foreign Direct Investment in Taiwan

Independent Variable	Approved FDI (1972–87)					Actual FDI (1958–85)	
	FDI	FDI in Nonoil LDCs (%)	FDI from Japan	FDI from U.S.	FDI in Electronics	FDI	FDI in Nonoil LDCs, 1965–85 (%)
Intercept	−355,871	7.9873	−76.2681	−6.0743	−244.66	0.2447	−0.0239
	(−1.095)	(2.3816)	(−0.590)	(−0.025)	(−1.616)	(0.385)	(−0.083)
GDP	1.6038	0.00002	0.0005	0.0003	0.0005		(RPCDGP) 0.2448
	(5.423)**	(4.958)**	(4.142)**	(1.374)	(3.276)**		(0.763)
ΔGDP						0.3313	(RΔGDP) −0.0331
						(2.783)*	(−0.153)
Export ratio	14,901	−0.1390	2.6505	0.9023	8.1398		
	(1.409)	(−1.274)	(.06299)	(0.114)	(1.708)		
Dummy for export orientation						−0.5953	0.7716
						(−2.646)*	(2.531)*
Wage index	−24,847	−0.2856	−7.5687	−4.0810	−7.5706		
	(−4.523)**	(−5.037)**	(−3.463)**	(−0.994)	(−2.686)*		
Dummy for export processing zones						1.3162	
						(3.739)**	
Tax preferences	4,871	0.1002	1.3916	0.6769	3.6975		
	(0.867)	(1.729)	(0.6228)	(0.161)	(1.156)		
Dummy for tax preferences						0.3769	
						(1.06)	
Adjusted R^2	0.9033	0.8301	0.8594	0.5543	0.7645	0.85	0.20
Durbin-Watson statistic	2.5396	2.5018	1.6656	2.6139	2.1260	1.54	1.95
N	16	16	16	16	16	28	20

Sources: Computational assistance for this study was provided by Hui-hse Chen. Actual FDI from Tsai (1991).

Notes: The numbers in parentheses are *t*-statistics; * and ** indicate results significantly different from zero at either the 5 percent or 1 percent levels, respectively. RPCGDP = (RCGDP/PCGDPW)·100, where PCGDP is per capita GDP in Taiwan and PCGDPW is the average of per capita GDP in all non-oil-exporting LDCs. RPCDGP = (RCGDP/PCGDPW)·100, where PCGDP is per capita GDP in Taiwan and PCGDPW is the average of per capita GDP in all non-oil-exporting LDCs. RΔGDP = (ΔGDP/ΔGDPW)·100, where ΔGDP is annual change of GDP in Taiwan and ΔGDPW is the average of annual change of GDP in all non-oil-exporting LDCs.

the increasing share of FDI going to domestic-oriented investment, particularly the service sector, as shown in table 12.5. However, both studies agree that the effect of tax preferences on FDI is insignificant.

12.5.2   Cross-sectional Studies

The data for the cross-sectional studies come from the financial statements of fifty-six foreign manufacturing firms that were eligible for tax holidays and reported their corporate income in 1984–86.[25] The dependent variable is the increase in net worth, which reflects both equity investment and reinvested earnings. The independent variables include the year of establishment, the before-tax profit rate, and tax preferences. Since the before-tax profit rate can be accounted for by a firm's characteristics, the following equation is estimated:

$$(2) \quad \triangle\text{Net worth} = c_0 + c_1 Y + c_2 ks + c_3 g + c_4 A + c_5 T_1 + C_5 T_2,$$

where $\triangle$Net worth = the average of the increases in net worth of a given firm during 1984–85 and 1985–86; Y = the year of establishment; ks = capital structure, measured by the average of liabilities divided by total assets of a given firm in 1984 and 1985; g = growth rate of a firm, measured by the average of the increases in sales divided by the total sales of a given firm in 1984 and 1985; A = size of a firm, measured by the average of total assets of a given firm in 1984 and 1985; T_1 = the average of tax holiday benefits divided by before-tax profits of a given firm in 1984 and 1985; and, T_2 = the average of other tax preferences divided by before-tax profits of a given firm in 1984 and 1985.

All c's except c_1 and c_2 are expected to be positive. Equation (2) is estimated for the manufacturing sector and for the electronics industry only.

The regression results, as presented in table 12.8, can be summarized as follows:

1. The effect of the year of establishment is mixed. In each equation, one of the alternative factors of the before-tax profit rate has the expected sign and is significant.

2. The effects of tax policy are also mixed. In the manufacturing equations, neither a tax holiday nor any of the other tax preferences is significant. However, for the electronics industry, we find that tax holidays have a significant effect. The corresponding elasticity of the increase in net worth with respect to tax holidays, calculated at mean values, is approximately 0.42. This seems to imply that the abolition of tax holidays would lead to a 42 percent cut in the increase of the net worth of the electronics industry. The marginal impact would be very strong. The overall adverse effect is not so great, however,

---

25. These data are confidential for tax purposes and are supposed to be more reliable than those obtained from surveys. The data source for this study is the subfile of data used by Lee and Chu (1990).

Table 12.8   **Cross-sectional Regression Results of Foreign Manufacturing Firms in Taiwan, 1985–86 (in millions of N.T. dollars)**

Independent Variable	Manufacturing Increase in Net Worth	Electronics Increase in Net Worth
Intercept	−490,680 (−0.54)	−1,328,100 (−0.83)
Year of establishment	−13,081 (−1.71)*	642.03 (0.05)
Liability/total assets	−34,342 (−0.38)	−323,890 (−1.79)*
Increase in sales/sales	4,224 (0.78)	1,470.5 (0.19)
Total assets	105,350 (2.69)**	114,130 (1.66)
Tax holiday preferences	392,540 (0.99)	908,630 (1.73)*
Other tax preferences	28,948 (0.06)	290,090 (0.35)
Adjusted R^2	26.74	20.41
N	56	31

Source: Computational assistance for this study was provided by Yon-chin Tsen. Data are from Lee and Chu (1990).

Notes: The numbers in parentheses are *t*-statistics; * and ** indicate results significantly different from zero for one-tailed tests at the 5 percent and 1 percent significance levels, respectively. All these firms were eligible for either five-year or four-year tax holidays during 1985–86.

since it accounts for only 6.7 percent of total net worth.[26] The adverse effect is also exaggerated in the sense that a firm not receiving a tax holiday can still enjoy the other tax preferences shown in table 12.1. Obviously, it is impossible for this study to project the whole potential impact of abolishing tax holidays on FDI in Taiwan, since the effects of tax incentives on other domestic-oriented industries would be much smaller, and the electronics industry's share of total FDI has decreased substantially in recent years.

The methodological inadequacy of this study is quite clear. No sophisticated theoretical model has been developed. D. Wu (1989) used a neoclassical model to study the determination of Japanese direct investment in Taiwan for the period 1970–84. However, a lag structure was not incorporated into the model due to data limitations.

Tsai (1991) pointed out that, to determine whether the demand-side determinants in Taiwan were relatively more important than those in other countries, all variables should be expressed in relative terms. Given the difficulty of estimating labor costs and tax preferences in various countries, a cross-national comparison is hardly feasible. Therefore, the findings of this study, using only the data of Taiwan, are at best tentative. However, these findings may be qualitatively valid if the twin trends of rising labor costs and increasing tax preferences in Taiwan continue.

In spite of these qualifications, the overall regression results seem to confirm the changing characteristics of FDI in Taiwan in recent years. As mentioned in section 12.4, the structure of Taiwan's FDI has become more ori-

26. This is calculated by multiplying 0.42 by 0.1588 (increase in net worth/total net worth).

ented to the domestic market, and it is expected that the effects of tax incentives are going to be less important than in the past. This conjecture is supported by the regression results of the time-series studies and by the firm-specific study on total manufacturing FDI in Taiwan. At the same time, high export-oriented investors have more countries to choose from nowadays, and they can expect to gain more from the provision of tax incentives. This is also confirmed by findings that tax holidays have a significant effect on increases in net worth in the electronics industry.

One important policy implication that may be derived from these findings can be related to income tax reform in Taiwan. As mentioned before, Taiwan currently has a relatively low corporate income tax, while it provides generous tax incentives. The questionable effectiveness of tax incentives and their costs in terms of equity and efficiency have raised growing doubts about their usefulness. The reforms proposed by the Tax Reform Commission (Chen and Cheng 1990) would broaden both the individual and business income tax bases, lower the income brackets for individual income tax, and reduce the highest marginal tax rate from 50 percent to 40 percent. Meanwhile, the business income tax rate would be raised from a marginal 25 percent to a flat rate of 35 percent, and complete dividend relief would be allowed for distributed profits.[27]

Under this reform package, current tax holidays and most of the other major incentives would be abolished. Therefore the effective tax rate for FDI in Taiwan would increase from 11.26 percent or 19.47 percent (table 12.2) to 35 percent or 48 percent, depending on whether the withholding tax on repatriated profits is paid out of business income tax. If the tentative results of this study are reliable, they imply that some highly export-oriented FDI would be heavily affected, while the overall impact on total FDI might be less substantial. This policy change, however, would improve the neutrality of resource allocation and meet the need for a more internationalized and liberalized economy.

12.6 Summary and Implications

This paper provides some observations taken from empirical studies and examines the possible effects of a change in tax policy on FDI in Taiwan. In theory, the fiscal incentives offered by a developing host country, which lower its effective tax rate, will in most cases be effective in attracting FDI. How responsively FDI reacts to these tax concessions, however, is a priori unclear.

In the case of Taiwan, we observe that the island increasingly attracted FDI during the 1980s, both in absolute and in relative terms. Meanwhile, the

---

27. In Taiwan all profit-seeking enterprises, including proprietorships and partnerships as well as corporations, are subject to a business income tax. In making comparisons with other countries, however, we have used the term "corporate income tax" as the equivalent of Taiwan's "business income tax."

structure of FDI has moved towards the service sector and other domestic-oriented industries.

Current tax incentives in Taiwan are very generous: eligible firms may, on average, enjoy approximately a one-third tax savings. On the basis of new data, the time-series regression for the period 1972–87 reveals that GDP has a positive effect on FDI, while rising labor costs have a negative effect. The effect of tax preferences is found to be insignificant, however, as was shown in previous studies.

The findings from firm-specific data are mixed. For all manufacturing firms, it is found that tax preferences have no significant effect on increases in net worth. On the other hand, tax holidays were found to have a significant effect on increases in net worth in the electronics industry. The marginal impact of abolishing tax holidays on investment in the electronics industry is predicted to be substantial, perhaps causing as much as a 42 percent reduction. However, the adverse impact is overestimated in the sense that other incentives may cushion or make up for part of the impact. The overall adverse impact on total FDI is also expected to be considerably less because of differences in the market orientation of industries and the electronics industry's decreasing share of total FDI.

While the limited supply of data is a severe problem, two basic policy implications can be derived from these findings. First, to understand whether and to what extent foreign capital may be withdrawn from Taiwan in response to the unilateral abolition of tax incentives, further studies should be performed focusing on those industries that face severe competition for foreign capital. Second, since Taiwan's domestic and foreign investment is now undergoing structural changes, both industrial and tax policies should be adjusted rapidly, in a coordinated way, by taking into account both domestic and international considerations. As Taiwan's economy becomes more internationalized, the neutrality of resource allocation should be more important than before, and thus dependence on tax incentives should be gradually reduced.

References

Agarwal, J. P. 1980. Determinants of Foreign Direct Investment: A Survey. *Weltwirtschaftliches Archiv* 116(4): 739–73.

Balasuramanyam, V. N. 1986. Incentives and Disincentives for Foreign Direct Investment in Less Developed Countries. In *Economic Incentives*, ed. B. Balassa, and H. Giersch, chap. 15. New York: Macmillan.

Boskin, M. J., and W. G. Gale. 1987. New Results in the Effects of Tax Policy on the International Location of Investment. In *The Effects of Taxation on Capital Accumulation* ed. M. Feldstein, chap. 6. Chicago: University of Chicago Press.

Chen, T., and P. W. Cheng. 1990. International Aspects of Taiwan Income Taxation. Paper given at International Symposium on Tax Policy and Economic Development among Pacific Asian Countries, Academia Sinica, Taipei, Taiwan, January 5–7.

Goldsbrough, D. 1985. *Foreign Private Investment in Developing Countries.* Occasional Paper no. 33. Washington, D.C.: International Monetary Fund.

Hartman, D. G. 1984. Tax Policy and Foreign Direct Investment in the United States. *National Tax Journal* 37: 475–87.

————. 1985. Tax Policy and Foreign Direct Investment. *Journal of Public Economics* 26: 107–21.

Lee, C., and T. Chu. 1990. Evaluating the Economic Benefits of Tax Holidays in Taiwan, (in Chinese). *Public Finance Review* 22(1): 81–95.

Lee, C. F., and S. C. Hu. eds. 1989. Introduction to *Advances in Financial Planning and Forecasting: Taiwan's Foreign Investment, Exports, and Financial Analysis,* 1–7. Greenwich, Conn.: JAI Press.

Lim, D. 1983. Fiscal Incentives and Direct Foreign Investment in Less Developed Countries. *The Journal of Development Studies* 19: 207–12.

Peat, Marwick, Mitchell and Co. 1987. *Investment in Taiwan.* Taipei: KPMG Peat Marwick Mitchell & Co.

Riedel, J. 1975. The Nature and Determinants of Export-Oriented Direct Foreign Investment in a Developing Country: A Case Study of Taiwan. *Weltwirtschaftliches Archiv* 14: 505–28.

Root, F. R., and A. A. Ahmed. 1978. The Influence of Policy Instruments on Manufacturing Direct Foreign Investment in Developing Countries. *Journal of International Business Studies* 9(3): 81–93.

Schive, C. 1987. The Dramatic Changes of Foreign Investment in Taiwan (in Chinese). In *Proceedings of the Fifth Seminar on Social Sciences,* 183–98. Taipei: Sun Yat-sen Institute for Social Sciences and Philosophy, Academia Sinica.

Shah, S. M. S., and J. F. J. Toye. 1978. Fiscal Incentives for Firms in Some Developing Countries: Survey and Critique. In *Taxation and Economic Development,* ed. J. E. J. Toye, chap. #12. London: Frank Cass.

Tsai, P. 1990. Demand-side Determinants of Foreign Direct Investment and Its Effects on Economic Growth (in Chinese). Paper given at Seminar on International Trade Policy in Taiwan, National Taiwan University, Taipei, Taiwan, March 2–3.

————. 1991. Determinants of Foreign Direct Investment in Taiwan: An Alternative Approach with Time-Series Data. *World Development* 19: 275–85.

Wu, D. 1989. An Empirical Analysis of Japanese Direct Investment in Taiwan: A Neoclassical Approach. In *Advances in Financial Planning and Forecasting: Taiwan's Foreign Investment, Exports, and Financial Analysis,* ed. C. F. Lee and S. C. Hu, 9–64. Greenwich, Conn.: JAI Press.

Wu, R. 1989. Economic Development Strategies and the Role of Foreign Investment in Taiwan. In *Advances in Financial Planning and Forecasting: Taiwan's Foreign Investment, Exports, and Financial Analysis,* ed. C. F. Lee and S. C. Hu, 65–89. Greenwich, Conn.: JAI Press.

Wu, R., et al. 1980. *The Influences of U.S. Firms on the Economy of Taiwan* (in Chinese). Taipei: Academia Sinica.

Comment   Kwang Choi

Overall, Ching-huei Chang's and Peter Cheng's paper is excellent, providing a good summary of theoretical issues in general and the characteristics of foreign direct investment (FDI) in Taiwan.

Kwang Choi is professor of public economics at the Hankuk University of Foreign Studies.

The contribution of the paper lies in its attempts, based on new data and new models, to ascertain the effects of tax policy on FDI in Taiwan. However, the attempts have been only partly successful for both theoretical and statistical reasons. Two technical points must be mentioned with regard to the time-series econometric testing of relationships between tax incentives and inflow of FDI into Taiwan.

First, I would like to ask whether Chang and Cheng have ever run time-series regressions based on time-lag specifications. Since it takes time for corporate managers or owners (particularly foreigners) to make decisions on FDI, one might say that there must be better specifications with regard to the time lag.

Second, one may ask a rather fundamental question about the role that tax preferences play in inducing FDI. Ceteris paribus, the decision to invest in the home country or a foreign country depends on the relative tax advantage between the two. Accordingly, tax preferences enjoyed by foreign firms should be measured by the difference between the effective corporate tax rate in the host country and the effective corporate rate in the rest of the world, including the home country, rather than by the difference between the highest marginal corporate income tax rate and the average effective tax rate.

With regard to the cross-sectional studies based on the financial statements from fifty-six foreign manufacturing firms in Taiwan, I cannot clearly see how the specifications (equations [2] and [3]) examine the effects of Taiwanese tax policy on inducing FDI. What equations (2) and (3) attempt is to examine the effects of tax preferences on the increase in net worth (not on FDI) within Taiwan (not between countries).

One important factor that might have exerted strong influences on the inflow of FDI into Taiwan but has not been mentioned at all is investment by overseas Chinese. It should be interesting to investigate the size of FDI in Taiwan by overseas Chinese and the area in which it is found.

Finally, I have one minor technical suggestion for presenting the average figure in the note to table 12.4. How about showing a simple average for 1952–1989, instead of a "simple average for the selected years shown in the table."

Chang and Cheng should be congratulated on their excellent efforts to elucidate tax policy and FDI in Taiwan.

Comment   Toshihiro Ihori

Ching-huei Chang's and Peter Cheng's paper investigates empirically the impact of tax policy on foreign direct investment (FDI) in Taiwan. Their review

Toshihiro Ihori is associate professor of economics at Osaka University.

of the literature shows that the tax incentives will in most cases be effective in attracting FDI. However, section 12.4 shows that the effect of tax preferences is actually insignificant. I found the empirical results quite interesting.

I think that there are three possible reasons why the theoretical conjecture is not confirmed by the empirical study. First, the real world may be characterized by "resident"-based taxation in the tax credit case, so that neither the home country tax nor the host country tax affects the firm's international investment decision, theoretically.

Second, the measurement of the tax preferences may be inaccurate. I am not convinced that the tax preferences can be measured by the difference between the highest marginal tax rate and the average effective tax rates.

Finally, even if the tax incentives are attracting FDI, it might take time or require some adjustment costs to make an actual investment. It seems quite possible that the short-term effect of the tax incentives on FDI is small but the long-term effect is large. I think that the paper would be improved by being more explicit about the dynamic behavior of FDI and by incorporating some lag structures into the regression.

Contributors

Thomas A. Barthold
Joint Committee on Taxation
United States Congress
1010 Longworth
Washington, DC 20515

Ching-huei Chang
Sun Yat-sen Institute for Social Sciences
   and Philosophy
Academia Sinica
Nankang, Taipei, Taiwan 11529
The Republic of China

Peter W. H. Cheng
Department of Public Finance and
   Taxation
National Chengchi University
Taipei, Taiwan 11623
The Republic of China

Kwang Choi
Hankuk University of Foreign Studies
270 Imun-Dong
Dongdaemun-Gu, Seoul 130–791
The Republic of Korea

Maria S. Gochoco
School of Economics
University of the Philippines
Diliman, Quezon City 1101
The Philippines 3004

Tatsuo Hatta
Institute of Social and Economic
   Research
Osaka University
Ibaraki, Osaka 567, Japan

Masaaki Homma
Faculty of Economics
Osaka University
1–1 Machikaneyama
Toyonaka, Osaka 560, Japan

Toshihiro Ihori
Faculty of Economics
Osaka University
1–1 Machikenayama
Toyonaka, Osaka 560, Japan

Hiromitsu Ishi
Department of Economics
Hitotsubashi University
2–1 Naka, Kunitachi, Tokyo 186, Japan

Takatoshi Ito
Institute of Economic Research
Hitotsubashi University
Kunitachi, Tokyo 186, Japan

Medhi Krongkaew
Department of Economics
Thammasat University
Prachan Road
Bangkok 10200, Thailand

Anne O. Krueger
Department of Economics
Duke University
Durham, NC 27706

Taewon Kwack
Department of Economics
Sogang University
Sinsu-dong, Mapo-ku, Seoul
The Republic of Korea

Kye-Sik Lee
Korea Development Institute
P. O. Box 113
Chongnyang, Seoul
The Republic of Korea

Joseph Y. Lim
School of Economics
University of the Philippines
Diliman, Quezon City 1101
The Philippines

Chuan Lin
Department of Public Finance
National Chengchi University
Taipei, Taiwan 11623
The Republic of China

Charles E. McLure, Jr.
Hoover Institution
Stanford University
Stanford, CA 94305

Hideki Nishioka
Department of Economics
University of Osaka Prefecture
4–804 Mozu-umemachi
Sakai-city, Osaka 591, Japan

Yukio Noguchi
Faculty of Economics
Hitotsubashi University
Kunitachi, Tokyo 186, Japan

Assaf Razin
Department of Economics
Tel Aviv University
Ramat-Aviv, Tel Aviv 69978
Israel

Efraim Sadka
Department of Economics
Tel Aviv University
Ramat-Aviv, Tel Aviv 69978
Israel

Parthasarathi Shome
Deputy Division Chief
International Monetary Fund
700 19th Street, NW
Washington, DC 20431

Toshiaki Tachibanaki
Kyoto Institute of Economic Research
Kyoto University
Yoshida-honmachi, Sakyo-ku,
    Kyoto 606
Japan

Vito Tanzi
Fiscal Affairs Department
International Monetary Fund
700 19th Street, NW
Washington, DC 20431

Irene Trela
Department of Economics
Social Science Centre
University of Western Ontario
London, Ontario N6A 5C2, Canada

John Whalley
Department of Economics
Social Science Centre
University of Western Ontario
London, Ontario N6A 5C2, Canada

Twatchai Yongkittikul
Director of Planning and Development
Thailand Development Research Insti-
    tute Foundation
Rajapark Building, 163 Asoke Road
Bangkok 10110, Thailand

Kun-Young Yun
Department of Economics
Yonsei University
Shinchon-dong, Suhdaemun-ku
Seoul 120–749, Korea

Author Index

Subject Index